History

for the IB Diploma

Authoritarian States

(20th Century)

Allan Todd and Sally Waller

Series editor: Allan Todd

Cambridge University Press's mission is to advance learning, knowledge and research worldwide.

Our IB Diploma resources aim to:

- encourage learners to explore concepts, ideas and topics that have local and global significance
- help students develop a positive attitude to learning in preparation for higher education
- assist students in approaching complex questions, applying critical-thinking skills and forming reasoned answers.

CAMBRIDGE
UNIVERSITY PRESS

University Printing House, Cambridge CB2 8BS, United Kingdom

One Liberty Plaza, 20th Floor, New York, NY 10006, USA

477 Williamstown Road, Port Melbourne, VC 3207, Australia

4843/24, 2nd Floor, Ansari Road, Daryaganj, Delhi – 110002, India

79 Anson Road, #06–04/06, Singapore 079906

Cambridge University Press is part of the University of Cambridge.

It furthers the University's mission by disseminating knowledge in the pursuit of education, learning and research at the highest international levels of excellence.

Information on this title: education.cambridge.org

First published 2011
Second edition 2015
20 19 18 17 16 15 14 13 12 11 10 9 8 7 6 5 4 3

Printed in the United Kingdom by Latimer Trend

A catalogue record for this publication is available from the British Library

ISBN 978-1-107-55889-2 Paperback

Dedication

In memory of 'Don' Houghton (1916–2008)
who first taught me to love History (AT).

Contents

Contents

Introduction

This book is designed to prepare students taking the Paper 2 topic – World history topic 10: *Authoritarian states (20th century)* – in the IB History examination. It will examine the various aspects associated with four different **authoritarian** states, including the origins of such regimes, the role of leaders and of **ideology** and the nature of the states concerned. It will also look at how such regimes maintained and consolidated power, the treatment of opposition groups and the range of domestic policies that were followed.

For many, such a state is typified by Nazi Germany under Adolf Hitler (1889–1945); while the Soviet Union under Stalin (1878–1953), though in many ways very different from Nazi Germany, was also clearly another authoritarian state. Especially during the early years of the Cold War (1945–91), some historians tried to argue that Nazi Germany and Stalinist Russia were essentially similar regimes. Some even argued that Stalin's regime was worse than Hitler's. As well as considering Nazi Germany, this book also examines the regimes of Benito Mussolini in Italy, Mao Zedong in China and Fidel Castro in Cuba.

authoritarian: This term refers to regimes that are essentially conservative and traditional and that try to defend existing institutions and keep all sections of society politically and organisationally passive.

ideology: This term usually refers to the logically related set of ideas that are the basis of a political or economic theory or system. In single-party states, ideology has often been promoted via propaganda and censorship.

Themes

To help you prepare for your IB History exams, this book will cover the themes relating to authoritarian states as set out in the IB *History Guide*.
For ease of study, it will examine each state in terms of three major themes, in the following order:

- the emergence of authoritarian regimes and the role of leaders and ideologies in the rise to power
- the methods used to consolidate and maintain power in such states – including propaganda and foreign policy
- the domestic economic and social policies of such regimes, their impact and the success or failure of such policies.

Each of the four detailed case study chapters has units dealing with the three major themes, so that you will be able to focus on the main issues. This approach will help you to compare and contrast the roles of the individual leaders and parties, and the main developments in the various states covered – and so spot similarities and differences.

Figure 1.1   A mass grave discovered by Allied troops when they liberated Belsen Concentration Camp in April 1945

States and regions

The case studies in this book cover four of the most popular states for study:

*   Italy and Mussolini
*   Germany and Hitler
*   China and Mao
*   Cuba and Castro.

IB History and regions of the world

For the purposes of study, IB History specifies four regions of the world:

*   Europe
*   Asia and Oceania

- the Americas
- Africa and the Middle East.

Where relevant, you need to be able to identify these regions and discuss developments that took place within them. They are shown on the map below, which also indicates the states covered by this book.

Remember that if you are answering a question that asks you to choose *two* different states or leaders, each from a *different* region, you *must* be careful and choose correctly. Every year, some examination candidates attempting such questions select two states from the *same* region. This limits them to a maximum of 8 marks out of the 15 available for Paper 2 questions.

The four IB regions are shown on this map, along with some of the states covered by this book.

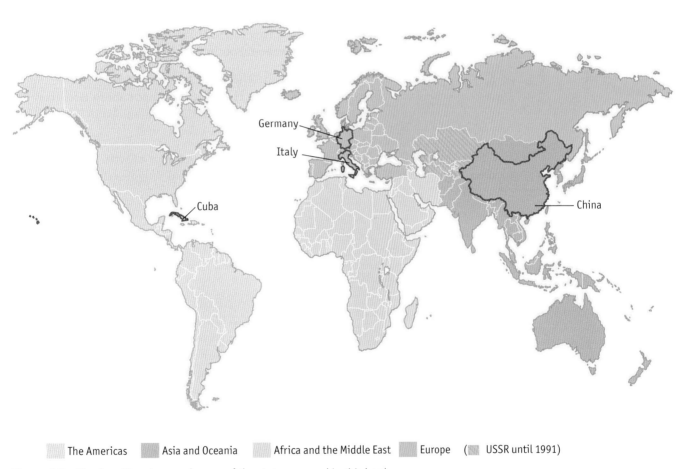

| The Americas | Asia and Oceania | Africa and the Middle East | Europe | (USSR until 1991) |

Figure 1.2 The four IB regions and some of the states covered in this book

Of course you may well study some other examples of authoritarian states specifically identified in the IB *History Guide* – such as Kenya and Kenyatta or Egypt and Nasser in Africa and the Middle East; the Soviet Union and Stalin in Europe; or Indonesia and Sukharno in Asia and Oceania. You may even study relevant regions that are not specifically mentioned here but are still acceptable, such as Russia and Lenin.

Key Concepts

To perform well in your IB History examinations, you will often need to consider aspects of one or more of six important Key Concepts as you write your answers. These six Key Concepts are:

- Change
- Continuity
- Causation
- Consequence
- Significance
- Perspectives.

Sometimes a question might require you to address two Key Concepts. For instance: Why did Mussolini introduce the Acerbo Law in 1923? What were the most significant consequences of this law for political developments in Italy between 1923 and 1926?

It is immediately clear with this question that the Key Concepts of Consequence and Significance must be addressed in your answer. However, it is important to note that although the word 'causes' does not explicitly appear in the question, words such as 'why' or 'reasons' nonetheless are asking you to address Causation as well.

To help you focus on the six Key Concepts and gain experience of writing answers that address them, you will find a range of different questions and activities throughout these chapters.

Theory of knowledge

In addition to the broad key themes, the chapters contain Theory of knowledge (ToK) links to get you thinking about issues that relate to History, which is a Group 3 subject in the IB Diploma. The 20th century authoritarian states topic has clear links to ideas about knowledge and history. This topic is highly political as it concerns opposing ideologies, and at times these have influenced the historians writing about the various states and leaders involved. Thus questions relating to the selection of sources, and to interpretations of these sources by historians, have clear links to the IB Theory of knowledge course.

For example, to make their case, historians must decide which evidence to select and use and which evidence to leave out. But to what extent do the historians' personal political views influence their decisions when they select what they consider to be the most important or relevant sources and when they make judgements about the value and limitations of specific sources or sets of sources? Is there such a thing as objective 'historical truth'? Or is there just a range of subjective historical opinions and interpretations about the past that vary according to the political interests and leanings of individual historians?

You are therefore encouraged to read a range of books giving different interpretations of the origins and development of the 20th century authoritarian states covered in this book in order to gain a clear understanding of the relevant historiographies.

Exam skills needed for IB History

Throughout the main chapters of this book, there are various activities and questions to help you develop the understanding and the exam skills necessary for success. Before attempting the specific exam practice questions that come at the end of the main chapters, you might find it useful to refer *first* to Chapter 6, the final Exam Practice chapter. This suggestion is based on the idea that if you know where you are supposed to be going (in this instance, gaining a good mark and grade) and how to get there, you stand a better chance of reaching your destination!

Questions and mark schemes

To ensure that you develop the necessary understanding and skills, each chapter contains a number of questions in the margins. In addition, three of the main Paper 1-type questions (comprehension, cross-referencing and reliability/utility) are dealt with in Chapters 2 to 5. Help for the longer Paper 1 judgement/synthesis questions and the Paper 2 essay questions can be found in Chapter 6.

For additional help, simplified mark schemes have been put together in ways that should make it easier to understand what examiners are looking for in examination answers. The actual IB History mark schemes can be found on the IB website.

Finally, you will find examiners' tips and comments, along with activities, to help you focus on the important aspects of questions and their answers. These will also help you to avoid simple mistakes and oversights that, every year, result in even some otherwise good students failing to gain the highest marks.

Terminology and definitions

The history of the authoritarian states that emerged in Italy and Germany after the First World War (1914–18), and in China and Cuba after the Second World War (1939–45), is often seen as extremely complicated. In part, this is the result of the large number of different political terms used to describe the ideologies and the forms of political rule that existed in those states. There is also the added complication that different historians have at times used the same terms in slightly different ways. To help you understand the various ideologies and the historical arguments and interpretations, you will need to understand the meaning of terms such as 'left' and 'right', 'communist' and 'fascist', and 'authoritarian' and 'totalitarian'. You will then be able to focus on the similarities and differences between the various single-party regimes.

Ideological terms

At first glance, understanding the various political ideologies appears to be straightforward, as the history of most authoritarian states can in many ways be seen as being based on one of two opposing political ideologies: 'communism' or 'fascism'.

Unfortunately, it is not quite as simple as that, as both communism and fascism have more than one strand. Consequently, historical figures and historians have often meant different things despite using the same terms. At the same time, some have argued that

Fact: The terms 'left' and 'right' are based on the political terminology that developed from the early stages of the French Revolution of 1789. At this time, the most radical political groups sat on the left side of the National Convention, while the most conservative ones sat on the right. Communists can be described as being on the far (or extreme) left, while fascists are on the extreme right, with fundamentally opposed ideologies.

communism and fascism should not be seen as two extremes at opposite ends of the political spectrum. Instead, they argue that the spectrum almost forms a circle. In this way, they stress the similarities rather than the contrasts between the extremes. However, this approach relates to practice rather than to political theory.

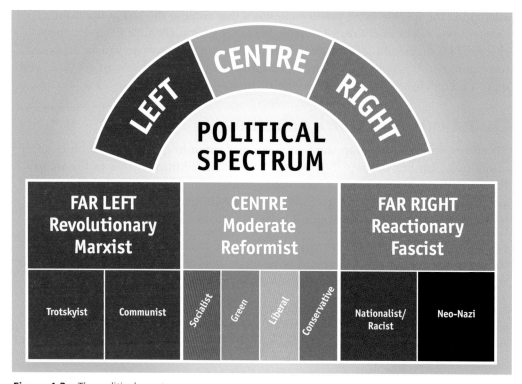

Figure 1.3 The political spectrum

Fact: The terms 'communism' and 'fascism' emerged during the 19th and 20th centuries. They are generally seen as two diametrically opposed ideologies or theories, at the opposite ends of the political spectrum. Generally, the fundamental difference between these two political theories is that communism is dedicated to destroying capitalism, while fascism in practice has often been described as capitalism's most ruthless defender.

Fact: The materialist conception of history was set out by Marx in his *Critique of Political Economy* (1859). Essentially he argued that the economic structure, based on the relations of production in any society (i.e. which class owns the important parts of an economy, such as land, factories, minds and banks), is the real foundation of any society, and on this are built the legal, political and intellectual superstructures of society. He went on to say that it is social existence that largely determines people's consciousness or beliefs, rather than the other way round.

Communism

The terms 'communism' and 'Marxism' are often used interchangeably by those who consider them to be the same thing. Yet Marx never referred to himself as a 'Marxist' – instead, he used the word 'communist', which indicated the ultimate ideal society. 'Marxism' in many ways is more an analytical and philosophical way of investigating society than a political programme with specific policies. Furthermore, as will be seen below, even communists have had – and continue to have – different ideas about what 'communism' and 'Marxism' mean. However, opponents of communism – such as Mussolini or Hitler – generally see these terms as being one and the same thing.

Marxism

The political roots of Marxism can be traced back to the writings of one man, Karl Marx (1818–83) – or two men, if Marx's close collaborator Friedrich Engels (1820–95) is included. The writings of Marx were based on the materialist conception of history that he developed, and on his theory that human history was largely determined by the 'history of class struggles' between ruling and oppressed classes. Marx believed that if the workers were successful in overthrowing capitalism, they would be able to construct a socialist society. This would still be a class-based society, but one in which, for the first time in human history, the ruling class would be the majority of the population (i.e. the working class).

From this new form of human society, Marx believed it would eventually be possible to move to an even better one: a communist society. This would be a classless society, and a society of plenty rather than scarcity because it would be based on the economic advances of industrial capitalism.

However, Marx did not write much about the political forms that would be adopted under socialism and communism, other than to say that it would be more democratic and less repressive than previous societies, as the majority of the population would be in control.

Marxist theory of stages

Marx believed in the idea of 'permanent revolution' or 'uninterrupted revolution' – a series of revolutionary stages in which, after one stage had been achieved, the next class struggle would begin almost immediately. He did not believe that 'progression' through the stages of society was inevitable. He also argued that, in special circumstances, a relatively backward society could 'jump' a stage. However, this would only happen if that state was aided by sympathetic advanced societies. He certainly did not believe that a poor agricultural society could move to socialism on its own, as socialism required an advanced industrial base.

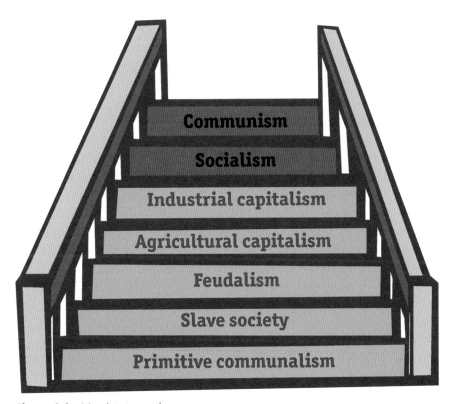

Figure 1.4 Marxist stages theory

Leninism

Marx did not refer to himself as a 'Marxist'. He preferred the term 'communist', as in the title of the book he and Engels wrote in 1847, *The Communist Manifesto*. However, many of Marx's followers preferred to call themselves Marxists as well as communists. In this way, they distinguished themselves from other groups that claimed to be communist, and emphasised that Marxism and its methods formed a distinct philosophy.

Introduction

Figure 1.5 Leon Trotsky (1879–1940)

Trotsky's real name was Lev Bronstein. He sided with the Mensheviks against Lenin when the RSDLP split in 1903. However, he joined the Bolsheviks in 1917 and was the main organiser of the November Revolution. He led the Red Army during the civil war. He became increasingly concerned about the increasingly authoritarian state being established by Stalin. Expelled from the Soviet Union in 1929, he set up the Fourth International, an international communist organisation, in 1938 while in Mexico. He was assassinated in Mexico by one of Stalin's agents in 1940.

socialism in one country: This theory was first developed by Stalin in his struggle against Trotsky after 1924. Before then, Lenin, and all Communist leaders, had believed that no single country – especially one with a relatively undeveloped economy – could construct a fully socialist society on its own. That was why Marxists stressed the importance of internationalism and world revolution. However, after Stalin's victory in the power struggle, 'socialism in one country' became an important part of official Soviet ideology.

One such Marxist was the Russian revolutionary Vladimir Ilyich Lenin (1870–1924). Lenin developed some of Marx's economic ideas, but his most important contribution to Marxist theory related to political organisation. His main ideas, based on the extremely undemocratic political system operating in tsarist Russia, were 'democratic centralism' (see Marxism-Leninism below) and the need for a small 'vanguard' party (a leading group) of fully committed revolutionaries.

However, **Leon Trotsky** (1879–1940), a leading Russian Marxist, disagreed with Lenin. From 1903 to 1917, Trotsky argued that Lenin's system would allow an unscrupulous leader to become a dictator over the party. Nevertheless, both Lenin and Trotsky believed in the possibility of a society moving through the revolutionary stages quickly to the socialist phase. This idea was similar to Marx's idea of 'permanent revolution', which argued that, as soon as one stage had been achieved, the struggle for the next would begin almost immediately.

Like Marx, Lenin and Trotsky both believed that Russia could not succeed in carrying through any 'uninterrupted revolution' without outside economic and technical assistance. When this assistance failed to materialise, despite their earlier hopes of successful workers' revolutions in other European states after 1918, Lenin proved to be an extremely pragmatic – or opportunistic – ruler. He was quite prepared to adopt policies that seemed to be in total conflict with communist goals and even with those of the 'lower' socialist stage: these policies were seen as adaptations to the prevailing circumstances.

Marxism-Leninism

The term 'Marxism-Leninism', invented by Stalin, was not used until after Lenin's death in 1924. It soon came to be used in Stalin's Soviet Union to refer to what he described as 'orthodox Marxism', which increasingly came to mean what Stalin himself had to say about political and economic issues. Essentially, Marxism–Leninism was the 'official' ideology of the Soviet state and of all communist parties loyal to Stalin and his successors. Many Marxists – and even members of the Communist Party itself – believed that Stalin's ideas and practices (such as '**socialism in one country**' and the purges) were in fact almost total distortions of what Marx and Lenin had said and done.

Stalinism

The term 'Stalinism' is used both by historians and those politically opposed to Stalin to describe the views and practices associated with Stalin and his supporters. Historians and political scientists use it to mean a set of beliefs and a type of rule that are essentially deeply undemocratic and even dictatorial.

Marxist opponents of Stalin and post-Stalin rulers were determined to show that Stalinism was not an adaptation of Marxism but, on the contrary, a qualitative and fundamental aberration from both Leninism and Marxism, and from revolutionary communism in general. In particular, they stress the way in which Stalin and his supporters – and later Mao in China – rejected the goal of **socialist democracy** in favour of a permanent one-party state. They also emphasise how Stalinism in practice and in theory placed the national interests of the Soviet Union above the struggle to achieve world revolution.

Fascism

Attempts by historians to agree on a definition of 'fascism' have proved even more difficult. Stanley Payne defined fascism as 'a form of revolutionary **ultra-nationalism** for national rebirth'. However, this definition says nothing about fascism being a movement committed to the destruction of all independent working-class organisations – especially socialist and communist parties and trade unions. Also absent is any reference to anti-Semitism or racism in general. Other historians stress these aspects as being core elements of fascism.

Fascism is certainly one of the most controversial and misused terms in the history of the modern world. For example, it is often used loosely as a term of abuse to describe any political regime, movement or individual seen as being right-wing or authoritarian. The issue is further complicated by the fact that, unlike with Marxism/communism, there is no coherent or unified ideology or *Weltanschauung* (world view).

Fascism and the 'third way'

Some historians and political commentators have seen fascism simply as a series of unconnected and uncoordinated reactions to the impact of the First World War and the Russian Revolution (1917), which varied from country to country and about which it is therefore impossible to generalise. Thus fascism is seen as an opportunistic form of extreme nationalism that in political terms lay somewhere between communism and capitalism. In other words, it was a political 'third way' or 'third force'.

Fascism and ideology

Unlike Marxism/communism, the 'ideology' of fascism does not appear to have existed before the end of the First World War. It was in Italy that Benito Mussolini (1883–1945) and other ultra-nationalists took the term *fascio* (meaning 'band', 'union' or 'group') for their own political organisation.

It is possible – with the benefit of hindsight – to trace the intellectual origins of fascism back to a rudimentary form of fascism that developed in the 19th century. Sometimes referred to as 'proto-fascism', this developed as a result of a 'new right' reaction against the late 18th century liberal ideas of the Enlightenment and early 19th century 'positivism'. Both of these philosophies had emphasised the importance of reason and progress over nature and emotion.

Fascism and Nazism

In addition to trying to establish a specific and coherent fascist ideology, there is the problem of comparing the different states of fascist Italy and Nazi Germany, and assessing to what extent they were similar. Those who argue that there is a general fascist category to which all fascist parties conform, to a greater or lesser extent, tend to see right-wing and left-wing dictatorships as being fundamentally different. One problem with the attempt to portray all fascist parties as being broadly similar is the question of racism and, more specifically, anti-Semitism. While anti-Semitism was not a core belief in Italian fascism, it was one of the main tenets of the German Nazi Party.

socialist democracy: This term refers to a form of democracy advocated by revolutionary socialists in which government is in the hands of the people who have the right of immediate recall of elected representatives who break their promises. In this system all parties that accept the goal of ending capitalist exploitation should be allowed to exist, and the state makes newspaper facilities available to all groups with sufficient support.

ultra-nationalism: This is an extremely strong belief in the superiority of one's own country and a desire to advance that country at the expense of others – including by waging wars.

1

Introduction

Dictatorships – authoritarian or totalitarian?

As well as having to understand the various political ideologies, it is also necessary to be familiar with several terms used by historians and political scientists. 'Dictatorship' is the term used to describe a regime in which democracy, individual rights and parliamentary rule are absent. Dictatorships have tended to be divided into two categories: authoritarian and totalitarian.

Authoritarian dictatorships

According to Karl Dietrich Bracher, authoritarian dictatorships do not come to power as the result of a mass movement or revolution. Instead, such regimes arise when an existing **conservative** regime imposes increasingly undemocratic measures, intended to neutralise and immobilise mass political and industrial organisations. Alternatively, they can arise following a military coup. Whatever their origin, authoritarian regimes are firmly committed to maintaining or restoring traditional structures and values.

Totalitarian dictatorships

In any comparative study of single-party states, it is important to understand the debate surrounding the application of the '**totalitarian**' label. In fact, the history of the term 'totalitarian' is complex. Those historians who argue that fascist and communist dictatorships were similar tend to believe that all such regimes were totalitarian dictatorships with many features in common.

> **SOURCE A**
>
> Stalin's police state is not an approximation to, or something like, or in some respects comparable with Hitler's. It is the same thing, only *more* ruthless, *more* cold-blooded … and *more* dangerous to democracy and civilised morals.
>
> Eastman, M. 1955. *Reflections on the Failure of Socialism*. New York, USA. Devin-Adair. p. 87.

However, such totalitarian theories were first developed by US theorists during the Cold War in the late 1940s and early 1950s. Several historians and political commentators from the 1960s onwards pointed out that the attempt to equate the Soviet Union with Nazi Germany was essentially a crude attempt to persuade public opinion in the USA and other Western countries to accept permanent war preparations and military threats against the Soviet Union after 1945.

The concept of totalitarianism – or total political power – was first developed systematically by Giovanni Amendola in 1923. In 1925, Mussolini took over Amendola's term and claimed that fascism was based on a 'fierce totalitarian will', stating that all aspects of the state, politics, and cultural and spiritual life should be 'fascistised': 'Everything within the state. Nothing outside the state. Nothing against the state.' Since then, several historians have attempted to define the meaning of the term 'totalitarian' by identifying certain basic features that are not normally features of authoritarian dictatorships. The following table provides a fuller explanation of the main features of a totalitarian state.

conservative:
A conservative political doctrine favours keeping things as they are and upholding traditional structures and values. It is a right-wing doctrine.

totalitarian: A totalitarian dictatorship is often defined as a system in which a dictator is able to impose their will on party, state and society – all of which are strictly disciplined. Such regimes come to power as the result of a mass movement or revolution and, at least in theory, are committed to a radical ideology and programme of political, economic and social change. The term is usually applied to regimes such as Hitler's Germany and Stalin's Soviet Union. However, many historians question whether all sections of society in such regimes were totally passive. Even the historian Robert Conquest, who used to advocate a stronger totalitarian interpretation, now concedes that Stalin was not always able to impose his will. Other possible examples of totalitarian dictatorships are those of Mao in China and – less convincingly – of Castro in Cuba.

Features of a totalitarian state

Views of Graeme Gill	Views of Leonard Schapiro
Graeme Gill sees authoritarian states (such as the Stalinist state) as having six components: 1. a personal dictatorship based on coercion, via the use of the secret police and repression 2. a total politicisation of all aspects of life which, at the same time, weakened the political control of state and party as it was the dictator who was seen as the embodiment of the country 3. tight political controls over cultural and artistic life 4. a static conservative ideology which, in theory, upheld but which, in practice, replaced earlier revolutionary ideals 5. a highly centralised economy, in which all important areas of the economy were state-owned 6. a social structure that, while at first allowing mobility from working-class occupations into scientific, technical, administrative and intellectual professions, soon saw the emergence of a privileged élite.	Gill's views correspond to the features of totalitarianism as set out by Leonard Schapiro's *Totalitarianism* (1973). Schapiro identified five main aspects as central to any totalitarian regime. These are as follows: 1. a distinctive, 'utopian' and all-embracing ideology that dominates and tries to restructure all aspects of society 2. a political system that is headed by an all-powerful leader, around whom a deliberate 'cult of personality' is created, and in which party, parliament and the state are under the control of the leader 3. a deliberate use of censorship and propaganda aimed at controlling all aspects of culture, and at indoctrinating (at times mobilising) all sections of society, but especially the young 4. a systematic use of coercion and terror to ensure total compliance with all decisions made by the leader and the regime 5. absolute state control and coordination of the economy, which is subordinated to the political objectives of the political regime.

Summary

By the time you have worked through this book, you should be able to:

- understand and explain the various factors behind the origins and rise of authoritarian states, and evaluate the different historical interpretations surrounding them
- show an awareness of the role of leaders and ideology in the rise to power of such regimes
- show a broad understanding of the nature of different authoritarian states
- understand the methods used by such leaders and regimes to maintain and consolidate power, including how opposition groups were treated, and the use of repression and propaganda
- understand the key economic and social policies of such regimes, their impact on society, and their successes and failures
- understand and explain the various policies towards women, ethnic minorities and organised religion
- understand the aims of authoritarian control and the extent to which they were achieved.

2 Mussolini and Italy

1 Unit — Emergence of an Authoritarian Regime in Italy

Overview

- Although independence had been gained from Austria in 1861, Italy remained a divided nation in many ways. The incorporation of the papal states in 1870 resulted in Catholic hostility against the new Italian kingdom, which lasted into the early 20th century.

- In 1900, the right to vote was still very restricted. This and the liberal domination of politics via the system known as *trasformismo* ('transformism') undermined support for parliamentary democracy. There was also opposition from the growing socialist movement.

- In addition, there were significant economic and social divisions in Italy, especially between the more prosperous industrial north and the poorer agricultural south.

- Another cause of unrest was the claims made by Italian nationalists for various territories in Europe, and their demands for Italy to establish colonies in Africa and Asia.

- These problems were worsened by Italy's entry into the First World War. There were divisions between interventionists and those who wanted to remain neutral. The war led to high casualties and inflation. After the war, there was disappointment at Italy's limited territorial gains from the peace treaties, as well as higher unemployment.

- Between 1919 and 1922, many socialist-led strikes and factory occupations took place. Right-wing groups such as the Arditi and the Fasci di Combattimento used increasing violence against the left.

- In 1921, Mussolini established the National Fascist Party (PNF) and then made an electoral pact with the liberals. A new wave of fascist violence was often ignored by the élites and the authorities.

- Many of the (often contradictory) ideas that eventually formed fascist ideology in Italy had their origins in 19th-century thought.

- Mussolini's own political views covered the entire political spectrum, from revolutionary socialism before 1914, to nationalism and then to fascism by 1919.

- In the early days of fascism, Mussolini placed much more emphasis on action than on ideology. From 1919 to 1922, the more radical elements of fascist programmes and policies were increasingly moderated.

- In 1922, local fascist leaders began to take over various towns and regions, and in October their 'March on Rome' resulted in Mussolini being appointed prime minister.

- After he became prime minister in 1922, Mussolini continued to distance himself from early fascism.

- From 1926 onwards, the more radical members of the PNF were purged, and the party came increasingly under Mussolini's personal control.

- Even the creation of the corporate state – although apparently a concession to party 'radicals' – was carried out in a way that emphasised the power of the Italian state and of employers over employees.

- During the 1930s, Mussolini made efforts to issue clearer statements of **fascist** ideology. However, by this point, Italy had become a personal rather than a party dictatorship.

fascist: A term deriving from the Italian word *fascio* (plural *fasci*), meaning 'group' or 'band'. In 1893, in Sicily, radical groups of mostly socialist workers formed *fasci* to organise demonstrations and strikes in protest at low wages and high rents. Mussolini adopted the term for his political movement in 1919. He later claimed that it referred to the *fasces*, bundles of rods carried by *lictors* (bodyguards) in ancient Rome.

KEY QUESTIONS

- How did the political and economic conditions in Italy before 1914 contribute to the emergence of an authoritarian regime?
- How did conditions between 1914–22 contribute to Mussolini's rise to power?
- What were the aims and ideology of the Fascist Party?
- What were the sources of support for Mussolini's Fascist Party?

QUESTION

What can you learn from this photograph about the nature of the Italian Fascist Party in 1922?

Figure 2.1 Fascists in Rome, November 1922, after their triumphant 'March' on the city

Figure 2.2 Benito Mussolini (1883–1945)

Mussolini followed an inconsistent political path in his early years. Initially more influenced by his father (a blacksmith with revolutionary socialist views) than by his mother (a school teacher and a devout Catholic), Mussolini drifted into socialist politics and journalism. Between 1904 and 1910, he developed a reputation as a militant as a result of articles in which he expressed traditional socialist views. The First World War led him to make a dramatic switch to extreme nationalism – which resulted in his expulsion from the Socialist Party – and then to fascism. Mussolini became Italy's first dictator, ruling from 1922 until 1943.

Risorgimento: This Italian word means 'resurgence' or 'rebirth', and refers to the literary and cultural revival that took place in Italy after 1815. The movement also campaigned against divisions within Italy and foreign domination, and called for political unification.

2.1 How did the political and economic conditions in Italy before 1914 contribute to the emergence of an authoritarian regime?

Italy was the first state anywhere in the world in which a Fascist Party developed, and the first to have a fascist dictator, in **Benito Mussolini.**

The problems of liberal Italy before 1914

Many of the long-term factors behind the emergence of Mussolini as fascist dictator of Italy can be found in the weaknesses of Italy's liberal monarchy in the period before 1914. In 1861, after many decades of struggle against the Austrian Empire, the *Risorgimento* nationalist movement succeeded in creating a unified and independent Italy. However, the Catholic Church retained its own separate state in Rome and the surrounding area.

The people of the new kingdom of Italy were far from united, though, and several serious underlying problems left the *Risorgimento* process incomplete in many ways.

Italian politics and the impact of trasformismo

After unification, Italian politics were dominated by the liberals, who hoped to modernise Italy through social reforms such as state education (to break the conservative influence of the Catholic Church), and by stimulating economic development and progress. However, although the liberals were split into progressives and conservatives – or 'left-liberals' and 'conservative-liberals' – they were united in distrusting the masses, who had played little part in the struggle for unification. The liberals also particularly feared the influence of socialists, anarchists and republicans on the left and the Catholic Church on the right. All of these groups were opposed to the new Italian state. Consequently, the liberals were determined to keep politics firmly under their control until the old internal divisions and rivalries were overcome and the new state was secure. The electorate was thus restricted at first, with only about 2 per cent of the adult population allowed to vote.

The resentment many Italians felt at this restricted franchise (the right to vote) was increased by the corrupt politics it encouraged. With no mass parties, and no real party discipline amongst the liberals, leading politicians formed factions that made deals with one another to alternate political control. This process became known as *trasformismo*.

Even though the franchise was gradually extended, and all adult males were allowed to vote by 1912, the practice of *trasformismo* continued.

Political disunity in Italy was intensified by the hostility of the papacy towards the new Italian state. The papacy's opposition to the liberal regime was moderated during the 1890s out of fear that it might give way to socialism, and in 1904, the pope permitted Catholics to vote in constituencies where abstaining might result in a socialist victory. However, there was no real harmony between the liberal and Catholic powers.

Regional divisions

In addition to these political problems, the people of the new kingdom of Italy were not really united. Many Italians felt more loyalty towards their own town or region than towards the national government. The mountain ranges and islands that dominated Italy's geography made communication difficult, hindering the development of a truly national identity among the country's 38 million people. This was especially true in the south, where earlier rulers had deliberately neglected road and railway development in an attempt to stop the spread of liberal and revolutionary ideas from the north.

The problems of communication and transport also contributed to economic divisions in Italy. The south was very poor in comparison with northern and central areas. Land suitable for farming in the south was restricted by geography and climate, and most of the fertile lands were part of large estates known as *latifundia*, which were owned by a small minority of wealthy landowners. The vast majority of the population was extremely poor.

In northern and central Italy agriculture was more developed, and more modern farming methods and machinery were used. Even here, however, productivity was much lower than in the countries of northern Europe. There were also significant social divisions in even the more advanced agricultural areas. Most of the land was owned by wealthy landowners known as the *agrari*, who rented out land to poorer farmers and peasant sharecroppers. At the bottom of the social scale was a large class of rural labourers. As in the south, poverty and discontent in rural areas often led to conflict between the classes. The biggest economic difference between north and south, however, was in industry.

The Fiat car company was established in 1899, and by 1913 it was exporting over 4,000 cars a year. Towns and cities in the north grew rapidly. This led to the creation of a large industrial working class, a sizeable lower-middle class, and a powerful class of rich industrialists and bankers. While industry expanded in the north, however, there was no real investment in the south.

As with agriculture, the social and economic inequalities in the industrial towns led to frequent clashes between employers and employees. Many workers joined the socialists or the anarchists, and in 1904 a general strike took place. The dissatisfaction felt by many Italians led them to emigrate – the majority going to the USA.

The problems of terra irredenta and the desire for empire

After 1870, many Italians came to realise that the *Risorgimento* was not complete. Firstly, there were the lands in Europe known as **terra irredenta**, which many Italians wanted Italy to reclaim.

In addition, many Italians hoped that unification would enable Italy to join the top rank of European powers by establishing its own empire. They looked to the example set by Germany – newly created in 1871 – which had started to obtain colonies in Africa and Asia. The first step in Italian empire-building was taken in 1885, with the acquisition of the port of Massawa on the Red Sea. By 1890, this had become the centre of the Italian colony of Eritrea. At the same time, Italy began the conquest of what became Italian Somaliland. However, tensions grew between Italy and the independent African state of Abyssinia (now Ethiopia), which bordered both of these regions.

In 1911, Italy invaded the Turkish colony of Libya in an attempt to increase the size of the Italian empire and to block growing French influence in North Africa. In 1912,

trasformismo: This political development began soon after Italy had obtained the papal states in 1870, and was first applied by Agostino Depretis who was prime minister for most of the period 1876–87. He wanted to unite all moderate Liberals, and was prepared to form coalition governments with politicians of conflicting views – provided they were not extremists of the right or left. He saw this as a way to 'transform' Italy's political life and bring about widespread national support for Italy's recent unification. In effect, however, it tended to result in different sections of the Liberals forming governments.

terra irredenta: This term means 'unredeemed land'. It originally referred to the areas inhabited by many Italian speakers but ruled by Austria-Hungary during the 19th and early 20th centuries. The most important of these were Trentino and Trieste, in the northern Adriatic. Later, this term would also designate other surrounding foreign territories to which Italy believed that it had a rightful claim. Those who advocated this policy of territory reclamation were called 'irredentists'.

QUESTION

How did the practice of *trasformismo* undermine support for parliamentary democracy in Italy before 1922?

Turkey formally accepted its loss. Many Italian nationalists, still angry at their defeat by Abyssinia in 1896, continued to press for a more aggressive imperial policy.

Fact: 'The papacy' refers to the office of the pope, while 'the Vatican' refers to the central administration of the Catholic Church. *Risorgimento* was not supported by the papacy, which had previously ruled a large part of central Italy. The creation of the new kingdom deprived the papacy of all its territory except that surrounding Rome itself – also seized by Italian troops in 1870 to complete Italy's unification. In 1873, the government confirmed the confiscation and in 1874, the pope retaliated by banning Catholics from all involvement in politics – even voting.

Fact: Industrial development in the newly unified Italy was limited. The north had some iron and steel concerns, but development was hindered by the lack of coal and iron ore. The south's traditional silk industry was soon wiped out by more efficient manufacturers in the north. In the 1880s, hydroelectric power in the north provided the basis for rapid industrialisation.

Figure 2.3 A postcard advertising a meeting of socialists in Bologna, 1904

2.2 How did conditions during 1914–22 contribute to Mussolini's rise to power?

Triple Alliance: The military alliance formed in 1882 between Germany, Austria and Italy. Opposed to this was the Triple Entente, consisting of Britain, France and Russia.

Although Italy was a member of the **Triple Alliance**, it did not join in when the First World War began in 1914. Instead, it decided to stay neutral.

The impact of the First World War and the peace treaties, 1914–19

Italian participation

While most Italians (especially the socialists) were in favour of neutrality, nationalists felt that intervention in the war would offer Italy an opportunity to gain more land and expand its empire. In view of its ambition to reclaim the country's *terra irredenta*, the liberal government decided to see which side would offer the best terms in exchange for Italy's support. Negotiations with the other two Triple Alliance nations in the period 1914–15 revealed that Austria would never concede Trentino or Trieste. However, the Entente nations promised that in the event of their victory, these territories would be granted to Italy, along with similarly contested Austrian territory in the South Tyrol, and Istria and northern Dalmatia on the Adriatic coast.

The Treaty of London

While the Italian parliament debated the issues, interventionists organised street demonstrations demanding Italian involvement in the war. Many were members of the *fasci*, a mixture of anarcho-syndicalists (see Mussolini and the Fascio di Combattimento below) and national socialists who believed war would hasten revolution. They were joined by the right-wing nationalists of the **Associazione Nazionalista Italiana (ANI)** – the Italian Nationalist Association – which had previously pushed for the conquest of Libya. However, the leading liberal politicians had already decided on Italy's participation in the war. Consequently, in May 1915, Italy signed the Treaty of London and promised to join the war on the side of the Triple Entente.

Italy's performance in the First World War

Despite the interventionists' hopes, the war did not go well for Italy. Over 5 million Italians were conscripted, and though most fought bravely they were ill-equipped and ill-supplied. In particular, military leadership was often poor and the Italian army found itself fighting a costly war of **attrition**.

In November 1917, the Italians suffered a terrible defeat at the hands of the Austrians at the Battle of Caporetto. Over 40,000 Italian soldiers were killed and about 300,000 were taken prisoner. The nationalists blamed the government for its inefficiency and for failing to supply the troops with enough equipment. Although the Italians won a costly victory at Vittorio Veneto in October 1918, this was overshadowed by previous defeats and the high casualties suffered. In addition, with the socialists maintaining strong opposition throughout, the war had clearly failed to unite Italians.

The economic impact of the First World War

The First World War had a significant impact on the relatively weak Italian economy. In order to finance its involvement, the liberal government had borrowed heavily from Britain and the US, and the national debt had risen from 16 billion lire to 85 billion. Even this proved inadequate, so the government printed more banknotes, causing rapid inflation – prices increased by over 400 per cent between 1915 and 1918. This inflation destroyed much of the middle class' savings, reduced rental incomes for many landowners, and caused a drop of more than 25 per cent in the real wages of many workers. At the end of the war the situation was worsened by high

Fact: In 1889, Abyssinia signed a Treaty of Friendship with Italy, recognising Italy's acquisition of Massawa and agreeing to use the city as its main port. However, the Italian conquest of Eritrea led the Abyssinians to oppose any Italian interference in their country's affairs. In 1895, Italy occupied the province of Tigre in Abyssinia, but after several military clashes the Italians were heavily defeated at the Battle of Adowa in 1896. This was seen by many Italians as a terrible national humiliation.

Associazione Nazionalista Italiana (ANI): Italy's first nationalist party, formed in 1910. It supported war against Austria as a way of gaining the terra irredenta. The ANI grew close to Mussolini's Fascist Party, and merged with it in 1923.

attrition: The process of wearing down the enemy by sustained attacks. Italian officers often sacrificed thousands of lives needlessly – in all, over 600,000 Italians were killed, about 450,000 were permanently disabled, and a further 500,000 were seriously wounded.

unemployment as war industries closed down and more than 2.5 million soldiers were demobilised.

The war also deepened the economic divisions between north and south Italy. Those industries linked to war production (especially steel, chemicals, motor vehicles, and the rubber and woollen industries) did extremely well before 1918, as they were guaranteed large state contracts. When inflation began to rise, industrialists simply passed on the price increases to the government.

The south, still predominantly agricultural, did not share in this prosperity. Farming was badly affected by the conscription of large numbers of peasants and farm labourers. However, during the last years of the war – in an attempt to limit the attraction of socialism and the ideology of the Russian **Bolsheviks** – the government promised a programme of land reform after the war.

The terms of the peace treaties

When the war ended in November 1918, many Italians thought that their sacrifices should be repaid by substantial territorial rewards. **Vittorio Orlando**, the Italian prime minister, went to the Paris Peace Conferences in January 1919 expecting to receive all that had been promised by the Treaty of London. Under pressure from the nationalists, he also demanded the port of Fiume on the border of Istria as it contained a large Italian-speaking population. Finally, Orlando wanted Italy to gain a share of the former German colonies in Africa.

Nationalists and the 'mutilated victory'

Although most of Italy's post-war demands were eventually met, there were some important exceptions. The country gained no African territory, and Britain and the US refused to grant Italy Fiume and northern Dalmatia, arguing that these were vital for the development of the new state of Yugoslavia.

Italy's long-term opponent, Austria-Hungary, had been defeated and its empire dismantled, leaving Italy the dominant power in the Adriatic. Yet Italian nationalists were disgusted once the likely terms of the peace agreements became clear, and accused the liberal government of allowing Italy to be both humiliated and cheated. The popular nationalist Gabriele D'Annunzio spoke for many Italians – especially war veterans – when he called it a 'mutilated victory'.

By 1919, it was clear that the liberal regime would face many problems in post-war Italy. In addition to the growing dissatisfaction of the nationalists, the liberals faced increased political opposition from other quarters. In January 1919, the papacy finally lifted its ban on the formation of a Catholic political party, leading to the foundation of the **Partito Popolare Italiano (PPI)**, or Italian Popular Party.

The Italian Socialist Party (PSI) – the socialist 'threat'

A more serious threat to the liberal regime was posed by the Italian Socialist Party (PSI). The economic problems resulting from the First World War caused great discontent among industrial and rural workers. The Socialist Party had moved increasingly to a revolutionary position. In 1917, inspired by the Bolshevik Revolution in Russia, it called for the overthrow of the liberal state and the establishment of a socialist republic. Industrial workers resented the imposition of wartime discipline in the factories, which increased working hours and banned strikes – to the benefit of the employers. With

Bolsheviks: The more revolutionary element of the Russian Social Democratic Labour Party (a Marxist party). Led by Vladimir Ilyich Lenin – later joined by Leon Trotsky – they took power in Russia in November 1917. The Bolsheviks later changed their name to the Russian Communist Party, and worked hard to aid and encourage socialist revolutions in other regions, especially in more advanced capitalist countries such as Germany.

Fact: Companies such as Pirelli (tyres) and Montecatini (chemicals) made huge profits during the war. Fiat continued to expand and, by 1918, it was the largest motor manufacturer in Europe. However, the end of the war meant the loss of lucrative state contracts as the government cut expenditure in order to cope with mounting debts.

QUESTION

What do you understand by the term 'mutilated victory'? What areas were claimed by Italian nationalists after 1919?

only about 50,000 members in 1914, Socialist Party membership had increased to over 200,000 by 1919. At its congress in that year, delegates talked of the need to use force in order to achieve 'the conquest of power over the bourgeoisie'. In practice, however, many socialist leaders were stronger on rhetoric than on action.

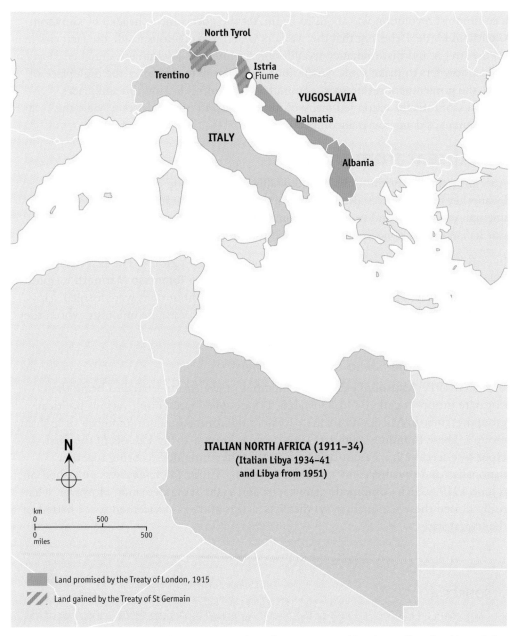

Figure 2.4 The land promised by the Treaty of London in 1915 and land actually gained by Italy in the 1919 peace treaties

The *biennio rosso*, 1919–20

Unemployment rose to over 2 million in 1919, and industrial workers began a wave of militant action that lasted from early 1919 to 1920. These years became known as the *biennio rosso* – the 'two red years'. Throughout 1919, strikes, factory occupations

Vittorio Orlando (1860–1952)

Orlando was appointed prime minister a few days after the Italian defeat at Caporetto in October 1917. At the Paris Peace Conferences, Italy had expected to be granted control of the Adriatic coastline. Orlando's failure to win this territory prompted his resignation in June 1919. His inability to secure all of Italy's territorial expectations at Versailles was used by Mussolini and the fascists in their campaign to demonstrate the weakness of the Italian government. Orlando initially backed Mussolini in 1922, but he withdrew his support in 1924.

Partito Popolare Italiano (PPI): Often known simply as the Popolari, this party was a coalition of conservative and liberal Catholics who wanted to defend Catholic interests and improve life for the peasants. It was led by the priest Luigi Sturzo, and was backed by Pope Benedict XV in order to oppose the Italian Socialist Party (PSI). In 1919, the Popolari won 20 per cent of the vote, and from 1919 to 1921 it was the second-largest party in Italy after the PSI. The Popolari was generally suspicious of liberalism because of the latter's history of anti-clericalism. Some members became ministers in Mussolini's fascist government.

and land occupations, organised by trade unions and peasant leagues and involving over 1 million workers, swept across Italy. By the end of 1919, socialist trade unions had more than 2 million members, compared to about 250,000 at the beginning of the year.

In many areas, especially in the north, socialists seized control of local government. To many industrialists and landowners, and to the middle classes in general, it seemed that a communist revolution was about to begin. Yet the government, headed by **Giovanni Giolitti**, did little. Believing that the workers were less dangerous inside the factories than on the streets, and that militancy would soon decline, the government urged employers and landowners to make some concessions. In response to riots over the high price of food, the government set up food committees to control distribution and prices. This lack of forceful action led many of the middle and upper classes to view the government as dangerously incompetent.

The threat from the right

After the war, the various militant and disaffected right-wing groups were joined by another force that was also in search of change. This comprised demobilised and unemployed officers and troops, who found it difficult to accept many aspects of post-war Italian society. One notable group was the **Arditi**.

In early 1919, the Arditi formed themselves into organised groups. The first Arditi Association was set up in Rome in January, while **Filippo Tommaso Marinetti** established another in Milan. Throughout February, many other Arditi groups were formed across Italy. They increasingly used weapons to attack socialists and trade unionists, whom they regarded as the enemies of the Italian nation.

Mussolini and the Fascio di Combattimento

In March 1919, Mussolini – himself a member of the Arditi – tried to bring these disparate groups together. On 23 March, 118 people, representing various political groupings, met in Milan and formed a Fascio di Combattimento ('combat' or 'fighting group'). These founding members later became known as the Fascists of the First Hour (see section 2.3, Fascist beliefs in 1919). They intended to bring together nationalists and socialists, and a militant-sounding *Fascist Programme* was published on 6 June 1919, which combined various left- and right-wing demands. However, what really united these nationalists, **syndicalists**, artists and ex-servicemen was a hatred of the liberal state.

SOURCE A

Comments on the backgrounds of the fascist squadristi by Angelo Tasca, a member of the Italian Communist Party in the early 1920s.

In the Po valley, the towns were on the whole less red than the country, being full of landowners, garrison officers, university students, rentiers, professional men, and trades people. These were the classes from which Fascism drew its recruits and which offered the first armed squads.

Tasca, A. *The Rise of Italian Fascism 1918–22*. Quoted in Macdonald, H. 1999. *Mussolini and Italian Fascism*. Cheltenham, UK. Nelson Thornes. p. 17.

Giovanni Giolitti (1842–1928)

Giolitti was prime minister of Italy five times between 1892 and 1921. Bowing to nationalist pressure, he agreed to the Italio–Turkish war of 1911–12. In 1915, Giolitti opposed Italy's involvement in the First World War, believing the country was unprepared. His last period as prime minister was 1920–21. He was supported by the fascist *squadristi*, and did not oppose their violent takeover of towns and regions. Giolitti backed Mussolini at first, but he withdrew his support in 1924.

Arditi: The term translates as 'the daring ones'. These were the black-shirted commando (or 'storm') troops of the Italian army, whose officers hated the liberal political system which they felt had betrayed their wartime sacrifices by failing to obtain the land promised to Italy. These troops were demobilised in 1920, but their name – and uniform – was used by D'Annunzio's supporters who took over Fiume in 1919.

Filippo Tommaso Marinetti (1876–1944)

Writer and artist Marinetti proclaimed the unity of art and life. The artistic movement he founded, futurism, incorporated elements of both anarchism and fascism. Marinetti was an early supporter of Mussolini. He later distanced himself from what he saw as the more conservative aspects of fascism, but he remained an important influence on fascist ideology.

Gabriele D'Annunzio (1863–1938)

D'Annunzio was a poet and writer. As an ultra-nationalist, he supported Italy's entry into the First World War on the side of the Triple Entente. He joined up as a pilot and became something of a war hero after dropping propaganda leaflets over Vienna. He was an irredentist (see section 2.1, The problems of *terra irredenta* and the desire for empire), and was angered when Fiume (now Rijeka in Croatia) was handed over to the new state of Yugoslavia after the First World War.

Figure 2.5 Benito Mussolini and Gabriele D'Annunzio in 1925

D'Annunzio and Fiume

Although Fasci di Combattimento were established in about 70 other towns, Mussolini's tiny network of militant agitators was soon overshadowed by the actions of **Gabriele D'Annunzio**, who led 2,000 armed men to the city of Fiume – one of the areas Italy had sought but not won in the peace treaties. D'Annunzio's force quickly took control, and in open defiance of the liberal Italian government and the Allies, they ruled the city for the next 15 months. This bold action made D'Annunzio a hero to Italian nationalists, and proved an inspiration to Mussolini. In particular, Mussolini decided to adopt the theatrical trappings used by D'Annunzio, especially the black shirts of the Arditi, the ancient Roman salute they used, and the many parades and balcony speeches they performed.

The relative weakness of Mussolini's Fasci di Combattimento was underlined by the results of the November 1919 elections. These were for appointments to the Chamber of Deputies – the lower house of the Italian parliament (the upper house was the Senate). For the first time, the elections were held using a system of **proportional representation**.

proportional representation: A method of voting whereby each party gains representation in parliament to a greater or lesser extent, according to the proportion of the total votes it receives in an election. Some proportional representation systems are more closely proportional than others.

ACTIVITY

Using what you have read, carry out some further research on D'Annunzio and the Arditi. Then write a couple of paragraphs to show the most significant ways in which they influenced Mussolini as he began to build his fascist movement.

Each local *fascio* was allowed to decide its own election manifesto but, despite this, not a single fascist candidate was elected. Mussolini himself won only 5,000 votes out of 270,000 in Milan. So great was his disappointment at this result that he considered emigrating to the US. In all, there were probably only about 4,000 committed fascist supporters throughout the entire country in 1919.

Fascist violence, the *ras* and Mussolini

By the end of 1920, the factory and land occupations had begun to decline. However, *squadristi* violence had not. Mussolini had not initially ordered the attacks, which had been organised by powerful *ras* leaders such as **Italo Balbo** in Ferrara and Dino Grandi in Bologna.

However, Mussolini soon realised the political – and financial – opportunities offered by a more organised use of *squadristi*. Support for Mussolini's Fasci di Combattimento increased when government military action against D'Annunzio forced the latter to surrender control of Fiume in January 1921. This removed a potentially powerful rival force for Mussolini. Slowly, with much resistance at first, he began to assert central control, arguing that without his leadership and newspaper (*Il Popoli*), the various groups would fall apart. In particular, Mussolini stressed the need to depict violence as necessary to prevent the success of a Bolshevik-style revolution in Italy. In April 1921, Mussolini made a speech in which he declared fascist violence to be part of an anti-socialist crusade to 'break up the Bolshevist State' (see **Source B**).

While attacking the state in public, Mussolini privately reassured Giolitti and other liberal politicians that talk of fascist revolution was not to be taken seriously. As a result, Giolitti offered the fascists an electoral alliance – an anti-socialist National Bloc – for the national elections due to be held in May 1921. During the election campaign, fascist squads continued their violence, and about 100 socialists were killed.

Figure 2.6   Italo Balbo (1896–1940)

A right-wing republican, Balbo joined the PNF in 1921. He became secretary of the fascist organisation in Ferrara, and soon the *ras* there. His fascist gangs – known as the Celbano – broke strikes for landowners and industrialists, and attacked socialists and communists. Balbo was one of the four main planners, known as the Quadrumirs, of Mussolini's 'March on Rome' (see The March on Rome, October 1922 below). In 1923, he became a member of the Fascist Grand Council.

> **SOURCE B**
>
> *Extracts from a speech about fascist violence by Mussolini to the fascists of Bologna, April 1921.*
>
> And, however much violence may be deplored, it is evident that we, in order to make our ideas understood, must beat refractory skulls with resounding blows … We are violent because it is necessary to be so …
>
> Our punitive expeditions, all those acts of violence which figure in the papers, must always have the character of the just retort and legitimate reprisal; because we are the first to recognise that it is sad, after having fought the external enemy, to have to fight the enemy within … and for this reason that which we are causing today is a revolution to break up the Bolshevist State, while waiting to settle our account with the Liberal State which remains.
>
> Robson, M. 1992. *Italy: Liberalism and Fascism 1870–1945*. London, UK. Hodder & Stoughton. p. 51.

Nonetheless, the socialists remained the largest party with 123 seats; the Popolari won 107 seats. Giolitti was disappointed by the results. Mussolini, however, was pleased with the outcome of the election – his group had won 7 per cent of the vote and had taken 35 seats. Mussolini himself was now a deputy and, significantly, all 35 fascist deputies

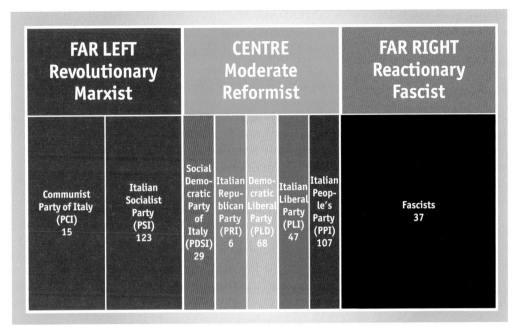

FAR LEFT Revolutionary Marxist		CENTRE Moderate Reformist					FAR RIGHT Reactionary Fascist
Communist Party of Italy (PCI) 15	Italian Socialist Party (PSI) 123	Social Democratic Party of Italy (PDSI) 29	Italian Republican Party (PRI) 6	Democratic Liberal Party (PLD) 68	Italian Liberal Party (PLI) 47	Italian People's Party (PPI) 107	Fascists 37

Figure 2.7 There were 535 seats in the Italian parliament in 1921. For these May elections, Mussolini entered the National Bloc, which was an anti-left alliance: led by Giolitti and the PLI, it also included the PPI. The remaining 105 seats were shared been several other less-important parties or political groupings

Fact: The action squads used knives, bayonets, firearms and even grenades in their attacks. They also beat up opponents with cudgels (known as *manganelli*). Often they would tie up their victims in town squares, and then – to humiliate them in public – force them to drink large quantities of castor oil, a powerful laxative that could cause severe diarrhoea, dehydration and in some cases even death.

were from the right of the movement. More importantly, holding positions in parliament gave the fascists an image of respectability as well as a foothold in national politics. With this success achieved, Mussolini announced that the fascists would not support Giolitti's coalition government after all.

The March on Rome, October 1922

Having obtained considerable control of northern and central Italy, the *ras* wanted to move from local to national power. Many of them had urged a coup after the collapse of the general strike, and Mussolini had struggled to restrain them. In early October 1922, the *ras* renewed their pressure. Balbo is said to have told Mussolini that the *ras* intended to march on Rome and seize power – with him or without him. To appease his more militant supporters, and to intimidate the liberal government into making concessions, Mussolini agreed to organise the March on Rome.

Local squads were organised into a national militia, under Balbo and Grandi, and a plan was drawn up by which four *ras* – Balbo, Bianchi, Cesare De Vecchi and General De Bono – would seize control of major towns and cities in northern and central Italy. Once this had been achieved, some 40,000 fascists would converge on Rome from three different cities.

On the night of 27 October, fascist squads took over town halls, railway stations and telephone exchanges across northern Italy. The following day, Prime Minister **Luigi Facta** persuaded the king, as commander-in-chief of the army, to declare a state of emergency. This meant that the government could use the military as well as the police to stop the fascist columns assembling in Rome.

Figure 2.8   Luigi Facta (1861–1930)

A liberal, Facta held various ministerial posts before and immediately after the First World War. He initially favoured neutrality, but later supported the war effort. Facta became prime minister in February 1922. Dismissed in July, he was soon reappointed, as no one else could form a government. He was the last prime minister of Italy before Mussolini began his rule.

Initially, roads and railways were blocked, and army troops met little resistance as they began to take back control of some buildings seized by the fascists. Fascist commanders, including De Vecchi, began to waver. The prefect of Milan was instructed to arrest Mussolini, who was in the city as a precautionary measure (Mussolini would be able to escape from Milan into Switzerland if things went wrong).

However, Mussolini was not arrested. The king changed his mind and refused to sign the papers authorising martial law. Facta resigned in protest. The king then asked the conservative Salandra to form a government, but Mussolini rejected the offer of four cabinet posts for fascists. He wanted the post of prime minister for himself. Salandra advised the king to appoint Mussolini and the king conceded. Mussolini accepted on 29 October 1922.

In fact, the March on Rome was more myth than reality. Mussolini himself did not march at the head of the fascist columns, but arrived in Rome by train, having already accepted the position of prime minister. The fascist militia did not reach the city until the following day, 30 October, when about 70,000 Blackshirts celebrated their victory in the streets of Rome.

2.3 What were the aims and ideology of the Fascist Party?

The question of fascist ideology, and the role it played in Mussolini's rise to power, is somewhat confused. This is firstly because there is no clear or consistent ideology connected to Mussolini's fascist movement, and secondly because Mussolini started on the left of the political spectrum and eventually moved to the extreme right. In fact, Mussolini once described fascism as 'action and mood, not doctrine'. As late as 1932, he wrote that when he formed the Fasci di Combattimento in 1919, fascism was 'not a doctrine'.

SOURCE C

Yet if anyone cares to read over the now crumbling minutes giving an account of the meetings at which the Italian Fasci di Combattimento were founded, he will find not a doctrine but a series of pointers.

Extract from *The Doctrine of Fascism*. 1932. Giovanni Gentile and Benito Mussolini. p. 23.

Fascism and ideology

Many historians argue that there is no coherent and unified ideological root for fascism, in the way that there is for Marxism, for example (see the Introduction). Mussolini did not make a concerted effort to define the basic beliefs of his movement until after he became prime minister. In fact, it was not until 1925 that Mussolini began to draw up a clear statement of fascist doctrine. Under the leadership of the philosopher

Giovanni Gentile, over 200 intellectuals met in Bologna and put together the *Manifesto of Fascist Intellectuals*.

However, this attempt to bring together the diverse and often contradictory ideas of fascism was not particularly effective. A more determined effort came in 1932, ten years after Mussolini became prime minister of Italy, when Gentile (with some help from Mussolini) wrote a lengthy entry on fascism for the *Enciclopedia Italiana*, of which he was editor. The first part of this was published separately as *The Doctrine of Fascism*, under Mussolini's name. However, this was as much a statement of what fascism was *against* (essentially liberalism, socialism, democracy and pacifism) as about what it stood *for* (action, the nation, authority and the state). In the section called 'Political and Social Doctrine of Fascism', Gentile explained that fascism was anti-communist, anti-socialist, and strongly opposed to the 'economic conception of history' and the centrality of 'class war' – both of which are fundamental to Marxist and communist ideology. He went on to explain that fascism was also opposed to democracy. The text stressed the authoritarian aspect of fascism: 'The foundation of fascism is the conception of the State. Fascism conceives of the State as an absolute.'

Figure 2.9   Giovanni Gentile (1875–1944)

Known as the 'philosopher of fascism', Gentile's philosophy of 'actual idealism' corresponded to the fascist liking for action. Gentile became minister of public education under Mussolini in 1923. He was also an important member of the Fascist Grand Council, and remained a loyal supporter of Mussolini after the foundation of the Salò Republic in 1943. He was killed the following year by anti-fascist partisans.

SOURCE D

Fascism [is] the precise negation of that doctrine which formed the basis of the so-called Scientific or Marxian Socialism.

After Socialism, Fascism attacks the whole complex of democratic ideologies …

Fascism denies that the majority, through the mere fact of being a majority, can rule human societies; it denies that this majority can govern by means of a periodical consultation …

Fascism is definitely and absolutely opposed to the doctrines of liberalism, both in the political and economic sphere.

Extracts from *The Doctrine of Fascism*. 1932. Giovanni Gentile and Benito Mussolini. pp. 30–32.

Yet Mussolini's fascism served as the model for many other fascist parties that emerged elsewhere in Europe during the 1920s and 1930s. In his early days, Adolf Hitler was an admirer of Mussolini. In 1934, Mussolini even set up Fascist International, which funded emerging fascist parties. While the main factors in Mussolini's rise were undoubtedly the instability in Italy, the violence of the fascist action squads and the supporting role of the élites, fascist aims and pronouncements also played a part.

Mussolini's early political views

It was during the wave of socialist militancy from 1919 to 1922 that the man who was to become the fascist prime minister of Italy founded his political movement. Yet, at first, Mussolini was involved with the Socialist Party. He frequently attacked the Roman Catholic Church and repeatedly called for a deepening of the class struggle and violent revolution.

At this time, Mussolini opposed militarism and Italian imperialism, supporting international solidarity instead. In 1911, during violent demonstrations against the Italian war on Libya, he was imprisoned for his part in attempting to provoke an insurrection in protest against the war. On his release in 1912, he became editor of the Socialist Party's newspaper *Avanti!* in Milan. His articles advocated revolutionary violence against the liberal state. He also helped expel pro-royalists and reformists from the Socialist Party. However, Mussolini was not a Marxist, and his 'socialism' was largely anti-clerical republicanism. Syndicalism and anarchism (see section 2.2, Mussolini and the Fascio di Combattimento) were far less important aspects of his 'ideology'.

The outbreak of the First World War soon led Mussolini to make a dramatic political U-turn – the first of many. The Socialist Party (like the Russian Bolsheviks) stuck to the principles of revolutionary internationalism and therefore condemned the war as an inter-imperialist conflict, urging the working class and the Italian government to remain neutral. Yet, in August, many of Mussolini's friends in republican and syndicalist groups supported Italy's entry on the Franco-British side. They set up the Fascio Rivoluzionario di Azione Internazionalista (Revolutionary Group of International Action). Mussolini soon dropped the idea of class struggle and rapidly moved towards an extreme nationalist position, advocating Italian involvement in the war.

In November 1914, Mussolini was sacked as editor of *Avanti!* and set up his own newspaper, *Il Popolo d'Italia* ('The People of Italy') to campaign in favour of war. The paper was financed by wealthy Italian companies such as Fiat (which expected to gain lucrative war contracts), as well as by the French government. Later, the paper was partly financed by Britain and Tsarist Russia. Shortly after the establishment of *Il Popolo*, Mussolini was expelled from the Socialist Party.

Despite advocating intervention in the war, Mussolini did not volunteer for the army. He was conscripted in September 1915, and invalided out of the army in 1917 after an accident during a training exercise. He then resumed his role as editor of *Il Popolo*, blaming the liberal government for military incompetence and calling for a dictator to take charge of the war effort. His *Manifesto to the Nation*, published in November 1917 after the defeat at Caporetto (see section 2.2, The impact of the First World War and the peace treaties, 1914–19), called for a 'national union' to work for victory in the war.

ACTIVITY

Write a couple of paragraphs to show the extent to which Mussolini's political beliefs between 1911 and 1918 both changed and remained the same.

The following month, some senators and deputies set up a Fascio Parlamentare di Difesa Nazionale (Parliamentary Group of National Defence). This coalition of nationalists, right-wing liberals and republican 'interventionists' set up various local *fasci* to take tough action against the 'enemy within' – for example neutralists and socialist revolutionaries. Although Mussolini still advocated social reform, he was rapidly moving away from a socialist position and closer to the emerging nationalist movement. In July 1918, he formally renounced socialism.

Fascist beliefs in 1919

Fascists of the First Hour: As the meeting took place in a hall on Piazza San Sepolcro, these early fascists were also known as the *sansepolcrista*. Historians disagree about the actual numbers who attended this foundation meeting. In 1923, Mussolini stated there were only 52.

Having already moved from his pre-war opposition to nationalism and imperialism to a pro-war expansionist position after 1915, Mussolini's political 'ideology' continued to shift. As seen above, in March 1919 Mussolini set up a Fascio di Combattimento in Milan. The founder members of this group later became known as the **Fascists of the First Hour.** Soon, over 70 such *fasci* had been established in northern and central Italy. Their *Fascist Programme*, published in June, was an incoherent mixture of left-wing and right-wing policies. It was designed to hold these very different groups together, and to appeal to as wide an audience as possible.

SOURCE E

1 A new national Assembly [will be set up] …

2 Proclamation of the Italian Republic …

4 Abolition of all titles of nobility …

6 Suppression of … joint stock companies … Suppression of all speculation by banks and stock exchanges.

7 Control and taxation of private wealth. Confiscation of unproductive income …

22 Reorganisation of production on a co-operative basis and direct participation of the workers in the profits.

Extracts from the 1919 Fascist Programme. Quoted in Robson, M. 1992. *Italy: Liberalism and Fascism 1870–1945*. London, UK. Hodder & Stoughton. p. 48.

Fact: In the 1919 elections, the results for the fascist candidates – and for Mussolini himself (his fascist list in Milan got only 1.7 per cent of the vote) – were so poor that the socialists in Milan organised a fake funeral for Mussolini and his fascist movement.

According to historian Alexander De Grand, Mussolini's fascism was a mixture of five, often contradictory, ideas and beliefs:

1 **National syndicalism.** At first republican, vaguely socialist and anti-clerical.

2 **Technocratic fascism.** Accepting and wholeheartedly embracing the industrial revolution and modernism (these included the futurists).

3 **Rural fascism.** Anti-urban, anti-modern and anti-industrial.

4 **Conservative fascism.** Essentially non-ideological and pragmatic, favouring tradition, monarchy and the Catholic Church.

5 **Nationalist fascism.** The most coherent element, favouring an authoritarian political system and an aggressive foreign policy in order to achieve territorial expansion.

As Mussolini's political ambitions grew after 1919, the more radical aspects of the *Fascist Programme* began to be dropped in favour of right-wing elements. This process began in earnest after the fascists' poor performance in the 1919 elections.

By 1921, Mussolini had cut the number of fascist 'enemies' down to the socialists and the alleged 'threat' of imminent communist revolution. Previously, the list of fascism's enemies had included capitalism and big business, the monarchy and the Catholic Church. In fact, one way in which ideology played a significant part in Mussolini's rise was the way he cleverly both exaggerated and exploited the people's fear of those who supported Marxist and communist ideologies.

SOURCE F

Our programme is simple: we wish to govern Italy. They ask us for programmes, but there are already too many. It is not programmes that are wanting for the salvation of Italy, but men and will-power …

Our [Italy's] political class is deficient. The crisis of the Liberal State has proved it … We must have a state which will simply say: 'The State does not represent a party, it represents the nation as a whole, it includes all, is over all, protects all.' This is the State which must arise from the Italy of Vittorio Veneto … a state which does not fall under the power of the Socialists … we want to remove from the state all its economic attributes.

Extracts from a speech made by Mussolini in Udine in September 1922. Quoted in Robson, M. 1992. *Italy: Liberalism and Fascism 1870–1945*. London, UK. Hodder & Stoughton. pp. 53–54.

QUESTION

How do you account for the differences between the two statements of fascist programmes and policies in **Source F** and **Source G**? What impact do you think **Source G** might have had on the conservative élites and classes?

Theory of knowledge

History, its study and language:
According to G. W. F. Hegel (1770–1831), '*The only thing we learn from history is that we learn nothing from history.*' Do you think that, since 1945, people have learned any 'lessons of history' from the study of fascist Italy and Nazi Germany? Do any fascist movements exist in the 21st century? Is it useful to apply labels to such political movements? Also, is it sensible in this case to stereotype such movements?

SOURCE G

The threat of Bolshevism was exploited cunningly by Mussolini and it is difficult to overestimate its importance in bringing Fascism to power. Yet in truth, the threat in Italy was almost entirely illusory. No master plan of revolution existed; peasants and workers acted without premeditation and on a local basis only … By the last quarter of 1921, the worst of the post-war depression was past; so was the worst of proletarian unrest. By the time, a year later, that Mussolini arrived in office to save Italy from Bolshevism, the threat, if it ever existed, was over.

Cassels, A. 1969. *Fascist Italy*. London, UK. Routledge & Keegan Paul. pp. 24–25.

Fascist 'ideology', 1921–22

After the May 1921 elections, in which Mussolini and 34 other fascist deputies from the right wing of the movement were elected, he became increasingly concerned with appeasing the conservative classes and controlling the *ras*.

In fact, Mussolini had been distancing himself from the more radical policies of early fascism since 1920. In October 1921, he successfully pushed for the establishment of a more disciplined political party – the National Fascist Party (PNF). This new party had a clear right-wing programme. It appealed to Mussolini's capitalist backers but it angered the *ras*, who wanted to destroy the existing political system, not participate in it. They became increasingly violent – a 'creeping insurrection', according to historian Philip Morgan. The socialists' general strike at the end of July 1922, which was intended to force the liberal government to take action against fascist attacks, merely served to frighten the conservatives and 'justify' further violence from the fascists.

Squadrismo

During 1921, Mussolini's 'ideology' was focused much more on the cult of fascist violence – which came to be known as *squadrismo* – than on political policies and programmes. After the bloc with the liberals and the May elections of 1921, Mussolini began to play on the conservatives' exaggerated fear of the socialists. In November, in another shift away from the radicalism of early fascism, Mussolini made a direct attempt to appease Catholics. The earlier left-wing and anti-clerical aspects of the 1919 programme were dropped: now the PNF opposed divorce and supported the Popolari's demands for better treatment of peasants.

From 1921 onwards, Mussolini's speeches and articles concentrated on what fascism was *against* – socialism and liberalism – rather than what it was *for*. However, Mussolini did stress fascism's commitment to strong government, patriotism and imperial expansion. Fascist violence increased during 1921–22.

Mussolini and fascism

Having looked at Mussolini's views and his movement's actions in the previous pages, it should now be possible to assess to what extent Mussolini himself can be described as a fascist. To draw any conclusions, it is necessary to examine how historians have attempted to define fascism, and to identify the movement's core beliefs. In particular, it is necessary to investigate what has been called 'generic fascism' – and how Mussolini's views relate to such academic definitions.

Generic fascism

In general terms, when considering 'generic fascism', many historians – such as Roger Griffin and Stanley Payne – have isolated a core set of aspects of fascist ideology, which identifies what fascists stood for. At the heart of fascism lie at least four key elements:

1   a populist – even revolutionary – form of ultra-nationalism
2   a desire to destroy the existing political system
3   a belief in a strong leader (the *Führerprinzip*, or 'leadership principle')
4   a belief in the positive values of vitalism (action) and violence.

However, Roger Eatwell and others have often found it easier to identify fascist ideology by isolating what they were *against*, thus focusing on the negative and reactionary aspects of the movement. These include a rejection of the liberal ideas of the 18th-century Enlightenment and 19th-century positivism, both of which had stressed rationalism, reason and progress.

Proto-fascism

Some historians have described the period before the First World War as the 'incubatory period of fascism'. Initially, the **proto-fascism** that developed from the late 19th century was opposed to the growth of liberal (i.e. unrestricted or 'free market') capitalism, which tended to negatively affect smaller businesses and artisans. Parliamentary democracy, which often came in the wake of industrial capitalism, was seen as a way for the wealthy – and for the organised labour movement – to influence politics in a way that harmed the 'small man' and 'the nation'. Certainly, it was from these quarters that Mussolini, and later Hitler, drew the majority of their active support and formed their mass movements.

Many nationalists and 'small men' were moving towards a form of reactionary ultra-nationalism. The nationalist and imperialist Italian Nationalist Association was particularly important in this shift. Dissatisfied nationalists and frightened conservatives longed to return to a more glorious Italian past (recalling the empire of ancient Rome), and feared the growth of socialism and the threat of communist revolution. Such views were widespread amongst the upper and middle classes in Italy – not just among the industrial, financial and landowning élites, but also shopkeepers, small farmers and clerical workers. Many despised the weak liberal coalitions and wanted a stronger, more authoritarian government to defend their interests.

proto-fascism: This early, incomplete form of fascism, which began to emerge before 1919, included elements of syndicalism found in the writings of philosopher Georges Sorel (1847–1922). However, fascists soon replaced Sorel's idea of a general strike fought by revolutionary unions (known as *syndicats*) with the 'big idea' of a powerful, united nation. There was also the idea of 'vitalism', which stated that emotion and action were superior to reason. It was the latter aspect in particular that led Mussolini and his followers to emphasise the need for action and violent combat.

ACTIVITY

Carry out further research on the historical debates surrounding proto-fascism and generic fascism.

QUESTION

What does **Source H** reveal about the importance of ideology in the Italian Fascist Party?

SOURCE H

We allow ourselves the luxury of being aristocrats and democrats; conservatives and progressives; reactionaries and revolutionaries; legalitarians and illegalitarians, according to the circumstances of the time.

Mussolini, commenting on the content of fascist ideology in 1919. Quoted in Pearce, R. 1997. *Fascism and Nazism*. London, UK. Hodder & Stoughton. p. 7.

ACTIVITY

Assess the value and limitations of **Source I** as evidence of the role played by fascist movements, and the reasons for fascist violence, in Italy during the 1920s.

SOURCE I

Born in the womb of bourgeois democracy, fascism in the eyes of the capitalists is a means of saving capitalism from collapse. It is only for the purpose of deceiving and disarming the workers that social democracy denies the fascistisation of bourgeois democratic countries and the countries of the fascist dictatorship.

Extract from the plenum on fascism of the Communist International, December 1933. Quoted in Griffin, R. (ed.). 1995. *Fascism: a Reader*. Oxford, UK. Oxford Paperbacks. p. 263.

Figure 2.10 Fascist Blackshirts from a Fascio di Combattimento (battle group)

2.4 What were the sources of support for Mussolini's Fascist Party?

After the May 1921 elections, and Mussolini's decision not to support Giolitti, Mussolini concentrated on gaining support from various quarters.

The economic élites and emerging fascism, 1921–22

The unrest of the *biennio rosso* 1919–20 had given a boost to Mussolini's organisation. In an attempt to end the factory and land occupations, he had offered to send in *squadre d'azione* (action squads) to help factory owners in the north and landowners in the Po Valley and Tuscany. These industrialists and landowners, frustrated and angered by the liberal government's stance of concessions and inaction, had been only too pleased to give money to Mussolini's groups in return for the *squadristi*'s violent actions against the left's strikes and occupations.

These action squads were controlled by local fascist leaders, known as **ras**. As well as attacking strikers, the *squadristi* burnt down the offices and newspaper printing works belonging to the socialists and trade unions in many parts of northern and central Italy. They also tried to destroy the influence of the peasant leagues, which were encouraged by the more liberal elements of the Roman Catholic Popolari (see section 2.2, Nationalists and the 'mutilated victory').

This growing alliance with industrialists, bankers and landowners began to finance the building of a mass base for Mussolini's Fasci di Combattimento among the middle and lower-middle classes, who feared socialist revolution. However, the more radical elements (such as Marinetti and the syndicalists) were increasingly alienated from this base. Instead, as time went by, the fascist squads were mainly composed of disaffected and demobilised army officers and non-commissioned officers (NCOs), and middle-class students. These supporters were united by their hatred of socialists and their belief in violent action, rather than by any coherent political ideology.

The practical appeal of the fascist *squadres* grew after September 1920, when a wave of factory occupations involving over 400,000 workers hit the industrial areas of the north. At the same time, agrarian strikes and land occupations continued to spread in central Italy. Then, in the local elections, the socialists won control of twenty-six out of Italy's sixty-nine provinces, mostly in northern and central parts of the country. All of this greatly increased the fears of the upper and middle classes. As the fascist action squads proved effective in suppressing leftist action, *squadristi* numbers were swelled by recruits from the ranks of small farmers, estate managers and sharecroppers.

From May 1921, Mussolini had hopes of achieving real power and he was determined to make full use of the opportunities to do so. He realised that he needed to convince the industrialists, landowners and the middle classes of three things: that the liberals were finished as an effective political force; that there was a real threat of socialist revolution; and that only the fascists were strong and determined enough to take the necessary action, and restore order and dignity to Italy.

Denied the support of the fascist deputies, Giolitti at first managed to form a coalition with the support of the Popolari, but this collapsed within a month. Between May 1921 and October 1922, there were three weak coalition governments, none of which managed to take effective action against industrial struggles and political violence.

The attitude of the political élites

The attitude of the élites now became increasingly crucial to the fascists' prospects of success. During the *biennio rosso*, the police and army leaders often turned a blind eye to fascist violence against socialists and industrial and agrarian militants. In fact, commanders in some areas even provided transport to take fascist squads to socialist demonstrations or congresses. In the first half of 1921, over 200 people were killed and more than 800 wounded by these action squads, and Emilia and Tuscany became fascist strongholds.

ras: An Abyssinian word meaning 'chieftain'. These were the regional fascist leaders who commanded their own action squads, and who often had a large degree of independence. They included Italo Balbo (Ferrara), Dino Grandi (Bologna), Roberto Farinacci (Cremona) and Filippo Turati (Brescia).

KEY CONCEPTS QUESTION

Causation and Consequence: How did the attitudes of Italy's political élite help to cause the rise of Mussolini's Fascist Party?

> **SOURCE J**
>
> There were sectors who assisted Fascism indirectly: although they could not bring themselves to support Fascism openly they were at least prepared to tolerate it in a way which would have been out of the question with, for example, socialism. One of these groups was the political establishment … Another was the aristocratic class, who were appeased by Mussolini's willingness to end his attacks on the monarchy. In fact, the Queen Mother, Margherita, and the king's cousin, the Duke of Aosta, were admirers of Fascism. A third sector was the Catholic Church, taking its cue from Pope Pius XI who, from the time of his election in 1922, remained on good terms with Mussolini. The Church undoubtedly considered a Communist revolution to be the main threat.
>
> Lee, S. 1987. *The European Dictatorships, 1918–1945*. London, UK. Routledge. p. 95.

Figure 2.11 Roberto Farinacci (1892–1945)

Farinacci was originally a radical nationalist, but he soon became involved in the emerging fascist movement. He was the *ras* in Cremona, publishing his own newspaper (*Cremona Nuova*), and his action squads were among the most brutal in 1919. In 1922, Farinacci declared himself mayor of Cremona. Mussolini made him PNF secretary in 1925. Farinacci was anti-clerical and anti-Semitic, and after 1938, he strongly enforced anti-Jewish legislation.

As *squadristi* violence continued to disrupt law and order into the summer of 1921, Mussolini began to worry that it might alienate the conservative élites and unify anti-fascists. His concerns grew on 31 July, when twelve *carabinieri* (police officers) managed to disperse over 500 fascists at Saranza, in north-west Italy. This was hardly the sign of a party able to impose law and order.

The formation and growth of the PNF

On 2 August, Mussolini surprised the opposition – and angered the *ras* – by signing a peace deal, known as the Pact of Pacification, with moderate socialists and the main trade union organisation, the General Confederation of Workers (Confederazione Generale del Lavoro, or CGL). He then resigned from the Fascist Central Committee in an attempt to outmanoeuvre the *ras*. This was successful, and in October 1921 Mussolini persuaded members of the Fasci di Combattimento to re-form the organisation into a political party, the Partito Nazionale Fascista (PNF).

Mussolini followed up this victory in November 1921 by persuading the Fascist National Congress to elect him as leader. In return, he agreed to end the truce with the socialists, and ordered all branches to organise action squads. Although the local *ras* still had considerable influence and some autonomy, Mussolini could now present himself as the clear and undisputed leader of an organised and united political party.

Mussolini and 'moderation'

Mussolini's growing control of this new party allowed him to drop what remained of the more left-wing elements of the 1919 *Fascist Programme*, especially those that had been hostile to the Roman Catholic Church. In doing so, Mussolini hoped to increase fascist support among conservatives. This was especially important as the new pope, Pius XI, did not support the leader of the Popolari and had previously – as archbishop of Milan – blessed the fascists' banners.

Mussolini kept fascist policy statements deliberately vague, declaring his party to be against socialism and liberalism and for a strong and ordered Italy. By the end of 1921, the Fascist Party claimed a membership of over 200,000 – many of whom were shopkeepers and clerical workers who had previously supported the liberals.

The fascists' 'creeping insurrection'

Despite Mussolini's growing control over the Fascist Party and its increasing appeal to conservatives, many of the local *ras* – including **Roberto Farinacci** and Italo Balbo – continued to endorse the violence of the action squads.

Determined to avoid a split in his party, Mussolini followed a dual policy throughout 1922. He encouraged the *ras* to continue their violent activities, but he made it known to the conservatives that he had no intention of pushing for a violent seizure of power. In the spring of 1922, there was a concerted campaign of *squadristi* violence in northern and central Italy. By July, street fighting was common in most northern towns, and soon Cremona, Rimini and Ravenna were under fascist control. Once again, the police either stood by or intervened on the side of the fascists. In some areas, the police even offered the fascists weapons if it looked as though the socialists might win.

The socialists and their trade unions decided to call a general strike for 31 July, in an attempt to force the government to take action against the fascists' violence and their 'creeping insurrection', which was giving the movement control of an increasing number of towns and other areas of Italy. Mussolini used this as an opportunity to prove that the socialists were still a threat and, more importantly, a threat that only the fascists could stop. Fascists immediately began to break the strike, taking over public transport and the postal service, and attacking strikers. The socialists called off the strike on 3 August.

The fascist success impressed the conservative middle classes, and led to renewed contact between Mussolini and former liberal prime ministers – such as Antonio Salandra, Vittorio Orlando, Francesco Nitti and Giovanni Giolitti – to discuss the possibility of the fascists entering a coalition government. To increase fascist respectability, in September Mussolini declared he was no longer opposed to the monarchy.

Victor Emmanuel III and fascism

Mussolini owed his success in October 1922 more to the role of the king, **Victor Emmanuel III,** than to the strength of his fascist militia. The king himself claimed that he refused to sign the declaration of martial law because he could not depend on the army's loyalty to him. However, he had been assured that his soldiers were faithful, and that they could easily disperse the fascist marchers.

Historians are still undecided as to why the king acted as he did. Some argue that he was uncertain of the reaction of the military, that he had little faith in the liberal politicians, that he genuinely feared the outbreak of civil war, and that he was worried about being replaced by his cousin, the duke of Aosta, a known fascist supporter. Other historians

Historical debate:
According to historians such as Renzo De Felice, Mussolini's rise to power in 1922 – and his ability to retain control until 1943 – had much to do with support from the élites (referred to as 'the Establishment men, the conservative trimmers and office-holders' by Martin Clark). Do you think this is a fair statement about the significance of the élites compared to popular support for fascism in Italy in explaining Mussolini's success?

Figure 2.12 Victor Emmanuel III (1869–1947)

Victor Emmanuel was the last king of Italy, largely due to his role during the rise and rule of fascism. After 1922, the king made little comment on fascist violence, anti-Semitic laws or the destruction of democracy. In 1944, he handed most of his powers to his son, Umberto, and abdicated in his favour in May 1946. In June, 54 per cent of Italians voted for a republic, and Victor Emmanuel went into exile in Egypt.

ACTIVITY

Was there any coherent ideology behind Italian fascism and Mussolini's fascist state? Divide the class into two groups. One group should prepare a presentation that argues that there was a coherent fascist ideology. The other group should argue that there was no clear or consistent ideological framework. After the presentation, take a vote on which argument was the most convincing.

have pointed out how leading industrialists, landowners and senior churchmen favoured compromise with the fascists (the queen mother, Margherita, was a fervent fascist) and how the king himself regarded the fascists as a bulwark against the threat of communist revolution.

Whatever the king's motives, by October 1922 Mussolini had become prime minister by legal, constitutional means – assisted by the fascist violence on the streets.

End of unit activities

1 Create a spider diagram to illustrate the economic, political and social conditions in Italy during the period 1900–19.

2 Divide into two groups. One group should present the case that Mussolini's rise to power in 1922 was inevitable, given the context of Italian history and politics in the period 1919–22. The other group should present arguments to show it was not inevitable – for example, could opponents of fascism have acted differently? Each group should present its findings in preparation for a class debate.

3 Use the internet and any other resources you have to find copies of Mussolini's speeches and interviews during the period 1919–22. Then carry out an analysis to show both consistencies and inconsistencies.

4 Carry out further research on the thinkers and ideas that contributed to the development of fascism. Then produce a poster to summarise this information.

5 Draw up a chart to show the extent to which Mussolini's fascist ideology seemed to offer:
   a a new form of society
   b a new economic and social structure
   c new values.

Consolidating and Maintaining Power

Overview

- By 1922, Mussolini was prime minister, but he was still not head of a fascist government. He began to take steps to increase his power over both the state and his own party.
- Securing the support of the Catholic Church and industrialists, in 1923 Mussolini pushed through a reform of the electoral system.
- In the 1924 election, using a variety of methods, the PNF became the largest party.
- After surviving the 'Matteotti crisis' of 1924, the following year Mussolini began a series of measures designed to establish an authoritarian one-party state, including banning trade unions and all opposition parties, and taking control of local government.
- Steps taken towards the creation of a corporate state also consolidated his power – including over the Fascist Party itself.
- At the same time, repression, censorship, control of the media and various forms of propaganda all helped to create Mussolini's personal dictatorship by the late 1920s.
- However, Italy's entry into the Second World War in 1940 led to increased opposition to Mussolini, and his downfall in 1943.
- Mussolini was eventually captured and shot by partisans in 1945.

KEY QUESTIONS

- How did Mussolini consolidate his power in the period 1922–24?
- What measures were taken after 1924 to maintain Mussolini's power?
- What role was played by personality and propaganda in the consolidation of Mussolini's power?
- How far did foreign policy help Mussolini maintain power?
- What was the nature and extent of opposition, and how was it dealt with?

TIMELINE

1922 Nov: Mussolini given emergency powers

Dec: Establishment of Fascist Grand Council

1923 Jan: Formation of national fascist militia

Jun: Corfu Incident

Jul: Acerbo Law

1924 Mar: Fascist violence against opposition

Apr: Elections held in which fascists and their allies win a large majority

Jun: Matteotti abducted and murdered

Aug: Aventine Secession

1925 Jan: end of 'Matteotti crisis'

Jul: control of press exerted

Aug: Fascist *podesta* control provinces

1926 Jan: Mussolini takes power to rule by decree

Oct: Trade unions and all opposition parties banned

1928 May: New electoral law restricts franchise to males belonging to fascist syndicates; powers of king reduced

1930 Mar: National Council of Corporations established

1935 Oct: Invasion of Abyssinia

1936 Jul: Italy intervenes with Nazi Germany in Spanish Civil War

Oct: Rome-Berlin Axis

1939 Jan: Chamber of Fasci and Corporations replaces Chamber of Deputies

Apr: Invasion of Albania

1940 Jun: Italy enters Second World War

1942 Allied bombing of Italy

1943 Jul: Mussolini brought down by coup

Sep: Italy surrenders; formation of Salò Republic (Italian Social Republic)

1945 Apr: Mussolini captured trying to flee and shot

2.5 How did Mussolini consolidate his power in the period 1922–24?

Although Mussolini was now prime minister, Italy was not a fascist state – for that to happen, he needed to change the constitution. To achieve this he set out to win new political allies, doing everything in his power to widen the political appeal of fascism. Such a move was crucial as Mussolini's government was essentially a Nationalist–Popolari–Liberal coalition that could fall at any time if one of these parties withdrew. There were only four fascists in the cabinet. In addition, the king had the power to dismiss Mussolini as prime minister. Both the king and the other political leaders believed Mussolini could be tamed, transformed and used to their own advantage.

Early consolidation moves

Mussolini had no intention of being tamed. Instead, he wished to establish a one-party fascist state, with himself as dictator.

SOURCE A

For all his willingness to compromise, at least temporarily, with the Italian establishment, Mussolini certainly had no wish or intention to relinquish the power he now held. Nor, however, can he be regarded as one of those fascist maximalists like Farinacci, Rossoni or Balbo who – in their different ways – from the start dreamed of a radical 'fascist revolution'. Probably, at this early stage, Mussolini envisaged, rather than a complete political revolution, a drastic revision of the existing system to ensure the repeated renewal of his authority. For a time at least this would have satisfied his new conservative supporters, for whom a fascist-led government may have been a blessing, and the prospect of greater authoritarianism attractive.

Blinkhorn, M. 2006. *Mussolini and Fascist Italy*. London, UK. Routledge. pp. 30–31.

In his first speech to parliament on 16 November 1922, Mussolini made a veiled threat about the strength of the Fascist Party (he claimed 300,000 armed and obedient members). He also spoke of his desire to create a strong and united Italy, and asked for emergency powers to deal with Italy's economic and political problems.

QUESTION

Study **Source B**. What do you think might be the hidden message behind Mussolini's speech? Can you identify any specific aspects of his speech that make you come to this conclusion?

SOURCE B

And so that everyone may know ... I am here to defend and enforce in the highest degree the Blackshirts' revolution ... I could have abused my victory, but I refused to do so. I imposed limits on myself ... With 300,000 youths armed to the teeth, fully determined and almost mystically ready to act on any command of mine, I could have punished all those who defamed and tried to sully fascism ... I could have transformed this drab silent hall into a camp for my squads ... I could have barred the doors of Parliament and formed a government exclusively of Fascists. I could have done so; but I chose not to, at least not for the present.

From Mussolini's first speech as prime minister, 16 November 1922. Quoted in Hite, J. and Hinton, C. 1998. *Fascist Italy*. London, UK. Hodder Education. p. 73.

The deputies, including ex-prime ministers Giolitti, Salandra and Facta, gave Mussolini an enormous vote of confidence and emergency powers for a year.

Controlling the Fascist Party

In order to increase his support amongst the conservative élites, Mussolini appointed the liberal Alberto de Stefani as finance minister. De Stefani's economic policies (reducing government controls on industry and trade, and cutting taxation) pleased the industrialists and shopkeepers. However, many on the left of the Fascist Party were angered, as they would have preferred to see significant social reforms. Partly as an attempt to increase his control over the Fascist Party, in December Mussolini established a **Fascist Grand Council.**

In January 1923, Mussolini succeeded in getting the Fascist Grand Council to agree that the regional fascist squads should be formed into a national militia, funded by the government. This militia, called the National Security Guards (MVSN), swore an oath of loyalty to Mussolini, not the king. This gave Mussolini a paramilitary organisation of over 30,000 men, which he could deploy against anti-fascists. At the same time, it considerably reduced the power of the provincial *ras*.

> **SOURCE C**
>
> What he did was to dissolve the squads and incorporate the *squadristi* into a new body, the Militia (Milizia Volontaria per la Sicurezza Nazionale, MVSN), organised by De Bono at the Interior. The Militia would 'defend the fascist revolution', would protect the fascist regime from its enemies, would give the *squadristi* status, pay and some local power, and would also discipline them: the ordinary ex-*squadristi* would supposedly find themselves serving under the command of ex-army officers. It was, therefore, an ambiguous body, part reward, part constraint; it was also part Fascist, part state, and it had ambiguous functions, part military, part police. However, it soon became clear that neither the army nor any of the various police forces was willing to let the MVSN muscle into its territory.
>
> Clark, M. 2005. *Mussolini*. London, UK. Pearson. p. 67.

However, the Fascist Grand Council also worked alongside the government's Council of Ministers – fascist ministers took important decisions, which were then passed on to the Council of Ministers for official approval. In addition to his role as prime minister, Mussolini also acted as interior and foreign minister.

By early 1923, the employers' organisation – the Confindustria – had pledged its support for Mussolini. This was largely due to his announcement that there would be no serious measures taken against tax evasion, which was widely practised by wealthy companies and individuals. In March 1923, the small Nationalist Party (a member of the coalition) merged with the Fascist Party.

This merger brought the fascists additional paramilitary forces (the Nationalists' Blueshirts), but it also confirmed Mussolini's increasing shift to the right, towards the conservative élites. Once again, this disturbed the more militant fascists.

The Vatican

At the same time, from April to June 1923, Mussolini worked to gain greater support from the Catholic hierarchy in order to widen the fascists' political base and to weaken

Fascist Grand Council: This was declared to be the supreme decision-making body within the Fascist Party. It could discuss proposals for government action, but Mussolini insisted on sole power over appointments to his council. In effect, he was attempting to establish total control over fascist policy-making.

QUESTION

How significant were the Fascist Grand Council and the MVSN in helping Mussolini to control his own party?

Fact: The Nationalist Party had close links to big business and the army. Ex-nationalists such as Enrico Corradini, Luigi Federzoni and Alfredo Rocco brought with them a desire for an authoritarian government and a much-enlarged Italian empire.

the position of the Popolari, another key member of the coalition government. Mussolini announced measures that included renouncing atheism, making religious education compulsory, banning contraception and punishing swearing in public places. Pope Pius XI, already a fascist sympathiser, signalled his willingness to withdraw his support for the Popolari.

> **SOURCE D**
>
> Mussolini alone has a proper understanding of what is necessary for his country in order to rid it of the anarchy to which it has been reduced by an impotent parliamentarianism and three years of war. You see that he has carried the nation with him. May he be able to regenerate Italy.
>
> Comments made by Pope Pius XI to the French ambassador, shortly after Mussolini was appointed prime minister. Quoted in Hite, J. and Hinton, C. 1998. *Fascist Italy*. London, UK. Hodder Education. p. 75.

In April 1923, Mussolini sacked all Popolari ministers from his government, claiming that they refused to give him full support. In June, the pope forced the priest Don Luigi Sturzo, a Popolari leader, to resign. Support for the Popolari among the conservative Catholics declined and by the summer of 1923 the party had lost most of its political importance.

Changing the constitution – the Acerbo Law

Fact: The Corfu Incident occurred when an Italian general was murdered on Greek soil while making maps of a disputed area. Mussolini took advantage of this to demand that Greece pay 50 million lire as compensation, and make a full apology. When Greece refused to pay (as they had not been responsible), Mussolini – ignoring criticism from the League of Nations – ordered Italian marines to invade the Greek island of Corfu. The Greek government paid the fine. Many Italians regarded Mussolini as a national hero after this incident.

More secure in his position, Mussolini announced his intention to reform the electoral system in a way that he hoped would strengthen his status even further. On his instructions, the under-secretary of state, Giacomo Acerbo, outlined a new electoral law that gave the party or alliance that won the most votes two-thirds of the seats in parliament, as long as the percentage was no less than 25 per cent of the votes cast. According to Mussolini, this would give Italy the strong and stable government it needed. In fact, the law was clearly intended to give the fascists total, but legally acquired, control over Italian politics. Given the intimidation and violence that could be expected from the fascists and the fact that, as minister of the interior, Mussolini could order the police not to intervene, there was little likelihood of the fascists' opponents ever being able to vote them out of office.

To ensure the passage of this law, Mussolini overcame the opposition (who greatly outnumbered the thirty-five fascist deputies) by threatening to abolish parliament, and by placing armed fascist guards on the doors to intimidate the deputies. Liberal leaders such as Giolitti and Salandra advised their supporters to approve the law, and it was passed by a large majority in July 1923. Most Popolari deputies abstained. With the Acerbo Law in place, Mussolini now needed to ensure his party would win the most votes in the next election. He was helped by the events of August 1923 that became known as the Corfu Incident.

The election of April 1924

It was not until April 1924 that Mussolini decided to hold new elections. In January he set up a secret gang of thugs and gangsters to terrorise anti-fascists both in Italy and abroad. Known as the Ceka, this group was led by **Amerigo Dumini**, who had his own office within the ministry of the interior.

The elections were announced in March, and Dumini's gang unleashed a wave of terror against anti-fascists in which over 100 people were killed. In addition to this, voting certificates were seized, fascists voted on behalf of dead people, and ballot boxes were stolen in areas where fascists feared electoral defeat. As a result, the fascists (and the right-wing liberals, including Salandra and Orlando, who had formed an electoral alliance with the fascists) won almost 65 per cent of the vote. The number of fascists in the 535-seat chamber rose from 35 to 374. Yet despite the intimidation and vote-rigging, over 2.5 million Italians still voted for opposition parties, mainly the socialists and the communists.

The Matteotti crisis

When the new parliament met for the first time, on 30 May 1924, **Giacomo Matteotti,** an independent and much-respected socialist, strongly condemned the fascist violence and corruption that had occurred during the election. He even dared to produce evidence, and called the results a fraud.

On 10 June 1924, Matteotti was abducted in Rome. Although there was no hard evidence, it was widely assumed that he had been murdered by Dumini's fascist thugs, and many began to distance themselves from Mussolini's regime. For a time, it seemed as though revulsion at Matteotti's murder might actually cause Mussolini's downfall. He was sufficiently worried to suspend parliament in order to prevent a debate. To win back support, Mussolini ordered the arrest of Dumini and his gang on 15 June, and on 18 August Matteotti's body was found. Although Dumini was found guilty of the murder and imprisoned, newspapers began to print evidence of Mussolini's involvement.

Figure 2.13 The body of Giacomo Matteotti is carried out of the woods outside Rome

Amerigo Dumini (1894–1967)

Dumini was born in the USA after his parents emigrated there from Italy. He travelled to Florence at the end of the First World War and became involved in the local Fascio di Combattimento. He was soon known as '*Il Duce's* hit man'. In 1924, Dumini headed the group that kidnapped and then murdered Giacomo Matteotti, leader of the Socialist Party. In 1943, after Mussolini's overthrow, Dumini gave his support to the establishment of the Salò Republic.

Figure 2.14 Giacomo Matteotti (1885–1924)

Born into a wealthy family, Matteotti studied law at the University of Bologna. He soon became active in socialist politics, and he opposed Italy's entry into the First World War, in line with the official position of the Italian Socialist Party. He was first elected to the Chamber of Deputies in 1919 and eventually became leader of the United Socialist Party. He was an outspoken critic of fascist violence.

Aventine Secession: This was named after similar events in ancient Rome, when a group of politicians set up a rival assembly on the Aventine Hills above Rome. The opposition deputies of 1924 walked out of the Chamber and set up an alternative parliamentary assembly, claiming they were now the true and democratic representatives of the Italian people.

Historical debate:
There has been some debate amongst historians about Mussolini's involvement in Matteotti's assassination. De Felice and Emilio Gentile argued that Mussolini had not ordered the death of Matteotti. De Felice even claimed that Mussolini was the victim of a political plot to threaten his power and frustrate his plans to create a more broad-based government. Other historians, including Denis Mack Smith, thought Mussolini was probably aware of the assassination plot but that it was ordered and organised by someone else. However, some studies have suggested that Mussolini did order the murder to stop Matteotti publishing documents containing details of corruption involving the selling of oil rights to a US company.

This evidence led most of the opposition deputies – mainly socialists, communists and radical Popolari – to boycott parliament in protest, under the leadership of the liberal Giovanni Amendola. This became known as the **Aventine Secession**, and was intended to force the king to dismiss Mussolini. At first, the king refused to consider such an action and instead blamed the opposition (most of whom were republicans, and thus disliked by the king) for unconstitutional behaviour.

SOURCE E

The Aventine [Secession] was undermined by its own contradictions. For the members of the opposition, genuine democrats who had not understood that Fascism represented a radically new element in political life, there was no choice but to await the constitutional monarch's pleasure ... Therefore, and as much in order to avoid frightening the king as out of fear of revolution, they rejected the call for a general strike and the proclamation of the Aventine as the sole legal Parliament of the country ... They hoped to bring about a Cabinet crisis and the dismissal of Mussolini. It was now December, seven months after the murder of Matteotti, and the Aventine moderates had not yet learned that on the parliamentary battleground Mussolini was bound to win because the king was determined to uphold him.

Gallo, M. 1974. *Mussolini's Italy*. London, UK. Macmillan. pp. 189–91.

The pope also supported Mussolini and condemned the Popolari deputies who had participated in the Aventine Secession. He was joined by Giolitti and Salandra and other leading liberals and conservatives, all of whom saw this as a way of reasserting influence over a now-weakened Mussolini. They also feared that Mussolini's fall might be followed by a revival of the revolutionary left-wing parties. Perhaps most significantly, leading industrialists were opposed to any change of government, especially as Mussolini had begun to reduce state involvement in the economy.

SOURCE F

Mussolini clearly feared his days were numbered. Yet the king declined to act ... He had quickly come to value Mussolini ...

Mussolini was under considerable pressure, but he was far from resigning. He countered by making changes in the government to reassure moderates ... Damage limitation was helped by the Vatican ... Many leading members of the clergy were grateful to Fascism for breaking the Left ... Industrialists too stayed largely faithful, reflecting their basic satisfaction with government policy.

Eatwell, R. 1995. *Fascism: a History*. London, UK. Chatto & Windus. p. 52.

In July 1924, industrialists, liberals and conservatives supported Mussolini's moves towards press censorship, and then his ban on meetings by opposition parties in August 1924. When further evidence of fascist violence emerged, Mussolini felt it necessary to promise to get rid of the thugs in the Fascist Party, and he sacked three fascist ministers from the government. However, in November, some leading liberals joined the opposition in criticising the continued press censorship.

These actions provoked a revolt by leading *ras* and some 50 senior officers of the MVSN in December 1924. At a meeting on 31 December, they presented Mussolini with a clear choice: either he had to stop any further investigations of fascist violence and become dictator of Italy, or they would overthrow him and replace him with a more hard-line fascist leader.

2.6 What measures were taken after 1924 to maintain Mussolini's power?

The establishment of the dictatorship, 1925–28

On 3 January 1925, Mussolini addressed the Chamber of Deputies. He denied having set up the Ceka, and condemned the actions of Dumini's gang. However, as prime minister and leader of the PNF, he assumed ultimate responsibility for Matteotti's murder. Nonetheless, he made it clear that, rather than resigning, he would continue to rule Italy – by force 'if necessary'.

SOURCE G

I declare before all Italy that I assume full responsibility for what has happened … If Fascism has turned out to be only castor oil and rubber truncheons instead of being a superb passion inspiring the best youth of Italy, I am responsible … Italians want peace and quiet, and to get on with its [sic] work. I shall give it all these, if possible in love, but if necessary by force.

Extract from a speech given by Mussolini, 3 January 1925. Quoted in Robson, M. 1992. *Italy: Liberalism and Fascism 1870–1945*. London, UK. Hodder & Stoughton. p. 66.

SOURCE H

For even as Farinacci continued to press for a Fascist takeover, his enthusiastic centralization of the party – intended to prepare it for its revolutionary destiny – actually had the effect of undermining the power and autonomy of provincial bosses like himself and neutralizing the *squadrismo* of which he had previously been chief spokesman. By the time he was manoeuvred into resigning in April 1926 he had fulfilled what Mussolini had expected of him and the PNF was well on the way to being domesticated.

Blinkhorn, M. 2006. *Mussolini and Fascist Italy*. London, UK. Routledge. pp. 36–37.

KEY CONCEPTS QUESTION

Causation: What reasons can you give for the failure of the Aventine Secession?

Remember – 'reasons' is a term commonly used in History questions: as it requires you to focus on explaining causes, it is thus a causation question, even though the word 'causes' is not used.

In February 1925, Mussolini became seriously ill. During his illness and recovery, power was exercised by Roberto Farinacci, the notorious *ras* of Cremona who had recently been appointed as party secretary by Mussolini. In fact, Mussolini disliked Farinacci, who was in favour of a total fascist takeover, but his appointment proved to be a shrewd move on Mussolini's part.

A new wave of violence

Farinacci launched a new campaign of *squadristi* violence against members of the Socialist and Communist Parties, as well as the more radical sections of the Popolari. Several people were killed, including Amendola, and many others decided to go into exile. Farinacci also supervised a purge of PNF members and local leaders (the latter in particular) who were considered to be insufficiently loyal to Mussolini.

Controlling the press

The first step in establishing a fascist dictatorship was taken in July 1925, when Mussolini, now recovered from his illness, imposed a series of laws designed to control the press. Anti-fascist newspapers were shut down, while other newspapers were only allowed to print articles approved by the government. From December 1925, all journalists were required to be on a register drawn up by the Fascist Party.

Local and central government

In August 1925, Mussolini began the next step in establishing his dictatorship, this time focused on local and central government. In the ninety-three provinces of Italy, elected mayors and councils of towns and cities were replaced by appointed fascist officials known as *podesta* (see section 2.15, Declining importance of the Fascist Party). Although the *podesta* were Fascist Party members, they were mainly conservatives, drawn from the traditional landowning and military élites. In this way, Mussolini excluded the more militant fascists from real power in the provinces. Fascist political control was further established on 3 August, when all meetings by opposition parties were banned.

Mussolini also moved to increase his personal power in central government. On 24 December 1925, he made himself 'head of government', a new official title. He also assumed formal powers over his ministers, who became responsible to him rather than to the Chamber of Deputies. In January 1926, Mussolini assumed the power to issue decrees without parliamentary approval, making him responsible only to the king. The new law also stated that the king must secure Mussolini's personal approval before appointing new ministers. Soon, Mussolini insisted on being called *Il Duce* ('The Leader').

By 1929, Mussolini held eight ministerial posts himself, thus excluding many other fascist leaders. However, in practice, it was the traditional conservative civil servants who ran these state departments rather than Mussolini or the Fascist Party.

Further steps, 1926

Despite increased control, Mussolini's position was still not totally secure. The king and the Chamber of Deputies still had influence, as did the increasingly harassed opposition parties. So in October 1926, after yet another failed assassination attempt on Mussolini, all parties other than the PNF were banned, and their deputies expelled from the Chamber. At the same time, trade unions were outlawed and a new law court (the Special Tribunal) was established to deal with political offences, some of which carried the death penalty. In 1927, Mussolini formed the Organizzazione per la Vigilanza e la Repressione dell'Antifascismo (Organisation for Vigilance and Repression of Anti-Fascism, or OVRA), a secret police force charged with suppressing political opponents.

In May 1928, when new elections were due, Mussolini took further measures to ensure that the Fascist Party won and that Italy remained a one-party, authoritarian state. These included changes to the electoral system so that only men aged twenty-one or over who belonged to fascist syndicates (see section 2.15, The corporate state) could vote. The Fascist Grand Council drew up a list of 400 candidates from lists approved by confederations of employers and employees, and voters only had the choice of voting either for or against this list. Fear of fascist violence meant most Italians voted 'yes', as fascist officials in the polling stations were able to identify those who voted 'no' (the voting slips were different colours). Having secured a clear electoral victory, Mussolini was established as dictator of Italy. The Chamber contained only fascist deputies, and the king's power was drastically reduced.

2.7 What role was played by personality and propaganda in the consolidation of Mussolini's power?

As well as these political measures, Mussolini took other steps to secure his power. These included methods of indoctrination and propaganda, as well as increased measures against opposition.

Controlling minds

Opera Nazionale Dopolavoro (OND)

The fascists believed that it was important to influence the minds of the adult population of Italy. To this end, they established organisations to control leisure activities. The Opera Nazionale Dopolavoro (OND), a national recreational club, was set up in 1925. *Dopolavoro* is Italian for 'after work'. The OND soon had a vast network of clubs, libraries and sports grounds, and organised concerts, dancing and summer holiday activities in most towns and villages. Overall, about 40 per cent of industrial workers and 25 per cent of peasants were members of the OND. Sport was given particular emphasis, and Italy began to do well internationally in motor racing, cycling, athletics and football.

The main function of the OND was to increase acceptance of fascist ideology. However, although its activities did lead to some popular support – many Italians enjoyed the subsidised sports, outings and holidays – most local organisers ignored the indoctrination aspects.

L'inquadramento

To build on the activities of the OND, and to increase fascist influence amongst the masses, there was a concerted attempt to expand membership of the party and its associated organisations. This process of uniting and incorporating the people was known as *l'inquadramento*. From 1931 to 1937, during the worst of the **Great Depression**,

Fact: The OVRA was not a specifically fascist organisation, being essentially an adaptation of the Interior Ministry's existing secret police section. So OVRA was not the equivalent of the Nazi SS or Gestapo, as it was under state, not party, control.

ACTIVITY

Carry out some further research on the methods and activities of the OVRA. To what extent was it similar to the Gestapo in Nazi Germany?

Great Depression: Following the 1929 Wall Street Crash, the entire world entered a prolonged economic downturn that resulted in a contraction of economic activity and mass unemployment. This became known as the Great Depression. All major countries – with the exception of the USSR – were badly affected during the 1930s.

ACTIVITY

Working in pairs, develop arguments for a class presentation on the effectiveness of the fascist policy of *l'inquadramento*. Concentrate on two aspects:

• the various policies connected to *l'inquadramento*

• the degree of success/failure of each one.

the Fascist Party established its own welfare agencies to provide extra relief, and also began setting up women's *fasci* to help run these agencies. Although these new agencies and networks led to increased party contact, surveillance and control, party membership did not increase dramatically. According to some, by 1939, only about 6 per cent of the population belonged to the party.

The Romanità movement

Another propaganda ploy to build up the prestige and popularity of Mussolini and the fascists was to link them to the earlier greatness of ancient Rome and its emperors. This became known as the Romanità ('Romanness') movement. Fascist writers, artists and scholars portrayed fascism as a revival of, and a return to, ancient Roman civilisation. From 1926, Mussolini was increasingly spoken of as a new Caesar.

In 1937, the Mostra Augustea della Romanità exhibition was held to celebrate the 200th anniversary of the birth of the emperor Augustus. Over the entrance to the exhibition was a quote from Mussolini: 'Italians, you must ensure that the glories of the past are surpassed by the glories of the future.'

QUESTION

How was the Romanità movement meant to create the fascist 'New Man'?

> **SOURCE I**
>
> Rome is our point of departure and our point of reference. It is our symbol and, if you like, our myth. We dream of a Roman Italy, an Italy that is wise and strong, disciplined and impersonal. Much of the spirit of Ancient Rome is being born again in Fascism: the Lictorian *fasces* are Roman, our war machine is Roman, our pride and our courage are Roman too. *Civis Romanus sum* ['I am a Roman citizen'].
>
> Extract from a speech delivered by Mussolini in 1935. Quoted in Hite, J. and Hinton, C. 1998. *Fascist Italy*. London, UK. Hodder Education. p. 106.

As part of this cult, Mussolini adopted the *fasces* as the fascist emblem, and had it incorporated into the national flag. In addition, much emphasis was placed on the need to establish a second empire – 'the resurrection of the empire'. According to Romanità, the fascist 'New Man' was a modern version of the idealised Roman centurion.

Ducismo: the personality cult of *Il Duce*

To create this 'New Man', Mussolini wanted fascism to penetrate every aspect of Italian life and society. To achieve this, he concentrated on building up and projecting his own image, and widely publicised the 'achievements' of fascism.

Almost as soon as Mussolini's dictatorship was established, he began to understand the importance of good publicity. Consequently, a press office was set up to ensure that photographs and newspaper articles projected a positive image of Mussolini and his activities. He was portrayed as youthful, energetic and an expert in a wide range of specialist areas and pursuits. He even gave instructions to the press on how he should be reported. Although initially sceptical of the value of radio, Mussolini eventually established a state radio network in 1924; this expanded rapidly. However, by 1939,

Fact: Unlike the efficient propaganda machine developed by Hermann Goebbels in Nazi Germany, propaganda in fascist Italy was marked by bureaucratic inefficiency. Mussolini's creation of a fascist propaganda machine was a gradual process. Significantly – and again unlike Nazi Germany – a number of non-fascist newspapers and radio broadcasts were allowed to continue, including those produced by the Vatican.

there were still only around 1 million radios in Italy – about one for every forty-four people. To deal with this, public-address systems were set up in cafés, restaurants and public squares, so that more people could listen to *Il Duce*'s speeches. Free radios were also given to schools.

Figure 2.15 Mussolini reviving the ancient glories of Rome; he is viewing a statue of Julius Caesar installed in the recently excavated forum

Mussolini was slow to realise the potential of film, but in 1924, a government agency (L'Unione Cinematografica Educativa, LUCE) was established to produce documentaries and newsreels. Soon, Mussolini was making full use of film. He insisted that the state-sponsored newsreel films (from 1926, these had to be played in all cinemas as part of the programme) showed him addressing large crowds of enthusiastic supporters, and that he was filmed from below, in order to disguise his lack of height.

Fascist propaganda

Throughout the 1930s, the press office extended its role to cover not just radio and film, but all aspects of culture. In 1933, Mussolini's son-in-law, Galeazzo Ciano, took over the running of the office. In 1935, it was renamed the Ministry for Press and Propaganda – in part an imitation of developments in Nazi Germany.

Two years later, in 1937, the office was renamed again, this time as the Ministry of Popular Culture (nicknamed Minculpop). This was an attempt to broaden its influence and ensure that all films, plays, radio programmes and books glorified Mussolini as a hero and the fascists as Italy's saviours. However, Minculpop's attempts to regulate the arts were not very successful. Traditional liberal culture proved too strong, and this led to compromises and thus only partial control by the fascists. While Minculpop managed to rally support for the Abyssinian War (1935–36), it failed to gain much popular support for Mussolini's alliance with Nazi Germany, or for the anti-Semitic policies he began to disseminate in 1938 (see section 2.13, Racism and anti-Semitism).

Figure 2.16 The *fasces* emblem was taken from ancient Rome; it consists of a bundle of rods and an axe were used by the *lictor* (Roman bodyguards) and symbolised authority, discipline and punishment

KEY CONCEPTS QUESTION

Significance: Using the material in this and the previous section, and any other resources available to you, make a list of the main methods used by Mussolini between 1925 and 1928 to consolidate his power. Place them in order of importance and then write a paragraph to explain your first choice.

At the same time, Achille Starace, appointed as party secretary in 1930, was also active in projecting an image of Mussolini as a hero. Lights were left on in the dictator's office to suggest that he worked twenty hours a day for Italy, while photographs and posters of *Il Duce* appeared in public buildings, streets and workplaces. Great prominence was also given to various catchphrases reflecting fascist ideals, such as *Credere, Obbedere, Combattere* ('Believe, Obey, Fight') and 'Mussolini is always right'.

At press conferences, Mussolini was always accompanied by Blackshirt bodyguards, while all public appearances were attended by what soon became known as the 'applause squad', who whipped up 'enthusiasm' for Mussolini's speeches, sometimes even resorting to prompt cards. Public events such as mass rallies and meetings were deliberately turned into political theatre, and full use was made of lighting and music to enhance the drama.

2.8 How far did foreign policy help Mussolini maintain power?

As was shown in the previous section, Mussolini deliberately tried to link his fascist state with the empire of Ancient Rome. The Romanità movement was part of this, and was closely connected to his foreign policy. The aims of his foreign policy were to gain what was called *spazio vitale* ('living space') for the Italian people, and to make Italy a great power in the Mediterranean, northern Africa and the Balkans. Although he hoped that his foreign policy would strengthen his regime, it actually ended up becoming what is generally regarded as the main factor in his downfall.

Peaceful diplomacy 1922–35

Mussolini's use of force in the Corfu Incident in August 1923 (see section 2.5, Changing the constitution – the Acerbo Law) is an example of how foreign policy *did* help him to establish and maintain power. Although, the Conference of Ambassadors eventually forced the Italians to withdraw, Greece made no official apology and Mussolini did obtain compensation from the Greeks. This increased his support within Italy, and having pushed the Acerbo Law through the previous month, it was an important factor in winning a big majority in the April 1924 elections.

Although the Corfu Incident had shown up the weakness of the League of Nations, Britain and France controlled important areas in the Mediterranean and in Africa. In addition, Yugoslavia was a potential obstacle to Italian ambitions along the Adriatic Sea. As Mussolini was not yet in a position to achieve his aim of a great new empire by force, he followed a largely peaceful foreign policy for the next eleven years. Some aspects of this also helped to increase support for his fascist regime. For instance, in 1924, as a result of the Pact of Rome with Yugoslavia, he gained Fiume. This was a valuable port city that Italy had originally hoped to gain by the peace treaties of 1919–20 – and which had long been an aim of Italian nationalists (see section 2.5, The terms of the peace treaties). Then, in 1926, talks with Britain and France resulted in parts of Kenya and Egypt being given to the Italian colonies of Somaliland and Libya, respectively.

However, after 1929 and the Great Depression, Mussolini's foreign policy began to change. He called for the 1919–20 peace treaties to be revised, and plotted (unsuccessfully) with Hungary to overthrow the king of Yugoslavia. Nonetheless, he was initially suspicious of Hitler, who came to power in Germany in 1933. As a result, he blocked Hitler's attempted takeover of Austria in July 1934 and then, in April 1935, formed the Stresa Front with Britain and France.

Mussolini's fascist 'crusades' 1935–39

Mussolini's preparedness to work with Britain and France ended when, later in 1935, he decided to launch fascist Italy's first imperialist war against Abyssinia (modern Ethiopia).

Mussolini and Italy

History, empathy and emotion:
The historian James Joll (1918–94) wrote: *'The aim of the historian, like that of the artist, is to … give us a new way of looking at things.'* But is it possible for historians to empathise with violent and racist regimes such as Mussolini's Fascist Italy without making moral or value judgements? If historians' personal views affect what they write, does this make history less valid as an academic discipline than, for example, the natural sciences?

This led to a breach with Britain and France and, more importantly for his regime, it saw him move increasingly closer to Hitler, his fellow fascist. In the end this would have disastrous consequences for Italy – and for his fascist regime.

The invasion of Abyssinia, 1935–36

Abyssinia lay between Italy's two existing colonies in East Africa – Eritrea and Somaliland – and Mussolini had been making plans to invade the country since 1932. The Italian invasion began on 2 October 1935, when 500,000 Italian troops invaded. The invading forces met little serious resistance: the Abyssinians were often only armed with spears, while the Italians had tanks, bombers and poison gas. By May 1936, Abyssinia had been conquered and it became part of Italian East Africa. Although it ended the Stresa Front and Italy's close relationship with Britain and France, this first successful attempt to create a new Roman Empire boosted the popularity of Mussolini's regime in Italy. It pleased Italian nationalists, many of whom had long wanted a chance for revenge after a defeat suffered at the hands of Abyssinian forces at Adowa in 1896. It also gained the support of the Catholic Church, which saw the invasion as a 'Christian crusade' against 'barbarism'.

However, one of the main outcomes of the invasion was that it made Italy increasingly dependent on Nazi Germany, which had supported it when the League had made half-hearted attempts to oppose Italy's aggression.

SOURCE J

Ethiopia proved a troublesome colony … Most of the western zones had not been conquered and guerrilla war continued there for years. In July Mussolini authorised … a terror policy of reprisals against rebels … But the cost was huge. Ethiopia provided no loot, indeed swallowed up Italian resources. By 1937–8 about 12.5 per cent of the total state budget was being spent in East Africa alone … Ethiopia bled Italy dry … The other consequences were diplomatic … and even more serious. When the Hoare-Laval scheme collapsed in December 1935, the 'Stresa front' against Germany collapsed with it.

Clark, M. 2005. *Mussolini*. Harlow, UK. Pearson. pp. 198–200.

Fact: Mussolini's involvement in Spain actually encouraged anti-fascist opposition in Italy. This was boosted by the news that Italian political exiles, fighting as volunteers in the International Brigades formed to fight Franco's forces, had played a big part in the defeat of Italian troops at the battle of Guadalajara in March 1937. Mussolini's response was to order his secret police to make greater efforts to assassinate Italian exiles abroad.

The Spanish Civil War, 1936–39

The growing links between fascist Italy and Nazi Germany were shown in 1936 when Mussolini informed Hitler that he would no longer object to a German *Anschluss* (union) with Austria, and did not oppose the German reoccupation of the Rhineland. Then, on 6 March, Mussolini followed Hitler's lead and withdrew Italy from the League. This shift to a pro-German policy was confirmed in July 1936, when Mussolini agreed to join Hitler in intervening in the Spanish Civil War to help General Francisco Franco overthrow the democratically elected Popular Front government. Although Italy gained the islands of Mallorca and Menorca, and Mussolini was supported once again by the pope and the Catholic Church in Italy which saw his intervention in the Spanish Civil War as another 'Christian crusade' – this time against communism – it brought Italy very few tangible benefits. In fact, it had negative effects on Italy, and thus on his regime.

Mussolini made a huge commitment in Spain: over 70,000 Italian troops were sent, along with 1,000 tanks and 600 planes. In all, this intervention cost over 10 billion lire, and more than 6,000 Italian soldiers were killed in the war. Given the impact of the Depression and the general economic situation in Italy, these were resources Italy could ill afford, and this was one of the reasons why Mussolini did not join in the Second World War in 1939.

The Rome–Berlin Axis

During the Spanish Civil War, Mussolini and Hitler confirmed their joint opposition to communism and agreed to divide Europe into spheres of influence. The Mediterranean and the Balkans fell within Italy's sphere. In October 1936, Mussolini moved closer to Nazi Germany when he signed the Rome–Berlin Axis. This marked a significant turning point in Italy's foreign policy, establishing cooperation and support between Italy and Germany. The two fascist dictators moved even closer in December 1937, when Mussolini joined Germany and Japan in their Anti-Comintern Pact. These steps would soon prove a disaster for Mussolini and his regime.

The Second World War

In March 1938, Mussolini had kept his promise not to oppose *Anschluss* with Austria: when Hitler ordered in German troops, Italy took no action to prevent the takeover. Mussolini's belief that Britain and France would never take any firm action against German expansion seemed to be confirmed when those nations made no response to Hitler's invasion of Czechoslovakia in March 1939 – despite the promises Hitler had made at the Munich Conference in September 1938 that he had no other territorial ambitions.

As a result, in April 1939, Mussolini attempted to annex Albania and turn it into an Italian protectorate. Ominously, Italian troops had difficulty in conquering even this small state – once again, this setback stimulated opposition to his regime in Italy. Despite these difficulties, in May 1939, Mussolini signed the Pact of Steel with Nazi Germany. This was a formal military alliance that committed Italy to fight on Germany's side in the event of war. However, Mussolini warned that he needed three years to prepare for war. He was shocked, therefore, when Hitler invaded Poland on 1 September 1939.

Because of Italy's serious weaknesses – and despite the Pact of Steel – Mussolini did not join Hitler in his attack on Poland. When Germany failed to supply Italy with the strategic resources it needed, Mussolini stated that Italy could not participate in the war, although he said he would send agricultural and industrial labourers to Germany. This, too, was unpopular in Italy.

Italy finally entered the war on 10 June 1940 – yet Italian forces had not recovered fully from the effects of the Abyssinian and Spanish wars. In addition, agricultural production declined in the period 1940–43. Wheat production, for instance, declined by about 1.5 million tonnes as so many peasants were conscripted into the armed forces. This led to food shortages and a growing dissatisfaction with the fascist regime. In particular, it led to the re-emergence of the first serious signs of opposition since the late 1920s. This is explored in more detail in the section which deals with opposition.

The resulting poor performances of the Italian army in France, Greece, Yugoslavia and North Africa played a large part in Mussolini's eventual overthrow on 24 July 1943. Although imprisoned, he was rescued by German paratroopers and, at Hitler's urging, Mussolini later set up a new fascist state in north-eastern Italy. However, this Italian Social Republic was little more than a German puppet state, and was bitterly opposed by many Italians who formed partisan groups to fight against his remaining forces.
When the Germans withdrew from Italy in April 1945, Mussolini tried to flee with them, but he was arrested on 27 April by a group of Italian partisans. The following day, he was

executed alongside fifteen other fascist leaders. Thus, in the end, Mussolini's foreign policy had not served to maintain his power – quite the reverse, it had eroded support and given those who opposed him a chance to bring about the end of his fascist regime.

Figure 2.17 Antonio Gramsci (1891–1937)

Born in Sardinia, in 1911 Gramsci went to the University of Turin to study literature and linguistics. In 1913, he joined the Italian Socialist Party, and in 1916 became co-editor of the Piedmont edition of the socialist newspaper *Avanti!* He supported the Socialist Party's decision to join the Communist Third International in 1919, and the establishment of the Italian Communist Party. Gramsci was a highly original Marxist theoretical thinker and wrote various important books, some while he was in prison. One of his most important theories was that of cultural hegemony, the idea that the ruling capitalist classes construct and manipulate cultural norms to maintain a state that protects private property and their own interests.

Figure 2.18 A photograph taken on 29 April 1945, showing the bodies of Mussolini (nearest to the camera) and other fascists, after their execution, hanging from the roof of a petrol station in Milan's Piazzale Loreto. The square was where fifteen anti-fascist partisans had recently been executed. The men on the roof are partisans – many in the crowd threw rotten fruit and stones at Mussolini's body

2.9 What was the nature and extent of opposition, and how was it dealt with?

Opposition to fascist rule, 1925–40

Although trade unions and all opposition parties had been banned in 1926, there was still limited opposition and resistance. One organised group that remained was the Communist Party of Italy, which had been set up in 1921. In 1924, with many leading Communist Party members already arrested by Mussolini's regime, **Antonio Gramsci** became its leader, and was even elected to the Chamber of Deputies.

Gramsci set up a Communist Party newspaper called *L'Unità* ('Unity') and called for a united front to defeat fascism. However, in November 1926 he was arrested and imprisoned under the new emergency laws (see section 2.6, The establishment of the dictatorship, 1925–28), and he eventually died in prison in 1937.

During the late 1920s and the 1930s, opposition to Mussolini in Italy, though often courageous, was weak. Such opposition mainly involved isolated individuals, small clandestine groups and remnants of the trade unions. After 1926, political opponents who were caught were often sent into internal exile (known as *confino*) to remote parts of Italy. While fascist treatment of active opposition was brutal, it was not as excessively repressive as in Hitler's Germany or Stalin's Russia, although it became more extreme after Italy's entry into the Second World War in 1940.

Several anti-fascist groups went into self-imposed exile so that they could organise opposition from abroad, especially in France. They smuggled anti-fascist literature into Italy and, during the Spanish Civil War (1936–39), over 3,000 Italian anti-fascist volunteers fought as part of the International Brigades on the side of the Republican government against Franco's forces, which included troops sent by Mussolini. Their Garibaldi Legion defeated Mussolini's troops at the Battle of Guadalajara in March 1937 – this greatly angered and embarrassed Mussolini.

Mussolini's Ceka often disrupted the activities of these *fuorusciti* (exiles or 'escapees'), sometimes by assassinating leaders in exile. For example, the Rosselli brothers, Carlo and Nello, established the Giustizia e Libertà (Justice and Liberty) group in 1929. They were murdered in France in 1937, probably on Mussolini's orders, by members of La Cagoule (The Cowl), a French fascist group.

The re-emergence of opposition at home, 1940–43

Italy's entry into the Second World War in 1940 initiated the first signs of real renewed internal opposition, characterised by the outbreak of strikes.

By 1942, Germany was taking more from Italy than it was offering in military aid. In addition to coal and iron, about 50 per cent of the 350,000 workers sent to Germany by Mussolini were skilled workers. The food he ordered to be sent to Germany caused serious shortages in Italy, and rationing was introduced in 1941. The inefficiency and inadequacy of the rationing system led to the rise of the black market (the ration of 150 grams of bread per person was the smallest in Europe with the exception of the USSR). Towards the end of 1942, Allied bombing of Italy increased. Poor anti-aircraft defences resulted in widespread destruction which in turn led to increased working hours and greater factory discipline. Inevitably, a great wave of strikes occurred in March 1943.

Italy's military situation deteriorated during 1943. Axis troops in Africa were forced to surrender in May, resulting in the loss of Libya. Then, in July, the Allies invaded Sicily and began bombing Rome. The invading Allies met only token resistance as many Italians blamed Mussolini for their army's defeats and the dire situation on the home front. They had also grown to dislike the German armies that had begun moving onto Italian soil. Most Italians, including the industrialists and lower middle classes who had been the backbone of fascism, were disillusioned by the regime's inefficiency and corruption. The **nepotism** that Mussolini frequently used was particularly unpopular.

Fact: Mussolini was persuaded by Hitler to declare war on Britain and France in June 1940, and then on the US in December 1941. However, Italy's forces performed badly in Greece and Yugoslavia and suffered several setbacks in North Africa in 1942–43, eventually losing control of Libya. Allied bombing of Italy began in 1942, and after the Allied invasion of Sicily in 1943, more and more Italians turned against the fascist regime. To help stop the Allied invasion, Nazi Germany sent troops into Italy in the early summer of 1943.

nepotism: The promotion of relatives because of their family connections rather than their ability to do a job. Many Italians resented the nepotism Mussolini demonstrated towards relatives of his mistress, Clara Petacci.

Between February and April 1943, Mussolini took a hard line in dealing with this disaffection – sacking or demoting several ministers and high-ranking members of the Fascist Party, including Grandi, Ciano and Bottai. However, this only led to plots against him. Many were critical of Mussolini's strategy, feared his close relationship with Nazi Germany, and wanted him removed from power altogether. However, another group of fascists, which included Farinacci and the new PNF secretary Carlo Scorza, wanted to forge closer ties with Germany.

The end of Mussolini's fascist state 1943–45

The military setbacks of May and July 1943 finally triggered a coup against Mussolini on 24 July 1943, when the Fascist Grand Council voted nineteen to seven to remove him from power. On 25 July, the king formally ordered Mussolini to resign. He was arrested and imprisoned. The ease with which his overthrow was achieved emphasised the fact that Mussolini had never been able to impose a totalitarian regime. He was replaced by Marshal Pietro Badoglio who, on 8 September 1943, announced Italy's surrender to the Allies.

The Italian Social Republic

Italian Social Republic: This was soon contemptuously known as the Salò Republic, after the town where Mussolini had his headquarters. It was little more than a German puppet state, despite Mussolini's claims to be returning to the social idealism of his original fascism.

In September 1943, Mussolini was 'rescued' from his enforced isolation in a mountainous region of eastern Italy by German paratroopers. They took him to Germany where Hitler persuaded him to set up the **Italian Social Republic**. This was a new fascist state in the German-controlled north-eastern part of Italy, which was not yet under Allied occupation.

Although Mussolini was nominally leader of the new republic, in practice the important decisions were taken by Rudolf Rahn, the German ambassador, and by SS general Karl Wolff. There was much SS and Gestapo brutality, especially against Jewish people, while thousands of Italian men were sent to Germany as forced labour. At the same time, fascist extremists made a determined effort to round up those who had planned and carried out Mussolini's overthrow. Several were captured, taken to the Salò Republic and then executed, including Mussolini's own son-in-law Galeazzo Ciano.

Mussolini's death

Historical debate: Immediately after the end of the Second World War, most histories of the Italian fascist movement focused on the periods of active opposition to Mussolini (1919–25 and 1943–45). However, some revisionist historians focused on the period 1926–43 when, they argued, the fascists achieved a degree of both success and at least passive support. In fact, Martin Clark has even compared Mussolini – in his defeat of the left and trade union power, and his attempts to increase patriotism – to Margaret Thatcher, the British prime minister from 1979 to 1990. How convincing do you find this argument?

During 1944, the Allies continued to push up through Italy from the south. In April 1945, they captured the northern city of Bologna, and the Germans decided to pull out of Italy. Mussolini tried to flee with the Germans, but was recognised by a group of Italian partisans and arrested on 27 April. The following day, he was taken by another, communist-led, group of partisans and he and his mistress were shot. Also executed were fifteen other fascist leaders and ministers, including Farinacci and Starace. The bodies were hung upside down outside a garage in Piazzale Loreto in Milan, where a group of partisans had previously been executed by the Germans for resistance activities.

End of unit activities

1 Create a diagram to show the various stages and steps in Mussolini's construction of a fascist dictatorship in the years 1922–29.

2 Carry out some additional research about the significance of the roles of both the king and the Catholic Church in the consolidation of Mussolini's control. Why do you think they acted in the ways they did?

3 Find out more about the Rosselli brothers. How far was what happened to them typical of Mussolini's regime and his treatment of opposition?

4 Construct a table showing Mussolini's foreign policies from 1922 to 1943. Draw up two main columns, listing which policies helped to increase support for his fascist regime and which eroded support. Make sure you include relevant details such as dates, actions and outcomes.

Theory of knowledge

History and bias:
There are various historical interpretations about Mussolini and his fascist state. Some recent reinterpretations have given a more positive view of his actions, considering Mussolini as one of Italy's most successful 20th century politicians. To what extent is it possible for historians and students of history not to be influenced by their own political views, or by the contemporary historical context in which they are writing?

Overview

- Once in power, Mussolini launched a number of economic 'battles', many of which were intended to make Italy self-sufficient and strong enough to pursue an aggressive and expansionist foreign policy.

- These 'battles' had varying degrees of success. In addition, other economic policies tended to benefit some social classes and groups more than others.

- From the late 1920s, despite various social policies and the creation of an Institute of Industrial Reconstruction (IRI) in 1933, many Italians experienced a decline in their standard of living.

- Women were particularly affected by fascist policies – the 'Battle for Births' attempted to restrict women to the traditional 'housewife/mother' role.

- Mussolini's government maintained generally good relations with the Catholic Church. However, disputes did arise – mainly over fascist attempts to control Catholic youth movements, and then over the introduction of anti-Semitic laws after 1938.

- Concerted efforts were made to control education and to establish strong fascist youth movements for boys and girls. In 1937, membership of these groups was made compulsory.

- Despite all of Mussolini's efforts to influence the views of different sections of Italy's social groups and organisations, he never managed to create a totally authoritarian state. This was confirmed in 1943 when internal opposition led to his dismissal as prime minister.

KEY QUESTIONS

- What were Mussolini's economic and social policies, and what factors influenced them?
- How successful were Mussolini's economic and social policies?
- What were the main religious policies in Mussolini's fascist Italy?
- What were Mussolini's policies towards women, ethnic and other minorities?
- What were the main fascist policies on education, young people and the arts, and what impact did they have?
- To what extent was authoritarian control established in fascist Italy?

2.10 What were Mussolini's economic and social policies, and what factors influenced them?

Mussolini had no real understanding of, or interest in, economics. However, he realised the importance of a strong economy to consolidate his regime, and lay the foundations for an aggressive and expansionist foreign policy. Thus, in many respects, Mussolini's main concern was not so much to create fascism as a viable '**third way**', as it was to make Italy a rich and great power.

To achieve this, Mussolini believed it was necessary to make Italy economically self-sufficient in both food and in raw materials for industry. This would require not only overcoming problems of poverty and improving agriculture at home, but also conquering a large empire to supply Italy with raw materials.

third way: In its early stages, fascist leaders often claimed that fascism was a 'third way' between capitalism on the one hand and revolutionary socialism on the other. However, most historians agree that, once it became the dominant power, fascism supported capitalist interests. This often caused problems with more radical fascists, who had believed earlier promises about helping the 'little man'.

SOURCE A

Fascism was not, and never claimed to be, an economic system … Throughout the life of the Fascist regime, it is true, a minority in the Party and the corporate structure continued to feed the guttering flame of Fascist 'leftism' with somewhat qualified anti-capitalist rhetoric. Such restlessness, and the implicit challenge to private wealth it contained, had its uses for Mussolini in his dealings with the captains of industry, agriculture and finance – just as long as he could be seen to possess the power equally to suppress, control or release it … From his crucial initial compromise with big business and the agrari in 1920–2 down to his fall in July 1943, Fascist 'leftism' was never allowed significantly to influence major policy decisions or initiatives.

Blinkhorn, M. 2006. *Mussolini and Fascist Italy*. London, UK. Routledge. pp. 43–44.

QUESTION

To what extent does **Source A** support the view that fascism did not represent a 'third way'?

Mussolini's economic 'battles'

To achieve the economic greatness he desired, Mussolini decided to launch a series of initiatives or campaigns that he called 'battles'. The first of these was announced in 1924 and was directed at the widespread poverty in southern Italy. It was known as the Battle over the Southern Problem, and promised the building of thousands of new villages in Sicily and the south. It also included attempts to destroy the power of the Mafia.

In 1925, a much more serious campaign, the Battle for Grain, was launched in response to a poor harvest and a consequent increase in grain imports. The aim was to get Italian farmers to grow more cereals (especially wheat), in order to reduce Italy's dependence on foreign imports.

As well as imposing import controls (which really just ensured that the inefficient farmers in the south could continue farming without having to modernise), more land

Fact: The poverty and social problems in the south gave criminals an easy field in which to operate, and the most notorious of these criminals belonged to the Mafia. Although a 'Battle against the Mafia' began in 1925, it soon stopped pursuing Mafia leaders because several important members of the Italian élites had connections to the Mafia. The Mafia leadership simply went underground. In 1943, they cooperated with US forces and soon reclaimed their former power.

was made available for growing grain. This was done by ploughing up pasture land, olive and citrus orchards, and vineyards. In addition, medals were awarded to the most productive farmers, and their stories were reported in the newspapers. In the more prosperous north, farmers began growing wheat rather than maize, and farms became more mechanised. The increased use of tractors and fertilisers also benefited industrial firms such as Fiat, Pirelli Rubber and Montecatini Chemicals.

Figure 2.19 Mussolini encouraging harvesters at Aprilla during the Battle for Grain

SOURCE B

Wheat was the vital commodity that could feed an army, and Italy did not grow enough of it. In the early 1920s about 2.5 million tonnes a year, nearly one-third of the requirement, had to be imported, at a cost of almost 3 billion lire. This was about one-fifth by value of all imports. Italy already had to import coal and oil; and could not import basic foodstuff as well.

Clark, M. 2005. *Mussolini*. London, UK. Pearson. p. 130.

The following year, 1926, saw the start of the Battle for Land – a further attempt to increase the amount of available farmland. Marshes and swamps were drained, most notably the Pontine Marshes near Rome. This allowed the establishment of many small farms. The farming itself, financed from public funds, created work for the unemployed.

On 18 August 1926, the Battle for the Lira began when the value of the Italian currency dropped. To restore its value abroad (and thus help stop internal price rises), and to increase Italian prestige, the lira was revalued. This allowed Italy to continue importing coal and iron for armaments and shipbuilding.

2.11 How successful were Mussolini's economic and social policies?

Were the battles won or lost?

Most of Mussolini's economic 'battles' were far from successful, often because they were fought inconsistently. New villages had been promised in the Battle over the Southern Problem, but none were actually built. Although the Battle for Grain succeeded in almost doubling cereal production by 1939, making Italy self-sufficient in wheat, it also involved misallocation of resources. This resulted in Italy having to import olive oil, while exports of fruit and wine, and numbers of cattle and sheep, dropped. The Battle for Land only reclaimed one significant area (the Pontine Marshes).

The Battle for the Lira, which involved artificially raising the value of the lira, also resulted in declining exports – and thus increased unemployment – as Italian goods became more expensive. Car exports, in particular, were badly hit. It also began a recession in Italy, which was worsened by the Great Depression (see section 2.7, Controlling minds).

Thus, most of Mussolini's 'battles', which were intended to achieve **autarchy**, caused at least as many problems as they solved.

Fascism and state intervention

Before the Depression, Mussolini had not interfered with private enterprise and had favoured large companies and heavy industry. However, once the Depression started to take effect, he began to consider some state intervention, at first by encouraging

autarchy: Sometimes spelled 'autarky', this means self-sufficiency. It usually applies to countries or regimes that try to exist without having to import particular foods, fuels, raw materials or industrial goods. It can also refer to the attempt to be totally self-sufficient in all important areas, as happened in Italy and Nazi Germany. Invariably, such attempts had limited success.

QUESTION

How did the IRI help large-scale private companies?

League of Nations: Set up by the peace treaties that ended the First World War, the League was intended to avoid future wars through 'collective security'. Member nations imposed economic sanctions on aggressive nations to force them to end conflict through negotiations.

job-sharing schemes. By 1933, unemployment had risen to over 2 million, while millions more (especially in the rural south) suffered from underemployment. More than 30 per cent of labouring jobs in agriculture were lost, and many women were forced to give up their jobs to unemployed men. The situation in the countryside was made worse by controls on migration to the cities. These were designed to keep the problem of unemployment hidden within less-populated rural areas. By 1930, Mussolini had to drop earlier claims that his regime had improved the living standards of working-class Italians. In 1931, Mussolini's government decided to use public money to help prevent the collapse of banks and industries hit by the Depression.

The Institute per la Reconstruzione Industriale (IRI)

The Institute per la Reconstruzione Industriale, or Institute of Industrial Reconstruction (IRI), was set up in 1933. At first, it took over various unprofitable industries on behalf of the state. By 1939, the IRI had become a massive state company, controlling most of the iron and steel industries, merchant shipping, the electrical industry and even the telephone system. However, Mussolini never intended for these industries to be permanently nationalised. Parts were regularly sold off to larger industries still under private ownership, resulting in the formation of huge capitalist monopolies. Examples of this were the large firms Montecatini and SINA Viscasa, which ended up owning the entire Italian chemical industry.

Autarchy in the 1930s

The effects of the Depression led Mussolini to adopt increasingly protectionist measures and to strengthen the push towards fascist autarchy. These policies became even more important to the fascists in 1935 when several countries belonging to the **League of Nations** imposed some economic sanctions on Italy after its invasion of Abyssinia (see section 2.7, Fascist propaganda).

As Mussolini involved Italy in more military actions, the push for autarchy increased – as did the problems associated with this struggle for self-sufficiency. Nonetheless, there were some moderate achievements: by 1940, for example, industrial production had increased by 9 per cent. As a result, industry overtook agriculture as the largest proportion of GNP for the first time in Italy's history. In addition, between 1928 and 1939, imports of raw materials and industrial goods dropped significantly. Overall, however, fascist economic policy did not result in a significant modernisation of the economy, or even increased levels of productivity. Italy experienced a much slower recovery from the Depression than most other European states. Once Italy became involved in the Second World War, its economic and industrial weaknesses grew increasingly apparent.

The social impact of fascism

According to the 'third way' ideal, fascism was supposed to replace class conflict with class harmony. It should have brought equal benefits to employers and employees, working in partnership for the good of the nation, the state and the Italian people. In particular, it was claimed that workers would no longer be exploited, and would enjoy an improved status under the corporate state.

How were the different classes affected?

Industrial workers

In the early years of Mussolini's rule (1922–25), male workers experienced a drop in unemployment and an improvement in living standards. This was due in part to the cautious economic policies followed by **Alberto de Stefani,** but the general economic revival in Europe in the early 1920s also contributed to this improved situation in Italy.

In 1925–26, workers lost their independent trade unions and their right to strike. The promises that had been made about the corporate state (see section 2.15, The corporate state) failed to materialise. Instead of ending class conflict, Mussolini's fascist state merely prevented workers from defending their interests, while employers were able to manage their companies without either interference from the state or opposition from their employees. For example, as the economy began to decline in the second half of the 1920s, employers ended the eight-hour day and extended the working week. At the same time, wages were cut – from 1925 to 1938, the level of real wages dropped by over 10 per cent.

By 1939, it was clear that only a small minority had benefited significantly from fascist rule. The standard of living and the general quality of life for most Italians, especially the working classes, declined under fascism.

Unemployment increased after the Great Depression, and even the public work schemes had little effect. Workers were afraid of protesting about their working conditions in case they lost their jobs altogether.

Some social welfare legislation was passed in the fascist era, including the introduction of old-age pensions and unemployment and health insurance. There was also a significant increase in education expenditure. However, these improvements did not make up for the loss of wages and poor working conditions experienced by many.

Peasants and agricultural workers

Despite Mussolini's claim to love the countryside and his promises to 'ruralise' Italy, the situation in rural areas actually worsened under the corporate state. Mussolini's policies clearly benefited large landowners rather than small farmers and agricultural labourers. In 1922, a law was introduced to split the large estates and redistribute the land, but this was never acted on. Agricultural wages dropped by more than 30 per cent during the 1930s.

In an attempt to escape rural poverty, many Italians emigrated. Over 200,000 Italians moved to the USA in the period 1920–29. The situation in rural Italy worsened when the US drastically reduced its immigration quotas from the mid-1920s, making it more difficult for Italians to find relief abroad. Not surprisingly, many rural workers ignored government decrees intended to stop migration to the towns. Those workers often ended up in the slums of Milan, Turin and Rome.

The lower-middle classes

The lower-middle classes, who had formed the backbone of the Fascist Party, were affected in different ways. Many small business owners were hit hard by the Depression and by Mussolini's economic policies. However, those who entered the administrative bureaucracy of the state or the Fascist Party enjoyed relative prosperity, with good wages and considerable benefits, as well as the opportunity to increase their income through corrupt means.

Fact: In October 1935, Italy launched an invasion of Abyssinia (now Ethiopia), which was sandwiched between the Italian colonies of Eritrea and Somaliland. Mussolini sent 500,000 troops, who used tanks, bombers and poison gas against people often only armed with spears. Abyssinia appealed to the League of Nations. Britain and France were reluctant to impose sanctions as, at this time, Mussolini was regarded as a useful ally against the rise of Nazism in Germany. In 1934, Mussolini had joined British and French leaders in opposing Hitler's attempted takeover of Austria. Some sanctions were imposed, but these were limited. For example, the League did not ban Italy from exporting oil or from using the Suez Canal.

Alberto de Stefani (1879–1969)

Originally a liberal, de Stefani later supported Mussolini, and was appointed minister of finance in 1922. He was in charge of Mussolini's economic programme from 1922 to 1925, favouring free trade, lower taxes (especially for private companies and the wealthier classes) and a reduction of government 'interference' in the economy. However, when wages started to drop and the economy began to show signs of crisis in 1925, de Stefani was replaced by Count Giuseppe Volpi.

2

Was there more change or more continuity as regards the living standards of most working-class Italian families under fascism?

Fact: There was no serious attempt to redistribute land. By 1930, 0.5 per cent of the population owned 42 per cent of land, while 87 per cent of the rural population (mainly small landowners) owned only 13 per cent.

Industrialists and landowners

Large industrialists and landowners benefited most in fascist Italy. The Vidoni Pact of 1925 and the Charter of Labour of 1927 increased the power and freedom of employers, while preventing workers from defending – let alone improving – their living standards. Even during the Depression, large firms benefited in many ways, either through government contracts or the IRI, which offered them financial assistance.

SOURCE C

While plainly damaging to some sectors of the economy, Fascist policies unquestionably benefited other, powerful interests whose ability to influence government long pre-dated fascism and on whose continued acquiescence the regime's chances of permanence partly depended: heavy industry, the *agrari* of the Po Valley, and the less enterprising big landowners of other regions.

Blinkhorn, M. 2006. *Mussolini and Fascist Italy*. London, UK. Routledge. p. 45.

Wealthy landowners flourished under the fascist system. In 1935, as part of an ongoing attempt to restrict the migration of rural workers to cities, special workbooks (*libretti di lavoro*) were printed. These had to be signed by the local prefect before a worker could move to a new area. Such measures kept unemployment high in rural areas, a situation exploited by landowners in order to cut wages.

2.12 What were the main religious policies in Mussolini's fascist Italy?

The Church

When it came to the Roman Catholic Church, Mussolini was a little more successful in widening the base of fascist support. Mussolini never really shed his anti-religious views, but as most Italians were Catholics he realised that he needed to reach an understanding with the Church. As early as 1921 (before he became prime minister), Mussolini began presenting the Fascist Party as an alternative to the traditionally anti-clerical liberals, and the atheistic communists and socialists. The Catholic hierarchy was particularly pleased by the fascists' defeat of the socialists and communists, and saw benefits in ending the conflict between Church and state.

Once installed as prime minister, Mussolini restored Catholic education in state primary schools, which encouraged the papacy to end its support for the Catholic Popolari. The real breakthrough, however, came in 1929, following a series of secret negotiations between the fascists and Cardinal Gasparri, a senior Vatican official.

These negotiations resulted in three Lateran Agreements, which finally ended the conflict and bitterness that had existed between the papacy and the Italian state since 1870. By the terms of the Lateran Treaty, the government accepted papal sovereignty over Vatican City, which became an independent state. In return, the pope formally recognised the Italian state, and its possession of Rome and the former papal states. In a separate but related agreement, the state gave the pope 1,750 million lire (£30 million) in cash and government bonds as compensation for the loss of Rome. Finally, the treaty agreed that Roman Catholicism would be the official state religion of Italy, with compulsory Catholic religious education in all state schools, and that the state would pay the salaries of the clergy. In return, the papacy agreed that the state could veto the appointment of politically hostile bishops, and that the clergy should not join political parties. It was also agreed that no one could get divorced without the consent of the Church, and that civil marriages were no longer necessary.

Figure 2.20   Mussolini and Catholic priests; as Mussolini's rule progressed he won over Church leaders, largely through the Lateran Agreements of 1929 (see section 2.12, The Church)

KEY CONCEPTS
QUESTION

Causation and Consequence: From what you have studied so far, what caused the Catholic Church in Italy to support Mussolini in the 1920s? What were the main consequences of this support?

Collaborators or rivals?

While the Lateran Agreements meant that Catholicism remained a potential rival ideology to fascism, thus preventing the establishment of a truly totalitarian dictatorship, Mussolini was satisfied. The pope and the Catholic Church gave its official backing to him as *Il Duce*.

The Lateran Agreements have led many people to regard the Catholic Church as a fascist collaborator. Indeed, priests would give the fascist salute and participated in Opera

Nazionale Balilla (ONB) activities (see section 2.14, Fascism and youth movements). However, relations were not always smooth. In 1928, rivalry between Catholic and fascist youth movements led to the banning of the Catholic Scout organisation, and this tension continued even after the Lateran Agreements. In 1931, the government attempted to suppress the Church's Catholic Action youth organisation, provoking further conflict. Eventually a compromise was reached, but only after the pope had publicly criticised the fascist oath of loyalty and interference in educational and family matters. From 1938, disagreements also emerged over the fascists' anti-Semitic policies. Thus it was clear that Mussolini never fully controlled the Church.

SOURCE D

To opponents of Fascism, the Church seemed … inextricably implicated in Fascist policy … Even the denunciations of particular Fascist policies were expressed in temperate tones …

Yet the Church … did resist the persistent attacks on the remaining forms of Catholic Action and did formally denounce Mussolini's racial policy in late 1938. No opposition to a complete totalitarianism was more formidable.

Grew, R. 'Catholicism in a Changing Italy'. In Tannenbaum, E. (ed.). 1974. *Modern Italy: a Topical History Since 1861*. New York, USA. New York University Press. p. 268.

2.13 What were Mussolini's policies towards women, ethnic and other minorities?

Women and families

One group that suffered more than most under fascism was women. Their status was deliberately and consistently downgraded, especially by the Battle for Births, which stressed the traditional role of women as housewives and mothers, and caused a downturn in employment opportunities for women.

SOURCE E

- Women must obey … In our state, she does not count.
- Intellectual women are a monstrosity.
- Higher education for women should just cover what the female brain can cope with, i.e. household management.
- Child bearing is women's natural and fundamental mission in life. [Women's work] distracts from reproduction, if it does not directly impede it, and foments independence and the accompanying physical-moral styles contrary to giving birth.

Various statements made by Mussolini during the 1930s. Quoted in Hite, J. and Hinton, C. 1998. *Fascist Italy*. London, UK. Hodder Education. p. 165.

The Battle for Births was launched in 1927, in an attempt to increase the Italian population to create a large future army that would help to expand Italy's empire. Mussolini aimed to increase the population from 40 million in 1927 to 60 million by 1950. To achieve this, the fascists encouraged early marriage, offered generous maternity benefits, exhorted women not to work, and gave jobs to married fathers in preference over single men. They also gave prizes to those women in each of Italy's ninety-three provinces who had the most children during their lives.

Fact: Some jobs held by women were seen by fascists as especially 'unnatural'. These included teaching in schools, office work and the professions. From as early as the mid-1920s, women began to be excluded from certain teaching jobs.

Theory of knowledge

History and emotion: Strong emotions can affect perception and reason. Study **Source E** again. Your attitudes to the position of women in society are probably very different from those put forward by Mussolini in the 1930s. Do his views make you angry? If they do, does this mean it is impossible for you to make an objective assessment of fascist policy towards women?

Figure 2.21 Mussolini with his wife and children, setting an example during the Battle for Births

Taxation policy was also used to encourage large families. Bachelors (especially those between the ages of thirty-five and fifty) had to pay extra taxes, while couples with six or more children paid none. Newly married couples were given cheap railway tickets for their honeymoon. Later, in 1931, same-sex relations were outlawed, and new laws against abortion and divorce were imposed.

A series of decrees was imposed to restrict female employment. In 1933, it was announced that only 10 per cent of state jobs could be held by women; in 1938, this was extended to many private firms. Although this policy was partly intended to solve the problem of male unemployment, it was also a reflection of fascist attitudes towards women.

Despite fascist statements and policies, however, many women were able to retain their pre-1922 positions in the economy. It is also important to note that the two key fascist policies relating to women (increasing the birth rate and reducing the number of women in the workforce) both failed to meet their targets. The number of births

ACTIVITY

Carry out research to find out how Italian fascist views about women compared to the views advocated by Hitler in Nazi Germany. To what extent do they differ from attitudes and policies relating to women in *either* Mao's China *or* Castro's Cuba?

actually declined – dropping from 29.9 per 1,000 in 1925 to 23.1 in 1940. In addition, nearly one-third of Italy's paid workforce was still female by 1940. In part, this was because Mussolini's military adventures resulted in the conscription of large numbers of men.

> **SOURCE F**
>
> The female experience of the Fascist period was marked by its sheer diversity … When they [the fascists] tried to intervene explicitly to mould gender roles, in their bid to stem or even reverse trends towards female emancipation through highly misogynous [anti-female] rhetoric and policy, they were far from successful … despite the enormous amount of attention paid to gender roles in Fascist rhetoric, it seems that particular patterns of industrialisation, commercialisation, and urbanisation had more power to shape female experiences in this period than the crude tools of Fascist ideology and policy.
>
> Willson, P. 'Women in Fascist Italy'. Quoted in Bessel, R. (ed.). 1996. *Fascist Italy and Nazi Germany.* Cambridge, UK. Cambridge University Press. pp. 92–93.

Racism and anti-Semitism

While neither explicit racism nor anti-Semitism were characteristics of the early fascist movement, there was a general racist attitude underlying the fascists' nationalism and their plans for imperialist expansion. Racism was also a strong element in the *Romanità* movement (see section 2.7, Controlling minds). Mussolini believed that the Italian 'race' was superior to those African 'races' in Libya and Abyssinia. In September 1938, in the newspaper *Il Giornale d'Italia*, Mussolini claimed that 'prestige' was needed to maintain an empire. This, he said, required a clear 'racial consciousness' that established ideas of racial 'superiority'.

Until 1936, when Mussolini joined Nazi Germany in the alliance known as the Rome–Berlin Axis, anti-Semitism had not played a part in fascist politics. In fact, in an interview given as late as 1932, Mussolini said, 'Anti-Semitism does not exist in Italy. Italians of Jewish birth have shown themselves good citizens and they fought bravely in the war.' In the *Historical Dictionary of Fascist Italy*, Mussolini dismissed anti-Semitism as 'unscientific'.

Furthermore, some leading fascists were Jewish, and almost 30 per cent of Jewish Italians were members of the Fascist Party. Mussolini had previously appointed the Jewish Guido Jung as minister of finance. At one point, Mussolini himself had a Jewish mistress, **Margherita Sarfatti**.

Mussolini's move towards anti-Semitism was signalled in July 1938 by the issue of the ten-point Charter of Race, which was drawn up by Mussolini and ten fascist 'professors', and issued by Minculpop (see section 2.7, Fascist propaganda). This manifesto claimed to offer a 'scientific' explanation of fascist racial doctrine, based on the fact that Italians were 'Aryans'. Thus, Jewish people were not members of the Italian 'race'. The charter was followed by a series of racial laws and decrees, initiated between September and

Figure 2.22 Margherita Sarfatti (1883–1961)

Sarfatti was a member of the wealthy Grassini family from Venice. Extremely intelligent, she was initially a radical socialist and feminist, as well as a talented art critic. Sarfatti first met Mussolini in Milan in 1911, before he was expelled from the Socialist Party, while she was working as a journalist and art critic for *Avanti!* She supported him after 1915, and is believed to have influenced the moderation of his policies after 1922. However, as Mussolini became more anti-Semitic after 1938, Sarfatti went into exile until the end of the Second World War.

November 1938. These anti-Semitic laws excluded Jewish children and teachers from all state schools, banned Jews from marrying non-Jews, and prevented Jews from owning large companies or landed estates. The laws also expelled foreign Jews, including those who had been granted citizenship after 1919.

Fact: There were few Italian-born Jews. Only about 37,000 Italians had two Jewish parents, while around 10,800 had one parent who was Jewish. Jews were well integrated in Italian society, and were not seen as a threat to established interests. Later, however, leaders of several anti-fascist opposition groups – such as the Giustizia e Liberta – were Jewish.

SOURCE G

Admittedly the definition of 'Jew' was not too rigorous: those with two Jewish parents, or with one but practising the Judaic religion. Hence the children of mixed marriages could become 'Aryan' by being baptised, and there were 4000–5000 conversions in autumn 1938 (many of them so that children might be admitted to Catholic schools, having been expelled from state ones). There were also plenty of 'exemptions' allowed for war service or exceptional merit, brought in to placate the king: more than 20 per cent of Jewish families were exempted in this way.

Clark, M. 2005. *Mussolini*. London, UK. Pearson. p. 221.

These laws were never fully implemented in the period 1938–43, mainly because at a local level they were largely ignored by many Italians. However, they were strongly and publicly opposed by the pope. As well as the Catholic leadership, several senior fascists were unhappy about the introduction of these racial laws.

In 1943, an extreme form of racial persecution began under the Italian Social Republic (Salò Republic), which was nominally ruled by Mussolini following his overthrow as prime minister (see section 2.8, The Second World War). In fact, it was mainly the German Gestapo and the SS who carried out this much more brutal persecution of the Jewish people living in northern Italy.

Many historians regard the adoption of anti-Semitism as either a momentary aberration or simply the consequence of Mussolini's desire to imitate and impress his new ally, Hitler. Other historians argue that anti-Semitism stemmed from certain deep-rooted aspects of fascism.

SOURCE H

His decision to formulate a policy which would weld together racism and anti-Semitism was purely voluntary and flowed naturally from the confluence of Italy's imperial policies, the ideological tenets of Fascism, and Italian national interests as enunciated by Il Duce …

The emergence of official anti-Semitism … must be viewed not as a momentary aberration on the part of Mussolini or the Grand Council … It was rather cut from the same cloth as the rest of Fascism's final costume.

Bernardini, P. 'The Origins and Development of Racial Anti-Semitism in Fascist Italy'. In Marrus, M. (ed.). 1988. *The Nazi Holocaust: the Final Solution Outside Germany*. Toronto, Canada. University of Toronto Press. pp. 230 and 238.

QUESTION

Why were the anti-Semitic laws of 1938 not rigorously enforced in fascist Italy before 1943?

2.14 What were the main fascist policies on education and young people, and what impact did they have?

'Fascistisation' – education and indoctrination

Central to Mussolini's 'Cult of Personality' was his portrayal of the fascists as the only force that could unite all Italians and make their country great. Mussolini also adopted various other methods to manipulate and control the public, including indoctrination. He gave prime importance to the younger generation, which – he believed – needed to be 'fascistised'.

In infant schools, children started the day with a prayer that began, 'I believe in the genius of Mussolini'. In primary schools, children were taught that Mussolini and the fascists had 'saved' Italy from communist revolution. In 1929, it became compulsory for all teachers in state schools to swear an oath of loyalty to both the king and to Mussolini's fascist regime. Two years later, this oath was extended to university lecturers. Only eleven chose to resign rather than take the oath.

Fact: In 1926, 101 out of 317 history textbooks were banned. By 1936, under the then minister of education, Giuseppe Bottai, there was only one official history textbook.

Mussolini's attempts at indoctrination were less successful in secondary education. However, all school textbooks were carefully reviewed, and many were banned and replaced with new government books that emphasised the role of Mussolini and the fascists.

In 1923, fascist attempts to indoctrinate secondary-school children were not helped by the first fascist minister of education, Giovanni Gentile, who decided to continue focusing on traditional academic education. Gentile also introduced exams that made it very difficult for most children to progress to secondary education at all. As a result, the number of children reaching secondary school, and thus university, declined significantly.

Fascism and youth movements

Mussolini and the fascists also tried to indoctrinate young people by setting up youth organisations. In 1926, all fascist youth groups were made part of the **Opera Nazionale Balilla (ONB)**. Within the organisation were different sections for boys and girls, according to age. For boys, there were the Sons of the She-Wolf (4–8), the Balilla (8–14) and the Avanguardisti (14–18). For girls, there were the Piccole Italiane and the Giovani Italiane. There was also the Young Fascists for boys aged 18–21, after which they could apply to become members of the Fascist Party.

Opera Nazionale Balilla (ONB): The main youth group in Italy from 1926, apart from those run by the Catholic Church. 'Balilla' was the name given to Giovan Battista Perasso, the Genoese schoolboy who – according to legend – began the revolt against Habsburg rule by throwing stones at Austrian troops in 1746.

In 1937, the ONB merged with the Young Fascists to form the Gioventù Italiana del Littorio (GIL), and membership was made compulsory for all young people aged eight to twenty-one. By this time, the ONB's membership had risen to over 7 million. While all groups followed physical fitness programmes and attended summer camps that included pre-military training, older children also received political indoctrination.

All members of the ONB – and of the GUF (the Fascist University Groups) – had to swear loyalty to Mussolini.

However, the impact on schoolchildren was not as great as Mussolini had intended. Some 40 per cent of 4–18-year-olds managed to avoid membership. In particular, private and Catholic schools tended not to enforce ONB membership. Also, because of the entrance exams required for secondary education, many children left school at the age of eleven. Contempt for – and even resistance to – fascist ideals was not uncommon in the universities.

Figure 2.23   Members of the Ballila (fascist youth) greet Mussolini in 1939

SOURCE I

The regime is and intends to remain a regime of the young ... The regime intends to prepare spiritually all the youth of Italy, from whom successive selections there must issue tomorrow the ranks of the governing classes of Italy, and for this purpose it has created, alongside the civil Militia of the party, the organisation of the Balilla, the Avanguardisti and the University groups. The totalitarian principle of the education of youth, systematically demanded by Fascism, responds to this supreme necessity of Fascist Revolution which intends to last.

Extracts from the 'Order of the Day', issued by the PNF secretary in 1930. Quoted in Hite, J. and Hinton, C. 1998. *Fascist Italy*. London, UK. Hodder Education. p. 157.

A regime that lasted twenty-one years could not fail to have some impact on the Italian youth. However, the speed with which support for fascism declined after Mussolini's downfall indicates that, for all the propaganda, the targeting of young people for fascist converts was ultimately yet another policy failure.

2.15 To what extent was authoritarian control established in fascist Italy?

The main characteristics of Mussolini's fascist state

When he became prime minister in October 1922, Mussolini almost immediately took steps towards the construction of his fascist state. By 1924, Italy was on the way to becoming a fascist dictatorship.

SOURCE J

The Fascist conception of the State is all-embracing; outside of it no human or spiritual values can exist, much less have value. Thus understood, Fascism is totalitarian, and the Fascist State – a synthesis and a unit inclusive of all values – interprets, develops, and potentiates the whole life of a people … The Fascist State lays claim to rule in the economic field no less than in others; it makes its action felt throughout the length and breadth of the country by means of its corporate, social, and educational institutions, and all the political, economic, and spiritual forces of the nation, organised in their respective associations, circulate within the State.

Extracts from the 1935 edition of *The Doctrine of Fascism*. Giovanni Gentile and Benito Mussolini. pp. 14 and 41.

Fact: In 1927, only about 15 per cent of the civil service were said to be fascists: both the interior minister (Luigi Federzoni) and the minister of justice (Alfredo Rocco) were conservative ex-nationalists. In the 1930s, civil servants often proclaimed loyalty to the Fascist Party merely to retain their jobs.

podesta: The *podesta* were the local mayors. After elected local councils were abolished in 1926, the prefects – whose powers were greatly increased – appointed all the mayors in their province. They usually chose 'respectable' landowners or ex-army officers, rather than local fascists. *Podesta* received no payment, so they needed to be financially independent.

Source J makes extravagant claims as to the nature of the state that Mussolini attempted to establish after 1922. However, such claims were often not an accurate reflection of reality. Nonetheless, by December 1924, the crisis following the murder of Giacomo Matteotti (see section 2.5, Changing the constitution – the Acerbo Law) had led some more militant fascists to present Mussolini with an ultimatum – establish a fascist dictatorship, or they would replace him with someone who would. After some hesitation, Mussolini had agreed to declare himself dictator, but only on his own terms. He was determined to enforce a dictatorship that would be independent of the *ras*. The authoritarian regime that Mussolini presided over between 1925 and 1945 was thus a personal rather than a Fascist Party dictatorship.

Declining importance of the Fascist Party

Mussolini deliberately restricted the influence of the PNF by using members of the traditional conservative élites to maintain law and order. This included the police, the judicial system, the civil service and the army. Mussolini made no serious attempt to 'fascistise' the system of government by restricting appointments to leading fascists, as some of his followers wanted.

However, Mussolini did instigate a purge of the judiciary, and many judges were sacked for lack of loyalty or for following an overly independent line. Mussolini frequently intervened in legal cases, and imprisonment without trial was common. The chief of police was another position filled by career politicians rather than fascists. In the provinces, it was the prefects (the senior civil servants who ran the administration, suppressed 'subversives' and controlled the police) who appointed the *podesta*. The prefects had to be loyal to the government, but also to the local élites. Between 1922 and 1929, only twenty-nine of the eighty-six new *podesta* appointed were fascists. Most were career civil servants.

At first, the *ras* resisted these developments, especially in central Italy. As late as 1927, local fascist leaders were able to insist on some power sharing. By 1930, however, Mussolini claimed this conflict had been resolved in favour of the prefects. Disputes between prefects and local party leaders still broke out occasionally though.

After Farinacci's forced resignation in October 1926 (ostensibly for another outburst of *squadristi* violence, but really because he had begun to push for a 'second wave' of fascist revolution), the prefects and the *podesta* set about stamping out *squadrismo*. In January 1927, Mussolini issued instructions that all Italians, including fascists, should offer the prefects total obedience.

The 'taming' of the PNF

In 1926, the new party secretary, **Augusto Turati**, began a purge of more militant fascists. At the same time, he opened membership to people who merely wanted to further their career. In just one year, party membership rose from about 640,000 to just under 940,000. For the first time, fascist branches were established in southern Italy.

Most of these new members came from the same local élites that had previously belonged to or supported the liberals. Soon there were very few Fascists of the First Hour left in important positions. At the same time, over 100,000 party members left – many of them disgusted by what was happening to their party.

These developments continued in the 1930s under Turati's successors, Giovanni Giuriati and Achille Starace. The PNF became a mass party, with almost 5 million (mainly inactive) members by 1943. However, most were white-collar employees, while the workers and peasants (who had once made up 30 per cent of the party's membership) dropped to a small minority. The Fascist Party thus increasingly became a tame and loyal base of support for Mussolini. At the same time, party posts were filled by appointment from above rather than through election by party members.

This gradual weakening of the PNF was due in part to internal divisions and disunity, which had existed from its foundation. According to the historian Richard Thurlow, there were at least five different factions within the party. These included the militant *ras*, who (like sections of the *Sturmabteilung* in Nazi Germany) wanted a 'second wave' of fascist revolution to replace state institutions with fascist ones, and the 'left' fascists, who wanted to establish a corporativist, or national syndicalist, state.

Opposed to these two factions were the fascist 'revisionists', led by Dino Grandi, Massimo Rocca and Giuseppe Bottai, who were prepared to cooperate and merge with the existing political system. Mussolini was able to play off these factions against each other to enhance his own power. At the same time, he manipulated different sectors of state personnel to ensure that no one could challenge his authority.

The corporate state

Those fascists who believed that their movement was a 'third way' between capitalism and communism favoured the creation of a corporate state. Sometimes known as the corporative state, the aim of corporativism was to replace the politics of traditional parliamentary democracy with that of corporations representing the nation's various economic sectors. These corporations, each with equal representation for employers

Figure 2.24 Augusto Turati (1888–1955)

Turati was an ex-syndicalist, an irredentist, a supporter of Italy's entry into the First World War, and a journalist. He joined Mussolini's Fascio di Combattimento in 1920, and became the PNF boss of Brescia. He was National Party secretary from 1926 to 1930. His purge of party members affected both provincial and non-provincial branches. In 1927, for example, 7,000 of Rome's 31,000 members were purged. In his first year as party secretary, Turati expelled 30,000 members, and by 1929 that number had risen to over 50,000. Later, he opposed Italy's entry into the Second World War and did not support Mussolini's Salò Republic.

and employees, were supposed to overcome class conflict. By thus avoiding strikes and other labour disputes, the corporate state would instead give prime consideration to the interests of the nation. Although there would be elements of increased state control, there was no thought of eradicating private ownership.

SOURCE K

Fascism is therefore opposed to Socialism to which unity within the State (which amalgamates classes into a single economic and ethical reality) is unknown, and which sees in history nothing but the class struggle. Fascism is likewise opposed to trade unionism as a class weapon. But when brought within the orbit of the State, Fascism recognises the real needs which gave rise to socialism and trade-unionism, giving them due weight in the guild or corporative system in which divergent interests are coordinated and harmonised in the unity of the State.

Extract from *The Doctrine of Fascism*. 1932. Giovanni Gentile and Benito Mussolini. p. 15.

The fascist syndicates

During their rise to power in the years 1920–22, the fascists closed down the traditional labour movement trade unions in the areas they controlled. They replaced these unions with fascist-controlled syndicates, which were still supposed to represent workers' interests. By 1922, a Confederation of Fascist Syndicates had been set up, headed by **Edmondo Rossoni,** who wanted to create corporations that would force industrialists to make some concessions to workers' demands. These corporations would be established for each industry, and made up of government representatives, employers' organisations and representatives from the fascist syndicates.

However, this 'leftist' fascist aspiration – unlike their attacks on the traditional trade unions – was opposed by the Confindustria, the organisation that represented the main industrialists in Italy. In December 1923, when Mussolini had been prime minister for fourteen months, the Chigi Palace Pact was made. In this agreement, the industrialists promised to cooperate with the Confederation of Fascist Syndicates, but they insisted on maintaining their own independent organisations.

Despite this, many employers were not prepared to make any significant concessions to workers, and this provoked a series of strikes in 1925. The resulting Vidoni Palace Pact confirmed that the Confindustria and the Confederation of Fascist Syndicates were the only organisations allowed to represent employers and employees respectively. It was also made clear that workers were not to challenge the authority of employers and managers. All workers' factory councils were closed down and non-fascist trade unions were abolished. In 1926, Alfredo Rocco's law made all strikes illegal – even those by fascist syndicates – and declared that industrial disputes must be settled in special labour courts. The law also stated that there could only be one organisation (a fascist syndicate) of workers and employers in each branch of industry, and identified seven main areas of economic activity.

The corporations

Following these developments, in July 1926 Mussolini established a Ministry of Corporations, with himself as the minister. Each corporation was made up of representatives of employers and workers of the same economic or industrial sector (e.g. mining), with the state's representatives acting as referees and final adjudicators. In practice, this new ministry was run by the under-secretary, **Giuseppe Bottai,** who produced the Charter of Labour (written

Edmondo Rossoni (1884–1965)

Rossoni was initially a revolutionary syndicalist, who was imprisoned for his activities in 1908. He became a socialist and then a nationalist, joining Mussolini's PNF in 1921. Rossoni was the most prominent of the fascist labour leaders and, as head of the Confederation of Fascist Syndicates, he wanted genuine workers' representatives who would share power with employers. After his dismissal in 1928, he continued in fascist politics, serving as under-secretary to the president of the Fascist Grand Council from 1932 to 1935. Later, he supported Dino Grandi's coup and voted against Mussolini in 1943.

Giuseppe Bottai (1895–1959)

Bottai met Mussolini in 1919 and helped set up a *fascio* in Rome, where he acted as editor of Mussolini's paper, *Il Popolo d'Italia*. In the March on Rome his unit was responsible for the deaths of several anti-fascists. From 1926 to 1929, Bottai was deputy secretary of corporations. From 1936 to 1943, he served as minister for education and mayor of Rome. He was responsible for implementing several anti-democratic and anti-Semitic measures. In 1943, Bottai sided with Grandi in the coup against Mussolini.

mainly by Rocco) in April 1927. This document guaranteed fair judgement of labour disputes and promised to carry out social reforms such as improved health care and accident insurance schemes (although none of these measures had the force of law).

In May 1927, Mussolini delivered a speech in which he claimed that a corporate state had been established. He even promised that the corporations would elect half of the members of the next Chamber of Deputies. In May the following year, a new electoral law was passed – a compromise between party and syndicalist views. It allowed for 1,000 names to be recommended to the Fascist Grand Council, which would select 400 as candidates for the March 1929 election.

As Mussolini feared, the corporations weakened the fascist syndicates. In 1928, Rossoni was dismissed and the Confederation of Fascist Syndicates was abolished. In 1929, Bottai took over as minister of corporations, and in March 1930 he set up the National Council of Corporations (NCC), which represented the seven largest corporations. In 1932, Mussolini resumed control of the Ministry of Corporations, and the number of corporations slowly grew, reaching twenty-two by 1934.

Despite all of the reorganisation, Mussolini usually made the important decisions himself. In particular, most of the decisions on policies to deal with the effects of the Great Depression (see section 2.7, Controlling minds) had nothing to do with the corporations – including the decision to cut wages. Furthermore, as most trade unionists experienced in industrial negotiations and disputes were socialists or communists (and were therefore either dead, in prison or in exile), the employers had a greater influence in the corporations. Many were 'tame' members of the fascist syndicates, or even middle-class careerists. In addition, the employers were nearly always supported by the three government-appointed Fascist Party members, who were supposed to remain neutral.

In 1938, in a belated attempt to give more credibility to the corporate state, Mussolini decided to abolish the Chamber of Deputies and to put in its place the Chamber of Fasci and Corporations. Mussolini hoped to establish a new form of politics, in which people were given a voice according to their economic function or occupation, rather than their territorial location. In reality, however, this had little substance or power, being dominated by fascists appointed from above.

Was Mussolini an all-powerful dictator?

Despite Mussolini's claims, and despite having established control over the PNF, the reality was that he had to share power with the traditional groups that had wielded power in Italy long before 1922. These included the monarchy, the Catholic Church, the civil service and the courts, and the industrial and financial élites and their organisations. For example, after other fascist leaders began moving against Mussolini, it was the king who eventually ordered his arrest on 25 July 1943. Thus Mussolini's aim to create a completely authoritarian state was largely unsuccessful.

Fact: In the March 1929 election, electors could only vote 'yes' or 'no' to the Grand Council's list. Of the original 1,000 names recommended by syndicates, employers' associations, ex-servicemen and a few other groups, the employers got 125 of their nominees 'elected', while the workers' syndicates only managed eighty-nine. Mussolini employed his usual methods of 'persuasion', resulting in a 90 per cent turnout, with 98.3 per cent voting in favour of the list presented to them. One of the few politicians to speak out against the new electoral law was Giolitti.

Historical debate: Historians are divided over the nature of Italian fascism and its ideology. One broad interpretation has tended to examine fascist ideology and its corporate state in a serious way, and largely on its own terms. Another has been much more sceptical, considering its ideology to be incoherent and its declared 'achievements' mainly unfounded propaganda claims. Since the works of historians Renzo De Felice and Emilio Gentile, a third 'revisionist' strand has returned to the idea of fascist ideology and its stated purposes as relatively coherent and worthy of serious study.

SOURCE L

The existence of autonomous, conservative interests – monarchy, industry, agrari, armed forces and Church – was thus integral to Mussolini's regime as it entered the 1930s. Their continued influence made the regime, in its essential character, less profoundly 'fascist' and less totalitarian in scope than it claimed to be and than outward appearances suggested.

Blinkhorn, M. 2006. *Mussolini and Fascist Italy.* London, UK. Routledge. p. 52.

ACTIVITY

In pairs, develop two
sets of arguments
about the role and
the attitudes of the
Catholic Church in
fascist Italy – one
to show they were
mainly collaborators,
and one to argue
that they were rivals.
Then present these
arguments in a class
debate. Make sure that
each of the two views
is critically examined
in relation to the
evidence presented.

SOURCE M

Mussolini gave the impression of being all-powerful, but he could not rule alone, and the
Fascist Party as such was little help to him in running the country. The civil service, the
courts, the armed forces and the police remained in the hands of career officials whose
commitment to Fascism was usually nominal.

Tannenbaum, E. 1973. *Fascism in Italy*. London, UK. Allen Lane. p. 93.

SOURCE N

The new system was a personal dictatorship under Mussolini, yet still legally a monarchy
… The government ruled by decree … Local elections were eliminated; all mayors were
now appointed by decree. Yet the basic legal and administrative apparatus of the Italian
government remained intact. There was no 'Fascist revolution', save at the top.

Payne, S. 1995. *A History of Fascism, 1914–45*. London, UK. UCL Press. pp. 116–17.

End of unit activities

1   Draw up a table to show the main economic problems facing Italy between 1922 and
    1943, and the degree of success Mussolini had in dealing with them. Use the table
    below as an example.

	Problem	Policy	Success?	Failure?
1922–24				
1925–43				

2   Divide into five groups, with each group researching the impact of Mussolini's
    economic policies on *one* of the various social groups:

    a   large landowners

    b   industrialists and bankers

    c   industrial workers

    d   agricultural workers

    e   peasants / small farmers.

    Each group should present their findings to the class.

3   Carry out some additional research to find out how Italian women were affected by
    the fascist regime.

4   Find out more about the reasons for the cooperation and conflicts between the fascist
    state and the Catholic Church.

5   Work in pairs to produce a PowerPoint presentation on how Mussolini's regime tried
    to indoctrinate young people.

6   Find out more about the various steps in the creation of the corporate state in Italy from
    1926 to 1932. Then write a few paragraphs to explain why the more radical sections of
    the PNF, such as Edmondo Rossoni, were disappointed by these developments.

End of chapter activities

Paper 1 exam practice

Question

What, according to **Source A**, were the roles of the PNF in Mussolini's Italy? **[3 marks]**

Skill

Comprehension/understanding of a source.

SOURCE A

Fascist Italy may thus have been a one-party state, but it was not a 'party state' along the lines of Soviet Russia or even, eventually, Nazi Germany … Quite apart from its mundane yet important role of providing job opportunities for the Italian middle class, the Party [PNF] came to perform numerous vital administrative and politically educative tasks …

Through the elaborate bureaucracy of the Dopolavoro ('After-work') organization it supervised and even enlivened the leisure and social activities of the working population, seeking to compensate workers for their falling wages with a variety of fringe benefits and in the process to 'cure' them of socialism.

Blinkhorn, M. 2006. *Mussolini and Fascist Italy*. London, UK. Routledge. p. 38.

Examiner's tips

Comprehension questions are the most straightforward questions you will face in Paper 1. They simply require you to understand a source and extract two or three relevant points that relate to the question.

As only 3 marks are available for this question, make sure you do not waste valuable exam time that should be spent on the higher-scoring questions by writing a long answer here. Just a couple of brief sentences are needed, giving the necessary information to show that you have understood the content/message of the source. Try to give one piece of information for each of the marks available for the question.

Common mistakes

When asked to show your comprehension/understanding of a particular source, make sure you do not comment on the wrong source! Mistakes like this are made every year. Remember – every mark is important for your final grade.

Simplified mark scheme

For each item of **relevant/correct information** identified, award 1 mark — up to a maximum of 3 marks.

Student answer

According to Source A, the main role of the Fascist Party (PNF) was to provide jobs for the middle classes.

Examiner's comments

The candidate has selected one relevant and explicit piece of information from the source that clearly identifies one important role of the PNF. This is enough to gain 1 mark. However, as no other point/role has been identified, this candidate fails to get the other 2 marks available.

Activity

Look again at the source and the student answer above. Now try to identify some other pieces of information from the source, and try to make an overall comment about the source. This will allow you to obtain the other 2 marks available for this question.

Summary activities

Draw your own spider diagram and, using the information from this case study and any other material available, make brief notes under the relevant headings to show how an authoritarian state emerged in Italy. Where there are differences between historians concerning these various areas, make a note of their names and a brief summary of their arguments.

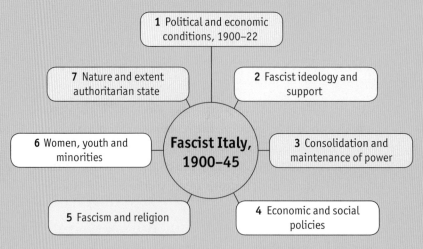

- **1** Political and economic conditions, 1900–22
- **2** Fascist ideology and support
- **3** Consolidation and maintenance of power
- **4** Economic and social policies
- **5** Fascism and religion
- **6** Women, youth and minorities
- **7** Nature and extent authoritarian state

Fascist Italy, 1900–45

Paper 2 practice questions

1 Examine the methods used and the conditions that helped Mussolini in his rise to power.
2 Compare and contrast the importance of ideology for Mussolini and Castro.
3 Examine the methods used by Mussolini to maintain his regime.
4 Evaluate the successes and failures of Mussolini's domestic policies from 1922 to 1940.
5 Compare and contrast the status of women in Mussolini's Italy's and *either* Mao's China *or* Castro's Cuba.
6 In what ways, and for what reasons, did the economic and social aims and policies of Mussolini and Castro differ?
7 'Mussolini's foreign policy played a significant role in helping to maintain his power.' To what extent do you agree with this statement?

Further reading

Bessel, R. (ed.). 1996. *Fascist Italy and Nazi Germany*. Cambridge, UK. Cambridge University Press.

Blinkhorn, M. 2006. *Mussolini and Fascist Italy*. London, UK. Routledge.

Cassels, A. 1969. *Fascist Italy*. London, UK. Routledge & Keegan Paul.

Clark, M. 2005. *Mussolini*. London, UK. Pearson.

Eatwell, R. 1995. *Fascism: a History*. London, UK. Chatto & Windus.

Gallo, M. 1974. *Mussolini's Italy*. London, UK. Macmillan.

Griffin, R. (ed.). 1995. *Fascism: a Reader*. Oxford, UK. Oxford Paperbacks.

Hite, J. and Hinton, C. 1998. *Fascist Italy*. London, UK. Hodder Education.

Lee, S. 1987. *The European Dictatorships, 1918–1945*. London, UK. Routledge.

Macdonald, H. 1999. *Mussolini and Italian Fascism*. Cheltenham, UK. Nelson Thornes.

Marrus, M. (ed.). 1988. *The Nazi Holocaust: the Final Solution Outside Germany*. Toronto, Canada. University of Toronto Press.

Payne, S. 1995. *A History of Fascism, 1914–45*. London, UK. UCL Press.

Pearce, R. 1997. *Fascism and Nazism*. London, UK. Hodder & Stoughton.

Robson, M. 1992. *Italy: Liberalism and Fascism 1870–1945*. London, UK. Hodder & Stoughton.

Tannenbaum, E. 1973. *Fascism in Italy*. London, UK. Allen Lane.

Tannenbaum, E. (ed.). 1974. *Modern Italy: a Topical History Since 1861*. New York, USA. New York University Press.

3 Hitler and Nazi Germany

1 Unit

Emergence of an Authoritarian Regime in Germany

TIMELINE

1918 Nov: Germany is defeated in First World War; a republic is declared

1919 Jun: Weimar Republic is forced to accept the harsh Treaty of Versailles

1920 National Socialists produce 25-point programme, reconciling nationalism and socialism

1923 Jan: French and Belgian troops invade the Ruhr; massive inflation results

Nov: Hitler attempts the Munich Putsch and fails

1924 Feb: Hitler is imprisoned in Landsberg Fortress and writes his semi-autobiographical *Mein Kampf* (released early in December)

1929 Oct: Wall Street Crash leads to unemployment in Germany

1930 Mar: Müller's Grand Coalition collapses and Brüning becomes chancellor

Sep: Nazis win 107 seats in elections (18.3% of the vote)

1932 Feb: unemployment reaches 6 million

Apr: Hindenburg beats Hitler in presidential elections

Jun: von Papen replaces Brüning as chancellor

Jul: Nazis win 230 Reichstag seats becoming the largest single party

Nov: Nazis win 196 Reichstag seats – a sign that their support has passed its peak

Dec: von Schleicher becomes chancellor

1933 Jan: Hitler becomes chancellor

Feb: Reichstag Fire is blamed on the communists

Mar: Nazis win 288 Reichstag seats; Enabling Act gives Hitler dictatorial powers for four years

Overview

- The Weimar Republic, which was set up in 1919, proved to be politically weak. It faced both left-wing communist rebellion and right-wing conservative and nationalist opposition, focused on the humiliating peace treaty, the Treaty of Versailles.

- Economic conditions also proved unfavourable. When the French and Belgians invaded the Ruhr in 1923, hyperinflation resulted, ruining middle-class savings. When US loans were withdrawn following the Wall Street Crash of 1929, Germany fell into depression.

- National Socialism thrived on the weaknesses of the Weimar Republic. Hitler's personal leadership, aims and ideology attracted a variety of supporters and his promises to restore German prosperity, provide jobs and 'smash' the Treaty of Versailles won increasing electoral success after 1930.

- In March 1930, the country's last democratic government – the 'Grand Coalition' – collapsed and subsequent chancellors relied on the president's right to issue decrees (under article 48 of the Weimar Constitution). By July 1932, the Nazis were the largest party in the Reichstag (parliament).

- President Paul von Hindenburg was persuaded to appoint Hitler as chancellor on 30 January 1933 following 'backstairs intrigue', which Hitler had worked to his own advantage.

- The Reichstag Fire permitted a further law that allowed the imprisonment of communists and helped to increase support for the Nazis in the March 1933 elections. Hitler forced through an Enabling Act, which gave him dictatorial powers over Germany.

KEY QUESTIONS

- How did political conditions in Germany after 1918 contribute to the emergence of a Nazi state?
- How did the economic conditions in Germany in the years 1919 to 1929 contribute to the emergence of a Nazi state?
- How did the aims and ideology of the Nazi Party develop between 1919 and 1929?
- How far did the conditions of 1929–33 contribute to the establishment of the Nazi state?
- Where did the support for National Socialism come from?

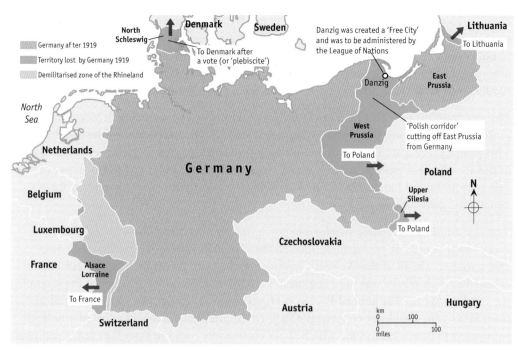

Figure 3.1 The impact of the Treaty of Versailles on the borders of Germany

3.1 How did political conditions in Germany after 1918 contribute to the emergence of a Nazi state?

Before the First World War, Germany had been ruled by the authoritarian Kaiser Wilhelm II. Although the German constitution of 1871 had made provision for a Reichstag (elected parliament), this had never been allowed to develop effectively, causing a good deal of political tension. The kaiser had pursued an ambitious foreign policy, partly to deflect attention away from political troubles, and this led to the First World War in 1914.

The war destroyed the imperial regime. As defeat threatened in 1918, the Kaiser tried to install a more liberal government. However, the country descended into chaos with strikes and mutinies. The Kaiser abdicated on 9 November 1918 and a republic was declared.

A new socialist government under **Friedrich Ebert** signed an armistice to end the war in November 1918, and in January 1919 a new democratic constitution was drawn up in the town of Weimar. The armistice came as a shock to the Germans, who had been encouraged to believe that their country would be victorious. Nationalists claimed that the German army had been 'stabbed in the back' by politicians who made peace when the army could have fought on.

The **Treaty of Versailles** in June 1919 caused further anger. Germany lost 13 per cent of its territory in Europe, plus all of its colonies. It was left with severely restricted armed forces, a demilitarised Rhineland in the west and a corridor of land given to Poland,

Figure 3.2 Friedrich Ebert (1871–1925)

Friedrich Ebert was a socialist leader who took over government in November 1918 after the Kaiser's abdication. As elected president of the Weimar Republic from February 1919, he faced political instability, the humiliation of the Treaty of Versailles, economic problems resulting from the war, the invasion of the Ruhr and hyperinflation.

Treaty of Versailles: This was the peace treaty imposed on Germany after the First World War by the victorious Allies – Britain, France and the USA.

self-determination: This term refers to the right of racial groups to be settled in a country of their own race and ruled by their own people.

Anschluss: This is the term used to refer to the joining together of Austria and Germany. Hitler carried this out in 1938 to create the greater German Reich (state).

proportional representation: Under this system of elections, electors vote for a party rather than a candidate. Parties can then choose deputies from a list, according to the number of votes cast for that party. The number of deputies in the Reichstag would therefore correspond proportionately to the number of votes that party received in the country as a whole.

Spartacus League: Led by Karl Liebknecht and Rosa Luxemburg, the Spartacus League was a radical socialist group. Its members were the founders of the KPD (German Communist Party), which was set up at a congress in Berlin held from 30 December 1918 to 1 January 1919. The group remained committed to violent revolution until about 1923, whereafter it contested Reichstag elections with some success. The KPD and SPD (Social Democratic Party) refused to work together, which was one factor that allowed the Nazis to come to power.

conservative élite: This is the name given to traditionally right-wing aristocratic landowners, industrialists, senior army officers, judges and civil servants.

dividing East Prussia from the rest of Germany. By forcing the Germans to accept war guilt and binding them to pay reparations (finally fixed at £6.6 billion in 1921), the humiliation of Germany seemed complete. Although **self-determination** was applied to other parts of Europe, Germany was left with many ethnic Germans living outside its borders, and **Anschluss** (union) with Austria was expressly forbidden.

The new constitution also contained some significant weaknesses, which were to cause problems in later years. The voting system was based on **proportional representation**. This produced coalition governments and allowed small parties to gain representation in the Reichstag. Constant governmental changes (with fourteen coalitions between February 1919 and June 1928) helped to weaken what support there had been for democratic government.

The constitution also gave considerable power to the president, who was to be elected every seven years. The president appointed the chancellor (who ran the government) and, under article 48 of the Weimar Constitution, had the power to rule by decree in an emergency. This power was used responsibly by the first president, Ebert, but the second, the old First World War general Paul von Hindenburg (1925–1934), chose chancellors from 1930 who could not command a majority in the Reichstag and allowed article 48 to be used to pass measures for which these chancellors could not get Reichstag approval.

The political weaknesses of the Weimar Republic left it exposed to continual political threats in its early years. The **Spartacus League** (*Spartakusbund*), an extreme left-wing socialist movement, attempted to overthrow the Republic in January 1919. There was also trouble from communists in the Ruhr in March 1920 and in Saxony and Thuringia in 1923.

Similarly, the right-wing **conservative élite** was lukewarm, if not hostile, towards the Republic. German conservatism and nationalism remained strong and most ex-army officers, judges, senior civil servants and university professors resented the new style of parliamentary rule. This continuation of nationalist values favoured the development of right-wing extremism, of which Nazism was to be one example, in Germany in this period.

Figure 3.3   Street fighting in Berlin between government troops and the Spartacus League, during the Spartacist uprising, January 1919

SOURCE A

In the eyes of the right, the Republic was associated with the surrender, a shameful and deliberate act of treachery, and the peace treaty, a further act of betrayal. The fact that the new republican institutions were democratic added to the hostility. It was openly said that loyalty to the fatherland required disloyalty to the Republic.

Bullock, A. 1962 (rev. edn). *Hitler, A Study in Tyranny.* Harmondsworth, UK. Penguin Books. pp. 58–59.

putsch: An attempt to overthrow the state.

Freikorps: These were volunteer groups of demobilised soldiers who continued to fight for right-wing values.

German nationalists showed their contempt for the Republic in the military Kapp **Putsch** of March 1920 and the 'White Terror' of 1920–22, when 400 political murders occurred, many committed by the **Freikorps**. Hitler's Beer Hall Putsch of November 1923 (see section 3.3, Adolf Hitler (1889–1945)), the first attempt of the Nazi Party to show its strength, was yet another incident in this long line of political challenges. Although a failure, it reinforced the picture of the Weimar Republic as a struggling parliamentary democracy.

The Republic enjoyed a more stable period between 1924 and 1929, when moderate parties made gains. From 1928 to 1930, a 'Grand Coalition' commanded over 60 per cent of the seats in the Reichstag. However, political problems had been submerged rather than going away. From 1929, as economic problems worsened, the parties of the Reichstag became so divided that in 1930 the Grand Coalition collapsed, opening the way for the total breakdown of the democracy.

KEY CONCEPTS QUESTION

Causation: Why was the Weimar Republic regarded as weak between 1919 and 1924?

3.2 How did the economic conditions in Germany in the years 1919 to 1929 contribute to the emergence of a Nazi state?

reparations: Compensation for war damage that was payable to Germany's former enemies.

passive resistance: A non-violent refusal to work – in the Ruhr, for example, this meant a refusal to work for the occupying troops of France and Belgium.

The costs of war and the impact of the wartime blockade, compounded by the Treaty of Versailles, undermined the German economy. Returning soldiers could not find work, and valuable industrial land was lost. In 1923, when Germany could not meet the impossibly heavy demands for **reparations** set by the victorious Allies in 1921, the French and Belgians occupied the Ruhr.

To pay welfare assistance to workers, who were ordered to meet the invasion of the Ruhr with **passive resistance**, the government over-printed paper money. This, plus the loss of production, provoked **hyperinflation**. Although hyperinflation was cured by a new currency in 1924, the loss of value in savings, which hit middle-class families particularly hard, caused lasting damage. Furthermore, a shortage of domestic investment, which forced the government to look for US loans under the 1924 Dawes Plan, was to place the economy in a dangerously dependent position.

hyperinflation: This term is used to describe a very high rate of inflation, when money is so devalued that prices rise constantly and excessive amounts are needed to buy everyday items. Effectively, the currency becomes worthless.

Although the years 1925–29 saw some improvements, agriculture never shared in the boom. Prices remained low as farmers faced competition from Canada and the USA. However, it was the Wall Street Crash of October 1929 that once again sent the economy into crisis as the USA recalled its loans. This created the desperate economic conditions in which democracy broke down and the Nazis were able to rise to power.

3.3 How did the aims and ideology of the Nazi Party develop between 1919 and 1929?

Adolf Hitler (1889–1945)

Table 3.1   Biography of early life

1889	Born in Branau, Austria, the son of a customs inspector
1907	Was refused admission to the Viennese Academy of Art
1908	Failed again to enter the Academy; lived rough in Vienna, painting scenes from postcards
1913	Moved to Munich in Bavaria, Germany
1914	Volunteered for military service and was sent to the Western Front as a dispatch runner; became a corporal
1918	Was recovering from a poison gas attack when he heard news of the armistice
1919	Returned to Munich and served in the army in an 'enlightenment project' to investigate new political groups

NSDAP:
Nationalsozialistische
Deutsche Arbeiterpartei:
This is the full name of the Nazi Party. Members were called 'Nazis' in the same way that the socialists were known as 'Sozis'. Nazi came from the NA of *National* and the ZI of *sozialistische*.

swastika: This term refers to an ancient religious symbol in the form of a cross with the arms bent at right angles. It had been used by right-wing groups in Austria and was associated with Aryanism even before Hitler chose to adopt it. It became the best-known symbol of the Nazi Party and was used on flags, arm-bands and badges.

ideology: This refers to a set of beliefs and ideas that characterise a political movement and provide the principles from which its policies derive.

The **NSDAP** (National Socialist German Workers' Party) or Nazi Party was just one of a number of right-wing political opposition groups that developed in Germany in the early years of the Weimar Republic. Founded in Munich as the *Deutsche Arbeiterpartei* or DAP (German Workers' Party) in 1919 by Anton Drexler, the party soon fell under the spell of Adolf Hitler.

After the war, Hitler worked as an army informant, 'spying' on left-wing political groups for the authorities. On 12 September 1919, he investigated Drexler's party. He was attracted by its philosophy and decided to join. By 1 April 1920, Hitler had left the army to become a full-time political agitator. He gave the party its new name, its drive and its **swastika** emblem. In July 1921, he became its chairman.

The **ideology** of National Socialism – the superiority of the German race, anti-Semitism, anti-communism, the survival of the fittest, the 'national community' and the cult of the leader – had already taken shape in Hitler's mind as a consequence of his own experience. His time living rough in Vienna before the First World War had helped to turn him into a fervent German nationalist and anti-Semite. His bitter disappointment that democratic socialist politicians should agree to an armistice in 1918 – and still worse, a humiliating peace treaty in 1919 – strengthened his convictions. He associated democracy with weakness, believing the German army had been 'stabbed in the back' by the 'November Criminals'. He saw the socialist politicians as communists, and tainted by association with Jewry.

Nevertheless, the 25-point programme embraced an element of 'socialism', probably in an effort to entice workers away from the communist groups that flourished in the aftermath of war. There were demands for the abolition of unearned income, the nationalisation of businesses and the closure of big department stores in favour of the small trader – although by the later 1920s, these elements had been largely forgotten.

Since the Nazis refused to recognise the Weimar government, no candidates were put up for election before 1924, but the party steadily increased its membership and influence through the 1920s. In 1921, the SA (*Sturmabteilung* – originally a 'gymnastics and sports division', although it became a paramilitary force) was created and the *Völkischer Beobachter* (*People's Observer*) was established as a Nazi newspaper. Regional branches or *Gau* were established, and by the end of 1923 the party had 55,000 members, although this was still a tiny number compared with a national German electorate of 38 million.

The Nazis attracted ex-soldiers and members of the Freikorps, who supported the nationalist views of the party and seized on the opportunities it provided for jobs. It also attracted conservative lower middle-class workers, lower-ranking Bavarian civil servants and students fired with desire for political change.

It was not until November 1923 that Hitler's name came to be known nationally when he attempted to seize control of the Bavarian government, as a preliminary to marching on Berlin. In 1922, Benito Mussolini had taken control in Italy through a 'March on Rome'. Hitler was eager to carry out a similar coup.

On 8 November 1923, Nazis interrupted a political meeting in a Munich beer cellar. Under duress, three right-wing Bavarian leaders, Gustav von Kahr, Otto von Lossow and Hans Ritter von Seisser, were persuaded to agree to Hitler's plan to march on Berlin and establish a new government. Immediately afterwards, however, Kahr contacted the police and army. On 9 November, Hitler and General Erich Ludendorff led a column of around 2,000 armed Nazis through Munich. Shots were fired and Ludendorff was arrested. Hitler dislocated his shoulder when his companion was shot and both fell. Hitler escaped but was found and arrested on 11 November.

The Munich Putsch, or Beer Hall Putsch, failed, but it proved a propagandist success. At his trial for treason, Hitler claimed that his actions had been taken out of patriotic concern for his country. He was convicted of high treason, but he was only condemned to the minimum sentence of five years, thanks to a sympathetic right-wing judiciary.

Hitler actually served just nine months, at Landsberg Fortress, which according to the historian Ian Kershaw was 'more akin to a hotel'. He spent that period writing a semi-autobiographical book *Mein Kampf* (*My Struggle*).

Fact: Nationalised industries are run directly by the state.

Theory of knowledge

History and ideology: How important is ideology for a political leader?

**KEY CONCEPTS
QUESTION**

Significance: What
is the significance of
the failed Beer Hall
Putsch?

Mein Kampf

The main messages of Hitler's *Mein Kampf* were:

- Germany had to fight international Marxism (communism – see Chapter 1) in order to regain its world power status.
- Communism was the invention of Jews intent on Jewish world domination.
- National Socialism was the only doctrine capable of fighting communism. Liberal 'bourgeois' or 'middle-class' democracy was the first stage to socialism and communism.
- Nazism had to prepare the population for war in order to obtain *Lebensraum* (living space) in the east. To achieve this there had to be racial unity, the elimination of Jews, authoritarian control and no tolerance of diversity or dissent.

Figure 3.4   A first-edition copy of Hitler's *Mein Kampf* (*My Struggle*), featuring the Führer on the frontispiece

Figure 3.5   Members of the SA during a training march outside Munich in 1923

Führerprinzip

After 1924, the Nazi Party changed tactics, tightening party discipline and contesting Reichstag elections. Hitler exerted his leadership (known as the *Führerprinzip)*, demanding obedience because 'he knew best'. The SS (*Schützstaffel*) was set up in 1925–26 as Hitler's personal bodyguard and the SA was refounded in 1926, with its distinctive brown uniforms.

New party organisations were also created, for women, students, young people and teachers. These helped the party to direct its appeal to a wide spectrum of society and to make more people and institutions aware of Nazism. Although the relative prosperity of 1925–29 did not help, Nazis pursued some energetic recruitment, concentrating on the middle class and the farmers of northern Germany who did not benefit from Weimar's '**golden years**'. This yielded some success, although the results of the elections of May 1928 were disappointing – the Nazis won only twelve seats (2.6 per cent of the vote).

Fact: Members of the SA were often called 'brownshirts' because of the colour of their uniforms. It was by chance that the SA adopted a brown uniform. A shipment of brown uniforms, intended for German troops in Africa, fell into Nazi hands and the historic decision was made to clothe the SA that way.

golden years: This refers to the period between 1925 and 1929 when the Weimar economy flourished with the help of US loans.

SOURCE B

No realist could have reckoned much to [the Nazis'] chances of winning power. For that, Hitler's only hope was a massive and comprehensive crisis of the state. He had no notion just how quickly events would turn to the party's advantage. But on 24 October 1929, Wall Street crashed. The crisis Hitler needed was about to envelop Germany.

Kershaw, I. 1998. *Hitler 1889–1936: Hubris*. London, UK. Allen Lane/Penguin Books. p. 311.

However, Hitler gained more publicity by joining the DNVP (*Deutschnationale Volkspartei*, the right-wing German National People's Party) in campaigns against the 1929 Young Plan, which had been negotiated to ease the reparations burden. By December 1929, membership had risen to 178,000. Nonetheless, it would have been hard to predict at the end of 1929 that Hitler would become the German chancellor just over three years later.

3.4 How far did the conditions of 1929–33 contribute to the establishment of the Nazi state?

The 1929–30 withdrawal of US loans and the collapse in the export market had catastrophic repercussions for Germany. The 'Grand Coalition', formed under Chancellor Müller in 1928, seemed powerless as unemployment soared from 2 million in 1929, to 4.5 million in 1931 and nearly 6 million in 1932.

Around one-third of all Germans found themselves with no regular wages. This was fuel for extremist parties, such as the Nazis (and also the communists), who mocked the government's inaction and made wild promises that they held the key to future prosperity.

The Nazis played on their claim to be a 'national party' that would keep out communism, uphold law and order, return to traditional middle-class values and restore national strength. However, they had no specific formula to end the slump and their promises of full employment, subsidies to help German peasants and aid to small-scale traders remained vague.

With the break-up of the Grand Coalition in March 1930, there followed five Reichstag elections in three years. Chancellors Heinrich Brüning (March 1930–May 1932), Franz von Papen (June 1932–November 1932) and Kurt von Schleicher (December 1932–January 1933) struggled to rule without parliamentary majorities and were propped up by the use of the president's decree powers.

Meanwhile, the Nazis kept up the pressure with, according to the historian Alan Bullock, 'a display of energy, demand for discipline, sacrifice, action and not talk'. In the Reichstag elections of September 1930, the Nazis obtained 107 seats – a huge increase on its previous 12. Hitler also used the presidential elections of 1932 to his advantage when he challenged von Hindenburg and forced a second vote.

In the Reichstag elections of July 1932, the Nazis won 230 seats and became the largest German party in the Reichstag. However, with just 37.3 per cent of the vote, they had less than an outright majority and they were financially exhausted after two elections in quick succession. Hitler refused Hindenburg's offer of the vice-chancellorship, wanting only the 'top job', but he found it increasingly difficult to restrain the impatient SA, who believed that they should grasp power by revolution.

Fact: Central to Nazism was the belief that the leader's 'will' was the source of all political authority. This *Führerprinzip* was cultivated even before Hitler became chancellor and could claim to be above the law. Hitler demanded unquestioning obedience. He was not prepared for others to challenge him – as the Strasser brothers tried to do in 1926 – nor was he prepared to bow to the will of the SA who pressed for a revolution in 1932–33, while he sought power by legal means.

Fact: Between 1928 and 1932 the political parties became increasingly divided. On the left, the Social Democratic Party (SPD) and communists (KPD) refused to work together. The formerly moderate Catholic Centre Party (*Zentrum*) became more right-wing. This left the moderate liberals without allies. The right-wing conservatives (DNVP) sought more authoritarian government and had some sympathy with the Nazis. Unable to agree on the necessary cuts needed after October 1929, the coalition broke up in March 1930.

SOURCE C

On 8 August 1932, Joseph Goebbels wrote in his diary:

The air is full of presage. The whole party is ready to take over power. The SA down everyday tools to prepare for this. If things go well everything is alright. If they do not it will be an awful setback.

Bullock, A. 1962 (rev. edn). *Hitler: A Study in Tyranny*. Harmondsworth, UK. Penguin Books. p. 218

Another Reichstag election, in November 1932, saw Nazi support decline to 196 seats. This suggested that the Nazis' electoral fortunes had peaked. Joseph Goebbels, director of propaganda from 1929, commented, 'This year has brought us eternal ill luck. The past was sad, and the future looks dark and gloomy; all chances and hopes have quite disappeared.' Furthermore, the KPD, which had won eighty-nine seats in July, increased its vote by 17 per cent to obtain 100 seats in November. However, it was to the Nazis' advantage that the communists refused to cooperate with the Social Democratic Party (SPD) (who had 121 seats) and that the KPD's electoral victories and huge presence in the streets had the effect of frightening the conservative élite and encouraging them to turn to Hitler.

Chancellor von Papen found himself faced by a hostile Reichstag and even considered using the army to force its dismissal as a prelude to adopting a new German constitution. However, this course of action was opposed by von Schleicher, minister of defence, who feared civil war. Hindenburg tried to prop up von Papen's government, but when this proved impossible he dismissed the chancellor and turned to von Schleicher to form a government. Von Schleicher became chancellor in December 1932.

Von Schleicher had rather optimistically hoped to be able to lure the more left-wing 'socialist' element of the Nazi Party, under Gregor Strasser, away from mainstream Nazism into a coalition with the SPD under his own control and, for a short time, a potential party split added to Hitler's anxieties. However, Hitler demanded and won 'total obedience' from his followers, and Strasser resigned. Von Papen, infuriated by von Schleicher's actions, was encouraged to look to Hitler as a potential ally in a Nazi–Nationalist coalition. The continuing difficulties faced by von Schleicher's government, whose refusal to increase tariffs on food imports had angered influential Prussian landowners, served to help Hitler's negotiations. By 28 January 1933, Hindenburg had no option but to dismiss von Schleicher and turn to von Papen once more. Both knew that a future government would have to include Hitler.

Both von Papen and Hindenburg were convinced, however, that the Nazis were in decline and that it was the right time to harness their energies. They believed the Nazi Party was still strong enough to counter the threat from the left, but that Hitler's position was too weak to threaten traditional élite rule. Consequently, they were prepared to offer Hitler the chancellorship, with just two Nazi cabinet posts for Wilhelm Frick and Hermann Goering, alongside nine nationalist ministers.

Hitler was summoned on 30 January 1933 to head a government with von Papen as his deputy. Hitler, Hindenburg and von Papen alike were content with their behind-the-scenes discussions and deals. Von Papen believed that he had made a good deal and would be able to push Hitler 'into a corner' within two months. Hindenburg, too, had little idea as to what the consequences of his action would be. Only Hitler had a clear idea of where he was going.

Hitler called for immediate elections and mounted another massive propaganda campaign. He was helped by the Reichstag Fire on 27 February 1933, which gave him an excuse to blame the communists and ask Hindenburg to issue an emergency decree, 'For the Protection of People and State' (28 February). With the power to search, arrest and censor 'until further notice', the Nazis were able to remove opponents before the elections took place.

On 5 March 1933, the Nazis gained 43.9 per cent of the total votes cast. While impressive, this left Hitler reliant on other parties to obtain the two-thirds majority needed to change the constitution. The conservative DNVP, which won 8 per cent, offered support, but a deal had to be struck with the Catholic Centre Party, which had won 11.2 per cent. This committed Nazism to protect the Church (see section 3.13). The emergency decree was also used to expel all communists from the Reichstag.

Fact: In the first round of the presidential elections, in March 1932, Hitler won 30.2 per cent of the total votes cast and forced a second ballot. He visited twenty-one different towns by plane in a week and increased his share of the vote in the second round in April to 36.7 per cent.

KEY CONCEPTS ACTIVITY

Change and Significance: Draw a horizontal timeline to illustrate the results of the Reichstag elections between September 1930 and November 1932. Beneath the line, add a few notes on each election to explain the significance of the result.

Fact: On 27 February 1933, the Reichstag building was burnt down. The Nazis claimed this was the work of a Dutch communist, Marinus van der Lubbe, acting on behalf of the KPD. However, there is no reliable evidence to prove this was the case. There has been speculation that Hitler or Goering and the SA provoked this incident as an excuse to act against their opponents. Almost fifty years later, the West German government pardoned van der Lubbe.

Table 3.2 The end of Weimar democracy

Chancellors	Developments
Figure 3.6 Heinrich Brüning **March 1930– May 1932**  	• No majority in the Reichstag; relied on president's emergency decrees • Nazis became the second-largest party with 18.3% of the vote in elections of September 1930 • Government seemed weak and unable to control street violence although SA was banned in April 1932 • Economic depression continued; proposed agrarian reforms angered the powerful Prussian landowners (Junkers) and Hindenburg; Brüning resigned
Figure 3.7 Franz von Papen **June 1932–November 1932**  	• Little Reichstag support and government formed from outside the Reichstag • Tried to gain Nazi support by lifting ban on SA (June 1932) – violence grew • Relied on presidential decrees and ended democratic government in Prussia • Nazis became largest party (37.3% of the vote) in July 1932; with communists, they held over half of the Reichstag seats • Nazis won 33.1% of the vote and communists 16.9% in November 1932; von Papen resigned
Figure 3.8 Kurt von Schleicher **December 1932–January 1933**  	• Persuaded Hindenburg to dismiss Brüning and von Papen, but reluctant to be chancellor • Tried to ally with Gregor Strasser and 'socialist' Nazis, but Strasser refused • Relied on presidential decrees • Von Papen schemed against von Schleicher to get Hitler made chancellor with von Papen as vice-chancellor; von Schleicher dismissed

As the SA and SS whipped up support in the localities, in a piece of cleverly timed propaganda President Hindenburg was persuaded to stand alongside Hitler, in full military dress, at a ceremony of national reconciliation in Potsdam on 21 March 1933. Consequently, on 23 March, the Enabling Act was passed with only ninety-four SPD members voting against it. This was to provide the basis for Hitler's dictatorship. It virtually destroyed the power of the Reichstag by allowing the chancellor to issue laws without consultation for a period of four years.

After the Enabling Act was passed it took Hitler just four months to set up a single-party, authoritarian state. He was able to combine his legal powers and the threat of force to remove or Nazify those groups or institutions that might limit his power in a process known as *Gleichschaltung*. The constitution of 1919 was never formally abandoned and the Reichstag survived, but in the first six months of 1933, what lingering democracy there had been was destroyed.

Gleichschaltung: This refers to a coordination process whereby all German institutions were to conform to Nazi ideals.

KEY CONCEPTS QUESTION

Significance: What was the significance of the Enabling Act?

3.5 Where did the support for National Socialism come from?

It used to be thought that most Nazi support came from the 'middle classes' (*Mittelstand*) who were frightened by communism, desperate after their losses in the 1923 hyperinflation crisis and disillusioned with the Weimar Republic. However, more recent thinking and the analysis of election results has shown that Nazi support came from a very wide spectrum of the community. Some were swayed by Nazi propaganda, some by self-interest and some by a genuine belief that National Socialism was the answer to the country's problems. (See section 3.8 for more information on the role of Nazi propaganda in the consolidation of power.)

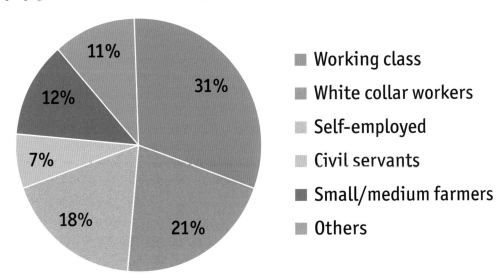

- Working class
- White collar workers
- Self-employed
- Civil servants
- Small/medium farmers
- Others

Figure 3.9 Support for National Socialism as a reflection of voting patterns

Another way of identifying support for National Socialism is to look at party membership, and this produces a similar picture.

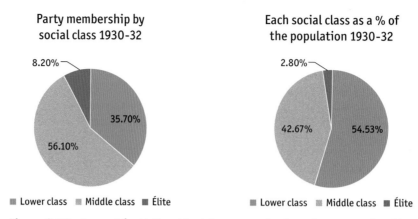

Figure 3.10 Support for National Socialism as a reflection of party membership

Whilst National Socialism failed to win over the mass of the working class – with its trade-unionist/socialist allegiances, whose support helped to increase the communist vote substantially in the same period as the Nazis' rise – it nevertheless attracted a substantial lower-class following. Working people were attracted by promises of work through interventionist economic policies and some saw the promise of a 'third way' between the state-controlled economy of the communists and rampant capitalism, as promising them a better life in the future.

Among the lower middle classes, self-employed shopkeepers, craftsmen and small traders saw National Socialism as protecting their traditional place within the economic structure, while the small/medium farmers welcomed the promise of controls on prices, the reduction of imports in the interests of self-sufficiency and financial controls to protect those in debt. The Nazis made much of their ideological commitment to the 'blood and soil' of the small farmer, promising 'any German who works and creates will be guaranteed not just a slave's ration of bread but an honourable life, decent earnings and the sanctity of his hard-earned property' in their Nazi Party election leaflets. (From a Nazi election leaflet in 1929 – given in Hite and Hinton, page 125.)

Historical debate:
The historians A. J. P. Taylor and William Shirer linked the rise of Nazism to the aggressive nature of the 'new' German state forged by war in 1871. Karl Bracher emphasised the circumstances of Europe in the 1920s and 1930s. Marxist historians associate the rise of Nazism with capitalists' attempts to resist communism. More recently, Alan Bullock and Ian Kershaw have emphasised the personality of Hitler.

Higher up the social hierarchy, the white collar office workers and professionals sought the protection from Marxism, big capitalists and the Jews of the banking world, which National Socialism promised. Similarly, civil servants, while supposedly 'neutral' and above party politics, tended to be right-wing in their attitude. They were fearful of communism and 'weak democracy' and anxious to return to the respectability they associated with the pre-Weimar era and which National Socialism promised to restore. It is sometimes said that it was the 'politics of anxiety' that attracted these middle ranks, in disproportionate numbers, to support National Socialism.

However, National Socialism also managed to appeal to the élites – to big businessmen and wealthier agrarian interests – who were deliberately targeted by the Nazis in the 1930–32 period in particular, in order to boost party funds. Some (although certainly not all) were attracted by the aggressive Nationalism of the party, its hostility to Marxism and commitment to self-sufficiency, whilst also being disillusioned by Germany's succession of unstable governments in the Depression. However, big business was divided in its attitude, and such financial support as they offered may have been more of an 'insurance premium' against a possible future Nazi government, rather than a true sign of support. Large landowners and the army also ranked among those élites that supported National Socialism and, in the political intrigue surrounding Hitler's final rise to power, these interests certainly played a role.

As well as looking at class and profession, it is also possible to identify other influences that affected support for National Socialism. Voting statistics have shown that, geographically, support was at its strongest in the north and east of the country, in the more rural and protestant areas. So, for example, the Nazis had a very high level of support in Schleswig-Holstein and Pomerania, but in the Catholic cities of the west, such as Cologne (Köln), they recorded their lowest levels of support. Rather interestingly, Nazism's birthplace, Catholic Bavaria, also had a fairly low Nazi vote. Quite apart from the ideological and economic appeal to the farming community, some of this may relate to the power of the Catholic Church, with its own ideology, strong organisational structure and powerful community influence – features that were much less in evidence in protestant areas.

Indeed, the voting patterns also reflect the influence of region on the electorate. There was, for example, a high Nazi vote in Silesia, even though it was a Catholic, urbanised and industrial area, but here a strong sense of nationalism and injured pride at the post-war loss of territory to Poland ensured that National Socialism had an overwhelming appeal.

Yet one further influence was age. Whilst National Socialism won support from the pre-war generation whose conservatism had been assaulted by Weimar experimentation, it also gained a strong following from those who were just coming of age when the Depression hit and jobs declined. Some 41–43 per cent of those who became party members before 1933 were aged 20–29, even though this group represented only 25.3 per cent of the national population.

QUESTION

Analyse the factors that led to Hitler's appointment as chancellor in January 1933.

Theory of knowledge

Historical determinism: Taylor has suggested that Hitler was a product of Germany's militaristic history and that the Germans never developed a democratic tradition because they preferred strong, authoritarian government – which Hitler continued. Is it possible to talk of 'national characteristics'? Can these account for, and perhaps excuse, a nation's actions?

End of unit activities

1 Make a diagram to illustrate why Germany became a single-party authoritarian state in 1933, using the following layout.

Long-term	Short-term	Catalyst	Specific event(s)

2 Marxist theory suggests that Hitler was the 'pawn' of self-interested capitalists – both businessmen and leading agrarian élites who 'used' him as a way of controlling the masses. Undertake some further research into the relationship between Nazism and big business, and in particular find out more about the significance of leading industrialists, Thyssen, Krupp, Siemens and Bosch.

3 Make a PowerPoint presentation for your class displaying a variety of election posters used by the Nazis to win support before 1933.

4 Make a spider diagram to illustrate why parliamentary government collapsed in Germany in the years 1930–33.

5 Divide into two groups. One group should seek to support the view that the establishment of the Nazi state was inevitable in the context of Germany in 1918–33. The other should seek to support the view that there was nothing inevitable about the Nazis' rise (considering, for example, that the Weimar Republic could have survived or that power might equally well have gone to the communists). Each group should present its findings for a class debate.

6 What was the personal contribution of Adolf Hitler to the rise of Nazism? Make a four-column table, with the headings, 'Personality', 'Leadership qualities', 'Ideology' and 'Political strategy'. Under each heading, try to record as many points and examples as you can to support the importance of this attribute.

Consolidating and Maintaining Power

Overview

- Without removing the old structures entirely, Hitler nevertheless ensured that the Nazi Party gained control over government at both central and local level.
- Hitler made sure that no sectional interests that might conflict with Nazism would be able to exist, by banning trade unions and other political parties, concluding a Concordat with the Catholic Church, purging the SA and, by 1938, bringing the army under control.
- Hitler's personality and the extensive use of propaganda helped to promote the dictatorship, although Hitler's fundamental laziness weakened the regime.
- National Socialist government combined state and party institutions and relied on the mighty SS to ensure the repression of dissident voices. However, the style of rule suggests that Hitler's position at the top of the party and state hierarchy was not as authoritarian as it might have appeared in theory. Some historians have described him as a 'weak' rather than a 'strong' dictator.
- Before 1939, there appeared to be little opposition to Nazi rule but, beneath the surface, political, ideological and religious hostility remained and an element of dissension continued in some groups of young people. Opposition grew appreciably in wartime.
- Foreign policy successes to 1940 added to Hitler's popularity and power, but failure thereafter weakened the regime and by 1945 few mourned Hitler's suicide.

KEY QUESTIONS

- How did Hitler consolidate his power to create an authoritarian regime?
- What part did personality and propaganda play in the consolidation of power?
- What were the main characteristics of National Socialist government?
- What was the nature and extent of opposition to Nazi rule and how was it dealt with?
- What was the impact of foreign policy on Hitler's consolidation and maintenance of power?

TIMELINE

1933 Mar: Enabling Act is passed; first concentration camp established

May: all trade unions are dissolved

Jul: Concordat is concluded with the Pope; Germany becomes a one-party state

Oct: Germany leaves League of Nations; rearmament begins

1934 Jun: Night of the Long Knives

Aug: Hindenburg dies; Hitler becomes Führer

1936 Himmler becomes Chief of German Police

Mar: remilitarisation of the Rhineland

Oct: makes Axis Alliance with Italy

Nov: Hitler makes anti-Comintern Pact with Japan

1938 Feb: army is reorganised; the Beck plot to overthrow Hitler

Mar: Anschluss with Austria

Sep: Munich Agreement

1939 Mar: invasion of the rest of Czechoslovakia

Aug: Nazi-Soviet Pact

Sep: invasion of Poland; Britain and France declare war

1940 Apr: invasion of Denmark and Norway

May: invasion of the Low Countries and France

1941 formation of the White Rose Group at Munich University

Apr: Nazi Germany occupies Yugoslavia and Greece

Jun: operation Barbarossa – invasion of USSR

Dec: Germany declares war on USA

1942 Nov: defeat at El Alamein

1943 Feb: defeat at Stalingrad

Mar: first allied bombing raid of German cities

1944 Jun: D-Day

July: failed bomb plot

1945 Apr: Hitler commits suicide

May: Germany surrenders

Figure 3.11   Hitler is welcomed by supporters at Nuremberg, 1933

Figure 3.12   Heinrich Himmler (1900–45)

Himmler became the head of the *Schützstaffel* (SS) in 1929 and head of all German political police outside Prussia in 1933. He helped to organise the Night of the Long Knives and in 1936 took over the Gestapo (the secret police). In December 1940, he established the Waffen SS. During the war, the SS Death's Head Units were put in charge of the concentration camps. In June 1944, Himmler took over the *Abwehr* (the military intelligence organisation) but his attempts to seek peace with the Allies led to his arrest. Himmler committed suicide at the end of the war.

3.6 How did Hitler consolidate his power to create an authoritarian regime?

Between March and July 1933, all other political parties were forced to disband. The KPD (German Communist Party) had been banned under the presidential decree of February, after the Reichstag Fire, shortly after Hitler became chancellor. Many less extreme socialists had also been imprisoned, although the SPD was not officially banned until 22 June. Similarly, the DNVP (the right-wing nationalist party) lost its role once it became part of the Nazi coalition, and disbanded itself. On 5 July the Catholic Centre Party followed as part of the Concordat with the Pope, which was signed later that month (see section 3.13, The Catholic Church). The culmination of this activity was the Law Against the Establishment of Parties of 14 July 1933. This made it a criminal offence to organise any party outside the NSDAP. Consequently, although there was an election in November 1933, only the Nazis were able to stand and so took all of the Reichstag seats.

The Nazi one-party authoritarian state was a centralised state. In the localities, the Nazis had begun to infiltrate state (**Länder**) governments from early in 1933, seizing public buildings and newspaper offices, and from March many state governments had been forced to resign since they had proved unable to control SA violence.

The Nazi government had already appointed many loyal commissioners to the states before a law passed in January 1934 formalised the situation. The old provincial assemblies of the *Länder* of Germany were abolished and all areas were placed under the control of Nazi governors (*Reichstatthalter*) and subordinated to the Reich government in Berlin. These Nazi governors often also had positions as local Nazi *Gauleiters* (the party representatives in the area).

By the Law for the Restoration of the Professional Civil Service of April 1933, non-Aryans were forced to retire and Jews and other opponents described as 'alien elements' were purged from positions in the administration, courts, schools and universities. However, it was not until 1939 that membership of the Nazi Party became compulsory, and in the interests of efficient government there was a remarkable continuity of personnel.

The left-wing socialist trade unions were dissolved in May 1933 and the German Labour Front (DAF) under Robert Ley was set up to replace them. Membership was compulsory and employees could no longer negotiate over wages and conditions with employers. New academies (or 'fronts') also controlled the professions, and teachers were, for example, required to join the National Socialist Teachers' League (NSLB), while in November 1933 university lecturers were required to sign a declaration in support of Hitler and join the Nazi Lecturers' Association.

Hitler's authoritarian state was legally established by the 'Law to Ensure the Unity of Party and State' (December 1933). However, the situation was not as simple as it sounds. Hitler allowed parallel institutions to develop rather than creating undiluted party rule, so there was competition within the state between different agencies, and sometimes between different branches of the Nazi Party itself. For example, in local government the minister-presidents of each *Land* were retained alongside the new Reich governors. Some intentionalist historians, such as Karl Bracher and Klaus Hildebrand, believe Hitler did this on purpose so that he could retain ultimate control. Structuralists such as Martin Broszat and Hans Mommsen believe that this situation was unintentional and resulted from Hitler's disinterest and neglect. Furthermore, although by the end of July 1933 most major interest groups had been brought under Nazi control and a one-party, authoritarian state had been created, Hitler was not secure until he had dealt with the radical wing of the SA, while the army had also largely survived Hitler's early measures unscathed.

Night of the Long Knives

Hitler had been content to use the paramilitary SA to destroy the communist movement when seeking power. However, he was concerned about the SA's violent and sometimes uncontrollable behaviour and about the demands of its leader, Ernst Röhm, who had ambitions to place himself at the head of a merged SA and army. Röhm openly condemned Hitler's compliance with the élite in 1933 and called for a second revolution to complete the 'Nazi uprising'.

Hitler could not afford to upset the army, whose loyalty he needed. Since the army was hostile to the SA, he increasingly took the view that the SA had served its purpose and was expendable. When **Heinrich Himmler** (head of the elitist and disciplined **SS (*Schützstaffel*)**) and **Hermann Goering** spread rumours of a planned coup by the SA, Hitler decided that it was time to take action.

According to official pronouncement, Röhm and eighty-five others were killed by SS men in the Night of the Long Knives on 30 June 1934 in order to forestall a revolt. In reality, the figure may have been nearer 200 and the reasons were far more complex.

SS (*Schützstaffel*): The SS – and its subsection the SD (*Sicherheitsdienst*), the security service – was a highly trained and élitist Aryan organisation with extensive powers as a military force and as political police.

Hermann Goering (1893–1946)

Goering joined the Nazi Party in 1923 and after 1933 became minister of the interior and prime minister of Prussia, taking control of the Gestapo. He helped to establish the concentration camps, arranged (with Himmler) the Night of the Long Knives and ran the 1936 Four-Year Plan. He was also behind the purge of Werner von Blomberg and Werner von Fritsch in 1938. In February 1938 he became head of Germany's armed forces and in 1939 Hitler's deputy and heir. He was in charge of the *Luftwaffe* (air force) during the war and was found guilty at the Nuremberg Trials of German war criminals in 1945–46. He committed suicide before he could be hanged.

Fact: Some members of the SA favoured a 'second revolution' that would bring more socialist change to Germany. They wanted to implement the 25-point programme, but Hitler could not afford to alienate big business and the élite on whom he depended.

93

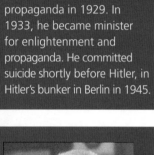

Figure 3.13   Paul Joseph Goebbels (1897–1945)

Goebbels joined the Nazi movement in 1924 and became director of Nazi propaganda in 1929. In 1933, he became minister for enlightenment and propaganda. He committed suicide shortly before Hitler, in Hitler's bunker in Berlin in 1945.

Figure 3.14   Paul von Hindenburg (1847–1934)

Paul von Hindenburg was commander-in-chief of Germany's forces on the Eastern Front from 1914. He retired from public life in 1918, but returned in 1925 to stand as president. He held this post until his death but grew increasingly senile and may not have appreciated the consequences of his decisions in 1930–33 to allow the use of article 48, which undermined parliamentary democracy and allowed Hitler to come to power.

Not all of the murders were of SA men. The Nazi Gregor Strasser (who had attempted to split the party in 1932) was shot, as was Kurt von Schleicher, the former chancellor. Von Papen was put under house arrest and was lucky to escape with his life.

The Night of the Long Knives helped to confirm Hitler's authority. He justified his actions to the Reichstag, two weeks after the event, by saying that he alone had acted on behalf of the German people at a time of emergency and he thus gained credit for a 'heroic' action. The Reichstag confirmed that Hitler's powers had no constitutional bounds and that his authority was derived from the will of the people and could not be challenged. In condoning his action, the Reichstag effectively made murder acceptable.

The purge also had other important consequences. **Goebbels** was able to portray Hitler as a man who had personally saved the country, and this helped in the growing cult of the Führer. The purge also left the way open for Himmler's SS to assume dominance in Germany, while Hitler gained the support of the army commanders. When **Hindenburg** died in August, all members of the armed forces swore a personal oath of loyalty to Hitler. Henceforward, Hitler combined the chancellorship and presidency.

Control over the army

Even after the Night of the Long Knives and the army's oath of loyalty in August 1934, Hitler knew that the army was the one institution that still retained the power to prevent his ambitions from being realised. Hitler was therefore careful not to cause trouble, and left the army structurally unchanged until 1938. However, every attempt was made to Nazify the institution through the adoption of the swastika insignia, Nazi training schemes and indoctrination. Hitler referred to the army as the 'second pillar

Figure 3.15   Adolf Hitler giving a Nazi salute to a crowd of soldiers at a Nazi rally, 1 May 1938

of the state', working alongside the Nazi Party and, since most officers shared Hitler's nationalist aspirations, the relationship was reasonably successful. The army favoured the Nazis' enforcement of law and order, and Hitler's repudiation of the disarmament clauses of the Treaty of Versailles in March 1935, restoration of conscription and promise to expand the peacetime army to more than 500,000 men also met with favour.

However, there was some friction, which grew in proportion to Hitler's military ambitions. Some generals condemned the pace of rearmament, and the commander-in-chief, Werner von Fritsch, complained that Hitler was 'rushing everything far too much and destroying every healthy development'. There was also concern about the role of the SS, which Hitler had always claimed to be a domestic police force, but which expanded markedly after the destruction of the SA. The *SS-Verfügungstruppe* (eventually known as the Waffen SS) was established to be 'part of the wartime army' in August 1938. This caused considerable unease among the professional army leadership. The *SS-Totenkopf* (Death's Head) units were also expanded as a reserve military force and, according to the historian Bernd Wegner, 'It was no longer a question of whether the SS units would be allowed to share in military conquests in the years to come; the disputes now concerned only their assignment, size and organisation.'

Another argument concerned Hitler's expansionist policies themselves. The army favoured the reversal of the Treaty of Versailles and limited conquest to restore the old empire. However, it was strongly against the idea of war with Russia, the traditional ally of the Prussian Junkers (the landed nobility of Prussia, who dominated the officer class of the German army), and did not support Hitler's policies of *Lebensraum*. Top army generals were critical when, at the Hossbach Conference of 5 November 1937, Hitler laid down aggressive plans for rapid expansion in the east. The plans were summarised in the 'Hossbach memorandum'. Only Goering spoke in Hitler's favour; von Fritsch and Hitler's war minister, General Werner von Blomberg, opposed the plans.

Consequently, in 1938 Hitler contrived to dismiss the war minister General von Blomberg, alleging that the woman he had just married in January had been a prostitute. Commander-in-Chief von Fritsch was also dismissed, on the grounds of allegedly being gay (which was later disproved, although he was never reinstated).

With the departure of von Blomberg and von Fritsch, Hitler became his own war minister, so combining his position as supreme commander (the president's role) with an additional political role. To reinforce his intentions, he changed the name of the War Ministry into the 'High Command of the Armed Forces' (the OKW) and Wilhelm Keitel was appointed as its chief. In practice, Keitel was little more than an office manager and worked under Hitler's direct control.

These changes were accompanied by a drastic reshuffle of those who had failed to support Hitler's ideas. Sixteen generals left the army and forty-four were transferred. Although many aristocratic officers still remained suspicious of Hitler, this effectively brought Hitler's consolidation of power to a close.

Hitler's popular triumphs, beginning with the remilitarisation of the Rhineland in 1936 and embracing Anschluss with Austria and entry into Czechoslovakia in 1938, made him virtually unassailable and the new generation of commanders such as Heinz Guderian and Erwin Rommel became his faithful followers.

3.7 What part did personality and propaganda play in the consolidation of power?

Personality

Hitler's own personality certainly helped in the creation of the National Socialist state. Quite apart from his own skills as an orator, his supreme confidence and faith in himself and the destiny of the German nation imparted a new optimism, which transformed a depressed and broken nation into what, at least to outside observers in the 1930s, appeared to be a happy and thriving state. Hitler's passionate commitment to the German nation and its people seemed to fulfil an emotional need for a strong figurehead to take the country forward. Policy success and propaganda combined to produce a carefully cultivated image of a man who had a unique mission. The 'will of the Führer' represented all that was best for the German nation. He, himself, was beyond petty and selfish interests and above criticism; this was reserved for lesser officials. This 'Führer Myth', as Ian Kershaw has called it in a book of the same name, contributed to Hitler's amazing popularity and brought Germans together in its emotional appeal.

QUESTION

By what means did Hitler consolidate his power in Germany?

This 'cult of Hitler' was almost like an alternative religious cult. Nazi propaganda portrayed Hitler as all-powerful and all-knowing. The media carried details of what he wore, said and did, and posters and books of photographs were sold. He was depicted as a father figure, a friend of children and a leader who really cared about his people. He was also portrayed as a strong man and a powerful statesman. Anything that showed a human 'failing', such as wearing glasses, was carefully erased.

However, although Hitler had plenty of fanaticism and charisma, routine governmental business failed to interest him. He was not an early riser and preferred to spend his days reading the newspaper, going for walks, watching feature films and talking with his cronies. It was well known that Hitler preferred to talk rather than to listen and that, when he did listen, he only heard what he wanted to hear – so much so that subordinates often withheld information they feared might displease him. From 1934, Hitler actually played very little part in the meetings of the Reich cabinet. From 1937, it ceased to meet altogether.

Hitler spent a considerable amount of time at his mountain retreat, the Berghof in the Bavarian Alps. Although government papers were conveyed to him for his signature, wherever he might be, there was no guarantee he would read them. Very often it was the case that individuals had to fight for access to the Führer to get approval for actions.

Hitler avoided making decisions as far as possible and, when he did so, often made them on the spur of the moment, perhaps over lunch or tea without full reference to all of the facts. He had to be caught at the right time and patient Nazi officials had to be prepared to wait for a chance or casual remark which they could then claim to be the 'authority' of the Führer (see section 3.18, Was Nazi Germany a totalitarian state and was Hitler 'Master of the Third Reich'?).

The use of propaganda

One of Hitler's first tasks as chancellor, in March 1933, was to set up a new Ministry for Popular Enlightenment and Propaganda under the control of Goebbels. Hitler believed that the masses, for whom he had little respect, could easily be won over through regular exposure to propaganda in schools, towns and the workplace, and in their leisure pursuits. Consequently, the ministry established separate chambers to oversee the work of the press, radio, theatre, music, the creative arts and film.

The ministry controlled the press through censorship and by allowing the Nazi publishing house, Eher Verlag, to buy up private newspapers until by 1939 it controlled two-thirds of the press. A German news agency regulated the supply of news and Goebbels held a daily press conference with editors to ensure the right messages arrived in print. Editors were held responsible for their papers and were liable for prosecution if they published unapproved material.

The Nazis made extensive use of the radio as a medium for reinforcing Nazi rule, with the Reich Broadcasting Corporation, set up in 1933, controlling all that was broadcast. Workplaces, shops, cafés and blocks of flats were expected to relay important speeches through loudspeakers for all to hear, while in the home, the *Volksempfänger* (people's receiver) became a standard item. These radio sets had a limited range, preventing individuals from listening to foreign broadcasts, and they were deliberately sold cheaply. Consequently, ownership of sets increased from under 25 per cent of households in 1932 to over 70 per cent by 1939 and the population could be subject to daily exposure to Nazi views.

Stamps carried Nazi slogans, and posters bearing Nazi quotations were put up in offices and public buildings. Furthermore, the 'Heil Hitler' salute became the official form of greeting and helped to reinforce enthusiasm for the leader.

Figure 3.16   A Nazi poster from c. 1935 depicting Adolf Hitler bearing the German flag at the head of a vast army, with the caption *'Es Lebe Deutschland!'* ('Long Live Germany!')

ACTIVITY

Find out about some Nazi films and the messages they tried to convey. You could start with films such as *Hitlerjunge Quex* (1933) about the Hitler Youth, *Triumph des Willens (Triumph of Will)* (1934) about the Nuremberg Rally, *Der Ewige Jude (The Eternal Jew)* (1940), *Jud Süss* (1940) reinforcing anti-Semitism, and *Ich Klage An* (1941) (*I Accuse*) about euthanasia.

The cinema was another propaganda tool, although the Nazis used film less effectively than the radio. Nevertheless, all films were censored and 'degenerate' artists were forbidden. Light-hearted entertainment – even romances, thrillers and musicals – had to conform to Nazi ideological principles.

It was hard to avoid the propagandist messages in Nazi Germany. Even culture became a form of propaganda, with concert halls bedecked in swastikas. There were constant meetings, rallies, festivals, such as that established to celebrate Hitler's birthday and the anniversary of his appointment as chancellor, and sporting events that provided opportunities to extol Nazism.

Of course, it is not easy to evaluate the success of propaganda since the German people were also subject to a number of other influences, most notably repression. However, the very ubiquity of propaganda must have played some role in strengthening the regime. According to the historian David Welch, propaganda was more successful at reinforcing than at countering existing attitudes. Insofar as it was able to do that, however, it must take some credit for the ease with which Hitler was able to consolidate his rule.

3.8 What were the main characteristics of National Socialist government?

From the establishment of the one-party state in July 1933, the Nazi Party exercised political authority over every aspect of German life. The 'Law to ensure the Unity of Party and State' of December 1933, decreed that the party was 'inseparably linked with the state' and party membership became essential for those wishing to advance themselves. For example, by 1939 all civil servants had to be party members.

Historical debate:
Tim Mason, a Marxist historian, has suggested that absenteeism, strikes and sabotage amongst workers were common, and Richard Overy has indicated that certain working-class areas were 'no-go' zones for Nazi officials. Kershaw has produced evidence of public grumbling, while Detler Peukert has identified extensive resistance among the young people of Cologne and Hamburg. Gellately, however, has produced evidence to reinforce the traditional picture that most ordinary Germans were ready to accept or support the Nazi regime.

However, the party-state cooperation was not as clear-cut in practice as it might have seemed in theory and Hitler's dislike of formal committees and paperwork meant that the governmental structure could be quite chaotic, with competing agencies and individuals. However, amidst this confusion, the SS maintained a constant vigilance and control that ensured there was an appearance, at least, of strong government.

During the consolidation of power in 1933–34, Himmler, who had been the leader of the SS since 1929 and had also set up the special Sicherheitsdienst (SD) security service in 1931, assumed control of all political police, including the Prussian gestapo. It was the SS that purged the SA in the Night of the Long Knives, and in 1936 all police powers were unified under Himmler as chief of police. As *Reichsführer* SS, Himmler commanded a huge SS-police-SD power block – sometimes described as a 'state within a state' – which controlled security, ran the concentration camps and eventually extended its influence into military and economic affairs.

In 1939, the Reich Main Security Department was set up to oversee all of this security apparatus. The individual was made well aware of the consequences of non-conformity, be it political, racial or moral. The state employed a stream of informants, including the dreaded 'block wardens', who paid regular visits to individuals' homes, creating an image of power that must have helped to reinforce obedience.

When those arrested were given a trial, the law courts were no longer impartial. Under the 1933 Civil Service Law, judges whose political beliefs conflicted with Nazism lost their positions. Lawyers had to be members of the Nazi Lawyers Association and were required to study Nazi ideology, so although the law itself did not always change, it was interpreted differently by Nazi lawyers. This was summed up by Ernst Hüber, who was at the time a prominent constitutional law professor at the University of Kiel. He defined the Nazi concept of law, stating that the individual can be judged by the law only from the point of view of the individual's value for the *völkisch* (people's) community. The law was reinterpreted according to the will of the Führer and the 'best interests' of the German community.

Theory of knowledge

History and emotion: If you had lived in Nazi Germany, would you have become involved in opposition?

3.9 What was the nature and extent of opposition to Nazi rule and how was it dealt with?

There would seem to have been very little opposition to Nazi rule in Germany after 1933–34. This has been explained by the propaganda, repression and general success of Hitler's policies both at home and, until 1943, abroad. However, there were acts of defiance, of both a private and public nature.

In private, individuals might read banned literature, listen to foreign news broadcasts, protect Jews and other Nazi victims or even refuse to join Nazi organisations or contribute to campaigns. Some, particularly among the young, listened to American jazz music or joined the Swing Movement or Edelweiss Pirates (see section 3.14), while others simply grumbled or told anti-Nazi jokes. Such 'opposition' is difficult to measure and, of course, not all such behaviour was politically inspired.

There was also more overt public opposition. Some brave socialists, for example, continued to distribute anti-Nazi leaflets or write slogans in public places. Others protested by emigrating and joining the SPD in exile, which operated from Prague and organised underground groups such as the Berlin Red Patrol and the Hanover Socialist Front. In November 1939, a socialist cabinet-maker, Georg Elser, planted a bomb in a beer hall where Hitler was speaking, although it failed to kill him as the Führer left the hall early. The KPD also formed underground cells, particularly in Berlin, Mannheim, Hamburg and central Germany, from where they issued leaflets attacking the regime. The *Rote Kapelle* (Red Orchestra) was a resistance network that gathered information to send to the Russians, but it was broken up in 1942.

Opposition to Hitler might also be seen in the action of judges who refused to administer 'Nazi' justice, and of churchmen, such as Bishop Galen (see section 3.13, The Catholic Church) and Pastor **Dietrich Bonhoeffer**, who spoke out against Nazi policies. One centre of opposition was the Kreisau Circle, which met at the home of Helmut von Moltke. Here, aristocrats, lawyers, SPD politicians such as Julius Leber, and churchmen such as Bonhoeffer engaged in discussion as to how to remove Hitler. The group held three meetings in 1942–43 before being broken up by the **Gestapo**.

Opposition also festered within the army. Between June 1940 and July 1944 there were six attempts on Hitler's life, all led by army officers. Following the last of these, the July Bomb plot of 1944, over 5,000 army officers were executed, including Ludwig Beck, Hans Oster and Colonel Claus von Stauffenberg. Even the Nazi's own intelligence agency, the *Abwehr*, was rife with resistance workers. The head of the agency, Admiral Wilhelm Canaris, supported resistance activities and did what he could to protect Jews.

The universities, most notably Munich University, were another centre of organised resistance in wartime. At Munich University, Hans Scholl formed the White Rose group in 1941. Members distributed pamphlets and revealed the truth about the Nazi treatment of Jews and Slavs. In 1943, they became even more daring and painted anti-Nazi slogans on public buildings. However, the members were caught, and Hans Scholl, his sister Sophie and other members of the movement were executed. Such activities and the alternative youth culture that flourished in a number of parts of Germany showed that not all young people were readily indoctrinated by the regime.

It is difficult to give any reliable estimate of the extent of opposition, but it certainly increased in wartime. Throughout the Nazi period, all opposition was firmly dealt with by the security police. From the earliest years, concentration camps were used as places for the 're-education' of dissidents, and although not extermination camps, they could be brutal places in which prisoners were forced to work for long hours on meagre rations. Between 1933 and 1939, around 225,000 Germans were convicted of political crimes and a further 162,000 were placed in 'protective custody' in prison without trial. Whether these were true opponents or merely victims of SS zeal it is difficult to say, but as a percentage of the population the figures are quite low.

In wartime, opposition was seen as treachery and usually involved execution or prolonged incarceration in camps that became increasingly inhuman. During these years, the army and the Churches provided the best opportunities for opposition, and Beck's plans of 1938 and the 1944 July Bomb plot were probably the most serious moments for the regime. For suspected involvement in the July bomb plot, for example, there were c. 5,000 executions, including nineteen generals and twenty-six colonels. However, apart from the assassination attempts, the Nazi regime remained secure to the end and was only ultimately toppled by the coalition of enemy powers.

Figure 3.17   Dietrich Bonhoeffer (1906–45)

Bonhoeffer was an academic theologian who strongly opposed Nazism. In 1940, he was banned from preaching and publishing. He joined the underground resistance, working with other opponents such as Ludwig Beck. He was sent to Buchenwald concentration camp in 1943 and was executed in 1945.

QUESTION

How might a historian measure the extent of opposition to Nazism?

ACTIVITY

Find out more about the resistance activities of Ludwig Beck, the Kreisau Circle and the July Bomb plotters. What impelled the participants to resist Hitler?

3.10 What was the impact of foreign policy on Hitler's consolidation and maintenance of power?

Gestapo (Geheime Staatspolizei): The Gestapo was the state secret police force, established by Goering in April 1933. It served to root out and intimidate potential opposition. However, the number of Gestapo officers was limited and many were engaged in routine bureaucratic work, so the regime had to rely on spies and informers. This has led to the conclusion that the survival of the Nazi regime rested on the compliance of the public, who were prepared to betray their colleagues and neighbours, rather than on an atmosphere of terror. For example, Robert Gellately put forward the theory that surveillance was dependent on the reports provided by ordinary German people rather than a ubiquitous force of the Gestapo.

SOURCE A

'If Germany is to become a world power, and not merely a continental state (and it must become a world power if it is to survive), then it must achieve complete sovereignty and independence. Do you understand what that means? Is it not clear to you how tragically mutilated we are by the restriction and hemming-in of our vital space, a restriction which condemns us to the status of a second-rate power in Europe? Only nations living independently in their own space and capable of military defence can be world powers. Only such nations are sovereign in the true sense of the word.'

Hitler's response to a question, in 1934 from Dr Hermann Rauschning, a member of Hitler's inner circle. From Rauschning, H. 1940. *The Voice of Destruction*. New York, USA. Putnam's Sons. pp. 121–22.

Foreign policy success 1933–39

Hitler made no secret of his desire to 'right the wrongs' of the Versailles Treaty and achieve '*lebensraum*' (living space) for the German people. Indeed, this had been one of the platforms on which he had achieved electoral success in 1930–32. His own personal interest lay in foreign affairs, so it is hardly surprising that one of his first actions, in October 1933, was to take Germany out of the League of Nations and begin rearmament. He even attempted a takeover of Austria in 1934, although he was hastily forced to withdraw when the Italians intervened against him, but he was able to take advantage of the Saarlanders' decision to vote in a plebiscite (as prearranged at the Treaty of Versailles) to join Germany, rather than France, to whom the region had been assigned for fifteen years from 1919 to allow the French to take its coal as reparations. The formal announcement of conscription at a huge public rally in March 1935 and a naval treaty with Britain in June won Hitler great acclaim at home. He was seen as a leader who was not scared to defy the 'unjust' peace treaty of 1919 and who could negotiate with Germany's erstwhile enemy, Britain, on an equal footing.

Mussolini's invasion of Abyssinia in 1935 provided the opportunity for Hitler to go further whilst the powers of Europe were distracted elsewhere. In March 1936, he defiantly marched his troops into the officially demilitarised Rhineland and scenes of joyous Rhinelanders – no doubt staged for domestic and international consumption – increased the belief that here was a man who was prepared to take on the world and win. The French, too timid to act without Britain's backing, and a Britain that was combating the effects of the Depression and dubious about the morality of the Versailles Treaty anyway, allowed Hitler to express his open defiance and with this confirm his authority at home.

Figure 3.18   Map showing areas of Nazi expansion

Hitler's next steps followed with such rapidity that it has left historians debating how far he had always planned a war of conquest and how far he was opportunistic in his actions. With Mussolini as an ally in the Axis alliance of October 1936, a partnership confirmed by their fighting together in the Spanish Civil War, Hitler was finally able to effect his Anschluss with Austria in March 1938. There swiftly followed a series of meetings with the British leading to the Munich agreement of September 1938, which allowed Hitler to take over the Czechoslovakian Sudetenland. An invasion of the whole of Czechoslovakia followed in March 1939 and, having surprised the world by signing a Nazi–Soviet Pact in August, Hitler ordered the German invasion of Poland in September 1939. With this, the Second World War began and patriotic Germans applauded the opportunity to show their 'master race' in battle.

At each step of the way between 1933 and 1939, the press hailed Hitler's victories. He moved from being the junior to the senior partner in his relationship with Mussolini. He duped Chamberlain at Munich. He absorbed 'true Germans' in Austria, the Sudetenland and Poland back into the German Reich and showed what he thought of a peace treaty that had offered self-determination to all European peoples except Germany. There were many good reasons why appeals to national values and German pride worked. After the lacklustre years of the Weimar Republic, the people of Germany finally had something to feel good about.

Foreign Policy Failure 1939–45

Hitler's triumphs were to continue through to 1942 and, in the closely guarded and heavily censored world of wartime Germany, belief in victory and success maintained its magic for longer. There was limited opposition to Hitler before 1944 and it was not until the first allied bombs began to rain down on Germany in March 1943 that most people started to learn the truth about what their Führer had brought them to. The seizure of Denmark and Norway (April 1940), the Netherlands, Belgium, Luxembourg and France (May 1940), Yugoslavia and Greece (April 1941) created a myth of invincibility that even Hitler probably came to believe in. However, by 1942, the German armies were overstretched. The decision to invade the USSR (Operation Barbarossa) in June 1941, to declare war on the USA (December 1941) – honouring the terms of the anti-Comintern Pact that had been signed with the Japanese in November 1936 – and to bail out the Italians in Northern Africa placed an intolerable strain on German resources which, despite Albert Speer's best efforts (see section 3.12, Speer's management of the wartime German economy) proved unsupportable.

The German people were largely shielded from news of defeats, as in the second battle of el Alamein in November 1942 and Stalingrad in February 1943, but they could not escape the impact of allied bombing, the food shortages and the loss of their menfolk as women and the young desperately tried to keep the German economy going. By the time of D-Day in June 1944, many illusions were already shattered. Some Germans welcomed the British/American advance (and all the more so because they feared the advance of the Soviet Red Army which swept against Nazi Germany from the east).

Nevertheless, the surprise is not that the German people finally lost faith in Hitler, but that they supported him for as long as they did. Hitler's sensational coups – initially effected without recourse to war – were fundamental to his hold on the German people. By employing the methods that had brought him success in his rise to power (high-risk gambles and unpredictable moves that caught his opponents off-guard) Hitler's foreign adventures paid off at least until the chain of success was broken. It took time before the Germans saw the truth behind Hitler's charisma, but whilst his foreign policy provided him with the highest peaks of adulation it also brought about his downfall.

Fact: General Ludwig Beck opposed Hitler's expansionist plans in 1938 and, following his dismissal, attempted to overthrow Hitler in a series of plots involving other army officers. These included two attempts to kill Hitler with a bomb in 1943. There were a number of army officers involved in other resistance activities, notably in the Kreisau Circle. Claus von Stauffenberg's bomb plot of July 1944 came very close to killing Hitler.

Theory of knowledge

History and bias:
How do historians know how the German people felt about Hitler's foreign policy? Why is it difficult for historians to write about people living in an authoritarian regime? Is it ever possible to discern the 'truth' about people's feelings?

End of unit activities

1 Draw a flow chart to show the stages by which Hitler consolidated his rule.
2 Write an obituary for Röhm (who died in the Night of the Long Knives). Comment on his significance. You could decide whether your obituary is for a pro-Nazi German newspaper or a more neutral British one.

Causation: Draw a diagram to show the reasons for opposition to Hitler's authority. Which groups in German society were most likely to oppose Hitler? Explain your answer.

Change and Continuity: Make a two-column diagram to record the ways in which Hitler's coming to power brought change in government, and the ways in which there was continuity.

Theory of knowledge

History and ethics:
What is a dictatorship? Is dictatorship always wrong? Is it possible to create a benign dictatorship?

3 Imagine you are interviewing Hitler for a TV news programme at the end of 1938. Produce ten questions and (after swapping scripts with another member of your group) fill in the replies that Hitler might have given.

4 Find one piece of visual propaganda and one piece of contemporary written evidence illustrating the 'cult of Hitler'. Explain your findings to your group.

5 Make a chart on which you can record the arguments that Hitler was a strong dictator and those that suggest he was a weak dictator. Try to add historians' names to the arguments and where possible find quotations from their books to support what you write.

6 Create a graph to illustrate Hitler's foreign policy successes and failures 1933–45. Identify three significant turning points and below your graph indicate how/why each turning point increased or decreased support for Hitler and the Nazi State.

Overview

- Nazi domestic and social policy was influenced by a belief in the national community – 'Volksgemeineschaft'.
- Nazi economic policy was incoherent and, despite having an ideological basis, was moulded by circumstances.
- The Nazis attempted to control the Churches through the Catholic Concordat and a separate Reich Protestant Church. However, neither was ever fully brought into line and attempts to spread an alternative pagan faith met with limited success.
- Young people were the focus of intense indoctrination through the education system and Hitler Youth.
- The experimental, modernist Weimar culture was rejected in favour of a controlled and conservative approach to the arts, which demanded that the arts should glorify Nazi values.
- Nazi policy towards women was conservative, aiming to keep women 'in the home', but it was inconsistent since women were encouraged back into the workplace in the war years.
- Minorities were persecuted for their social, religious and racial non-conformity, with policies becoming ever more radical as the regime grew more secure. Attempts to create a 'Jew-free' society ultimately led to the Holocaust and the deaths of 6 million Jews.

KEY QUESTIONS

- What factors influenced domestic and social policy?
- How successful was Nazi economic policy?
- What was the relationship between the Nazis and the Churches within Germany?
- How did the Nazis see the role of education and try to ensure the support of youth?
- How did Nazism affect the arts and the media?
- How were social, religious and racial minorities treated within the Nazi State?
- What was the position of women in the Nazi State?
- To what extent did the Nazi authoritarian regime achieve its aims?

TIMELINE

1917 Nov: Bolshevik Revolution in Russia

1933 Apr: one-day boycott of Jewish shops and businesses; Civil Service Law

May: public burning of 'un-German' books; Law for the Protection of Retail Trade

Jul: Concordat with Catholic Church

Sep: the German Chamber of Culture, Reich Food Estate and Reich Economic Chamber are created; Reich Entailed Farm Law

1934 Aug: Schacht becomes minister of economics

Sep: New Plan comes into effect

1935 Sep: Nuremberg Laws – Jews are deprived of rights

1936 Apr: *Lebensborn* (Spring of Life) programme is launched

Oct: Four-Year Plan is drawn up with Goering in charge

Dec: membership of Hitler Youth becomes compulsory

1937 Mar: Pope issues Mit Brennender Sorge (*With Burning Anxiety*) criticising racism

Nov: Schacht resigns as minister of economics and is replaced by Goering

1938 Nov: *Reichskristallnacht* (Night of the Broken Glass) – anti-Jewish pogrom

1939 Aug: euthanasia programme is launched

1941 Aug: Bishop Galen protests against euthanasia

Dec: gassing of Jews in mobile vans in Chelmo begins

1942 Jan: Wannsee Conference to coordinate 'final solution' of Jewish question; Speer takes control of the economy

Figure 3.19 A Hitler Youth group, 1939

3.11 What factors influenced domestic and social policy?

From 1933, the National Socialists set out to create a state that would fulfil their ideological aims and transform society. They wanted to change the way in which people behaved and thought by imposing a new concept of 'Volksgemeineschaft'. This was an attempt to create a 'national community', in which every member of the society worked to support others and to contribute to the greater good of the nation or 'Volk'. This involved controlling how people lived, worked and spent their leisure time. It required a change in the consciousness of the German people so that they would act as one.

There was no intention to destroy old class divisions but to subordinate them to the new Nazi way of thinking, which in many respects was backward-looking. It perceived women fulfilling their traditional role as mothers and housewives, for example. It was, however, intolerant of alternative institutions, such as the Church, which the Nazis constantly tried to mould to their own way of thinking and only worked with under sufferance.

Volksgemeineschaft was based on blood and race. The 'Volk' was made up of racially pure Aryans, and one aim was to encourage every pure German to think of themselves as part of a master race, in which the state was superior to the individuals that comprised it. Nationalism and a common world view (Weltanschauung) was to bind the people together. The 'Volksgenossen' (members of this community) would be Aryan and politically and socially committed, and every member would strive towards the goals of the state. In this way, Germans would be prepared for expansion and world domination.

The ideal German was seen as the German peasant farmer, whose very life was dependent on the German soil and whose background was in a traditional German way of life. In contrast, the Nazis sought the eradication of social outsiders, and in particular racial outsiders. Aryan Germans were to be united around common nationalist and anti-Semitic goals and, for the most part, all other policy decisions were subordinate to this aim. However, since Hitler had come to power promising to restore Germany's economic fortunes, this was also a driving force behind domestic policy in the 1930s.

> **KEY CONCEPTS QUESTION**
>
> **Significance:** Draw a diagram to show the many significant ideas which shaped Nazi policies.

3.12 How successful was Nazi economic policy?

Hitler had no clear economic programme when he became chancellor in 1933. In the 25-point programme of 1920, the Nazis had claimed to want to respond to the needs of small farmers (29 per cent of the working population) and smaller urban traders. However, as with much of what Hitler said in his quest for power, he displayed little depth of commitment once he reached the top – despite his avowed ideological commitment to the traditional peasant working on the soil. Indeed, as the likelihood of power had grown nearer, he had increasingly looked to reassure big business, which could fund his campaigns and make his dreams a reality.

There was some token acknowledgement of the 'socialist' aspects of National Socialism in the policies of early 1933. All peasant debts – a total of 12 billion Reichsmarks – were suspended between March and October 1933 and high tariffs were put on many imported foodstuffs. The setting up of the **Reich Food Estate** under Richard Darré, the minister of food and agriculture, gave peasant farmers guaranteed prices for their produce. The Reich Entailed Farm Law (September 1933) provided small farmers with security of tenure by forbidding the sale, confiscation, division or mortgaging of any farm between 7.5 and 10 hectares (18.5 and 25 acres) that was owned by Aryan farmers. Similarly, there was a gesture towards helping urban traders in the Law for the Protection of Retail Trade (May 1933). Among other measures, the law forbade the setting up of new department stores.

> **Reich Food Estate:** This was an organisation that controlled food production and sales, setting targets, quotas and prices.

Although such measures fulfilled one aspect of the Nazis' professed concerns, they always took second place to the Nazis' predominant desire, which was to strengthen Germany to fight a future war. It was the 'national' aspect of the party's name that was the real driving force behind Nazi economic policy. This produced the concept of *Wehrwirtschaft* – a defence economy that would provide for Germany's needs in a future war.

cartel: A cartel is an agreement between companies to work together to reduce production costs and improve efficiency.

guns and butter: This phrase had been used by historians writing about the Nazis' preparations for war. The Nazis could not invest heavily in rearmament (guns) while maintaining standards of living (butter). There was also literally a shortage of fats in Germany – both for consumption (butter, margarine and lard) and for industrial purposes (grease).

Fact: Krupp factories supported Hitler with weapons and armaments, while I. G. Farben built chemical plants. During the war, Krupp ran factories using slave labour in occupied countries and in 1943 Alfred Krupp was made minister of the war economy. I. G. Farben built a plant producing synthetic oil and rubber at Auschwitz, where 83,000 slave labourers worked. I. G. Farben also held the patent for the Zyklon B gas, which was used in the gas chambers. At the Nuremberg Trials, Krupp was sentenced to twelve years in prison and thirteen directors of I. G. Farben were sentenced to one to eight years.

> ### SOURCE A
>
> *In February 1933, a week after coming to power, Hitler announced:*
>
> For the next four to five years the main principle must be everything for the armed forces. Germany's position in the world depends decisively upon the position of the German armed forces. The position of the German economy in the world is also dependent on that.
>
> Noakes, J. and Pridham, G. (eds). 2000. *Nazism 1919–45: Vol. 2, State, Economy and Society 1933–39: A Documentary Reader*. Exeter, UK. University of Exeter Press. p. 263.

This principle became even more important after 1936 and necessitated a 'managed economy' whereby the state regulated economic life. *Wehrwirtschaft* included the pursuit of self-sufficiency, or autarky, which drove out 'socialist' ideas by demanding the development of modern large-scale farms. It also encompassed the acceleration of rearmament, which required the support of big business. Hence, between July 1933 and December 1936, over 1,600 new **cartel** arrangements were put in place.

The historian Richard Grunberger has estimated that, while only 40 per cent of German production was in the hands of such monopolies in 1933, it was 70 per cent by 1937. Many industrialists and companies became closely associated with the regime – for example, Krupp, the arms and steel manufacturer, and I. G. Farben, which produced chemicals.

However, as Hitler said to building workers in May 1937, 'the decisive factor is not the theory but the performance of the economy'. Bracher has echoed this point, arguing that 'at no time did National Socialism develop a consistent economic or social theory'. Ideological ideas could be contradictory and there was a conflict between the continuance of private ownership and increased state direction.

Furthermore, the practical need to provide the German people with a reasonable standard of living was difficult to reconcile with a commitment to rearmament. Hitler never fully resolved this conflict between '**guns and butter**'.

Unemployment had peaked at 6 million (one-sixth of the working population) in July 1932, and when Hitler became chancellor in 1933, Germany's exports were just 39 per cent of the 1928 level. Reducing unemployment, stimulating the economy and addressing the balance of payments problem, which resulted from the collapse of the export market, were issues the Nazis had to address if they were to retain credibility and support. To help with this, in March 1933, Hitler appointed **Dr Hjalmar Schacht** as president of the Reichsbank. Schacht was a non-Nazi who was well respected by the business community.

In June 1933, a law to reduce unemployment was passed. This included:

- government spending on public works schemes – *Arbeitsdienst*
- subsidies for private construction/renovation
- income tax rebates/loans to encourage industrial activity.

Other measures that helped to combat unemployment included:

- emergency relief schemes
- recruitment into the Reich Labour Service (RAD) formed in 1934 – through which the unemployed were sent to work on various civil, military and agricultural projects
- a law for the construction of 7,000 km (4,350 miles) of motorway – the *Autobahnen*
- specific regulations – for example, that no machinery could be used for road-building when surplus labour was available
- an expansion of the party and national bureaucracy
- discouragement of female labour (see section 3.17), including marriage allowances to remove women from the labour market
- in March 1935, conscription and an increase in rearmament.

In order to stimulate the economy, tax concessions were offered to businesses, and Schacht also raised money for investment through 'mefo bills'. These were credit notes, issued by the Reichsbank and guaranteed by the government. The bills were a means of '**deficit financing**'. They were paid back with interest after five years from the increased government tax revenue they helped to generate. Repayments on mefo bills accounted for 50 per cent of government expenditure in 1934–35.

Mefo bills permitted subsidies and agreements, such as that to match private investment in the car industry. This helped to stimulate housing, road construction and a variety of industries. Among these was the rearmament industry, although it was not the main growth area before 1936.

Schacht also took action to erode Germany's debt and improve the balance of payments position. In 1933, controls were introduced to limit the drain of Germany's foreign exchange by paying foreign debts in Reichsmarks.

In July 1934, debt repayment was stopped altogether and creditors were given **bonds** instead. Although creditor countries opposed this move, they failed to cooperate to put pressure on Germany. Consequently, the Nazis were able to push ahead with the New Plan of September 1934, devised by Schacht, who was promoted to minister of economics that year. The New Plan supported:

- increased government regulation of imports
- the development of trade with less-developed countries
- the development of German trade with central and south–east Europe.

The New Plan led to a series of trade agreements, particularly with the Balkan and South American states, which provided for the import of vital raw materials. Since these were paid for in Reichsmarks, they encouraged such countries to buy German goods in return. According to William Shirer, 'Schacht's creation of credit, in a country that had little liquid capital and almost no financial reserves, was the work of a genius.'

Other influences that helped the revival of the economy included the avoidance of labour troubles with the dissolution of the trade unions, the banning of strikes and the creation of the DAF in May 1933, and the Nazis' continued use of propaganda to increase the illusion of success and prosperity and maintain confidence. There were also other 'windfalls', such as the seizure of Jewish property and Austrian assets, following the Anschluss of 1938.

Figure 3.20   Dr Hjalmar Schacht (1877–1970)

Although not a Nazi Party member, Schacht helped to raise funds for the party in the 1930s. In August 1934, he was made minister of economics. However, he protested against extreme anti-Semitism and opposed Hitler's demand for increasing expenditure on rearmament. He resigned as minister of economics in November 1937 and as president of the Reichsbank in January 1939. In 1944, he was charged with being involved in the July Bomb Plot. At the Nuremberg Trials, he was found not guilty of war crimes.

deficit financing: This refers to the practice of spending more government money than is received. The difference is made up by borrowing.

bond: A bond is the contract accompanying a loan. The creditor is promised that they will be paid back at some point in the future and in the meantime annual interest is paid on the amount lent.

3

Did the Nazis perform an 'economic miracle'?

Unemployment fell from 6 million to 2.5 million within eighteen months of Hitler coming to power. By 1936, it stood at 1.6 million and, with subsequent expansion, by 1939 it had fallen below 200,000. Economic investment increased and public expenditure reached 23.6 billion Reichsmarks in 1939 – a considerable advance on 17.1 billion Reichsmarks in 1932 and 18.4 billion in 1933.

SOURCE B

What we have achieved in two and a half years in the way of a planned provision of labour, a planned regulation of the market, a planned control of prices and wages, was considered a few years ago to be absolutely impossible. We only succeeded because behind these apparently dead economic measures we had the living energies of the whole nation.

From a speech by Hitler to the Reichstag, 1935. Quoted in Hite, J. and Hinton, C. 2000. *Weimar and Nazi Germany*. London, UK. John Murray. p. 217.

However, despite Hitler's talk of a new 'determination', the economic situation when he took office was not as bad as he liked to suggest. Thanks to Brüning, reparations had ended and unemployment had started to fall after July 1932. Work creation schemes had been established and the world economic recovery from late 1932 had laid the basis for the so-called 'Nazi economic miracle'. Furthermore, despite considerable economic achievements, the Nazis' economic policies were not a total success. Reserves of foreign currency remained low and the balance of payments continued to be in deficit – and this grew worse after 1936, when Schacht's influence declined. Rearmament put a strain on the economy, and although real wages increased overall, the price of food rose to the detriment of the poorer peasants and urban workers.

Figure 3.21 Inside the Krupp factory in Essen, 1933

Historians who question the strong dictator theory (e.g. Kershaw and Overy) would argue that there was no coherent Nazi economic policy, so it is wrong to ascribe the term 'Nazi economic miracle' to what happened after 1933. Despite Nazi claims, most economic policies were not carefully thought through and evolved according to political whims.

How ready was Germany for war in 1939?

By 1936, Schacht was urging a curb in public expenditure and a slowdown in the pace of rearmament, as it was straining the balance of payments. Hitler disagreed, and in August 1936 the Four-Year Plan was announced, with Hermann Goering as its director.

- Emphasis was to be placed on self-sufficiency, or autarky; plants were to be built for the production of *ersatz* (substitute) synthetic materials, such as artificial rubber (known as Buna), which could be made from acetylene.

- Special encouragement was to be given to the chemical industry and the development of synthetic fuel (such as using coal to produce oil).

- Steelworks were to be developed, using the lower-grade ores that were available within Germany (the Hermann Goering steelworks was erected in compliance with this).

- Emphasis was to be placed on the production of heavy machinery.

- The office of the Four-Year Plan was to issue regulations controlling foreign exchange, labour, raw materials distribution and prices.

- Targets for private industry were to be established through six sub-offices with special responsibilities for production and distribution. (These were: raw materials; labour force; agriculture; price control; foreign exchange; and the Reichswerke Hermann Goering, the steel plant that coordinated rearmament.)

The Four-Year Plan extended Nazi control by setting up a 'managed economy' in cooperation with big business. Private industry continued, but failure to conform and meet expectations could result in the business being taken over. The plan had some success and there was a growth in output in all of the key areas. However, overall targets were not met (especially those for synthetic fuel, rubber, fats and light metals) and the production of synthetic substitutes proved costly. For example, to produce one tonne of oil, it took six tonnes of coal. By 1939, Germany still imported a third of all its raw materials, including iron ore, oil and rubber, and there remained a shortage of foreign exchange to buy necessary imports.

The development of the plan was also impeded by bureaucratic inefficiency and internal rivalry, while the need to maintain the production of consumer goods for the German people impeded the priorities of the plan.

Tim Mason, a Marxist historian, has argued that the German economy had reached a crisis point by 1938 and that this was so serious that it drove Germany to war. Mason claims that the economy had been put under strain by rearmament. He argues that the regime, which had consistently favoured capitalist big business over the workers, was unable to demand the 'sacrifices' necessary to pursue its

Fact: Between 1932 and 1939 unemployment in Germany fell from around 6 million to less than 200,000. However, around 4 million had been absorbed into the *Wehrmacht* (armed forces). This meant that, in reality, only about 2 million extra jobs had been created over six years. These were mostly in the manufacture of armaments, which was necessary to equip the 4 million members of the *Wehrmacht*.

Fact: The Four-Year Plan was designed to gear the economy in support of the Nazis' political objectives, but its actual significance has provoked debate. According to Overy, 'It was the foundation of preparation for total war.' E. H. Carr has claimed, 'It was not an attempt to switch from rearmament in breadth to rearmament in depth.' Nevertheless, the memorandum that launched the plan asserted that 'the German armed forces must be operational within four years' and 'the German economy must be fit for war within four years', suggesting a more gradual development.

111

Blitzkrieg: This refers to 'lightning warfare' – an attack conducted with such speed that the enemy is overwhelmed before it can put all of its forces into action.

Fact: In August 1939 Germany and the Soviet Union signed a non-aggression pact, under which both nations agreed not to go to war with each other and (in a secret clause) to divide Poland between them. Hitler's invasion of Poland began on 1 September 1939, while the Soviet Union's invasion from the east began on 17 September.

Figure 3.22 Albert Speer (1905–81)

Speer, a young architect, joined the Nazi Party in 1932 and became a member of the SS. Hitler commissioned him to design the Reich Chancellery in Berlin and Party Palace in Nuremberg. In 1942, Speer was made minister of armaments. He increased production but clashed with other leaders. At the Nuremberg Trials he was sentenced to twenty-five years in prison. On his release in 1966 he published his memoirs in which he claimed to be uninterested in politics and to have known nothing of the Holocaust. However, Trevor-Roper has described him as 'the real criminal of Nazi Germany', because he saw faults and did nothing.

ends, such as wage reductions. Consequently the conflict between 'guns and butter' threatened unrest among the working classes and led Hitler to divert attention by going to war before he was really ready to do so. However, according to Overy, the decision to go to war caused, rather than was caused by, an economic crisis. He argues that the outbreak of war was decided by the ending of appeasement, not an economic need.

Most historians agree that, whatever the reason, Germany was not fully prepared for war in 1939. Taylor, for example, has stressed that Hitler was unable to concentrate on rearmament because he needed to keep up consumer production. Burton Klein has put forward the view that Germany was ready for a short war of **Blitzkrieg**, but not for total war, which Hitler never intended. In support of this view, he has pointed to the 'quite modest' scale of economic mobilisation in 1939 and to the 30 per cent rise in the production of consumer goods between 1936 and 1939.

Overy has also argued that, although Hitler was undoubtedly preparing for war, he was not ready in 1939. This theory is backed up by Hitler's speech at the Hossbach Conference in November 1937. In this speech, Hitler argued that Britain and France would not fight for Czech independence and that Poland could be taken without a general war.

The Nazi–Soviet Pact of 1939 (Hitler's 'deal' with Joseph Stalin to divide Poland between them) also fits the view that Hitler planned to absorb Poland peacefully and use Polish resources for economic build-up before launching into full-scale war, perhaps in 1942. When Hitler's plans for peaceful expansion failed in September 1939, Hitler told Goering that he wanted 'complete conversion of the economy to wartime requirements'. It is likely that it was at this stage that target dates had to be brought forward and a new acceleration applied.

Speer's management of the wartime German economy

When war broke out, the Nazi rearmament programmes were only half completed. Consequently, the early German victories were more the result of their enemies' weaknesses and their own military tactics than that of superior German armaments. However, these victories gave a false sense of confidence. Resources within Germany were not used efficiently. For example, the army could call up any worker, regardless of his skills or employment, women remained in the home, and few prisoners of war were set to work. (The proportion of prisoners in work had still only reached 40 per cent by 1942.) Furthermore, there was no central authority to direct labour.

Hitler's failure to defeat Britain at the end of 1940 and the Soviet Union after the invasion of June 1941 created a situation that the German economy had never been prepared to deal with. Rather than a short war of Blitzkrieg, it had to sustain a long war. To achieve this, Fritz Todt was made minister of armaments and munitions in March 1940. He died in February 1942 and was replaced by **Albert Speer**.

Todt laid the foundations for Speer by setting up a series of committees with chairmen from industry to rationalise production. However, he had only limited success because of military interference. Erhard Milch (Goering's deputy at the air ministry) also organised aircraft production through committees linking producers and contractors, but he suffered the same level of army bureaucracy.

Speer's role in enabling Germany to continue the war to 1945 was to be of immense importance. Although he fought constant battles against other Nazi leaders, such as Goering, Himmler and Martin Bormann, as well as obstructive local *Gauleiters*, he managed to turn wartime production round.

In April 1942, Speer persuaded Hitler to establish a Central Planning Board to organise the allocation of raw materials and ensure that a larger proportion went into armaments. The Central Planning Board:

- set norms for the multiple use of separately manufactured parts to reduce unnecessary duplication
- provided for substitution in raw materials and ensured the development of new processes
- increased industrial capacity (sometimes by converting existing plants)
- placed bans or limits on the manufacture of unnecessary goods
- set schedules and issued output comparisons
- organised the distribution of labour, machinery and power supplies.

Speer worked extremely hard, overseeing everything himself. Hitler remained unrealistic and never fully understood Germany's economic position. He was reluctant to endorse rationing or to cut consumer production, which was kept at only 3 per cent below peacetime levels in 1942.

In the organisation of labour, Speer had to counter the prejudice of both Hitler and Fritz Saukel, who was officially responsible for the supply of labour. In January 1943, it was agreed that German women could be conscripted into the factories, but the order continued to be frequently ignored.

However, labour supplies were maintained with the use of 7 million foreign workers (both male and female) transferred to German factories. Although forced labour could be unreliable (particularly when workers were living on meagre rations), statistics would certainly support Speer's success in increasing wartime production.

In the first six months of Speer's control, overall armament production rose 50 per cent – guns 27 per cent, tanks 25 per cent and ammunition 97 per cent. Work continued despite military losses, defeats and allied bombing raids. On average, in the second quarter of 1944, 111,000 tonnes of bombs were dropped on Germany every month – many falling on fuel plants and refineries. Yet, from the production of 3,744 aircraft in 1940, factories reached a peak production of 25,285 planes in 1944. By rebuilding works to protect the factories from enemy bombing raids, 5,000 new planes were still built in the first four months of 1945.

However, not even Speer could overcome Germany's inherent disadvantages in the war. In the end, bombing and shrinking resources, as Germany's enemies advanced from east and west, caused the economy to crumble in 1945. By 1945, 400,000 civilians had been killed in bombing raids, and towns, cities and factories lay in ruins. The transport network had completely broken down with roads and railways destroyed or in a state of total disrepair, and oil was unobtainable.

Fact: Todt was killed in an air crash, having just left Hitler's headquarters. It has been suggested that Hitler wanted to get rid of him in order to promote Speer, who was immediately given Todt's job. When Goering arrived shortly afterwards, Hitler ordered him to remain in charge of the Four-Year Plan and air force. This was probably because Goering was closely associated with the military, while Speer was a personal protegé and seen by Hitler as more pliable. Hitler hoped Speer could bring the party and industry into closer partnership through his contacts.

Theory of knowledge

History and economics:
Are economic needs the driving force of History?

3

QUESTION

Did the changes in economic policy which took place in the years 1933–42 constitute an 'economic miracle'? To what extent was Nazi economic policy driven by ideology?

KEY CONCEPTS QUESTION

Consequence: How successful was Nazi economic policy?

Ludwig Müller (1883–1946)

Ludwig Müller held strongly nationalist and anti-Semitic views and was a staunch Nazi supporter. He became influential in the association of German Christians and in 1933 was appointed as the country's Reich bishop of the Protestant Church. However, he was increasingly marginalised and committed suicide in 1946.

According to Mommsen's view of Nazism's destructive capacity, economic destruction was the product of Hitler's personal obsession, as summed up in his order to Speer in 1945 to destroy transport and factories lest they fall into enemy hands. He claimed, 'The Germans have failed to prove worthy of their Führer. I must die and all Germany must die with me.' Fortunately, Speer countermanded the order, but there is no doubt that the Nazi economy had ultimately failed.

3.13 What was the relationship between the Nazis and the Churches within Germany?

Germany contained both Protestants (58 per cent of the population) and Catholics (32 per cent) as well as other religious groups.

Hitler's determination to set up an Aryanised social community left little room for religion, but since both the Protestant and Catholic Churches shared a good deal of common ideological ground with Nazism, in their dislike of Marxism, their conservatism, belief in family values and underlying anti-Semitism (even if in principle they spoke against it), he sought to 'use' rather than attack them, but he wanted to restrict the Churches to a purely spiritual role. This ran counter to the desire of most churchmen to maintain the Church's role in other activities such as youth groups.

The Protestant Church

The Protestant Church, which had Lutheran and Calvinist branches, had never been fully united, and with the rise of Nazism, a 'German Christian' movement emerged calling for a new national 'People's Church'. This was mainly supported by young pastors and theology students who saw the Nazis' 'national uprising' as the opportunity for religious as well as political renewal. The German Christians described themselves as the SA of the Church and adopted uniforms, marches and salutes. Their motto was 'the swastika on our breasts and the cross in our hearts'.

In May 1933 Hitler set up the Reich Church with the help of the German Christians, and he appointed a Reich bishop to coordinate the Protestant churches under his authority. In July, **Ludwig Müller** took this position and German Christians were appointed as state bishops and given other senior positions in the Church.

Some German Christians even wanted to remove the Old Testament from religious practice, calling it 'Jewish'. However, not all members of the Protestant Church approved of the German Christians and certainly not of their more outspoken devotees.

In September 1933, a group of 100 pastors headed by **Martin Niemöller** set up the Pastors' Emergency League to resist the German Christians and defend traditional Lutheranism. Some members of this League were arrested, including

Bishop Meiser of Bavaria and Bishop Wurm of Württemberg in 1934, provoking mass demonstrations.

In October 1934, the Pastors' Emergency League formally broke with the Reich Church to form its own Confessional Church. This led Hitler to abandon his attempt to impose direct control on the Protestant Church through the Reich bishop. The bishops of Bavaria and Württemberg were reinstated and orthodox officials and bishops were allowed to continue in their positions.

This left the Protestant Church divided into three:

- the 'official' Reich Church under Müller, which cooperated with the regime but tried to retain organisational autonomy
- the German Christians, who tried to control the Reich Church but whose influence declined
- the Confessional Church, which formed an oppositional Church and was subject to harassment from both the state and other Church authorities but had strong support in some areas.

From 1934, the Church suffered less from direct persecution than from attempts to curb its activities. **Confessional schools** were abolished, religious teaching was downgraded in schools, and young people's time was taken up with the Hitler Youth to such an extent that attendance at Sunday services as well as participation in other Church activities was hindered. The weakening of the Church was, however, sporadic and uncoordinated because of the way the Nazi state was run, with some *Gauleiters* being far more anti-religious than others.

The Catholic Church

The Catholic Church came to terms with the Nazis, agreeing to the dissolution of the Centre Party and, in July 1933, signing a Concordat. According to the Concordat, the Vatican recognised the Nazi regime and promised not to interfere in politics. In return, the state promised not to interfere in the Catholic Church, which would keep control over its educational, youth and communal organisations.

However, between 1933 and 1939, the Nazis increasingly tried to go back on their promises. They used propaganda, insulting the clergy and Catholic practices to encourage anti-Catholic feeling. Catholic schools were closed and had almost disappeared by 1939. Catholic organisations and societies were also removed. For example, in 1936, Church youth organisations were disbanded when the Hitler Youth became compulsory.

In 1937, Pope Pius XI issued the encyclical *With Burning Anxiety* (*Mit Brennender Sorge*), attacking Nazi beliefs. This was smuggled into Germany and read out in Catholic churches. However, his successor in 1939, Pius XII, failed to condemn Nazism outright and has been criticised for his tolerance of the regime.

Bishop Galen's protest against euthanasia in 1941 was the most outspoken criticism to come from a Catholic prelate but, although between one-third and half of Catholic clergy were harassed by the regime, only one Catholic bishop was expelled and one was imprisoned for any length of time, suggesting that protest against the Nazis was limited.

Martin Niemöller (1892–1984)

Niemöller was a co-founder of the Confessional Church. In 1933, he was working as a Protestant pastor in Berlin where he initially welcomed Hitler as chancellor. However, he opposed Hitler's efforts to politicise the Church. He was arrested in 1937 for his outspokenness and sent to Sachsenhausen concentration camp. During his time in prison he repudiated his earlier anti-Semitism. He was released by the Allies in 1945.

confessional school: A state school in which specific Church teaching was allowed. During the Weimar Republic, confessional schools dominated the education system, with 55 per cent of primary and secondary schools being Lutheran, 28 per cent Catholic, 15 per cent non-denominational, and 2 per cent secular and Jewish.

Theory of knowledge

History and guilt:
The Catholic Church faced post-war accusations of collaborating with the Nazis, and in 1998 the Vatican issued a formal apology for failing to oppose the Holocaust. Were these accusations fair? Has the apology made any difference? Can an apology ever atone for mistakes made in the past?

3

Fact: Other pagan influences included the use of ancient Germanic names for the names of the months, the removal of Church holidays from special status and campaigns against the use of the crucifix.

The German Faith Movement, neo-Paganism and 'positive Christianity'

Moves to weaken the Church were not always well coordinated. In the mid-1930s a 'Church Secession' campaign deliberately encouraged Germans to abandon the Churches. Some members of the Nazi Party, though not Hitler himself, encouraged the pagan German Faith Movement. This embraced several beliefs that fitted well with Nazism, including a belief in *Blut und Boden* (blood and soil) ideology and the rejection of Christian ethics.

Although it remained a small sect, at its height the German Faith Movement had around 200,000 supporters and was particularly strong among the SS. Paganism also influenced policy. For example, carols and nativity plays were banned from schools in 1938 and the word 'Christmas' was forbidden and replaced by 'Yuletide' in the war years.

Overall, the record of the Churches in the period of Nazi domination is not one of which they were to feel proud in later years. As organisations, they almost completely surrendered to the Nazi political leadership, although the breakaway Confessional Church and some individual clergymen (see the profiles of Niemöller and Bonhoeffer) were able to stand out as symbols of religious opposition to Nazism.

However, Christianity as such does not seem to have been affected. Church attendance remained steady, and even increased in the war years, making Christian belief an obstacle to a fully totalitarian state.

Fact: Tests for admission to the *Pimpfen* included:
- recitation of Nazi dogma and all the verses of the 'Horst Wessel Song' (the Nazi Party anthem)
- map reading
- participation in pseudo war games and charitable collections
- sporting standards – 60 metres (66 yards) in 12 seconds; long jump of 2.75 metres (3 yards)
- participation in a cross-country march.

Fact: Members of the Hitler Youth took an oath and vow to the Führer:

You, Father, are our commander! We stand in your name.

The Reich is the object of our struggle, It is the beginning and the Amen.

3.14 How did the Nazis see the role of education and try to ensure the support of young people?

Young people were very important to the Nazis. According to Hans Schemm, leader of the Nazi Teachers' League, 'those who have youth on their side control the future'. Consequently, much effort was put into winning over this new generation through youth movements and the control of education.

In July 1933, Hitler appointed Baldur von Schirach as 'youth leader of the German Reich'. By the end of 1933, von Schirach had control over all youth organisations except for those Catholic organisations exempted under the Concordat (see section 3.6, The Catholic Church).

Membership of the Hitler Youth (*Hitlerjugend*: HJ) became compulsory in 1936, and in March 1939 the Catholic youth groups were finally closed down. The Hitler Youth was divided into various sections.

Boys		Girls	
Pimpfen (cubs)	6–10 years	*Junge Mädel* (JM)	10–14 years
Deutsches Jungvolk (DJ)	10–14 years	*Bund Deutscher Mädel* (BDM)	14–18 years
Hitlerjugend (HJ)	14–18 years	*Glaube und Schönheit* (League of Faith and Beauty)	18–21 years

Nazi youth organisations were governed by two basic aims: to train boys for war and girls for motherhood. At every level there were uniforms, competitions, expeditions, sports, musical activities, theatrical productions and artistic displays to take part in. There was incessant activity and competition, which penalised the weak or uncommitted. Values of honour, discipline and self-sacrifice were encouraged, with contempt for moderation, intellect and sensitivity. Youths were even encouraged to spy on their parents and report aberrant attitudes.

Generally, the *Hitlerjugend* was well received by young people. However, some young people disliked the regimentation, and by the later 1930s alternative, illegal youth groups began to attract growing numbers. These included the working-class Edelweiss Pirates, and the middle/upper-class Swing Movement, whose members rejected Nazi values by dancing to American jazz (black) music and wearing American-style fashions.

The German education system was also used to inculcate Nazi values, and in May 1934 a centralised Reich Education Ministry was established under Bernhard Rust. No substantial change was made to the structure of the education system, apart from the establishment of a new series of élite schools including *Napolas*, Adolf Hitler Schools and the *Ordensburgen* (see the Fact box). However, there was a radical revision of the curriculum.

Biology, history and German became the means for conveying Nazi philosophy. In biology, racial differences and the Nazis' interpretation of Darwin's theory of selection and survival of the fittest were emphasised. History was designed to 'awaken in the younger generation that sense of responsibility towards ancestors and grandchildren that will enable it to let its life be subsumed in eternal Germany'. German lessons encouraged a consciousness of the nation and there was an emphasis on folklore. Ideology even entered the curriculum in a lesser way in Maths, where problems were posed in ideological language. At further education colleges and universities, new subjects such as genetics, racial theory, folklore, military studies and the study of German borderlands made an appearance. There was also a huge emphasis on sport, which occupied a minimum of five hours a week, giving the gymnastics teacher a new status. This was at the expense of religious education, which ceased to exist as a subject in the school-leaving examination in 1935. There was also differentiation between the curriculum for males and females, with the latter emphasising home economics.

Teachers and lecturers were also subject to Nazi controls. Some were dismissed under the 1933 Civil Service Law, and in 1939 all teachers became Reich civil servants. The National Socialist Teachers' League and National Socialist Lecturers' League organised special 'camps' to reinforce Nazi values. At these camps, all teachers below the age of fifty were expected to participate in sport. The teaching profession was required to

Fact: *Napolas* (national political educational institutions) were set up from April 1933 and in 1936 fell under the influence of the SS. They produced highly trained youngsters for the armed forces. Classes were known as platoons and the routine of the school was based on that of a military camp with a communal style of living and sporting drill before breakfast. The Adolf Hitler Schools were strongly influenced by the Hitler Youth. The ten *Ordensburgen* were party-controlled Nazi colleges, set up from 1937, with an emphasis on physical training.

Fact: A pupil had to reach the required standard in sport before they could move to the next class. Sport was an examination subject for grammar school entry (a child could be refused entry to secondary school if they had a serious physical handicap) and for the school-leaving examination. Persistently unsatisfactory sporting performance could be grounds for expulsion.

Theory of knowledge

Teaching history:
Is it right for governments to control what is taught in schools? What is acceptable and what is not? Does the teaching of History serve a specific purpose? If so, what?

3

Fact: Many scientists emigrated from Nazi Germany, including twenty past or future Nobel Prize winners. Among them was Albert Einstein.

be actively anti-Semitic, and 'Jewish' theses, such as Einstein's theory of relativity, were banned.

It is hard to gauge the effect of Nazi youth policies, but the willingness of millions of young people to fight for the Nazi cause when war broke out must suggest some degree of success. However, the quality of educational provision declined and extra youth activities sapped young peoples' energies. Furthermore, there was active discrimination against women and Jews and, in wartime, evacuations and the conscription of teachers further disrupted education.

3.15 How did Nazism affect the arts and the media?

The Nazis believed that Germany's impressive cultural history placed the arts in a unique position in German society. Both élite art, such as classical music, paintings, sculpture and theatre, and the more popular arts such as film, radio broadcasting and light entertainment were perceived as media for reinforcing Germans' shared statehood and race. Nazis despised the modernist styles of the 'decadent' Weimar era and looked to exploit 'traditional' art forms that were unadventurous, of high moral standing, dominated by Aryanism and that glorified a mythical past.

The main themes of the arts included:

- 'blood and soil', in which the peasant was cast as the representative of the 'pure' Aryan blood of the German people and his struggles with the soil and the weather were glorified
- anti-feminism, with its emphasis on preindustrial images of women
- anti-Semitism, which permeated all aspects of composition and performance as well as colouring the themes of literature and film
- order, as reflected in a return to the classical tradition (particularly in sculpture and architecture), with solidity of style and a sense of dominance and purpose which served to underpin Nazi notions of the superiority of the state and the permanence of the Reich.

Goebbels was made minister of propaganda and popular enlightenment in 1933 and his office imposed rigorous censorship on all art forms, encouraging only those that conveyed a suitable propaganda message. In May 1933, Goebbels coordinated a 'burning of the books'. This symbolically and physically destroyed works associated with Jews, Bolsheviks and 'Negroes', as well as anything seen as 'decadent' and 'un-German'.

The annual Great German Art exhibition was another propaganda pageant, and the Reich *Kulturkammer* (Reich Chamber of Culture) ensured that only arts 'suitable' for the masses were permitted. An individual's artistic tastes could become the subject of a report by their local block warden.

Many artists were expelled or went into voluntary exile. For example, the conductors Bruno Walter and Otto Klemperer, the composers Schönberg, Hindemith and Kurt Weill, and the singers Marlene Dietrich and Lotte Lenya all left the country.

In the concert hall, the works of the Jewish composers Mahler and Mendelssohn were banned. Modernist paintings were removed from art galleries. The Nazis also tried to prohibit American jazz and foreign dance-band music, which was referred to as *Niggermusik*.

However, some artists remained and helped to give the regime respectability. Composers such as Richard Strauss, who became the first president of the Reich Chamber of Music, and singers such as Elizabeth Schwarzkopf, performed for the regime.

The spread of the *Volksempfänger* (people's receiver), a mass-produced radio found in over 70 per cent of German homes by 1939, increased the number of listeners who could enjoy German classical music, which was mixed with light entertainment and traditional Germanic tunes and songs. Composers such as Anton Bruckner and Richard Wagner became popular heroes and attracted a mass following, as concerts were filmed to reach a wider audience, and skilfully edited shots of the audience reaction were displayed to reinforce the desired patriotic message.

The Wagnerian Bayreuth Festival was turned from an élitist minority interest into a great popular festival, as were art exhibitions and some theatrical performances. Attendance at arts events was subsidised and encouraged through works outings and special 'Strength through Joy' or Hitler Youth events. However, in popularising the arts, the Reich *Kulturkammer* often resorted to commissioning second-rate artists, as well as forcing those who possessed real talent into narrow and restrictive paths.

Films were seen as a useful popular diversion – partly propagandist and partly to provide relaxation and to offer a 'shared experience', binding the community together. Sound was relatively new and was developed to great effect in feature films. The Reich Film Chamber controlled both the content of German films and the foreign films that could be shown.

Some great producers, such as Leni Riefenstahl, flourished and produced works of art, even if the ideological themes were controversial. However, some films lacked subtlety, and *The Eternal Jew* was so horrific that members of the audience fainted and box office receipts fell away. The cinema was used to show newsreels before the main picture and admission was restricted to the beginning of a programme, so all filmgoers had to sit through a certain amount of propaganda.

The impact of Nazism on the arts was contradictory. Not everything produced in Nazi Germany was an artistic disaster, but much individual creativity and inspiration was lost in the interests of *Gleichschaltung* (see section 3.4, The end of Weimar democracy) and the desire to use culture as a propagandist tool. Some positive advances occurred despite, rather than because of, Nazi values. Music suffered the least, since it was played as written, but other art forms were reduced to fake posturing. After the war, artistic expression in West Germany seemed to pick up where the Weimar Republic had left off, almost as though the Nazi era had never existed.

Fact: The most famous films of the era, *Hitler Youth Quex* (1933), *Jud Süss* (1940) and *Ohm Krüger* (1941) (which was about British atrocities during the Boer War), all had clear political messages. However, the messages were conveyed subtly and the films are deemed to have some artistic merit. Leni Riefenstahl, who produced the *Triumph of Will* (1935) about the Nuremberg Party Rally and *Olympia* (1938) on the 1936 Olympic Games held in Berlin, was a particularly innovative and talented director.

ACTIVITY

Weimar culture is epitomised in the works of the playwright Bertolt Brecht, the musician Kurt Weill, the artist George Grosz and the architects of the Bauhaus movement. Investigate some of their works and compare them with what followed during the Nazi era.

3.16 How were social, religious and racial minorities treated within the Nazi state?

Volksgenossen: Literally 'race comrade', this term refers to a person who was racially pure and was therefore considered worthy of German citizenship.

Fact: In the 1930s, the term 'homosexual' was commonly used to describe a sexual relationship between people of the same sex, which was then illegal. Nowadays, following changes in attitudes and the law, the term is now regarded as offensive and the terms 'gay', 'lesbian' and 'bisexual' are widely used and regarded as more acceptable.

Fact: Prisoners in Nazi concentration camps were made to wear badges, usually triangles, to identify them. These were sewn on jackets and shirts and were seen as badges of shame. Political prisoners (socialists, communists) had red triangles; habitual criminals, green; gay men and lesbians, pink; and certain religious people, purple.

Those who failed to fit Nazi criteria for **Volksgenossen** were subject to intimidation and persecution. Political enemies have already been considered (see section 3.9), but two other important minority groups suffered:

- asocials such as habitual criminals, the work-shy, tramps and beggars, alcoholics, prostitutes, gay men and lesbians, and juvenile delinquents
- biological outsiders, including those suffering hereditary defects that were considered a threat to the future of the German race and those who were regarded as a threat because of their race, such as Roma, Sinti and Jews.

'Asocials'

In September 1933, 300,000–500,000 so-called beggars and tramps were rounded up. Some (mainly the young unemployed) were given a permit (*Wanderkarte*) and had to perform compulsory work in return for board and lodgings, but the 'work-shy' were dealt with under the Law Against Dangerous Habitual Criminals, 1933. They were sent to concentration camps and made to wear a black triangle. They could also be compulsorily sterilised, since 'social deviance' was considered to be biologically determined. In the summer of 1938, another big roundup took place under the 'Work-shy Reich' programme. Those arrested were mostly sent to Buchenwald. Of the 10,000 tramps incarcerated during the Third Reich, few survived.

In 1939, the Reich Central Agency for the Struggle Against Juvenile Delinquency was established and a youth concentration camp was set up in Moringen near Hannover in 1940. Here, youths were subjected to biological and racial examination and those deemed unreformable were sterilised. If the 1940 Community Alien Law had been carried out, all those considered deficient in mind or character would have been similarly treated, but this policy was abandoned because of the war.

'Biological outsiders'

In July 1933, the Nazis introduced a law demanding the compulsory sterilisation of those suffering from specified hereditary illnesses. These included some illnesses that had a dubious hereditary base, such as schizophrenia and 'chronic alcoholism'. Heredity courts were established to consider individual cases, and between 1934 and 1945 around 350,000 people were sterilised under this law. People who had been sterilised were forbidden to marry fertile partners.

Euthanasia

The Nazis also launched a propaganda campaign to devalue people with mental or physical disabilities as 'burdens on the community'. This culminated in the euthanasia programme, which began in the summer of 1939. Practised in secret, the programme initially targeted children under three, but it was later extended to children up to sixteen years of age. By 1945, 5,000 children had been murdered by injection or deliberate starvation. In order to extend this programme to adults, carbon monoxide gas was used in six mental hospitals in various parts of Germany. By August 1941, when the programme was officially stopped because of public outrage, 72,000 people had been murdered. However, between 1941 and 1943, the secret programme '14F13' led to the gassing of 30,000–50,000 in the concentration camps on the grounds of mental illness or physical incapacity.

Roma and Sinti

The Nazis persecuted Roma and Sinti people, then called Gypsies, because of their alleged inferior racial character. The term 'Gypsy' is now seen, in many countries, to be offensive. There were only around 30,000 'Gypsies' in Germany, but they were included in the Nuremberg Laws of 1935, which banned marriage between Aryans and non-Aryans. Physical traits were analysed and efforts were made to distinguish between pure 'Gypsies' and half-'Gypsies' (*Mischlinge*) at the Research Centre for Racial Hygiene and Biological Population Studies.

From December 1938, gypsies were registered, and from 1940 they were deported to Poland to work in camps. In December 1942, they were transferred to Auschwitz and subjected to medical experiments carried out by Dr Josef Mengele, a Nazi German SS officer known as the 'Angel of Death'.

Mengele supervised the selection of incoming prisoners to determine who should be killed, who would become a forced labourer, and who would be used for human medical experiments. Most of those Mengele experimented on died, either from the experiments or later infections. He also had people killed in order to dissect them afterwards.

It was not just the Roma and Sinti who suffered such cruelty, but of the 20,000 sent to Auschwitz, around 10,000 were murdered. Probably a total of around half a million gypsies were killed in occupied Europe.

Fact: The euthanasia programme began when the parents of a severely disabled boy petitioned Hitler for the right to kill him. Hitler agreed and ordered that other cases be dealt with in the same way.

Fact: Protests against euthanasia were led by the Catholic Bishop Galen. However, there was no similar Church-led protest against attacks on Jews.

Fact: Gypsies were given different-coloured papers according to their origins. The pure, *Sinti*, Gypsies received brown papers, the *Mischlinge* were given blue papers and 'nomads' received grey papers. There was a suggestion that the *Sinti* (who had kept their race 'pure') should be assigned areas in Bohemia and Moravia where they could live traditionally as 'museum specimens'. However, the war stopped this from becoming more than a plan.

Fact: Mengele's 'research' included an attempt to change eye colour by injecting chemicals into children's eyes, experiments involving the amputation of limbs, or the injection of deadly viruses and shock treatments.

Figure 3.23   Nazi troops hold anti-Semitic placards in front of a locked shop in an organised boycott of German Jewish businesses in Berlin, 1933. One of the signs reads 'Germans defend yourselves! Don't buy from the Jews!'

121

Religious minorities

Although the Nazis exercised a cautious policy towards the main Christian religious churches, they were far less sympathetic to minority religious sects. The Salvation Army, Christian Scientists and Seventh Day Adventists were all attacked while astrologers, faith healers and fortune tellers were banned (despite the SS interest in paganism – see section 3.13, The German Faith Movement, neo-Paganism and 'positive Christianity'). The Jehovah's witnesses, who refused to compromise with the regime and stood out against military service, were subject to particular persecution and most perished in the concentration camps.

The Nazis also closed down the German Freethinkers League (an atheistic association, but outside National Socialism) and persecuted Freemasons – partly because of their political associations, but also because they espoused values of tolerance and equality and were, in Nazi eyes, associated with Jews.

Jews

Although there were only about 500,000 Jews in Germany itself (less than 1 per cent of the population), and most had been thoroughly assimilated into the German community, Jews were portrayed by the Nazi regime as a serious racial threat and the root cause of Germany's ills.

The first state-sponsored act of persecution was a one-day boycott of Jewish shops and businesses in March 1933. The action was largely taken to fulfil SA demands and was not repeated, since the economy was too fragile and fear of international repercussions was too great. The government continued to issue contracts to Jewish firms, although Jewish civil servants were dismissed under the Law for a Restoration of a Professional Civil Service, 1933. Persecution increased from 1935, with the announcement of the 'Law for Protection of German Blood' (Nuremberg Laws), which banned marriage between Jews and Germans and deprived Jews of German citizenship.

In 1938, persecution escalated as the regime grew increasingly radical:

- Jews were no longer awarded public contracts
- all Jewish property valued at over 5,000 marks had to be registered and could not be sold
- Jews could no longer be employed in businesses
- it was forbidden for Jewish doctors, dentists and lawyers to offer services to Aryans
- all Jewish children were required to bear the names Israel or Sarah in addition to other names
- Jews were obliged to carry identity cards and have their passports stamped with a 'J'.

On *Reichskristallnacht* (Night of the Broken Glass), 9/10 November 1938, there were attacks on synagogues, businesses, homes and shops – leaving broken glass (like 'crystal') everywhere. Hundreds of Jews were injured, ninety-one were murdered and 20,000 were sent to concentration camps on 'the night the national soul boiled over'. The official excuse for the attacks was the murder by a Jew of Ernst von Rath, a German diplomatic official in Paris. In reality, this orgy of violence was orchestrated by Goebbels.

Increasing numbers of Jews emigrated between 1934 and 1939 as they were expelled from economic life, schools, cinemas, universities, theatres and sports facilities. In cities,

Fact: Before 1933 in Germany, 17 per cent of bankers, 16 per cent of lawyers and 10 per cent of doctors and dentists were Jews. Jews were also influential in the clothing and retail trades.

Fact: Himmler had encouraged an emigration policy for Jews since 1934, but it met with limited success. Only 120,000 of around 500,000 Jews had left Germany by 1937 – and many had subsequently returned. The annexation of Austria in 1938 had added 190,000 Jews to the German Reich and led to an intensified emigration policy whereby 45,000 were forced to leave Austria in six months. During 1939, 78,000 more Jews were forced out of Germany and 30,000 from Bohemia and Moravia in Czechoslovakia.

they were even forbidden to enter areas designated 'for Aryans only', and in January 1939 Hitler threatened 'the annihilation of the Jewish race in Europe' in the event of war.

The invasion of Poland in September 1939 added 3 million Jews to the German empire. Jews were placed in ghettos where they were forbidden to change residence, were subject to a curfew, had to wear a yellow star on their clothing and were compelled to perform labour service.

A final attempt to rid the German Empire of Jews – the Madagascar Plan of summer 1940 – had to be abandoned after Hitler's failure to conquer Britain left the British in control of the sea. This left millions of European Jews facing death – through malnutrition and hard labour, and by mass shootings as the Germans advanced into Russia from June 1941. Following the Wannsee Conference of January 1942, Jews were gassed in the extermination camps created at Auschwitz, Chelmo, Majdanek and Treblinka, an event ambiguously referred to as the 'final solution'. Around 6 millions Jews died in the camps. The operation was shrouded in secrecy, but the fact that scarce resources were diverted to facilitate this Holocaust at a time when the Germans were struggling in the war gives some indication of the irrationality of Nazism.

3.17 What was the position of women in the Nazi state?

Hitler had very clear views about the position that women should hold in the Nazi state.

Hitler looked back on female emancipation during the Weimar Republic with disfavour. According to Nazi propaganda, the duties of women were as mothers, housewives supporting their husbands, and community organisers.

Historical debate:
No written order to exterminate the Jews exists. However, intentionalists such as Christopher Browning and Andreas Hillgruber believe orders were given in the summer of 1941 when it was felt Russia would soon collapse. Goering's order to Reinhard Heydrich, Himmler's deputy in the SS, on 31 July 1941, 'to bring about a complete solution of the Jewish question within the German sphere of influence in Europe' supports this. However, structuralists such as Mommsen and Broszat believe the order came in the autumn when the policy of Jewish resettlement east of the Urals was wrecked by Germany's failure to defeat Russia.

Fact: During the years of the Weimar Republic, women had been granted the vote and enjoyed greater equality with men than under the Nazis. They had been encouraged to pursue higher education, to take up professional posts and to participate in politics as members of the Reichstag.

Figure 3.24 According to Nazi ideology, a woman's primary role was as a mother, whose duty was to bear further Aryans

Fact: Prolific mothers were awarded medals with the inscription 'The child ennobles the mother.' These were given annually on 12 August, the birthday of Hitler's own mother. The recipients had to be 'of German blood and hereditarily healthy'. There were three categories:
- bronze – for those who had four or five children
- silver – for those who had six or seven children
- gold – for those who had eight or more children.

To encourage motherhood, birth control centres were closed, abortion was made illegal unless necessary for the eradication of 'genetic defects', and maternity benefits were increased. Income tax allowances for dependent children were raised and large families enjoyed concessions on expenses such as school fees and railway fares. In 1935, the *Lebensborn* (Spring of Life) project encouraged unmarried women with good racial credentials to become pregnant, with selected SS men as the fathers. 'The Honour Cross of German Motherhood' or 'Mothers' Cross' was established in May 1939 to encourage all women to 'bear a child for the Führer'.

However, only the genetically pure were allowed to procreate. From 1935, couples needed a certificate of 'fitness to marry' before a marriage licence could be issued. From 1938, 'unproductive' marriages could be ended. After 1941, couples found cohabiting after their marriage had been banned were sent to concentration camps. Mothers who failed in their duty to support their children's education as 'national comrades', for example attending the Hitler Youth (see section 3.14), could also face having their children removed.

To facilitate their role as mothers and alleviate male unemployment, legislation and propaganda were used to remove women from the workplace. By the Law for the Reduction of Unemployment of June 1933, women were encouraged to leave work on marriage with the support of generous loans. Marriage loans provided just over half an average year's earnings. They had a low interest rate of 1 per cent per month over eight-and-a-quarter years. They were reduced by one-quarter and repayments delayed by a year on the birth of each healthy child, so after having four children a couple owed nothing. At first, loans were only granted if a wife gave up her job, but the regulations changed in 1937. By 1939, 42 per cent of all marriages were loan assisted.

SOURCE C

The slogan 'Emancipation of Women' was invented by Jewish intellectuals. If the man's world is said to be the state, his struggle, his readiness to devote his powers to the service of the community, then it may perhaps be said that the woman's is a smaller world. For her world is her husband, her family, her children and her home.

From Hitler's speech to the National Socialist Women's League, 8 September 1934. Quoted in Noakes, J. and Pridham, G. (eds). 1984. *Nazism 1919–1945: Vol. 2, State, Economy and Society 1933–1939: A Documentary Reader*. Exeter, UK. University of Exeter Press. p. 449.

In 1934, all married women were forced out of careers in medicine, the legal profession and the Civil Service. They were even declared ineligible for jury service, supposedly because they could not think logically. Similar beliefs placed politics out of women's reach. In a striking contrast with the 1920s, women were banned from senior positions in the Nazi leadership and there were no female Nazi members of the Reichstag. Education also discriminated against women. Only 10 per cent of university entrants were female until a shortage of professional and technical experts in the later 1930s led to a relaxation of policy.

Similarly, when a labour shortage began to affect rearmament plans in 1936, some women were once more drawn back into factories. Compulsory agricultural labour service was introduced for women under twenty-five in 1939, and from January 1943 women aged 16–45 could be conscripted for the war effort.

Speer later wrote of his struggle to get Hitler to agree to the need for female mobilisation, but leading Nazis justified the apparent change in policies by arguing that in wartime the whole of Germany had become the 'home' where women were required to serve.

Nazi policies towards women were therefore contradictory. While they claimed to promote the importance of family values, they encouraged an independent youth that placed the party above the family. While they extolled conventional morality and the importance of marriage, they also permitted illegitimate births and easier divorce, and advanced compulsory sterilisation for those with genetic defects. While they told women to stay in the home, from 1936 women were encouraged to return to the factories. While female education was initially discouraged, by the war years women were encouraged to enter universities and train for professional roles.

3.18 To what extent did the Nazi authoritarian regime achieve its aims?

Goebbels once wrote that 'the aim of the National Socialist Revolution must be a totalitarian state, which will permeate all aspects of public life.' In practice, the National Socialist regime never created such a state. Whilst Nazi Germany was a one-party state, dependent on propaganda and repression and bound by clear ideological principles, National Socialist power was never 'total'. Whilst it sought the 'blind obedience' of the authoritarian state, the regime was, in practice, based on a number of compromises. The chaotic governmental structure (see section 3.8) left a confusion of authority, while the practicalities of creating a Germany capable of waging war meant that obedience to the dictates of Nazi ideology sometimes had to be overlooked. There was comparatively little outright opposition in Nazi Germany, but it never disappeared altogether.

Furthermore, the Nazis never achieved the authoritarian control over society that they had hoped for with their Volksgemeineschaft ideas. There were certainly some major social changes, but these fell short of creating a truly 'National Community'. Compromises were made over the Churches and the position of women, while the Euthanasia Project had to be abandoned and the persecution of minorities was often veiled in secrecy, suggesting the mass of the population had not been reconciled to Nazi ideas.

Even though Nazi Germany was radicalised, through a mixture of ideology and Hitler's own personality, to create a state upheld by the SS-Police-SD system and capable of conducting the savage persecution of social and racial outsiders culminating in the Holocaust, it is hard to categorise it as 'authoritarian' in every sense of the word.

ACTIVITY

Look back at the material you have studied and create a diagram to record evidence of:

- Nazi authoritarian control
- limits to Nazi control.

Divide your chart thematically, looking at aspects of political, economic, religious and social policy and developments.

125

3

polycrat: This is a system of government made up of overlapping bodies such as ministries, party organisations and special agencies.

cumulative radicalism: This is the process whereby policies and actions become more extreme.

Theory of knowledge

Historical interpretation: Broszat and Mommsen were the first to put forward a 'structuralist' interpretation of Nazi Germany as a mixture of competing institutions. These views ran contrary to those of Bracher.

Was Nazi Germany a totalitarian state and was Hitler 'Master of the Third Reich'?

By 1938, outward appearances gave the impression of an effective and successful totalitarian regime. At its head was an all-powerful Führer with unlimited power that filtered down through his Reich cabinet and state governors to keep everyone in line. In theory, the party and state worked together, but studies of Nazi rule both at local level and in central government have suggested that the regime was not run as effectively as was once thought.

It is now more common to see the Nazi regime as a confused, **polycratic** system. This is because Hitler superimposed the party structure on to the state that he took over and deliberately generated competition within it. For example, within the chancellery, made up of Hitler's close friends and followers, he allowed competences to overlap so that no one was quite sure who was responsible for what. There was, for example, considerable conflict between the authority of Goering and Albert Speer (see section 3.12, Speer's management of the wartime German economy) over the economy. Similarly, the civil service found some of its work was bypassed by party members.

According to the historian Broszat, Hitler created a 'confusing system of "empires"'. He believes this accounts for the '**cumulative radicalism**' that marked the Nazi regime.

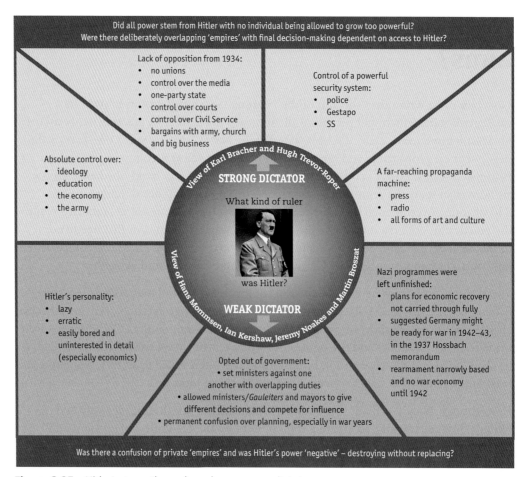

Figure 3.25 Hitler's strengths and weaknesses as a dictator

Broszat claims that policies grew more extreme because party leaders were constantly trying to go one stage further to please or impress Hitler.

This confusion fitted with Hitler's ideological belief in the survival of the fittest. Hitler encouraged competition. It provided an opt-out if things went wrong and left him to intervene only when it suited him. Having no clearly organised pattern to government also appealed to Hitler's fundamental laziness and lack of interest in bureaucratic detail.

This state of affairs did not help a regime that depended on Hitler's decisions to run smoothly. According to structuralist historians such as Mommsen, Kershaw, Jeremy Noakes and Broszat, the Third Reich was not a powerful totalitarian state and Hitler was a 'weak' dictator. Although the authority of the Führer was never questioned, these historians argue that the formation of policy and decisions about its implementation were such a matter of guesswork, as ministers and officials sought to 'work towards the Führer', that the regime was chaotic.

SOURCE D

In the twelve years of his rule in Germany, Hitler produced the biggest confusion in government that has ever existed in a civilised state. During his period of government he removed from the organization of the state all clarity of leadership and produced a completely opaque network of competencies.

Hitler's press chief, Otto Dietrich. Quoted in Williamson, D. and Fulbrook, M. 2008.*OCR Democracy and Dictatorship in Germany 1919–1963*. Oxford, UK. Heinemann. p. 19.

Intentionalist historians, such as Bracher and Hugh Trevor-Roper, suggest that the overlapping of interests was deliberate and that Hitler was a powerful integrating figure at the centre of government. According to them, internal rivalries generated a degree of effectiveness, reinforcing Hitler's position and power. Hitler was able to take the praise for effective policies and blame others for ineffective ones – making himself a 'strong' dictator.

KEY CONCEPTS ACTIVITY

Significance: Make a two-column table. In one column record the arguments that suggest Hitler was a strong dictator; in the other record those that suggest he was a weak dictator. Add the names of historians and quotations to support each view. At the bottom of each column, record the significance of that interpretation for an understanding of Hitler's government.

QUESTION

Is the phrase a 'weak dictator' a contradiction in terms? Explain your views.

End of unit activities

1   Draw a table to show the economic concerns of the Nazi government at key dates during the Nazis' time in power and their success in dealing with these issues:

	Key stages in the development of the Nazi economy		
	Main policies	**Success?**	**Failure?**
1933–36			
1936–42			
1942–45			

2 Find out more about Schacht, Goering and Speer. Make a case for which of these men most significantly helped the Nazi government in his economic policies and actions. This could lead to a class debate.

3 What was the Nazi relationship with the Church? Why did the German Churches not offer more resistance to the Nazi regime? Undertake some research for a class discussion.

4 Draw a diagram to show the various influences to which young people were subject in Nazi Germany.

5 Choose one aspect of Nazi culture and prepare a PowerPoint presentation for your class in which you show how that art form was used as propaganda in this period.

6 Who gained most from the Nazi Germany? Research the impact of National Socialist policy on each of the following groups (you may like to divide these between members of your class). You should consider change and continuity under the Nazi regime.

 a Big business

 b Peasant farmers

 c Factory workers

 d Women

 e Young people.

7 Find out more about alternative youth movements – the Swing Movement, the Edelweiss Pirates and the White Rose group.

8 Make a summary chart assessing whether the consequence of Nazis' social policies in the following areas was success or a failure:

Area	Policies	Success?	Failure?	Comment
Women				
Youth				
Education				
Religion				
Minorities				
Culture and the arts				

What are the problems in assessing the success of Nazi social policy?

9 Prepare and hold a debate on the motion: 'National Socialist Germany was not an Authoritarian state'.

End of chapter activities

Paper 1 exam practice

Question

What message is suggested by **Source A** below about the *Führerprinzip* (the personal importance of Hitler in Nazi leadership)? **[2 marks]**

Skill

Comprehension of a source.

SOURCE A

My German comrades! I speak to you today … first, in order that you should hear my voice and should know that I am unhurt and well and secondly that you should know that there has been a crime unparalleled in German history. A very small clique of ambitious, irresponsible and, at the same time, senseless and stupid officers have concocted a plot to eliminate me and, with me, the staff of the High Command of the *Wehrmacht* [armed forces]. The bomb planted by Colonel Count Stauffenberg … seriously wounded a number of my true and loyal collaborators … [but] I myself am entirely unhurt, aside from some minor bruises, scratches and burns. I regard this as a confirmation of the task imposed upon me by Providence … The circle of these traitors is very small and has nothing in common with the spirit of the German *Wehrmacht* and, above all, none with the German people. It is a gang of criminal elements, which will be destroyed without mercy.

From a personal radio broadcast made by Hitler to the German people on 21 July 1944, following the failure of the July Bomb Plot. Quoted in Noakes, J. 1998. *Nazism 1919–1945: Vol. 4, The German Home Front in World War II: A Documentary Reader*. Exeter, UK. University of Exeter Press. p. 111.

Examiner's tips

Comprehension questions test your basic understanding of a source and your comments need to be supported by some specific detail from that source. Ideally, you should try to make two or three separate points, providing a sentence on each. Since there are only 2 marks available for this question, answers should not be too long.

Common mistakes

It is easy to comment about the topic of the source rather than the source itself. Try to keep to the specific content of the source rather than providing extraneous own knowledge.

Simplified mark scheme

For each item of **relevant/correct information** identified, award 1 mark – up to a maximum of 2 marks.

Student answer

Source A is about the Führerprinzip, which means 'leadership principle'. Hitler had created a one-party, authoritarian state in Germany dependent on his all-powerful leadership. Without this, he believed the state could not function. That is why it was important that the Führer survived the bomb plot on his life.

Examiner's comments

The candidate has shown an excellent knowledge of the *Führerprinzip*, but has failed to comment directly on the source. There is a brief link in the last sentence to the occasion, but there is no direct reference to the specific timing, relevance or detail of the speech. This answer would therefore only be worthy of 1 mark.

Activity

Look closely at the source and see how many examples of statements demonstrating or explaining the *Führerprinzip* you can find. Look at the content and the meaning conveyed in Hitler's use of language and the references he makes. Could you, for example, comment meaningfully on the sentence: 'I regard this as a confirmation of the task imposed upon me by Providence …' or draw a message from the last sentence?

Summary activity

Nazi Germany has been the subject of much historiographical debate. The diagram below raises some key questions that have taxed historians trying to understand the truth of the Nazi German state. Having considered the issues they raise in the course of this chapter,

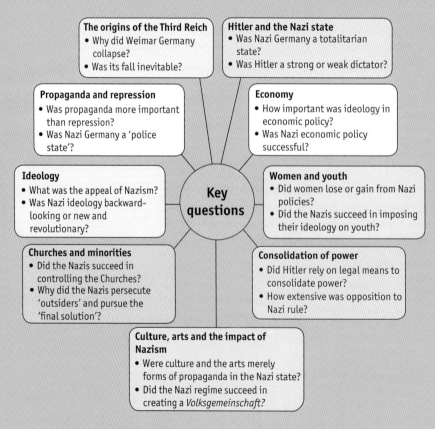

The origins of the Third Reich
- Why did Weimar Germany collapse?
- Was its fall inevitable?

Hitler and the Nazi state
- Was Nazi Germany a totalitarian state?
- Was Hitler a strong or weak dictator?

Propaganda and repression
- Was propaganda more important than repression?
- Was Nazi Germany a 'police state'?

Economy
- How important was ideology in economic policy?
- Was Nazi economic policy successful?

Ideology
- What was the appeal of Nazism?
- Was Nazi ideology backward-looking or new and revolutionary?

Women and youth
- Did women lose or gain from Nazi policies?
- Did the Nazis succeed in imposing their ideology on youth?

Key questions

Churches and minorities
- Did the Nazis succeed in controlling the Churches?
- Why did the Nazis persecute 'outsiders' and pursue the 'final solution'?

Consolidation of power
- Did Hitler rely on legal means to consolidate power?
- How extensive was opposition to Nazi rule?

Culture, arts and the impact of Nazism
- Were culture and the arts merely forms of propaganda in the Nazi state?
- Did the Nazi regime succeed in creating a *Volksgemeinschaft*?

you should be in a position to tackle them yourself. There are no easy answers. As with so much in History, the answers are likely to involve a compromise between support for different sides of the debate. However, it is in thinking through these compromises that you can hope to get nearer to understanding the complexities of the Nazi state.

Paper 2 practice questions

1 Examine the conditions that enabled Hitler to rise to power in Germany.
2 Evaluate the importance of ideology in Hitler's rise to power.
3 Evaluate the way in which the Nazis were able to consolidate power between January 1933 and the end of 1938.
4 Examine the success of National Socialist economic policies?
5 Examine the status and role of women in Nazi Germany.
6 'Under Nazism, the lives of ordinary German families were significantly affected in the years 1933 to 1939.' To what extent to you agree with this statement?

Further reading

Try reading the relevant chapter/sections of the following books:

Bessel, R. 1987. *Life in the Third Reich*. Oxford, UK. Oxford University Press.

Evans, R. J. 2003. *The Coming of the Third Reich*. London, UK. Penguin Books.

Evans, R. J. 2005. *The Third Reich in Power*. London, UK. Penguin Books.

Evans, R. J. 2008. *The Third Reich at War*. London, UK. Penguin Books.

Grunberger, R. 1971. *A Social History of the Third Reich*. London, UK. Penguin Books.

Housden, M. 1996. *Resistance and Conformity in the Third Reich*. London, UK. Routledge.

Kershaw, I. 1985. *The Nazi Dictatorship – Problems and Perspectives of Interpretations*. London, UK. Arnold.

Kershaw, I. 1998. *Hitler 1889–1936: Hubris*. London, UK. Penguin Books.

Kershaw, I. 2000. *Hitler 1936–1945: Nemesis*. London, UK. Penguin Books.

Overy, R. 2004. *The Dictators: Hitler's Germany, Stalin's Russia*. London, UK. Allen Lane/Penguin Books.

Stackelberg, R. and Winkle, S. A. (eds). 2002. *The Nazi Germany Sourcebook: An Anthology of Texts*. London, UK. Routledge.

4 Mao and China

1 Unit Emergence of an Authoritarian Regime in China

Overview

- In the early 20th century, China suffered from a lack of unity and was politically unstable. It was dominated by foreign powers that had gained land, rights and privileges there.

- China became a republic in 1912 but its nationalist government was ineffective. A period of warlordism ensued between 1916 and 1928, when the Guomindang (GMD) captured Beijing and established a central nationalist government, with Nanjing as the capital and Jiang Jieshi as president.

- The Chinese Communist Party (CCP) was established in China in 1921, but Mao Zedong was not initially dominant. His ideology, which centred on the importance of the peasants, was at variance with mainstream Marxist thinking.

- Mao's ideology became defined during his time at Jiangxi when the communists were forced to set up base areas and form a Red Army to defend themselves against the GMD.

- A large group (including Mao) broke out and undertook the Long March of 1934–35. They established a new base at Yan'an where Mao became undisputed leader and implemented his social policies, such as land reform.

- The Second Sino-Japanese War (1937–45) briefly reunited the GMD and CCP forces and the CCP grew. After Japan's defeat in 1945, the CCP fought a civil war against the GMD. This ended in complete victory for the communists and placed Mao in the position of ruler of China.

KEY QUESTIONS

- How did political conditions in China in the early 20th century contribute to the emergence of a communist state?
- How did Mao Zedong achieve leadership of the Chinese Communist Party?
- How did the aims and ideology of the Chinese Communist Party develop under Mao?
- How did the Second Sino-Japanese War and Chinese Civil War increase communist support and bring about political change in China?

4.1 How did political conditions in China in the early 20th century contribute to the emergence of a Communist state?

China had endured '100 years of humiliation' by foreigners following its defeat in the Opium Wars of 1839–42 and 1856–60 and by the Japanese in 1894–95. Industrialising nations, led by Britain, sought to make profits in China and divided the country into 'spheres of influence'. Resentment of foreign domination provoked the Boxer Rebellion of 1898–1901.

In the early 20th century, peasants in China were struggling to survive and consequently resented heavy government taxes. Townspeople were under pressure from inflation and hostile to the corrupt government officials. Students were resentful of foreign influence and in despair at the failure of the dynasty to bring about effective reforms.

In 1911, a revolutionary uprising started in central China that brought together peasants, townspeople and students. The recognised leader of the young revolutionaries was **Sun Yat Sen**, who had formed a revolutionary league in 1905. Most of southern China was swept up in the movement that led to the proclamation of a Chinese republic. The Qing Dynasty, which had ruled China since 1644, collapsed.

Sun Yat Sen was declared president of a new National Assembly and the republic was formally established on 1 January 1912. The last emperor, six-year-old Puyi, abdicated in February. Sun resigned in March in favour of Yuan Shikai, a conservative army leader who had the loyalty of China's military forces. In August 1912, the nationalist **Guomindang** (GMD) party was formed, with Sun as its leader. The party brought together Sun's revolutionary league and other smaller revolutionary parties.

Yuan failed to live up to expectations and even tried to have himself crowned emperor. On his death in 1916, many of his former subordinates took the opportunity to seize control of their own provinces. They refused to acknowledge the authority of the republic and behaved as independent **warlords**.

The end of the First World War in Europe in 1918 increased Chinese humiliation. The 1919 Treaty of Versailles gave former German concessions in China to the Japanese, which provoked a patriotic march of students in Beijing on 4 May 1919. This was followed by nationwide demonstrations.

In 1925, the army officer **Jiang Jieshi** took over leadership of the GMD and in 1926 he undertook a campaign against the warlords. Among those supporting his efforts were communists such as the young **Mao Zedong**, who worked among the peasants of Hunan, and Zhou Enlai, who helped to organise a strike among Shanghai workers, thus allowing the GMD to take the city in 1927.

Sun Yat Sen (1866–1925)

Sun Yat Sen came from a peasant background. He was a Christian and was educated in the West. He founded the first anti-imperial organisation in 1894 and campaigned for a republic. In 1905, he founded a revolutionary league and advocated nationalism, democracy and the improvement of livelihoods through socialism. In January 1912, he became president of the new Chinese republic, but he resigned in March 1912 to avoid civil war.

Guomindang: This was the nationalist political party founded in China in 1912; it governed China from 1928 to 1949.

warlords: These were generals who commanded bands of soldiers who terrorised peasants into giving them food and paying taxes.

Jiang Jieshi (1887–1975)

(Also known as Chiang Kai-Shek) Jiang became leader of the GMD in 1925, and from 1928 he dominated the nationalist government as president and commander-in-chief of the army in China. He lost popularity by failing to enforce reforms or prevent the Japanese invasion. After the GMD's defeat by the communists, he fled to Taiwan in 1949, which he ruled until his death.

Fact:
- China is nearly fifty times the size of Britain, larger than the whole of Europe and slightly smaller than the total land area of the United States.
- In the early 20th century, the majority of the population barely had enough to eat.
- Foreigners dominated industry and trade and had settlements (concessions) where they lived by their own laws.
- Society was very structured and valued scholarship. Trade was ranked as a lowly profession.

KEY CONCEPTS QUESTION

Cause and Consequence: Draw a spider diagram to show why China was an unstable state in the early 20th century.

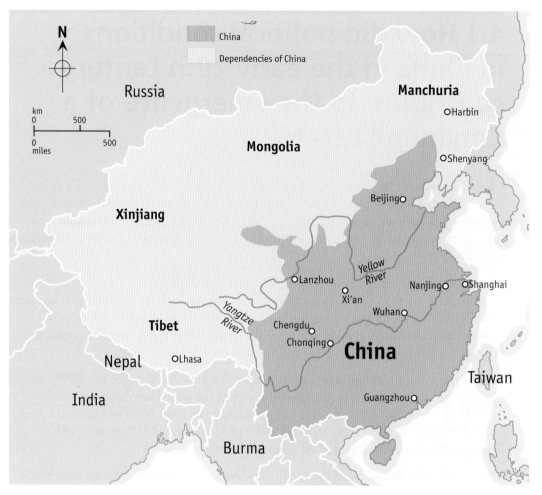

Figure 4.1 A map showing the Chinese Empire at the end of the Qing Dynasty

Nevertheless, Jiang regarded the communists as a threat to his authority. He spoke of the Japanese as a 'disease of the skin' but of the communists as 'a disease of the heart'. Consequently, after taking Shanghai, Jiang turned his army on the striking workers and their communist leaders. Thousands were killed. Jiang also expelled the GMD's Russian advisers. Such moves were popular with China's business class, who provided the GMD with financial support. Similarly, Western powers also provided loans in an attempt to keep communism out of China.

By 1928, Jiang had overcome the warlords sufficiently to capture Beijing and establish a central government with Nanjing as the capital. Jiang's nationalist government brought China a new, more stable currency and some industrial growth, but the Japanese remained in Manchuria and set up a puppet administration, Manchukuo, headed by Puyi, the former emperor.

4.2 How did Mao Zedong achieve leadership of the Chinese Communist Party?

Mao became a Marxist whilst studying and working as a library assistant at Beijing University in 1919. He came to believe that 'all power grows out of the barrel of a gun' and that violence was the only way to achieve change in China. He met and corresponded with other communist thinkers, helped to organise strikes and took part in the 4 May protest movement in 1919 against the granting of former German territory in China to Japan.

Figure 4.2 Members of the Red Army in 1927, with newly supplied Russian equipment; the Red Army was created from willing peasant recruits

The Russian **Comintern**, established in 1919 in order to spread Marxist revolution beyond Russia, encouraged the formation of the Chinese Communist Party (CCP) in 1921. The party was led by Chen Duxiu and Li Dazhao, but Mao was one of twelve delegates who attended the first National Congress of the party in July 1921.

As ordered by the Comintern, CCP members also joined the GMD in order to drive the 'imperialists' from China and bring about Chinese unity. Mao worked as a GMD political organiser in Shanghai, and in 1924 he was elected to both the Central Committee of the CCP and that of the GMD.

When Jiang Jieshi broke the alliance with the CCP in 1927, Mao developed his own brand of communism in the rural areas. He believed (contrary to Comintern advice) that communism had to be established among Chinese peasants if it was to succeed.

Mao attempted a revolt of peasants in his native Hunan in 1927, but this was bloodily suppressed. He then led his followers to a more secure base in the remote mountains of Jinggangshan. Here, he formed the communist Red Army.

Mao built up a well-disciplined and reliable force by providing basic provisions and pay and insisting that all generals, including himself, shared the hardships of the ordinary men. Although the ranks had to obey orders, they were otherwise treated as equals and could not be beaten by officers. Unlike the GMD army, the force was ordered to help the peasants. By 1928, the Red Army consisted of 12,000 men.

However, the army was poorly equipped and relied on bamboo spikes more commonly than guns. This led the army to develop guerrilla tactics. Small, lightly armed bands of Red Army soldiers merged with the civilian population, disguised as peasants, or retreated into underground tunnels linking villages to attack the larger enemy forces when and where they least expected it.

In 1929, Mao's band moved to more fertile land in the south of Jiangxi province around Ruijin, where they established a base and in 1931 set up the Jiangxi Soviet. Mao referred to the area as the 'Chinese Soviet Republic'. It contained a population of 1 million.

Mao became CCP party secretary and ordered land redistribution. Poorer peasants were encouraged to kill their richer peasant neighbours and landlords, and those who disagreed with Mao's line and those he suspected of disloyalty were purged. In 1930, Mao ordered 2,000 Red Army soldiers to be shot for staging a revolt at Futian, for example.

The Long March

Despite four different campaigns from 1930 onwards, Jiang Jieshi failed to defeat the Red Army. However, when the GMD surrounded the communist stronghold in an attempt to starve the red forces into surrender, Mao recognised the need to move elsewhere. Consequently, in October 1934, Mao and the main body of the Red Army broke through where Jiang's forces were weakest, to the west, and began their Long March. On 20 October 1935, the marchers arrived at Shaanxi. Around 5,000 of 100,000 original marchers survived the 13,000 km (8,000 mile) ordeal.

Figure 4.3 The route of the Long March

QUESTION

Why do you think that the Long March was later afforded such an important place in Maoist propaganda?

Fact: In 1936, Mao asked a US sympathiser, the Beijing school teacher Edgar Snow, to write the story of the communist movement in China. His *Red Star Over China* romanticised Mao's movement, and tens of thousands of young, educated Chinese went to Yan'an in a spirit of idealism. However, they found themselves suspected as 'bourgeois intellectuals', class-enemies or nationalist spies.

KEY CONCEPTS QUESTION

Significance: How important was the Long March in Mao's emergence as the unchallenged leader of the CCP by 1945? Make a two-column table, picking out key factors supporting the significance of the Long March on one side and listing other significant factors on the other.

collectivisation: The creation of a socialist economy by removing private ownership and making peasants work together or 'co-operatively' in order to cultivate the land.

nationalisation: State ownership of industry with control over supply and production.

The Yan'an Soviet

The surviving marchers settled in the Yan'an Soviet. Here, peasants were won over by land redistribution and rent control (a slightly milder approach than that used at Jiangxi, with no mass killings of rich peasants or landlords). Campaigns were undertaken to improve literacy and stamp out corruption, while homes, schools, hospitals and factories were created in cliff caves and huts.

Mao and the communist leadership undertook all political decision-making, but peasants and others participated in 'revolutionary committees'. Mass meetings were also held that helped to build support and increase the number of military recruits for the anti-Japanese struggle.

Mao wrote a number of political and philosophical works here, which helped him impose his personal authority. A series of 'rectification campaigns' in 1942 removed any suspected disloyalty, as men and women were forced to confess to 'crimes' that went against Mao's orders and beliefs, and were publicly stripped of possessions or posts. There were regular 'self-criticism' sessions at which everyone was encouraged to air their doubts and secrets. Not to speak at such a meeting brought even greater suspicion on an individual, but to air too many faults could lead to demotion and punishment. No outside press or radio communication was permitted to witness what was going on, and no letters could be sent to or received from the outside world.

4.3 How did the aims and ideology of the Chinese Communist Party develop under Mao?

Figure 4.4 One of the earliest editons of *The Little Red Book*, printed in 1963 prior to formal official publication in 1964

Maoist ideology, or 'Mao Zedong Thought', was the product of Mao's own peasant background and early career. Mao was introduced to Marxism at Beijing University in 1919 and developed his belief in the masses as a source of energy that could transform China. He attended the first CCP Congress in July 1921 and joined the Central Committee in 1923. However, Mao remained detached from the mainstream communist group who attributed little importance to the Chinese peasantry. While the party concentrated on the cities, Mao saw the numerically strong peasants as the leaders of revolution, and from 1924 he worked in the newly created GMD Peasant Movement Training Institute, where he increasingly formulated his own ideology, believing a vigorous organisation of the peasantry under communist leadership and a radical land policy were needed.

By the time of the Long March (1934–35) Mao's ideology was clear. His adaptation of Marxism–Leninism for a peasant mass base won support as it was seen to work. In Yan'an, he also encouraged voluntaryism, mass mobilisation and self-criticism.

The key elements of 'Mao Zedong Thought' are illustrated in Table 4.1.

Table 4.1 Mao Zedong Thought

Orthodox Marxist beliefs	
Marxist revolution	Progress would come through class struggle in which the landowners and bourgeoisie had to be overthrown. This would lead to the 'dictatorship of the proletariat' (or masses). There should be collective ownership of the means of production. Socialist states should promote worldwide communist revolution.
Specific Chinese elements	
The importance of the peasants	The peasant masses could overthrow capitalism and create a socialist society.
A two-stage revolution, as explained in Mao's *On new democracy* (1940)	The first revolution could incorporate elements of the bourgeoisie. During this stage private ownership could continue. A second revolution would bring about the **collectivisation** and **nationalisation** of property and economic resources and remove remaining elements of the bourgeoisie.
Mass mobilisation and voluntaryism	The party should 'learn from the people'. Campaigns should be people's campaigns and not be imposed from above. Properly guided, the people would support campaigns voluntarily and work in the best interests of all.
Continuous revolution	Revolution should not cease once a party achieved power but should be a constant process of renewal, to avoid complacency and corruption.
Self-criticism and rectification	Officials should undergo regular criticism to prevent them becoming self-satisfied and élitist and regular purges of the party would keep it pure. Only through self-criticism would individuals see the wisdom of mass campaigns and 'rectify' false thoughts.
Ruthless determination	Willpower and determination would be sufficient to bring about change provided everyone showed total commitment. Violence was a necessary element of revolution.
The primacy of 'Mao Zedong Thought'	Mao Zedong was always right and people could find the solution to any problem if they studied his thought sufficiently.

Fact: Mao said: 'The Red Army lives among people as a fish dwells in water.' And, in reference to tactics:
'The enemy advances, we retreat.
The enemy camps, we harass.
The enemy tires, we attack.
The enemy retreats, we pursue.'

Fact: The 'Six Principles of the Red Army' were:
- Put back all doors when leaving a house.
- Rice-stalk mattresses must all be bundled up and returned.
- Be polite. Help people when you can.
- Give back everything you borrow, even if it is only a needle.
- Pay for all things broken, even if only a chopstick.
- Do not help yourself or search for things when people are not in their houses.

Fact: Jung Chang and Jon Halliday calculated that, between 1931 and 1934, 700,000 people died at the Ruijin base. Half were murdered as 'class enemies'; the rest were worked to death or died from other causes attributable to the regime.

Fact: The Long March from Jiangxi was much celebrated in later Maoist mythology. However, there is evidence that Mao was not the initial leader of the march – nor even automatically selected to take part in it (see Xinran, *Chinese Witness*). Hurdles included crossing the swollen Dadu River by a suspension bridge that had been sabotaged and had no planks on the first section.

4

4.4 How did the Second Sino-Japanese War and Chinese Civil War increase communist support and bring about political change in China?

A full-scale attack on China by the Japanese in 1937 led Jiang Jieshi to approach the CCP once again to form a United Front. This enabled the communists to expand their army and develop their guerrilla tactics, tying down some Japanese forces in the north. However, in 1941, Jiang broke his agreement and again attacked communist forces in the south – an action portrayed by the communists as unprincipled. When the USA and Britain entered the war in the Far East, following the Japanese attack on Pearl Harbour in December 1941, Jiang's government was accused of dependence on foreign allies. The CCP, on the other hand, was able to advertise itself as the only true Chinese patriot.

The outbreak of civil war between the GMD and CCP followed the ending of the Second World War. In 1945, the Allies recognised the legitimacy of Jiang Jieshi's government in China (even though it only controlled a fraction of that country's territory) and gave China a seat on the Security Council of the United Nations.

The USA continued to supply aid, arms and advisers to Jiang and helped the nationalists to move back into areas of northern China and Manchuria that had been liberated by the Soviet Red Army. The communists resisted this move and reinforced their soldiers with weapons captured from the Japanese and handed over to them by the former Russian occupation forces.

Despite US attempts to bring agreement between Mao Zedong and Jiang Jieshi, fighting broke out over the nationalists' attempt to reclaim Manchuria. A ceasefire, agreed under US auspices in January 1946, failed to hold and in July 1946 the GMD launched a major offensive against the communist forces in Manchuria and a full-scale civil war broke out.

Fact: Mao's most influential writing was *On new democracy* (1940), which suggested that China had to adopt a 'third form' of democracy, involving a two-stage revolution that was different from both the democracy of the capitalist West and the communist system as practised in Soviet Russia.

Although the nationalists and communists had been struggling for power since 1927, it was the civil war of 1946–49 that, against all the odds, secured Mao as ruler of China. In 1946, Mao's communist military forces were reorganised as a single army, known as the People's Liberation Army (PLA), and given a unified command. In the fierce four-year struggle, the PLA defeated Jiang Jieshi's forces, despite Jiang's US aid and the fickleness of Soviet Union leader Joseph Stalin, who, to the end, engaged in negotiations with Jiang.

The table below illustrates some of the strengths and weaknesses of each side and helps to explain the ultimate communist victory in the civil war.

Strengths and weaknesses of the GMD and CCP/PLA in the civil war, 1946–49

Issue	Nationalists – GMD	Communists – CCP/PLA
Troops	Army larger and better equipped than the communists' army (2,800,000 troops at the start of the war); had an air force; experienced in conventional fighting; able to take initiative in the early stages. But troops were largely conscripts with low morale and poor training.	Had fewer troops than the nationalists (no more than 800,000 at the start of the war); were poorly equipped and had no aircraft. But by June 1948 armies were roughly equal in size; soldiers trained as pilots; experienced in guerrilla warfare; morale and discipline were good.
Territory	Controlled most territory and population/most large cities/most of railway network and main waterways at outbreak of war. But control could depend on local warlords; behaviour of soldiers lost some support from local populations.	19 base areas with main base at Yan'an at outbreak of war. But from 1948 took cities; key railway junction (Jinzhou) gave control of Manchuria; controlled whole of northern China including Beijing by January 1949 and most of the south and west during 1949.
Foreign powers	Recognised by other powers (including Soviet Union) as legitimate government; the USA gave almost $3 billion in aid, provided equipment and military assistance; Soviet Union signed treaty of alliance and tried to curb Mao. But the USA was critical of Jiang's style of rule and the Russian Red Army aided the PLA in the early stages.	Soviet troops in Manchuria gave PLA forces training (e.g. as pilots), and equipment at the outset. But Stalin ordered that cities be given to the nationalists in November 1945 (although the PLA retained Harbin). Stalin urged Mao not to send forces across the Yangtze River to the south in 1949, but Mao ignored him.
Popular support	Had ten years' experience of running a one-party state; used police, army and harsh reprisals to keep peasants and workers in check. But noted for corruption, inefficiency, minimal reform, inflation and rationing; had poor reputation from struggle against the Japanese; were reliant on wealthy businessmen and landlords; did not try to build up mass support.	Supported by peasantry who feared revenge if an area was recaptured by the GMD; had a good reputation from the struggle against the Japanese; kept troops restrained, took steps to control prices; used propaganda to win support (particularly targeted at the young). But only controlled Harbin and a few cities at the outset; dealt harshly with those who did not conform.

(continued)

QUESTION

Which elements of 'Mao Zedong Thought' do you think would be most effective in attracting support to get into power?

KEY CONCEPTS QUESTION

Significance and Perspectives: With a partner, consider whether Maoist ideology was constructive or destructive. Justify your views to the rest of the class.

ACTIVITY

Using the information contained in the table, explain why the communists won the civil war that took place in China between 1946 and 1949.

Theory of knowledge

History and the masses: Is it realistic to be able to run a state through mass mobilisation?

ACTIVITY

Draw a diagram to show the long- and short-term causes of the civil war that broke out in China in 1946.

Issue	Nationalists – GMD	Communists – CCP/PLA
Leadership	Jiang: experienced, hard-working, confident, ruthless; controlled military strategy. But could be stubborn, inflexible, not good at delegation, poor judge of character, relied on corrupt advisers.	Mao: personality cult, inspired confidence; allowed field commanders to fight without interference. But insisted on defending a pass between China and Manchuria (November 1945), which failed; not good in dealings with foreign powers.
Military factors	Early advantages – Yan'an taken, March 1947. But sent best troops to Manchuria before establishing control of northern and central China; lost Manchuria in early 1948; no retreats allowed; generals corrupt, incompetent; communication lines long; troops in cities had to be supplied by air; increasing surrenders without fighting (e.g. Beijing, January 1949).	Guerilla warfare maintained pressure, and once men were trained, from 1948, began conventional warfare; in spring 1948, retook Yan'an, which was a psychological boost; **Lin Biao** organised the army, capturing transport links to isolate GMD forces in cities. But initially inferior in equipment and numbers.

Lin Biao (1908–1971)

Lin Biao attended the Whampoa Military Academy and became an able military commander for the CCP. He transformed the PLA into a modern army. In 1949, he was ranked second in the governing hierarchy and recognised as heir to Mao. He became minister of defence in 1959 and was responsible for the support that some army units gave Mao during the Cultural Revolution. However, he apparently died in a plane crash in Mongolia in September 1971, after what was declared to be a failed coup to oust Mao.

Zhou Enlai (1898–1976)

Zhou Enlai attended university in Japan, but returned to China in 1919 and became involved in the 4 May movement (see section 4.2). He went to France and returned to join the Military Academy at Whampoa in 1924. He worked there as a deputy political director during the United Front period. In 1927, he joined the Central Committee of the CCP and from 1949 he served Mao as prime minister and third in the hierarchy (after Lin Biao). He was regarded as a moderate, particularly in foreign affairs.

On 1 October 1949, Mao Zedong gave a triumphant victory speech from the Gate of Heavenly Peace (formerly the entrance to the Imperial Palace) in the capital of Beijing. The crowds cheered as Mao, **Zhou Enlai** and other communist leaders watched a procession of Red Army soldiers, peasant fighters and other party workers. As they did so, the communist forces were still sweeping west and south almost unopposed. Jiang, with the remaining members of his army and government, fled to Taiwan (a group of islands off the east coast of mainland China) and declared it to be the seat of the legitimate Chinese government. Jiang Jieshi ruled Taiwan as the Republic of China (ROC) and until 1971 it was recognised by many Western nations and by the UN as the only legitimate government of China, with a seat on the security council. However, it seemed only a matter of time before he would be ousted.

SOURCE B

We announce the establishment of the People's Republic of China. Our nation will from now on enter the large family of peace-loving and freedom-loving nations of the world. It will work bravely and industriously to create its own civilisation and happiness and will, at the same time, promote world peace and freedom. Our nation will never again be an insulted nation. We have stood up.

An extract from Mao Zedong's victory speech, 1 October 1949. Quoted in Schools Council. 1977. *Rise of Communist China (Modern World Studies)*. Edinburgh, UK. Holmes McDougall. p. 41.

Figure 4.5 Mao Zedong proclaiming the founding of the People's Republic of China (PRC) in Beijing, 1 October 1949

End of unit activities

1 Make a thematic chart to illustrate why China became a communist state in 1949.
   You could look at:
   a political factors
   b economic factors
   c social factors
   d military factors
   e the influence of individuals.

**Cause and
Consequence:**
The class should work
in two halves. One half
should make a case
that the Nationalists
were responsible
for the outbreak of
the civil war and the
other half should
make a case for the
communists. After
hearing the views from
each side, take a class
vote on the issue.

Theory of knowledge

History and the value
of evidence:
According to Harrison
Salisbury, 'I don't think that
there was much natural
cruelty in Mao's make-up. He
didn't exercise cruelty for the
sake of cruelty. He didn't mind
using it if it was necessary, but
he was not a man who got his
kicks that way. He was a man
who saw life as being very
cruel.'

Was the way Mao ruled in
Jiangxi and Yan'an cruel?
From what standpoint
should a historian judge
Mao's behaviour? Most of
the material we have on
Mao's early life comes from
interviews that he gave
while at Yan'an. What are
the problems posed by such
evidence?

2 Imagine you were a student arriving at Yan'an in the late 1930s. Write a few
pages of your diary, giving your impressions, hopes, fears and other relevant
details.

3 Find out more about Mao's own writings. Collect and share extracts from
his works, explaining what these extracts can tell you about Mao and his
ideology.

4 Write two speeches:
   a a speech that Mao might have given on winning the civil war and taking control
      of the Chinese government
   b a speech that Jiang Jieshi might have given after losing the civil war and fleeing to
      Taiwan.

5 Who supported Mao's brand of Chinese communism? Look back through the
chapter and make a list of supporters and the reasons for their support.

Consolidating and Maintaining Power

Overview

- The CCP set up a new structure of government that paid lip service to 'democratic principles' but in which the party was dominant and shared many of the personnel of the state government.
- The army was used to secure unity and dominance over outlying areas, such as Tibet.
- Mao had a vision for the future of China which he pursued single-mindedly and with the support of extensive propaganda campaigns.
- Mass movements, local committees and rectification campaigns ensured surveillance and control over the population.
- Although there was virtually no outright opposition to the regime, Mao persecuted 'rightists' and 'bourgeois elements' through struggle sessions and mass campaigns.
- The police, courts and legal system were entirely in the party's hands and the prison camps removed opponents and kept others in check.
- Mao conducted purges within the Chinese Communist Party, including the removal of former colleagues and loyal supporters.
- Mao wanted China to be its own master in international diplomacy; his achievements helped to reinforce China's independent path to Communism and had propagandist value in binding the state.

KEY QUESTIONS
- How did Mao consolidate his power to create an authoritarian regime between 1949 and 1954?
- What part did personality and propaganda play in the consolidation and maintenance of power?
- What were the main characteristics of Mao's political control between 1954 and 1976?
- What was the nature and extent of opposition to Mao's communist rule and how was it dealt with?
- What was the impact of international affairs and foreign policy on Mao's consolidation and maintenance of power?

TIMELINE
1949 Oct: Mao becomes Chairman of the People's Republic of China (PRC)

1950 Mar: suppression of counter-revolutionaries begins

Jun: launch of land reform programme

Nov: 'resist America and aid Korea' campaign is launched

1950 Sino-Soviet treaty

1951 Dec: the Three Antis campaign is launched

1952 Jan: the Five Antis campaign is launched; all political parties except CCP are banned

1954 Feb: purge of Gao Gang and Rao Shushi

1956 May: the Hundred Flowers campaign is launched

1957 Jul: the Anti-Rightist campaign is launched; MoscowConference

1958 Jul: Great Leap Forward is launched; Mao and Khrushchev meet in Beijing

1959 Apr: Mao steps down as chairman of the People's Republic of China

Sep: Peng Dehuai is purged

1961 Soviet advisers withdrawn from China; China's walkout from Moscow Conference

1962 Sep: Socialist Education Movement is announced; Sino-Indian war

1963 Chinese attack on USSR's policy of peaceful coexistence

1964 China produces atom bomb

1966 May: Cultural Revolution begins

1966 Jul: Liu Shaoqi is dismissed from the post of party deputy chairman

Dec: Deng Xiaoping is forced to withdraw from public life

1971 Sep: Lin Biao dies in mysterious circumstances; PRC replaces Taiwan on UN Security Council

1972 Visit of President Nixon to China

1973 Apr: Deng Xiaoping is rehabilitated

1976 Jan: Zhou Enlai dies

Jul: Deng Xiaoping is removed again

Sep: Mao Zedong dies

Figure 4.6 Chinese athletes carrying a huge portrait of Mao Zedong at a parade in Tiananmen Square, Beijing, 1 October 1955

4.5 How did Mao consolidate his power to create an authoritarian regime between 1949 and 1954?

After 1949, Mao had to act with speed and efficiency to maintain his hard-won position. He needed to establish stable and effective government, restore unified control over the former Chinese Empire and fulfil promises of social reform and economic recovery after the war with Japan and the civil war.

Government

The Chinese People's Political Consultative Conference met in September 1949, bringing together non-communist parties and other groups that had opposed the GMD under communist leadership. This produced a temporary constitution that allowed the participation of other parties in a multi-party 'people's democratic dictatorship'. However, the dominance of the communists was without question.

Five 'black' categories were identified:

- reactionary elements
- feudal elements

Fact: The constitution of 1949 was not democratic in the Western sense of the word. Although non-reactionaries were granted a vote to an elected National People's Congress, there was seldom a choice of candidates, although voters were able to discuss beforehand, at public meetings, who should appear on the ballot paper.

- lackeys of imperialism
- bureaucratic capitalists
- enemies of the people.

These groups were considered 'non-people', and had no political rights, although they were still subject to state law. Most country landlords, people with big businesses and prominent ex–GMD supporters found themselves classified in this way. However, the 'national bourgeoisie' and 'petty bourgeoisie' were given civil rights, alongside the peasants and workers, in an attempt to harness their expertise. Mao needed their businesses and skills in these early years and was prepared to compromise, although taxes were used to limit private profit.

The country was divided into six regions, each under the control of a bureau dominated by the military. Most of the 2 million officials who had served the GMD government were retained, as at first there were only 750,000 party cadres available to take on essential administrative responsibilities. As CCP membership and administrative competence increased, the non-communists were gradually removed. (The outbreak of the Korean War in 1950 encouraged this process as fears about the reliability of non-communists were heightened.)

In 1954, a formal constitution established China as a single-party state. The chairman of the National People's Congress, Mao, became the head of government. Beneath him were two vice-chairmen and a council of ministers headed by the prime minister. Zhou Enlai was prime minister from 1949 until his death in 1976. The provincial administration, which had local powers, supported the Congress.

Fact: Party cadres were important at all levels of government and administration, in the legal system, in education and in the PLA. They organised the mass organisations and local committees and meetings, providing a means of surveillance and control. In return they enjoyed a privileged lifestyle with an 'iron rice bowl' – guaranteed employment and income for life in return for their absolute loyalty.

Theory of knowledge

The meaning of democracy: What is the difference between 'democracy' in China and democracy in Western states? Is one better than the other? Why?

Figure 4.7   A retouched picture released in 1953 by the Chinese official news agency showing Zhou Enlai (right) and Mao Zedong (left); notice the favoured 'communist' style of dress

Mao and China

Fact: In the Korean War (1950–53) the North Koreans tried to extend their communist regime to South Korea. The southerners, aided by the USA, drove them back and invaded their territory. Mao chose to help North Korea, possibly to provide further reasons to demand solidarity and loyalty from his people.

Fact: The fines imposed on businessmen during the mass campaigns were often used to push them into going 'state-private'. Private owners sold part of their business to the state and a state manager was appointed to work alongside the private businessman.

An important feature of the new state was the organisation of the population into groups. Everyone in a village, street, office, factory or school was required to meet regularly to hear about and comment on policies. The local party cadres were expected to 'educate' their groups and to pass views to branch secretaries and up through an ascending pyramid to the central committee – the politburo in Beijing. Consequently, in accordance with Maoist ideology, peasants in the villages and soldiers and workers on the factory floor could influence official decisions.

Mao's consolidation of power was built on a series of mass mobilisation campaigns, in the course of which, propaganda, self-criticism, rectification and purges (see section 4.8, Historiography) were used to stamp out any opposition or 'bourgeois individualism'.

Between 1950 and 1952 there were four mass mobilisation campaigns.

The resist America and aid Korea campaign, 1950

Rallies were held to increase Chinese suspicion of foreigners, particularly those from the West. People from the USA were singled out because of their involvement in Korea. Many foreigners, including missionaries, were arrested. Christian churches were closed and priests and nuns were expelled. By the end of 1950, the country was closed to all foreigners except Russians, and institutions with links to the West were watched or closed down.

The Suppression of Counter-Revolutionaries campaign, 1950–51

This focused on those with links to the GMD, criminal gangs and religious sects. There were numbers of denunciations and public executions.

The Three Antis campaign, 1951

This was a campaign against corruption, waste and obstruction, and was directed against communists and non-communists. Managers, state officials, police and cadres were obliged to take part in struggle sessions. Humiliation and group pressure were employed to bring them into line.

The Five Antis campaign, 1952

This was a campaign against bribery, tax-evasion, theft of state property, cheating in government contracts and economic espionage. Workers' organisations were invited to investigate employers' business affairs, forcing employers to provide self-criticisms and undergo 'thought reform'. The accused faced fines, property confiscations and periods in labour camps. If they confessed and paid their dues, they were (unlike the landlords) usually allowed to return to their work. Few were executed although around 2–3 million committed suicide because of the shame and humiliation.

Unified control

KEY CONCEPTS QUESTION

Change and Continuity: What changed, and what remained the same in China between 1949 and 1954?

In 1949, the GMD still controlled much of south-west China. Fighting continued in 1950, by which time only British Hong Kong, Portuguese Macao, Outer Mongolia, Taiwan and a few small GMD-controlled islands lay outside communist control. Mao's plan to invade Taiwan at the end of 1950 had to be called off when the Korean War broke out, although success in that war enhanced Mao's reputation further. He also made administrative arrangements to bring different ethnic groups into the PRC (see section 4.17).

Strong resistance in Tibet (see section 4.17) took six months to crush. The nation was captured and renamed Xizang in 1950 and its people were subjected to severe repression in an attempt to eradicate all traces of the Tibetan language and culture. Tibetans were also moved to other parts of China and **Han Chinese** were brought in.

By 1954, the CCP had built up its membership to 6.1 million and there was no longer a shortage of ideologically trustworthy officials. Industrial and agricultural production were showing signs of strong growth and the budget was balanced. Thus Mao felt the time was ripe to push the revolution into its second stage with the full implementation of communism in both the economic and social spheres.

Han Chinese: The Han were the dominant Chinese race (and the largest ethnic group in the world) comprising 92 per cent of the population of mainland China.

4.6 What part did personality and propaganda play in the consolidation and maintenance of power?

Personality

There is no doubt that Mao was an ideologically committed individual who was driven by the desire to make China a powerful, self-sufficient and influential state. He proved an inspirational leader in the struggle for power, and once in power he achieved cult status and became a figure of reverence.

His portrait appeared on public hoardings and in the newspapers. Peasants, industrial workers and soldiers were expected to learn Mao's quotations by heart and, during the Cultural Revolution (refer to section 4.7, Political control during the Cultural Revolution, 1966–76), to study *The Little Red Book* of Mao's speeches and writings. Mao was portrayed as the saviour of the nation, the voice of truth, the source of all wisdom and the benefactor of the people. The Chinese were persuaded that a careful study of 'Mao Zedong Thought' could solve their problems and enable them to carry out their tasks more effectively. Carefully stage-managed rallies and meetings showed Mao addressing the adoring crowds. Events, such as Mao's swim down the Yangtze River in July 1966 (see section 4.10), symbolising his strength and purpose, occupied the media for weeks.

However, whether Mao was a 'visionary reformer', as his supporters have maintained, or whether he was driven by an ambition that overrode all moral scruples, as has been the view of critics, remains an area for debate (see section 4.18, What kind of ruler was Mao?).

Fact: Mao Zedong launched a 'Cultural Revolution' in 1966 in order to reassert his authority and beliefs. He called on China's youth to rise up in order to purge the nation of the 'four olds' (old customs, old culture, old habits and old ideas) and revive the revolutionary spirit. This 'revolution' continued until Mao's death in 1976.

SOURCE A

Backed by the immense cult of his personality, Mao, who thought himself capable of changing human nature through his mass campaigns, could demand complete loyalty to the cause of revolution as he chose to define it. Nobody and nothing could be excused from utter dedication and readiness to contribute whatever was demanded. Private life meant nothing. People were a blank sheet of paper, mere numbers to be used as the leader saw fit. Marxist autocracy reached heights of totalitarianism unparalleled by Hitler or Stalin.

Fenby, J. 2008. *The Penguin History of Modern China 1850–2008*. London, UK. Allen Lane/ Penguin Books. p. 526.

Theory of knowledge

History and cult of personality:
How important is individual personality in politics?

Propaganda

The propaganda system was central to communist rule in China. Propaganda was controlled by the CCP's Central Propaganda Department, which commanded a network of local branches that were used for mass indoctrination. The aim was to bring about 'thought reform' so that the population would support mass campaigns such as the Great Leap Forward of 1958 (see section 4.12, Collectivisation and the Great Leap Forward,

Figure 4.8 'Hail the defeat of revisionism in our China', a propaganda poster from 1967

1958) and the 1966–76 Cultural Revolution. The PLA, which remained the largest army in the world, also helped indoctrinate and reinforce political messages. Although thought reform was practised in other totalitarian states, according to William Bradbury (1968), the CCP 'set about it more purposefully, more massively, and more intensively than have other ruling groups'.

Propaganda was used to spread ideology, encourage activism and hold out examples of selfless model workers and soldiers. An example is Lei Feng, a possibly fictitious soldier of the civil war years, whose overwhelming sense of duty embodied the desired image of self-sacrifice. Highlights of the communist past, such as the Long March or the struggles of Mao at Jiangxi and Yan'an, were spread as inspiration. Revolutionaries in the Developing World and allies such as Albania and North Korea were praised, while the 'imperialists' of the USA and the 'revisionists' of the Soviet Union, who had betrayed communism, were attacked.

Ideological messages and the cult of Mao were spread through posters, the media, the education system, literature, films, theatre, music, radio and television (although TV ownership was not common). It was also disseminated by the work of local groups, committees and propaganda teams. There was a particular emphasis on political study groups, led by party cadres, where everyone would be persuaded of the value of particular policies through the study of political articles.

A nationwide system of loudspeakers reached into every village, and reading newspapers was regarded as a 'political obligation'. China Central Television (set up in 1958) offered a diet of televised propaganda, while the *People's Daily* (established in 1948) conveyed propaganda in print. Political campaigns were launched through leading articles in the *People's Daily*, and reports criticised political adversaries, while controversial news stories were censored.

Fact: The PLA comprised 5 million soldiers in 1950, and despite a partial demobilisation to release more men into productive work, it still comprised 3.5 million soldiers in 1953. Some 800,000 conscripts were added each year, with each serving three years. This gave young Chinese men training in warfare and indoctrination in communist ideology. The force itself served a propagandist role – its achievements were celebrated and its heroes held up as role models.

KEY CONCEPTS QUESTION

Significance and Perspectives: How important was propaganda in the Maoist state? Find a propaganda poster and explain its significance to your class.

4.7 What were the main characteristics of Mao's political control between 1954 and 1976?

Political control in China was based on the Chinese Communist Party, which made all policy decisions. The party administration, under Mao, paralleled the administrative structure of the state. Ministers and provincial officials were usually members of the CCP. When they were not, they were assisted by a communist adviser. Most army officials (assisted by political commissars), heads of factories and heads of villages were Chinese Communist Party cadres, as were most heads of schools and universities.

The state constitution of 1954 provided a framework for the development of a legal system in China, modelled on that of the Soviet Union. A committee of the National People's Congress was given the power to appoint and dismiss judges and enact legal codes. Each citizen was granted the right to a public trial and defence by a 'people's lawyer' and there was, in theory, equality before the law. However, none of this was practised until after Mao's death.

Historical debate: With the Hundred Flowers campaign, Mao may have wanted to experiment by allowing some 'democratic check' on the party, spurring it to still greater endeavours (the view of Philip Short), or he may have simply felt it necessary to provide an outlet for critics to 'let off steam'. Jung Chang, however, believes that he intentionally set a trap to flush out intellectuals and opponents.

During the Maoist era party committees replaced courts, and despite some effort to make the legal system work between 1954 and 1957, the belief that different standards should be applied to class enemies destroyed any real sense of justice. The party leadership declared itself to have absolute power in legal matters and gave an increasing amount of control and judicial authority to the masses. Many judicial functions were passed to local cadres and by the 1960s the court system existed only for public 'show trials' during the Cultural Revolution. Throughout his years of political control, Mao never allowed himself to feel that his position was secure. He was continuously concerned that officials were backsliding or plotting against him. Consequently, Mao continued to look for ways to consolidate his power further and ensure the 'revolution' was never forgotten.

The Hundred Flowers campaign, 1956–57

In 1956, Mao lifted censorship restrictions and encouraged open criticism of the way the party had been working. In February 1957, he announced: 'Letting a hundred flowers blossom and a hundred schools of thought contend is the policy for promoting progress in the arts and the sciences and a flourishing socialist culture in our land.'

Participation was slow at first, and in February 1957 Mao told the people that they could vent their criticisms as long as they were 'constructive' ('among the people') rather than 'hateful and destructive' ('between the enemy and ourselves').

In May and June 1957, the central government received a deluge of letters. Magazine articles and posters appeared and there were rallies in the streets. Students at Beijing University created a 'Democratic Wall' and complained about political corruption, Russian influence, low living standards, censorship of foreign literature, economic corruption and the privileged lifestyle of party cadres and the leadership of the CCP itself.

Mao claimed such activity went beyond 'healthy criticism'. In early July 1957, he called off the campaign and reimposed censorship and orthodoxy. He had either achieved his aim of entrapment or severely misjudged the scale of criticism that the campaign would unleash.

The Anti-Rightist campaign, July 1957

The crackdown that followed the Hundred Flowers campaign ended any criticism by the intellectuals, who never again trusted Mao. Around half a million were branded as 'rightists' and subjected to persecution, ranging from imprisonment, time in labour camps and spells in the countryside for 're-education', to public shootings as a warning to others. Many committed suicide.

Mao's disappearance from public life

In 1959, once it was clear the Great Leap Forward had failed (see section 4.12, Collectivisation and the Great Leap Forward, 1958), Mao gave up his position as PRC chairman and the mass mobilisation campaigns ceased for a while. Mao claimed this time away from public life gave him the opportunity to think and plan rather than worry about daily administration. However, Philip Short has suggested that he still remained a powerful influence, and the purge of **Peng Dehuai** in 1959 would seem to support this.

In July 1959, Peng criticised Mao's economic policies (see section 4.12, Did Mao succeed in making China a great economic power?). His removal from the politburo

Peng Dehuai (1898–1974)

Peng joined the CCP in 1927 and participated in the Long March. He served in the civil war and he was a member of the politburo, China's defence minister from 1954 to 1959, and marshall of the PLA from 1955. He was removed from all posts in 1959 and placed under house arrest. He was brutally treated during the Cultural Revolution including being beaten in public spectacles 130 times.

Deng Xiaoping (1904–97)

The son of a peasant, Deng joined the Chinese Communist Party while on a work-study programme in France in the 1920s. He studied in Moscow from 1926 to 1927 and was one of the members of the Long March. He was a military leader during the civil war and after 1949 became an important figure in the economic restructuring. He became general secretary of the party's Central Committee in 1956, but he was denounced at the beginning of the Cultural Revolution in 1966. He was purged twice, but was paramount leader of the People's Republic of China from 1978 to 1992.

and his position as minister of defence set an example to others of the dangers of independent thought.

From 1962, Mao again became obsessed by a fear that the party was turning to the 'capitalist road' – a euphemism for the more moderate policies being pursued by **Deng Xiaoping** and **Liu Shaoqi**. He tried to mobilise the masses in the Socialist Education Movement of 1962. However, it was not until 1966 that he had the power base from which to launch the Cultural Revolution.

Political control during the Cultural Revolution, 1966–76

The launch of the 'great proletarian Cultural Revolution' brought a dramatic purge of Mao's rivals. Mao mobilised the Red Guards, who were bands of radical students, and ordered them to attack the 'four olds' (thought, culture, practices and customs) and remove 'bad elements' among the party, teachers, intellectuals and former bourgeoisie. Terrifying assaults were permitted and the police were instructed not to intervene. Public denunciations, struggle sessions at which victims were expected to 'confess' to their crimes, and mass mobilisation were practised in their most extreme form. Tens of thousands died in prison (for more information on the Cultural Revolution, see unit 4.3).

During this period, Mao removed many of his opponents from the party and retook absolute control of the party hierarchy. His 'cult' rose to new extremes and Mao Zedong Thought was even written into the Chinese constitution in 1969. In May 1966, Mao purged the '**Group of Five**'. Originally set up to carry through the Cultural Revolution, the group's members supported Deng Xiaoping and Liu Shaoqi. Mao replaced the group with the Central Cultural Revolution Group, which he packed with his own supporters including his wife Jiang Qing. In July, Liu Shaoqi was dismissed from his post of party deputy chairman and in December Deng Xiaoping was forced to withdraw from public life.

In December 1968, when the Cultural Revolution threatened to get out of hand, Mao ordered the Red Guards to leave the cities and go to the countryside. The struggle continued, but Mao's grip on developments may not have been as firm as he would have liked. Furthermore, Mao was still concerned about rivals in the party. He confirmed Lin Biao as his successor in 1969, but in September 1971 Lin died in an air crash over Mongolia. The story was put about that he had been planning a coup to overthrow Mao. Whether that was true or not, it showed Mao's fear of challenge. Lin had opposed Mao's decision to seek cooperation with the USA, a move which led to both nations pledging to work towards full diplomatic relations. Deng Xiaoping, on the other hand, had spoken in favour of this new beginning in Chinese–US relations. Consequently, Deng was allowed back as vice-premier in 1973.

However, after Deng's close colleague, Prime Minister Zhou Enlai, was diagnosed with cancer and looked close to death, the radicals turned on Deng again. In 1975, he was asked to draw up a series of self-criticisms, and following Zhou's death in January 1976 the **Gang of Four** launched the 'criticise Deng and oppose the rehabilitation of right-leaning elements' campaign. Mao therefore selected the relatively obscure Hua Guofeng, in preference to Deng, as the new prime minister. When mass mourning for Zhou sparked disturbances in Tiananmen Square, Deng was held responsible and demoted from all leadership positions. Deng was saved further disgrace by Mao's death in the same year and returned as the dominant figure in Chinese politics from 1978.

Liu Shaoqi (1898–1969)
Liu Shaoqi joined the CCP in 1921 and trained in the Soviet Union as a communist organiser and theorist in the 1920s. He was a close ally of Mao during the Yan'an years and was recognised as Mao's chosen successor in 1943. He succeeded Mao as chairman of the republic in 1959, but he was denounced during the Cultural Revolution for 'taking the capitalist road', opposing the communes. He was expelled from the CCP in October 1968 and died in prison.

Group of Five: This term refers to the committee established in January 1965 to initiate a revolution in China's culture. It was led by Peng Zhen (the fifth most senior member of the politburo and mayor of Beijing). However, only one of its five members (Kang Sheng) was a firm supporter of Mao. Their failure to act vigorously enough led to the dismissal of Peng as mayor and the dissolution of the committee in May 1966.

Gang of Four: This term refers to a powerful political group that was created in 1974. It consisted of four CCP officials who oversaw the suppression of a wide variety of traditional cultural activities during the Cultural Revolution. Its members were Jiang Qing (Mao's wife), Zhang Chunqiao, Yao Wenyuan and Wang Hongwen.

4

Fact: Mao commanded the loyalty of Lin Biao, who had replaced Peng Dehuai as minister of defence in 1959 and led the PLA. He also had powerful support from his wife, Jiang Qing, and a group of radicals in Shanghai who were determined to rid China of bourgeois and Western influences and create a proletarian society.

Fact: Red Guards broke into Liu Shaoqi's house, physically attacked him and forced him to write his own confession. Liu was removed from all his positions and expelled from the party in October 1968. He died in prison in November 1969 after being refused proper medical treatment for diabetes and pneumonia.

Fact: After Liu's death in 1969, power was concentrated in the hands of the CCP chairman (Mao himself) and he assumed the ceremonial duties associated with the head of state. Not until after Mao's death was a new head of state appointed when Soong Ching-ling, the widow of Sun Yat Sen and former vice-chairwoman of the PRC, was made honorary president as confirmed by the constitution of 1982.

4.8 What was the nature and extent of opposition to Mao's communist rule and how was it dealt with?

Mao deliberately cultivated an atmosphere of vigilance, fear and uncertainty within China. Although there was virtually no outright opposition to Mao after his success in the Civil War, opposition to Maoist thinking was identified with 'bourgeois and intellectual elements', the landlord class and complacent members of the party, all of which were subject to persecution. The term 'rightist' was used to refer to those with bourgeois, intellectual or foreign connections, and these became the victims of both mass and individual campaigns.

There was a central investigation department within the CCP from 1949, a military intelligence wing of the PLA and, during the Cultural Revolution, the Central Case Examination Group (headed by Kang Sheng) was also set up. From 1951, official residence permits were needed for those over fifteen years old and a special government department was created to draw up a *dangan* (dossier) on every suspect Chinese person.

From the earliest days, citizens were encouraged to inform on others. For example, in the autumn of 1951 6,500 intellectuals and university professors were obliged to undertake courses in communist thinking, artists and writers who refused to support the remove them after struggle sessions.

The repressive methods used followed those that had been practised at Yan'an. Group criticism sessions, or struggle sessions, where individuals were required to practise self-criticism and invite the criticism of others, were organised daily or weekly by work units and neighbourhood and street committees. There were also larger mass meetings (of which there were no fewer than 3,000 in Shanghai in February 1952). Individuals admitted crimes or publicly denounced colleagues and neighbours.

Admissions of guilt led to 'rectification', ranging from ritual humiliation, fines, loss of job, property and housing, a period in the countryside undertaking physically strenuous and menial tasks to reform habits, or a prison sentence in a *laogai* (labour camp). Although executions were not a normal outcome of such activity, many committed suicide rather than face further humiliation.

Activity

Find out more about a struggle session and present your findings to the class. *Wild Swans: Three Daughters of China* (1991) by Jung Chang has plenty of material on this.

Historiography

Chang and Halliday have observed that the **struggle sessions** differentiated Mao's China from Stalin's Soviet Union and Hitler's Germany. While other dictators carried out purges through an élite secret police force, which removed victims silently to prison, camps or death, Mao enforced ritualised public humiliation. Meetings proved a potent force of control, leaving people with little free time for 'private thoughts'. He increased the number of persecutors by having his victims tormented by their own associates and used party members to terrorise their own party.

Labour camps

A network of labour camps, known as *laogai* or 're-education through labour', was created soon after Mao came to power. Initally the CCP used Soviet advisers in establishing the camps and, as in the Russian Gulags, prisoners were used as slave labour for back-breaking projects. On average, 10 million prisoners per year were held in the camps under Mao, and by 1976 there were more than 10,000 labour camps spread across China.

Many of the worst camps were deliberately built in the most inhospitable regions, unbearably col Historiography d in winter and correspondingly hot in summer. Food rations were dependent on confessions. Refusal could lead to solitary confinement, beatings and sleep deprivation, when prisoners were interrogated at night. Threats to their families or signed 'confessions' from colleagues or families increased the pressure. Many prisoners died from hunger, ill-treatment or suicide.

The camps helped to terrify others into obedience. If a prisoner was executed, the family could be sent the bullet and a bill for the cost. Even released prisoners faced a constant threat of re-arrest and families of those imprisoned were deemed guilty by association and shunned by their neighbours. Ex-prisoners would have difficulty finding housing and jobs, as well as shops that would sell to them and schools to which they could send their children.

Repression

The notion of 'continuous revolution' (see 4.3) also meant that some of those who had served the party loyally in its early years eventually became its victims in political

Figure 4.9 A poster depicting Mao as the peasants' hero, 1951

KEY CONCEPTS QUESTION

Change and Continuity: Create a timeline of Mao's rule indicating the key ways in which he asserted his authority and forced change. How different was communist China in 1976 compared to what it had been in 1954?

struggle session: This term refers to a session in which 'accused' individuals were taken before a panel, usually in public, to listen to a catalogue of their alleged crimes and moral failings. They were deliberately humiliated and required to look down. Sometimes guards held the victims in the 'jet-plane' position, with the head down and arms thrust back. They had placards placed around their necks or wore a necklace of ping-pong balls to symbolise their bourgeois love of jewellery, and were beaten with bamboo sticks. They were expected to make full confessions and agree with their accusers.

Theory of knowledge

History and autobiography: How should a historian use autobiographies such as that of Chang? Can an autobiography (or even a biography) ever be truly impartial?

Fact: According to Chang and Halliday's figures, 38 million died in the famine of 1958–61 (see section 4.12, Did Mao succeed in making China a great economic power?); 27 million died in labour camps between 1950 and 1976; about 3 million were killed by execution, mob violence and suicide between 1950 and 1951 and a further 3 million died during the Cultural Revolution. These figures may be exaggerated, but several Chinese estimates, and even that of the official investigator in 1979, have put the figure at more than 40 million. (Chinese authorities to this day are reluctant to release 'classified material'; problems also stem from the size of the country and a lack of well-kept records.)

purges. The first of these was in 1954 when **Gao Gang**, who already held several senior government and party posts, having backed Mao against Zhou Enlai and Liu Shaoqi in support of Mao's economic policy, put himself forward to replace Zhou as vice-chairman of the CCP. He and his colleague **Rao Shushi** were accused of 'underground activities'. Gao Gang committed suicide rather than face disgrace in 1954, while Rao Shushi was arrested and imprisoned until his death in 1974. This purge was the first of many, including Peng Dehuai in 1959 and Deng Xiaoping and Liu Shaoqi in 1966 – with Deng undergoing a second purge in 1976 (see Political control during the Cultural Revolution, 1966–76 above). As Lin Biao's son put it, 'today he [Mao] uses sweet words and honeyed talk to those whom he entices; tomorrow he puts them to death for fabricated crimes'.

However, for all the repression, the PRC never had a highly centralised security apparatus like the KGB in the Soviet Union. This was partly because of Mao's reliance on mass campaigns, orchestrated through the media, and his expectation that individuals would expose those whose background or behaviour appeared at variance with the expectations of the regime. Mao believed that, given 'correct' guidance, the people could police each other, thus avoiding the need to create an alternative power base within the state.

4.9 What was the impact of international affairs and foreign policy on Mao's consolidation and maintenance of power?

In 1949, Mao was more interested in establishing his own brand of Communism within China than in exporting it elsewhere. Whilst he accepted the Marxist premise of 'world revolution', he knew that China was too poor and too isolated to lead an international revolution. Nevertheless, he was determined that China should be recognised as a 'great power' and he was committed to modernising China so that it could play a part in the Cold War world. His Chinese nationalism endeared him to his people who had an inherent dislike and distrust of foreigners who had once occupied and belittled their nation. So, whilst his dealings with foreign powers may have been less important in his consolidation and maintenance of power than they were, for example, for Hitler, Mao's independent stance in international affairs nevertheless reinforced his authority and provided a focus for the Chinese that, at times, distracted them from problems at home.

Relations with the USSR

One of Mao's first actions was an official visit to Moscow where he concluded a treaty with the USSR in 1950. This not only created a symbolic tie between the two world leaders in Communism (which in itself was a boost to Mao's reputation), it also provided much-needed Soviet economic (and military) aid. However, the treaty merely papered over deep underlying conflicts between China and the USSR that related to their shared border and different views of communism. Whilst China's participation in the Korean War (1950–53) provided an opportunity for Mao to reinforce suspicion of foreigners within China, particularly Americans and westerners, through his 'resist America and aid Korea campaign' of 1950 (see section 4.5, Government), it also showed the limitations of the USSR's support. Not only was China required to pay for its military assistance, it has been suggested that the Soviet Union deliberately sabotaged an early armistice in order to exhaust the Chinese.

How much the average Chinese person was aware of such double-dealings is a matter for conjecture. On the whole, citizens accepted what they were told – whether it was the support of 'brother Russia' or anger at the USSR's treacherous move towards 'peaceful coexistence' with the West under Khrushchev. Certainly the official rhetoric changed after Khrushchev's denunciation of Stalin in 1956 (which Mao interpreted as an attack on any single-minded leadership, such as his own). Beginning with Deng Xiaoping's outspoken criticism of Soviet détente at the Moscow conference in 1957, the technical advisers sent to China were portrayed in the media as 'foreign spies', and whilst the media conveyed the affability of Mao as host during Khruschev's visit to Beijing in 1958, it hid deeper tensions. When the USSR refused to back Mao as he prepared a provocative attack on Taiwan in 1958 (the attack on this remaining nationalist stronghold was subsequently called off) and condemned Mao's much-vaunted Great Leap Forward, relations reached a low point. The Chinese people were left in little doubt as to the

Rao Shushi (1903–75)

Rao joined the CCP in 1925 and studied in the Soviet Union and the West. He was a political commissar during the civil war, and in 1949 he was made chairman of the Military and Political Committee of East China, general secretary of the East China Bureau of the CCP and governor of East China. In 1953, he became minister in charge of party organisation. However, his association with Gao Gang led to his downfall and he spent the last twenty-one years of his life under arrest – in prison and on a working farm.

Figure 4.10   Poster of 1965: The text reads: 'Imperialism and all reactionaries are all paper tigers'

Mao and China

KEY CONCEPTS QUESTION

Significance: Which was the more significant for Mao's authoritarian control – propaganda or repression?

Theory of knowledge

History and national characteristics:
It has been suggested that the Chinese education system, which relied on rote learning rather than critical reasoning skills, made 'self-policing' possible. Do you think styles of education system affect people's behaviour? Is it possible to generalise about 'national characteristics'?

QUESTION

How did the Chinese Communist Party ensure continuing loyalty from the Chinese people?

KEY CONCEPTS QUESTION

Significance: Do you agree with Chang that Mao should be regarded as a greater mass murderer than either Hitler or Stalin?

righteousness of Mao's position against the 'scheming' USSR which withdrew aid from Albania in 1961 (which the PRC promptly stepped in to supply) and, whilst officially neutral in the Sino-Indian war of 1962, actually provided the Indians with planes and moral support. Khrushchev's 'weak' withdrawal after the Cuban missile crisis of 1962 and agreement to the 1963 Test Ban treaty produced a fierce Sino-Soviet propaganda war, largely conducted on the meaning of revolution and the 'correct' path to socialism. The detail might have been beyond the comprehension of the average Chinese person, but the message left no doubt.

Mao also won great public acclaim when China detonated its first atomic bomb in 1964. Hsinhua, the Chinese Communist press agency, reported that Mao presided over a display involving more than a thousand young people, who sang and danced in a performance entitled 'The East Glows Red' in celebration.

SOURCE B

Under the signboard of 'peaceful coexistence', Khrushchev has been colluding with U.S. imperialism, wrecking the socialist camp and the international communist movement, opposing the revolutionary struggles of the oppressed peoples and nations, practising great-power chauvinism and national egoism and betraying proletarian internationalism. All this is being done for the protection of the vested interests of a handful of people, which he places above the fundamental interests of the peoples of the Soviet Union, the socialist camp and the whole world.

The line Khrushchev pursues is a revisionist line through and through. Guided by this line, not only have the old bourgeois elements run wild but new bourgeois elements have appeared in large numbers among the leading cadres of the Soviet Party and government, the chiefs of state enterprises and collective farms and the higher intellectuals in the fields of culture, art, science and technology.

From an article by Mao Tse-Tung July 1964 called, 'On Khrushchev's Phoney Communism and Its Historical Lessons for the World' published in *Renmin Ribao (People's Daily)* and *Hongqui (Red Flag)*, China on 14 July 1964.

Relations with the USA

Until the 1970s, Maoist China maintained a bitter rhetoric against the USA, which had supported the GMD, protected Taiwan, refused to recognise the PRC, opposed the Chinese in Korea and was ideologically opposed to Communism. Such behaviour provided ample ammunition for mass campaigns. An attack on American Imperialism was easier to 'sell' to the Chinese than the attack on communist USSR. Americans were portrayed as 'paper tigers', and from 1950 schoolchildren were made to chant, 'Death to the American imperialists and all their running dogs' daily. The Anti-American campaigns reached a peak during the Vietnam war (from 1963) when China, although not actively involved, supported the Northern Communist forces under Ho Chi-Minh against the US-backed south. Indeed, fear of a direct American attack helped to unite the Chinese people under their Chairman.

Although his anti-American rhetoric no doubt helped Mao in his maintenance of power, he was forced to reverse some of his former outbursts in the early 1970s.

The USA's acceptance, in 1971, of the PRC's right to representation in the UN (in preference to Taiwan) set the scene for improved relations. A series of table-tennis tournaments provided the forum for talks and 'ping pong diplomacy', which culminated in a successful visit by President Nixon to Beijing in 1972. However, like everything else in Maoist China, this too was portrayed as a Maoist triumph, with Chairman Mao shown in the press as the equal or more of the most powerful man in the world. The Chinese scarcely needed more proof of his greatness than that.

End of unit activities

1 Make a two-column table to show the ways in which the 'new democracy' of the PRC differed from democracy in Western states such as Great Britian.

2 Draw a table illustrating (a) the main challenges faced by Mao in the 1950s, and (b) how he dealt with these. A third column could offer some comment on his success/failure.

3 Undertake some research into the People's Liberation Army (PLA). Create a poster showing how the PLA was used as a role model for civilians in communist China.

4 Create two tables showing (a) Mao's mass campaigns, and (b) Mao's political purges. For each, record their aims, developments and outcomes.

5 Research the life of any one of Mao's victims and write an obituary for that person.

6 Recreate a struggle session. Think carefully about who the victim might be and the accusations that might be made.

7 Mao's foreign policy can be drawn as a triangle – one side is relations with the USSR, another is relations with the USA and the third is China's independent stance. Draw a triangle like this and add some key dates along each side. Next to each side of the triangle, indicate how that aspect of Mao's foreign policy contributed to his maintenance of power within China.

Theory of knowledge

History and bias:
The impact of foreign affairs on Mao's maintenance of power in China was largely the result of propaganda. How can we distinguish between knowledge, opinion and propaganda?

Theory of knowledge

Politics and behaviour:
Is it realistic to think that human behaviour can be modified?

QUESTION

What is totalitarianism? Can China under Mao be labelled totalitarian?

3 Unit   Mao's Policies and their Impact

Overview

- Mao believed he could turn China into a great world power by putting his specifically Chinese version of Marxism into practice. Living standards were raised, but Mao's methods often mitigated against the effective implementation of policies.

- Collectivisation was introduced in gradual stages. It began with co-operative farms before moving to higher-level collectives and finally communes during the Great Leap Forward from 1958.

- The first Five-Year Plan began the process of central planning, but this model was abandoned in the Great Leap Forward, which proved to be a disastrous mistake. The economy was gradually revived under the direction of Liu Shaoqi and Deng Xiaoping but suffered again in the dislocation brought about by the Cultural Revolution from 1966.

- The communists tried to weaken the power of organised religion within China and only 'patriotic Churches' were allowed to operate. However, the party's success was limited overall.

- There was a successful drive to increase literacy, but the growth of education was limited by the party's dislike of intellectualism and the disruption caused by the mass campaigns.

- Youths were indoctrinated through youth organisations and played a major part in the Cultural Revolution, although this proved detrimental to their broader education.

- Culture suffered as it became a branch of Maoist propaganda, and the Cultural Revolution not only destroyed some of China's heritage but also led to the persecution of intellectuals and creative minds.

- Mao's China granted 'equality' to women, but in practice their lives sometimes became more onerous than before.

- Although there was some toleration of ethnic and religious minorities, the Tibetans suffered enormously and the Cultural Revolution affected such groups.

KEY QUESTIONS

- What factors influenced domestic and social policy?
- How far did Mao raise living standards in China?
- How successful was Mao's economic policy?
- What was the relationship between the communists and the Churches within China?
- How did the CCP view the role of education and try to ensure the support of youth?
- How did Maoism affect the arts and the media?
- What was the position of women in Mao's China?
- How were social, religious and racial minorities treated within Mao's communist state?
- To what extent was authoritarian control achieved?

Figure 4.11   A photograph published in 1967 by the Chinese official news agency; the original caption read 'Every day, prior to starting work in the field, young people and young girls read and meditate together some of "Mao Zedong Thought"'. Chinese workers were constantly taught that they were working not for themselves, but for their country and for their great Chairman Mao. Consequently, a typical working day would begin with a period of reflection on the tasks ahead, and meditation on Mao's thoughts and inspiring words. In this picture, we can see the group leader directing an early morning session

QUESTION

Mao's picture has been brought to the field to inspire the workforce. Do you think such activities would be effective?

161

4.10 What factors influenced domestic and social policy?

Mao believed he could transform China by implementing his unique version of communism, with its emphasis on the peasants, mass mobilisation, self-criticism and continuous revolution. He believed anything could be achieved by ruthless determination. However, whilst such a doctrine had served him well in his rise to power, it proved more controversial once he was in power. Indeed, his ideological goals tended to become a destructive force that detracted from his avowed desire to strengthen China and better the lives of its people.

Mao's belief that 'sheer commitment' was sufficient to drive the country forward and make up for China's lack of capital and industrial technology showed an acute lack of real understanding. Mao's policies hindered proper industrial management, deprived China of the trained experts it needed to direct its social and economic programmes, wasted natural and human resources and brought horrendous famine (see section 4.12, Did Mao succeed in making China a great economic power?). Furthermore, his belief in himself and his own leadership was mitigated against good policy-making. Others were only permitted a say when policies went wrong and he always found a scapegoat – particularly among the '**bourgeois elements**', '**capitalist roaders**' and '**backsliders**'.

bourgeois elements, capitalist roaders and backsliders: These are derogatory terms, given to individuals or groups who exhibited 'middle class' or bourgeois characteristics, such as private ownership, working for profit or intellectualism. They were believed to be preventing the development of socialism by pulling the country in a capitalist direction.

Mao's policies were driven by his commitment to 'continuing revolution'. He believed he could 'remould the souls of the people' and that ruthlessness *and* violence were an integral part of the cleansing process. Nothing was allowed to stand still. Whenever 'stability' threatened, Mao would launch a new campaign. Every generation, he believed, should have a new commitment and he even said that 'great disorder across the land leads to great order'. However, trying to carry through a programme of economic and social reform in conditions such as those produced by the Cultural Revolution, was virtually impossible.

Similarly, his anti-intellectual belief that only the masses were capable of carrying the revolution forward, proved damaging. The school system was based around a work-study programme, with universal participation in manual labour. This hindered academic achievement and creativity. 'Intellectuals' were despised and anyone suspected of thinking for themselves was subjected to struggle sessions, forced to undertake manual labour and persecuted. Thus the very people whom he needed to create his new China suffered most at his hands.

This was Mao's essential paradox. It proved impossible to reconcile voluntaryism – whereby men and women were re-educated to participate willingly in the 'mass struggle' to carry through policies – with Mao's determination to stamp out 'bourgeois thinking', and to achieve this he was forced to resort to extensive repression, brainwashing and an unparalleled level of violence.

It would probably be fair to say that the social and economic improvements that occurred between 1949 and 1976 took place largely despite, rather than because of, Mao's strong ideological principles. His view that unless the Chinese Communist Party was regularly purified it would cease to be a revolutionary force, and China would cease to be truly socialist, threatened to defeat his own objective of making China strong and prosperous.

KEY CONCEPTS QUESTION

Change and Consequence: How successful was Mao in fulfilling his ideological aims in the years 1949–76?

KEY CONCEPTS QUESTION

Significance: Was Maoist ideology constructive or destructive? Divide the class in two. One half should try to think of the ways in which Maoist ideology was 'constructive' and the other half of the class should consider its 'destructive' tendencies. When you have exchanged ideas, write your own considered appraisal, advancing your supported judgement.

Figure 4.12   A picture released by the Chinese official news agency shows Mao Zedong (centre, bottom) surrounded by his bodyguards, swimming in the Yangtze River near Wuhan, 16 July 1966

Theory of knowledge

History and ideology: Does knowledge of Maoist ideology help the historian to justify and excuse Mao's actions?

4.11 How far did Mao raise living standards in China?

The years after the establishment of the People's Republic of China (PRC) saw an impressive rise in standards of living in China. Inflation was curbed and crime and corruption were checked as drug dealers, prostitutes and criminal gangs were outlawed. Citizens themselves were involved in building the 'new society', although under the direction of the local party cadres.

Most Chinese people gained job security and a stable income. Each employed citizen in an urban area was required to belong to a Danwei (work unit); those who were not employed came under the supervision of a residents' committee. These units controlled food supplies, the allocation of housing and permits for travel, marriage, jobs, military service and university. Their work was complemented by the establishment of a variety of mass organisations such as the National Women's Association, the New Democratic Youth League and the Children's Pioneer Corps.

Residents' committees dealt with public health, policing and the resolution of disputes. Water supplies and sanitation were improved in cities and the countryside, and mass 'patriotic health campaigns' were used to focus attention on improving hygiene and reducing cholera, typhoid and scarlet fever. Teams went into rural areas to educate people about healthy living, and death rates fell steadily.

More doctors and nurses were trained, although there was some conflict with Maoist ideology, which regarded doctors as 'bourgeois intellectuals' in the 1960s and expected them to subordinate medical duties to factory work. However, they were replaced by the 'barefoot doctors', who underwent short practical training sessions of six months and worked among the peasants, giving inoculations and basic treatments.

4.12 How successful was Mao's economic policy?

Mao's economic policy was governed by:

- his basic belief in the 'collective ownership of the means of production' (i.e. the nationalisation of industry, and collective farming)
- the desire to make China a great world power, to equal and surpass the Soviet Union's economic achievement and avoid dependency on an outside power
- the immediate need for recovery after the damage caused by war.

Mao knew that, to achieve these ends, China would need to increase its capital for industrial investment. He planned to do this by reducing foreign imports and boosting the export market in Chinese agricultural goods. He never trusted scientific experts and believed that manpower alone could make his plans a success.

Land reform, June 1950

In June 1950, a programme of land reform was launched, but in accordance with his ideological principles Mao wanted the peasants to lead the change themselves. Party cadres stirred up hostility in 'speak bitterness' campaigns, with the slogan, 'Dig the bitter roots, vomit the bitter waters'. These campaigns encouraged peasants to turn on their landlords – executing them on the spot or subjecting them to a 'trial', following which they lost their civil rights, land, animals and household goods, which were distributed among the poor peasants of the area. Up to 2 million were killed. Ownership of land remained private, but landlords that were spared held only as much as the poorest peasant.

Following redistribution, the average farm remained too small for efficient farming. So, from 1951, the cadres encouraged the peasants to farm land co-operatively. Profits were distributed according to what land, tools and animals the peasant contributed and how much work they did. Although not compulsory, most peasants favoured cooperation since they stood to gain. By 1952, grain production was 10 per cent higher than in 1936. By 1953, almost 40 per cent of peasant households belonged to 'mutual aid teams' (see the table below) and increasingly the traditional farming of individual plots ceased.

Official policy was not entirely consistent. At first, Mao condemned what he referred to as 'rash advance', but when the increase in the number of co-operatives threatened to fall as wealthier peasants began buying up land to consolidate individual farms, he railed against the 'rash retreat' and ordered the cadres to quicken the pace towards cooperation.

From 1954, the cadres tried to encourage peasants to create higher-level Agricultural Producers' Co-operatives (APCs). However, this scheme proved impossible to implement because of the turmoil and food riots that followed a poor harvest that year. The APC plan was suspended for eighteen months, but in the summer of 1955 a new drive began and the first higher-level APCs were established that year. In these, land was pooled and no longer privately owned. Rich peasants were excluded and profits were distributed only according to levels of work. The new drive was supported by Mao. Liu Shaoqi favoured a more cautious approach. There was limited opposition, partly because there was already less difference in wealth among the peasants than there had been in Stalinist Russia, and partly because propaganda successfully persuaded peasants of the advantages of higher level cooperation. Furthermore, individual peasant proprietors soon found themselves unable to obtain bank loans, buy seed and fertiliser or get neighbours' help at harvest time.

Fact: The situation in the countryside provoked debate in the Central Committee in 1955. In Jiangsu (a fertile province), for example, the farmers were angered that they were left with only 35 per cent of their output after government procurements. They reacted by under-reporting their harvest yields, trying to bribe officials and even attacking them. As a result, procurement was cut by one-third.

Table 4.2 Percentage of families in China in different types of co-operative farms

Year	Mutual aid (5–10 households): equipment and animals pooled but private ownership retained	Lower-level co-operatives (30–50 households): pooling of land but share of profits partly based on how much land/ equipment contributed	Higher-level co-operatives (collectives/APCs) (200–300 households): land collectively owned/small allotments permitted
1953	39.3	0.2	–
1954	58.3	1.9	–
1955	32.7	63.3	4.0
1956	3.7	8.5	87.8
1957	–	–	93.5

By the end of 1956, most villages had formed collectives, and by 1957 over 90 per cent of peasant families were incorporated into APCs. The state had become the sole purchaser of grain from 1953 and peasants were obliged to sell fixed quotas to the state. This gave the CCP greater control over the countryside than any previous regime. John King Fairbank referred to this as a 'modern serfdom under party control'.

communes: This was more than an agricultural unit. Each was equipped with nurseries, old people's homes (Happiness Homes), health clinics, schools and open-air cinemas. Peasants abandoned private possessions, slept in unisex dormitories and ate in communal canteens. ('Marriage rooms' had to be booked by married couples.) Communal teams dealt with house cleaning, mending and the preparation of food.

Fact: Trofim Lysenko was a Soviet agronomist who claimed to have developed methods for increasing the crop yields. His methods included increased fertilisation of the land and pest control. His advocacy of sparrowcide almost wiped out the sparrow population and allowed an explosion of caterpillars and other vermin, which devastated crops.

KEY CONCEPTS QUESTION

Causation and Consequence: By what methods, and with what results did the CCP attempt to reform agriculture and bring about collectivisation in the years 1950–58?

Collectivisation and the Great Leap Forward, 1958

Agricultural output grew 5 per cent in 1957, but Mao felt this was not enough. From January to April 1958, Mao toured China visiting the more enterprising APCs, and concluded that efficiency could be best achieved by amalgamating co-operatives into much larger **communes**.

This scheme was launched in 1958 as one part of the Great Leap Forward. It involved the setting up of 70,000 communes, each divided into about 750,000 brigades, with each brigade representing around 200 families. Private farming was to cease and all aspects of production were to be centrally directed by the party.

Co-operative projects for irrigation and flood control, electricity schemes and road building were encouraged and each commune was to contain a number of small factories, providing work for women and children, and for the men during slack times of the farming year.

There followed a spate of Mao-endorsed campaigns such as 'the four pests campaign' (which 'outlawed' flies, mosquitoes, rats and sparrows) and 'Lysenkoism' (which it was claimed would produce yields up to sixteen times greater than by using traditional methods).

However, communal farming failed to work. By tradition, most peasants in China were subsistence farmers and neither they nor the officials trying to lead them had the knowledge to farm on a large communal scale. Some peasants became too involved in industrial enterprises and they neglected agriculture. Others, influenced by the propaganda, left the fields fallow because they thought grain was plentiful, or neglected pig breeding, poultry raising or vegetable growing because an emphasis was placed on the production of grain.

How did Mao apply communism to industry?

The GMD had already taken control of a considerable amount of industry before 1949, so the moderate period of National Capitalism between 1949 and 1953 involved minimal disruption. During this period the state took over the ownership of heavy industry and the banking system only. Wages and prices were regulated, but members of the 'national bourgeoisie' were still able to make profits. In 1953, 20 per cent of heavy industry and 60 per cent of light industry was still privately owned.

China turned to the Soviet Union for support at this time. The Sino-Soviet friendship treaty of February 1950 provided $300 million in Russian loans (repayable at low interest – largely by food exports). During the 1950s, 11,000 Soviet experts arrived in China, while 28,000 Chinese received training in the Soviet Union.

Between 1949 and 1952, the value of industrial output more than doubled and 300 modern industrial plants were planned, including factories for iron, steel, motor vehicles and aircraft.

The first Five-Year Plan, 1953–57

The period of National Capitalism ended with the launch of the first Five-Year Plan in 1953, which was intended to speed up China's industrial growth. Over the next two years all private industries and businesses were nationalised, although many former owners were still kept on as managers and were given an annual share of the profits.

Sectors such as iron and steel, energy, transport, communications, machinery and chemicals were prioritised and given production targets, at the expense of consumer industries. In addition to Soviet loans, which represented 3 per cent of total investment, capital was raised by setting low prices to be paid to peasants for grain, so as to produce a large surplus for investment.

Vast new industrial schemes were planned for areas in the north-east (former Manchuria) and north-west, far from the old centres of development in the port cities such as Shanghai. Iron and steel mills were set up in former small market towns, such as Lanzhou and Baotou. Roads and railways were built, including a spectacular new rail link from Lanzhou across the Gobi Desert to Urumqi, capital of Xinjiang, where oil, coal, iron ore and other minerals were found.

In the north-east, the factories and mines formerly operated by the Japanese were developed, creating more industrial expansion. According to official statistics, heavy industrial output nearly trebled and light industry increased 70 per cent during this period. Overall targets were exceeded by 20 per cent. These figures cannot necessarily be trusted, but for the first time China produced its own cars, tractors, aeroplanes, cargo ships, machine tools and penicillin. The urban population grew from 57 million (in 1949) to 100 million (in 1957).

Industrialisation and the Great Leap Forward, 1958

In May 1956, Mao delivered a speech, 'On the Ten Great Relationships', indicating his desire to abandon the centralised, industry-based Soviet model in favour of a mass campaign combining agricultural and industrial growth. In 1957, he described his idea as a 'great leap' and predicted that China would become a new world superpower that would challenge the USA and overtake Britain in fifteen years.

Mao had a number of reasons for favouring a Great Leap Forward.

- He wanted to reassert China's independence from the Soviet Union.

- He wanted the Chinese people to take responsibility for their own future; he believed success resulted from determination, not money and expert advice.

- He was sixty-four and 'in a hurry'; he believed the pace of change had been too slow and he wanted to prove himself after the failure of the Hundred Flowers campaign.

- He was worried that the CCP was becoming bureaucratic and wanted to reduce the influence of central planning ministries and revive the 'Yan'an spirit'.

In urban areas, the cadres were expected to increase output beyond the levels previously considered feasible. There was an increase in the number of State-Owned Enterprises (SOEs), which operated with state subsidies, fixed rates of pay, conditions and output targets. Managers were no longer to receive a share of the profits and any surplus went to the state. These enterprises were organised rather like the countryside communes, with accommodation, schools, hospitals and other facilities for workers.

The development of the rural communes was part of the same drive. Here, rural peasants were expected to contribute to industrial growth, with a particular emphasis on the production of steel. A target of 10.7 million tonnes a year by 1959 and 60 million tonnes by 1960 was set. Peasants were told they would get rich quickly if they concentrated on iron and steel production and were inspired by the slogan 'twenty years in a day' and the song:

Fact: Members of the 'national bourgeoisie' were restricted in their right to dismiss workers (even if there was no job for them) and were ordered to improve working conditions and provide paid holidays, canteens, restrooms and other facilities. Some suffered under the Three Antis and Five Antis campaigns, launched in 1951–52 (see section 4.5, Government), but after confessing, most returned to their businesses.

Fact: The Anshan steel complex, with 35,000 workers, was a new showpiece. In 1954, the British reporter James Cameron travelled the north-east and wrote: 'The train-ride to Anshan was fantastic; a lunar landscape of new bricks and drifting smoke, heavily guarded bridges, great gangs and communities of people laying immense girders over riverbeds.'

Fact: Gao Gang's demise (see section 4.8, Repression) in December 1954 was partly because of his strong support for Soviet-style industrialisation.

'Produce more faster, better.

Three years of bitter struggle!

Ten thousand years of joy!'

The 'drive to produce metals locally' involved around 90 million peasants. Small-scale, 'backyard' industrial projects began on farm units and peasants abandoned other work to build brick furnaces in their yards. Whole communities contributed to the smelting of crude steel. Children collected peasants' donations of metals, including pans, tools and even bicycles to add to the ore. Adults stoked and tended the cauldrons or helped to push barrows or drive buffalo carts to bring in the raw materials and carry away the finished product. Around 600,000 furnaces reddened the rural skies as brigades competed with one another to produce the most.

Figure 4.13 Backyard furnace construction in Beijing during the Great Leap Forward, October 1958

Did Mao succeed in making China a great economic power?

Fact: China began developing nuclear weapons in the late 1950s and the first Chinese nuclear test was carried out in 1964.

There was undoubtedly an unprecedented period of economic growth in China after 1949, and during the Great Leap Forward rural industrialisation spread and China's infrastructure was developed.

However, in most respects, the Great Leap Forward and its aftermath was little less than disastrous. Steel production increased, but barely 1 per cent of what was produced was usable – the remaining 99 per cent being of such poor quality that it had to be abandoned as 'slag'.

Table 4.3   Production of manufactured goods, 1959–62

Using a base of 1959 = 100	1959	1960	1961	1962
Light industry	100	91.2	78.4	70.0
Heavy industry	100	90.0	66.4	44.2

Table 4.4   Production figures, 1957–62 (in millions of tonnes unless otherwise stated)

	1957	1958	1959	1960	1961	1962
Grain	195.1	200.0	170.0	143.5	147.5	160.0
Steel	5.4	8.0	10.0	13.0	8.0	8.0
Oil (millions of barrels)	1.5	2.3	3.7	4.5	4.5	5.3
Chemical fertilisers	0.8	1.4	2.0	2.5	1.4	2.1
Cotton (billions of metres)	5.0	5.7	7.5	6.0	3.0	3.0
Coal	131.0	230.0	290.0	270.0	180.0	180.0

KEY CONCEPTS QUESTION

Significance and Change: Look at the tables on this page showing production figures. What do these figures suggest about agricultural and industrial production in China in the years following the Great Leap Forward?

In the towns, political interference made it difficult to operate a national plan. The disappearance of private managers weakened the drive for profits, and guaranteed wages reduced the incentive to work hard and produce better-quality goods.

Nikita Khrushchev, leader of the Soviet Union from 1953 to 1964, warned that the Great Leap Forward was a 'dangerous experiment'. However, Mao refused to back down and in 1960 the Soviet experts working in China left and Russian loans ceased. Factories were left half built or closed as capital disappeared and spare parts ceased to arrive from the Soviet Union.

In the countryside the results were even worse. In 1959, the government took 28 per cent of peasants' grain, as opposed to 17 per cent in 1957, and the price paid was kept low in both 1959 and 1960. Some overenthusiastic peasants almost abandoned farming altogether in order to meet the drive to work the furnaces. Some even consigned their own tools to the flames.

Government policies and the worst drought for a century in northern and central China in 1960, plus flooding in the south, produced a catastrophic famine. The years

Mao and China

Fact: Chang and Halliday have accused Mao of confiscating Chinese harvests during the Great Leap Forward in order to export food in exchange for armaments, irrespective of the sufferings of the Chinese. They write of cases of cannibalism in Anhui and Gansu provinces, and a daily intake of 1,200 calories in Chinese cities in 1960 (compared with 1,300–1,700 calories a day fed to prisoners in Auschwitz). Not all historians accept this, but conditions were clearly very bad.

Fact: A million Tibetans perished in the famine, representing around a quarter of the total population (see section 4.17). In Anshui 8 million died, in Henan 7.8 million died and in Sichuan 9 million perished in the famine.

Theory of knowledge

Luck in history:
It is sometimes said that Mao suffered from 'bad luck' insofar as his Great Leap Forward policy coincided with a terrible drought in central and northern China and flooding in the south. Is it appropriate to talk of 'bad luck' when apportioning blame for historical events?

KEY CONCEPTS QUESTION

Consequence: How successful were Mao's economic policies in the years 1949 to 1976?

---

between 1959 and 1961 became known as the 'three bitter years' when between 20 million and 50 million died. However, Mao's government refused to acknowledge what was happening, let alone admit responsibility. The Lushan Conference in July 1959 provided an opportunity for delegates to address the famine, but only Peng Dehuai spoke out. Mao reacted badly to Peng's criticism and dismissed him as defence minister (see section 4.7, Mao's disappearance from public life). Mao resigned as head of state in 1959, allowing Liu Shaoqi and Deng Xiaoping to deal with the crisis.

The PLA was called upon to stand by to suppress rebellion. However, the situation eased before this became necessary as grain was imported from Australia and Canada to feed the starving. Highly centralised economic planning and wage differentials for skilled and unskilled workers were brought back and 25 million unemployed urban workers were forced to return to the countryside.

In 1961, the communes were reorganised, reduced in size and made less regimented (for example by ending communal dormitories). Pay rates were changed to take work and output into account. Backyard steel furnaces were quietly abandoned, and irrigation and dams were left incomplete. Peasants' time was no longer wasted on unnecessary industrial work or military marches around the fields.

Small private plots reappeared, and in some areas families reclaimed farmland to cultivate independently under a 'household responsibility scheme'. By January 1962, 20 per cent of arable land was being farmed individually. Deng justified the new approach as serving the same ends, saying, in 1962, 'It doesn't matter if the cat is black or white; so long as it catches the mouse it is a good cat.'

It took at least five years just to recover from the damage to agriculture. The revival of industry was faster, aided by discovery of huge oil and gas fields in Daqing, doubling output by 1965. However, factories continued to be run inefficiently. Technical and managerial skills were lacking, outdated equipment continued to be used and a rigid adherence to socialist concepts, including lack of contact with the West, hindered development so that overall production declined in the 1960s.

Although Mao's Cultural Revolution from 1966 did not officially change economic policies, the chaos it produced affected economic growth. The requisitioning of trains and trucks to carry Red Guards around the country created shortages of raw materials, slowing factory production. Even the Anshan blast furnace (see section 4.12, The first Five-Year Plan, 1953–57) had to be stopped. Furthermore, almost all engineers, managers, scientists, technicians and other professional personnel were 'criticised', demoted, sent to the countryside or jailed. This meant their skills and knowledge were lost. Imports of foreign equipment ceased and the closure of the universities created more problems for the future. The immediate result was a 14 per cent decline in industrial production in 1967.

The economically progressive Zhou Enlai and Deng Xiaoping were attacked in the press and described as 'poisonous weeds' by supporters of the Gang of Four. Output for 1976, the year Mao died, showed continuing stagnation. Only after the fall of the Gang of Four in October 1976, a month after Mao's death, did China really begin to develop its potential as an economic powerhouse.

4.13 What was the relationship between the communists and the Churches within China?

The official communist view was that religion was a capitalist invention, used to keep the lower classes in their place with promises of a better afterlife. Mao was particularly hostile to organised religion, referring to it as 'poison'.

Confucianism, Buddhism, Islam and Christianity alike were condemned as superstitions, and Maoist China saw the closure of churches, temples, shrines and monasteries. Foreign priests and missionaries were expelled and Chinese ones were forbidden from wearing distinctive dress.

Religious toleration was officially guaranteed by the Chinese constitution, but the government had its own definition of 'religion' and a campaign against 'superstition' began in 1950. Ancestor worship was condemned and traditional religious rituals were banned. However, religious establishments could become 'patriotic Churches' operating under government control, provided they did not endanger the security of the state and broke all links with overseas Churches. Clergy had to profess support for the communist regime and allow the government to vet appointments. Some Buddhist temples, Muslim mosques and, less often, Christian churches were even given state money.

During the Cultural Revolution, religion was denounced as belonging to the 'four olds'. The first monument to be wrecked in August 1966 was a Buddha in the Summer Palace in Beijing. No public worship or ceremony was allowed and the remaining clergy were rounded up and imprisoned. Temples, churches, religious images and shrines were destroyed everywhere, although it was in Tibet that some of the worst excesses of the regime were felt.

Confucianism was accused of representing the worst of China's past and 'Confucius and Co.' became a standard term of abuse, referring to everything and everybody that belonged to past culture.

There was, however, a limit to how much Mao could reshape private belief. In the more remote areas it remained strong, and in Tibet the Lama Faith inspired continued resistance to Chinese occupation.

Fact: The Christian Protestant Church created the 'Three-Self Patriotic Movement' (TSPM), which was the only legal Protestant denomination in China. However, Chinese Roman Catholics were subject to repeated persecution. In 1955, the Roman Catholic Bishop of Shanghai and his followers were accused of plotting against the state and arrested.

Fact: In 1973, in the Anti-Confucius campaign, Lin Biao was accused of being 'one of the Confuciuses of contemporary China'.

KEY CONCEPTS QUESTION

Causation and Consequence: For what reasons and with what success did Mao attempt to eradicate religious influences from public life?

4.14 How did the CCP view the role of education and try to ensure the support of youth?

Education

In 1949, only about one in ten Chinese could read and many could not write because there was no standardised form of written Mandarin. Only 20 per cent of children went to primary school and around 1 per cent went to secondary, and the number of female

Mao and China

Fact: Written Mandarin is expressed in ideograms (pictures of the ideas described) and every word has to be learned separately. There is also considerable difference in the way Mandarin is spoken in different parts of China, so it is hard for people from different areas to communicate.

Fact: Pinyin is a written form of Mandarin in which sounds are given symbols and written expression is standardised and simplified, making it much easier to learn than traditional Mandarin.

Fact: Mao instructed his own daughter to tell peasants, 'Papa says that after studying for a few years we become more and more stupid. Please be my teachers. I want to learn from you.'

students beyond primary level was negligible. The CCP was determined to increase literacy rates and expand educational provision for both practical and ideological reasons, although there was some conflict between their drive for education and disdain for intellectualism.

Schools were set up for all children except those in the 'black' categories (see section 4.5, Government). Study groups and night schools were set up, and the 'little teacher' scheme was established, whereby schoolchildren visited adult peasants and workers and shared their learning.

Chinese characters were simplified for quick learning. Pinyin was approved by the National People's Congress, and in 1964 the Committee for Reforming the Chinese Written Language released an official list of 2,238 simplified Chinese characters.

Secondary schooling expanded, helped initially by teachers and textbooks from the Soviet Union and scholarships to Soviet universities. However, this Soviet help ceased after the Sino-Soviet split, which began in the late 1950s (see section 4.9, Relations with the USSR). After this, new Chinese textbooks were carefully vetted and foreign languages were studied only in Maoist translations of literature. There was an emphasis on practical 'work experience'. Students were required to spend part of their days in the fields and factories.

'Key schools' were given priority in the assignment of teachers, equipment and funds and provided for the children of the party cadres. They monopolised places at top universities, although in theory peasant and workers' children were given preferential admission.

In the later 1960s, various experiments were undertaken in which peasants and industrial workers were made 'teachers' and pupils were encouraged to criticise their teachers for unacceptable political statements, failing to help the more backward or even failing to mark work properly.

The results appeared impressive:

- Literacy rates increased, reaching 50 per cent of the population in 1960, 66 per cent in 1964 and 70 per cent by 1976.
- By 1957, most village children had some primary education and the number in secondary education had almost tripled.
- By 1976, 96 per cent of children aged 7–16 were in schools.

However, a number of factors limited the degree of educational advance:

- Education was neither compulsory nor free and was never a budget priority.
- The quality of education varied and provision in the villages was often rudimentary.
- The emphasis on practical education, the anti-intellectualism of the regime, and the politically oriented criteria for admission to better schools and universities held back some of the able individuals that China needed.
- Despite the lip service to equality, the children of the party cadres were advantaged.
- Schools became centres for indoctrination, encouraging the cult of the leader.
- During the Cultural Revolution most schools and universities were closed down.

The communist youth associations

The communists had a Youth League for young people aged 14–28, run by Lu Hao, and a subsection, the Youth Pioneers, for children aged 6–14. Schools and villages ran units and children wore red scarves to symbolise the blood that had been shed by revolutionary martyrs. However, despite these attempts at indoctrination, students were among the forefront of those who criticised the regime during the Hundred Flowers campaign in 1956–57. Consequently, the Cultural Revolution aimed to reinvigorate the youth with revolutionary fervour, and the Red Guards (for the older age group) and 'little Red Guards' were formed.

After being encouraged by Mao to go and destroy the 'four olds' in 1966 (see section 4.6, Personality), youths took over the streets – banging gongs and shouting slogans. Enjoying special priority on public transport, Red Guards travelled across China spreading the revolution and destroying old culture. They invaded people's houses, smashed 'antique' possessions and forced those wearing Western clothing or hairstyles into the ubiquitous grey Maoist baggy pants and tunics. They even forced teachers to wear tall dunces' caps and paraded them through the streets to be spat at and insulted.

Figure 4.14 Red Guards marching to spread the revolution and destroy the old culture during the Cultural Revolution, 1967

Fact: The youth organisations helped to politicise the young. Pioneers recited the motto: 'Be prepared to struggle for the cause of communism!' To which others replied 'Always be prepared!' They pledged: 'I am a member of the Young Pioneers of China. Under the Pioneers' Flag I promise that I love the Communist Party of China, I love the motherland, I love the people. I will study well and keep myself fit to prepare for contributing my effort to the cause of communism.'

KEY CONCEPTS QUESTION

Consequence: How effective were the communist attempts to spread literacy and education after 1949?

Perspectives: In what respects was Maoist educational policy contradictory?

Cause: Can you explain why tens of thousands of young people were prepared to join the Red Guards?

Fact: The attack on the play *Hai Rui Dismissed From Office* was not just an artistic criticism. It was a thinly veiled attack on officials at the top of the party leadership – Peng Zhen, the mayor of Beijing, politburo member and minister responsible for culture, as well as his allies Deng Xiaoping and Liu Shaoqi.

Fact: Model plays that were permitted during the Cultural Revolution included:
- *Taking Tiger Mountain by Strategy,* a play about communist soldiers infiltrating a bandit camp during the Chinese Civil War
- *The Legend of the Red Lantern,* a play about the communist resistance against Japan in Hulin during the Second Sino-Japanese War
- *Red Detachment of Women,* a pre-Cultural Revolution era play about the women of Hainan Island who rose up in resistance on behalf of the CCP
- *The White-Haired Girl,* a play exploring the miseries of peasants in 1930s China.

When matters got totally out of hand, Mao used the PLA to break up the Red Guard units in July 1968. Thereafter, schools began to function again and students were ordered to the countryside for re-education. Universities reopened in the early 1970s, but here and in the higher schools the decline in educational quality was marked. Exams were abolished and Deng Xiaoping wrote in 1975 that university graduates were 'not even capable of reading a book'.

4.15 How did Maoism affect the arts and the media?

Mao associated China's rich traditional culture with feudal and imperial society and believed it needed to be swept away and replaced by a communist culture, which exulted the common man. Writers and artists were expected to educate the masses – not create artistic works for their own sake.

In the 1950s, traditional Chinese art was allowed to continue alongside more modern Soviet-inspired art that imparted propagandist messages, such as happy peasants celebrating the abundant harvest in a village co-operative. Old-style poetry also continued, although younger poets were encouraged to write about new agricultural and industrial achievements in a more modern style. Plays and films were overtly propagandist, while all literary works were carefully censored and the news media was centralised, with Xinhua as the PRC's news agency. The state controlled which newspapers and journals could be published, and what could appear in print.

Although the Hundred Flowers campaign brought a burst of freedom (see section 4.7, The Hundred Flowers campaign, 1956–57), repression followed in the anti-rightist campaign and persecution was at its most intense during the Cultural Revolution (1966–76) when **Jiang Qing** was made the 'cultural purifier of the nation'.

In November 1965, the play *Hai Rui Dismissed From Office* was performed in Shanghai. The play was written by Wu Han, deputy mayor of Beijing and an intellectual. The parallels between this play, set in imperial times, and Mao's dismissal of Peng Dehuai (see section 4.7, Mao's disappearance from public life) were obvious, and one of the Shanghai critics, Yao Wenyuan, wrote a fierce attack on the play, with Mao's approval.

Yao Wenyuan was one of the 'Shanghairadicals' with whom Jiang Qing, Mao's wife, associated. He and his circle asserted that the struggle over culture was part of the wider struggle between classes. Consequently, they seized the opportunity to demand a campaign against the 'four olds', including old culture. Lin Biao, an ally of Mao, declared, 'If the proletariat does not occupy the positions in literature and art, the bourgeoisie certainly will. This struggle is inevitable.'

Rigid censorship forbade all but works with relevant contemporary Chinese themes. The sale or possession of foreign literature became punishable and libraries and museums were closed. For two years almost nothing new was printed except Mao's *Little Red Book*. Western music, both classical and popular, was banned and traditional Chinese opera, with its satirical style, was replaced by a repertoire of specially commissioned contemporary opera-ballets, which depicted the triumph of the proletariat over its class enemies.

Artists of all sorts were terrorised into silence and made to submit to 'struggle sessions'. By the early 1970s, China was an artistic wasteland. Old culture had been destroyed but nothing of value had arisen to take its place.

4.16 What was the position of women in Mao's China?

The CCP had always advocated female equality, with Mao famously proclaiming that 'Women hold up half the sky'. Traditionally, women had been expected to stay at home and to obey their menfolk while the practices of concubinage, foot binding and arranged marriages had given women a second-class status.

From 1950, the traditional practice of killing unwanted baby girls was officially abolished (although not always enforced), foot binding was outlawed, and girls were expected to go to school and women to work. The 1950 Marriage Law forbade arranged marriages and child betrothals, the payment of dowries and concubinage. Official registration of marriage was introduced and new laws made divorce permissible by mutual consent or on the complaint of either husband or wife. Those who had been subject to an arranged marriage were allowed to petition for divorce.

The 1953 Election Law gave women the right to vote and some joined the government and PLA. Women were actively encouraged to train for jobs formerly held only by men. There was a drive to curb prostitution. In the 1950s, laws gave women the same property rights as men. Some were even granted land in their own name in the redistributions that followed the campaign against landlords (see section 4.12, Land reform, June 1950). In the communes, communal eating and shared cleaning released women from traditional household chores and here, and in the larger factories in the towns, communal nurseries and kindergartens allowed them to escape child minding and return to work.

However, communist policy towards women did not always bring positive results.

- There was a huge increase in the numbers of divorces – 1.3 million divorce petitions were filed in 1953, many from ill-treated wives, and a drive against hasty action had to be launched.
- Although the number of women in work increased from 8 per cent to 32 per cent, jobs could be physically demanding and many women had to act as both workers and mothers.
- In rural and Muslim areas, government interference was resented and arranged marriages continued.
- Women provided only 13 per cent of the party membership and 14–23 per cent of the deputies in the National People's Congress between 1954 and 1975.
- Communes and schools, where children were taught that love for Mao was more important than love for their family, undermined the family unit. Young people were encouraged to speak against their parents in the Four Olds campaign (see section 4.15) and many youngsters were sent far from home to experience rural work. The outlawing of ancestor worship also hit at the family unit.

Fact: Although a well-off man would only have one 'official' wife, concubines or 'other women' were recognised and sometimes seen as the way to produce a male heir. The practice of foot binding, to preserve dainty female feet (regarded as sexually attractive), had spread from élite women to families of lesser means from the later 19th century.

Theory of knowledge

A historian's standpoint: Should governments intervene to outlaw cultural practices such as foot binding? If we applaud Mao's attempts to 'liberate' women, do we do so through Western eyes?

Fact: Modern feminist writers such as Xiufen Lu, in *Chinese Women and Feminist Theory* (2005), have suggested that the communists overplayed the picture of former feminine subordination in order to glorify their own achievements.

ACTIVITY

Was the campaign to limit population growth an unnecessary attempt by the state to limit freedom of choice or a sensible policy to keep the population size to a manageable level? Discuss this question in groups.

Figure 4.15 A young woman operating a precision machine at a factory in Beijing, October 1955

Initially, the communists favoured the large families that swelled the population in the early 1950s. However, with the coming of the famine, women were told that two children was the ideal. Late marriage – at 25–27 years for men and twenty-three years for women – was encouraged and couples who had large families, or did not allow sufficient time between pregnancies, were criticised in their group meetings. Partly because of this campaign, the Chinese population grew more slowly than had been expected, although between 1953 and 1964 it increased to 112 million as death rates fell and birth rates remained high.

4.17 How were social, religious and ethnic minorities treated within Mao's communist state?

The 'bourgeois' social minority (see section 4.10) was not the only group to be persecuted in Maoist China. While they suffered for their social standing, there were others who suffered for their religion or ethnicity. There were a number of ethnic and religious minority groups of non-Han ethnicity within communist China including Tibetans (Lama-Bhuddist), Uighurs (Muslim), Hui Muslims and Mongols (of Buddhist, Islamic and other faiths). The existence of different sectarian interests was seen as hostile to the Maoist/communist ideology, although, for the most part, Mao was prepared to let the minorities continue their own way of life.

In his struggle for power in the 1940s, Mao promised the minorities independence, but he changed his mind once in power. Tibet was forced into the PRC in 1950 and its Buddhist culture was suppressed (see section 4.5, Unified control). In 1950 also, the government called on other ethnic minorities to identify themselves and promised them a degree of autonomy. Four hundred ethnic groups did so. From these, officials created fifty groups, which were subsequently placed under military supervision and forced to accept communist rule, although they were, within limits, given the right to express and develop their own culture.

From 1959 the oppression of religious and ethnic minorities increased. In Tibet, measures to outlaw the Lama Faith and Tibetan culture provoked a national uprising in 1959, which was brutally crushed. Even speaking of the Dalai Lama (the leader of the Buddhist faith who fled to northern India to win international support) in public, was a criminal offence. The communists imposed extreme policies. Tibetans were forced to grow wheat and maize (even though these proved indigestible) and herders were made to farm high ground and not allow their yaks to roam. This severely cut supplies of milk, cheese, meat, and yak hair, which was used for clothes and tents. Such policies provoked a famine in which a quarter of the Tibetan population died. When the Panchen Lama (second to the Dalai Lama) sent Mao a letter detailing the suffering and accusing Mao of genocide, he was accused of lying.

Other groups also suffered in the Cultural Revolution, as the Four Olds campaign led to attacks on religious buildings, statuary and books. In 1974, the PLA forced the closure of mosques and burned religious books in Shadian Town. This contained around 7,200 Hui people who took matters into their own hands and seized the local PLA barracks. This led to a military attack by a 10,000-strong force of PLA soldiers in July 1975 who used guns, cannon and aerial bombardment. Within a week 1,000 Huis had been killed and 4,400 homes destroyed.

4.18 To what extent was authoritarian control achieved?

Mao's state would appear to meet most of the criteria for authoritarianism (see Chapter 1, Dictatorships – authoritarian or totalitarian?). Mao came to power through victory in Civil War. He was never elected leader, nor did he ever hold a plebiscite to give himself legitimacy. However, given the limitations of China's political past, this is, perhaps, understandable and the very fact that he amassed so much popularity in wartime could be taken as a sign of genuine popular support.

Nevertheless, he certainly expected blind submission to his authority and there was no room for individual thought or action in Mao's China. The country was a one-party state, with no elected authorities at the national level. Power was concentrated in the hands of the National People's Congress which represented the party and acted in accordance with the dictates of Mao. It was not constitutionally responsible to the body of the people and its orders were passed down through a strong chain of party command.

Mao exercised power arbitrarily, according to his strong ideological beliefs. Political and civil rights were non-existent, traditional legal bodies were dispensed with and opposition was virtually non-existent. Those who did not comply either had their privileges taken away (if they had any), or were forced to undergo struggle sessions and sent to hard labour camps or prisons. There was tight control of the media and even the army was under Mao's political control.

However, Mao did tolerate some pluralism from ethnic and religious minority groups, although such groups had to be state sanctioned. Furthermore, episodes such as his own removal from public life between 1959 and 1962 – accompanied by his own self-criticism, and the power wielded by the Gang of Four in the last years of the regime, might suggest that Mao's authoritarian control varied in its intensity. It would certainly be true to say that despite his attempts to mobilise the entire population in pursuit of national goals, the size of the country and limits to his authoritarian apparatus (for example his ability to keep the Red Guards in check) made authoritarian government difficult to achieve.

KEY CONCEPTS QUESTION

Change and Continuity: Draw up a balance sheet of the ways in which Mao exercised authoritarian control and the limits of that control.

What kind of ruler was Mao?

Some early authors, particularly those on the left, suggested that Mao was a visionary reformer whose mistakes were outweighed by his positive achievements. Jean-Paul Sartre referred to Mao as 'profoundly moral', Simone de Beauvoir claimed he was 'no more dictatorial than, for example, Roosevelt was', whilst Edgar Snow portrayed Mao as a hero who liberated the Chinese peasants from feudalism and Japanese invasion. The US historian Stuart Schram also praised Mao's 'unique vision' and 'strong continuous nationalism' and suggested that many of his apparently unreasonable decisions were logical responses in the circumstances of the time.

These authors were writing before the Cultural Revolution, and since then authors have been more critical. However, until recently, most felt Mao should not be regarded as harshly as Hitler or Stalin. Philip Short, author of *Mao: A Life* (1999) excused some of Mao's excesses because 'one has to understand the context, which is of an autocratic tradition'. Short wrote of Mao as a 'visionary, statesman, political and military strategist of genius who combined a subtle, dogged mind, awe-inspiring charisma and fiendish cleverness' to produce remarkable achievements for China. Jonathan Spence, in *Mao* (1999), claimed that 'despite the agony he caused, Mao was both a visionary and a realist'. Lee Feigon, in *Mao: A Reinterpretation* (2002), claimed that Mao grew 'increasingly original and creative in the late 1950s and the 1960s, when he set China on the road to fundamental change'.

However, Jung Chang (who wrote *Wild Swans: Three Daughters of China* (1991) and, with her husband Jon Halliday, *Mao: The Unknown Story* (2005)) as well as Jasper Becker, author of *Hungry Ghosts: China's Secret Famine* (1995), have countered these views. Becker accused Mao of starving 30–40 million people to death during the Great Leap Forward of 1958–61, whilst Chang has called him the greatest mass murderer in human history, responsible for the deaths of over 70 million people – more than Hitler and Stalin combined. Given the huge size of the Chinese population (around 600 million in

1960), Mao clearly had more potential victims than either Hitler or Stalin, but according to Chang, Mao persecuted individuals simply because of their thoughts, thus making him more tyrannical.

The recent reinterpretations of Mao's rule, including that of **Jung Chang** (although coloured by her family's own sufferings during Maoist China), would suggest that, with the benefit of hindsight, Mao's personality shaped Chinese political development in a destructive way. He sought authoritarian power in order to impose this 'vision' on the people, but it came at the cost of millions of lives. Mao's attempt to stir the masses by ideological commitment actually made his aim of a prosperous, stable and successful China more difficult to achieve.

End of unit activities

1 Draw a diagram to show the various stages in the reorganisation of agriculture in communist China.

2 Design a communist-style propaganda poster advertising the industrial changes brought in by the communist government.

3 Undertake some further research to assess the reasons for and the significance of the great Chinese famine. Try to obtain some statistics, sources and historiographical extracts to build up a full picture of what happened and how its causes have been the subject of debate.

4 Make an illustrated poster to compare the lives of Chinese women in imperial times with conditions after the arrival of the communists. Indicate the positives and negatives for both eras.

5 Choose a section from Nien Cheng's *Life and Death in Shanghai* or Jung Chang's *Wild Swans* to illustrate the Cultural Revolution. Justify your choice to the class and explain what it has taught you about the period.

6 Draw a table to show the advantages and disadvantages of being a young person growing up in Mao's China through the 1950s and 1960s.

7 Choose one religious faith or ethnic minority and consider the change and continuity across the Maoist period. Research how it was treated and affected by Chinese communist policies.

8 Complete the summary table below to show the result of Maoist attempts to control culture:

Aims	Targets	Methods	Victims	Results

9 Chose a significant event, issue or development and write two press articles on this – one for a communist Chinese newspaper and the other for a Western newspaper.

Activity

Find out more about those who suffered during the Cultural Revolution by reading *Wild Swans: Three Daughters of China* by Jung Chang and *Life and Death in Shanghai* by Nien Cheng.

Jung Chang

(b. 1952) the daughter of two prominent members of the CCP cadre, was brought up in Maoist China. Having moved to London, she has devoted her life to writing about her experiences and Chinese history. Her best-known work is her family autobiography, *Wild Swans*, which is still banned in China. She has also written (together with her historian husband, Jon Halliday) *Mao: the Unknown Story*. Her work has been strongly criticised by some academic experts, both on the grounds of factual accuracy and also selective use of evidence.

QUESTION

To what extent was China under Mao a totalitarian state?

QUESTION

Who benefited and who suffered the most from Mao's rule in China?

Theory of knowledge

History and personal prejudice:
To what extent is our perception of Mao coloured by our own political and national prejudices? Is it important to try to empathise with Mao in order to understand his policies and actions?

End of chapter activities

Paper 1 exam practice

Question

With reference to origin, purpose and content, assess the value and limitations of **Source A** for historians studying the impact of the Great Leap Forward of 1958.

[4 marks]

Skill

Value/limitations of sources

> **SOURCE A**
>
> *From an official report by Mikhail Klochko, a Soviet scientist visiting the Chinese countryside in 1958.*
>
> 'But where are those 500 million peasants?', my Soviet colleague wondered. 'Why are they not in the fields? It's the spring planting season, isn't it?' The answer to that query could be found in the thousands of smoking chimneys we saw each day, and in the fires that were visible every night over the horizon. The peasants were carrying out the orders of the party, working day and night at the mines and home blast furnaces to fulfil the 'Drive to produce metals locally'. And we know the results: they did not obtain any more iron than before, and there was much less bread and rice to go round.
>
> Quoted in Williams, S. 1985. *China Since 1949.* London, UK. Macmillan. p. 18.

Examiner's tips

Value/limitations questions require you to assess a source and comment on its value (or usefulness) to a historian studying a particular topic. The question is explicit as to what you must consider:

- origin, purpose and content
- value and limitations.

Before you write your answer, jot down some ideas on the value and limitations of the source's origin (author, place/time of origin) and on the value and limitations of the source's purpose (reason for writing or speaking and intended audience/scope).

Common mistakes

Do not fall into the trap of writing out what the sources say. Ensure that your comments are specific. Do not simply say that the source is limited because it leaves a lot out. Finally, take care to address both sides of origin and purpose. If you only concentrate on value, with just a passing reference to limitations, you will be unable to obtain the higher marks.

Simplified mark scheme

Band		Marks
1	**Explicit/developed consideration** of **BOTH** origin, purpose and content **AND** value and limitations.	3–4
2	**Limited consideration/comments** on origin, purpose and content **AND** value and limitations. **OR** more developed comments on **EITHER** origin, purpose and content **OR** value and limitations.	0–2

Student answer

The source is from an official report by Klochko, a soviet scientist visiting the Chinese countryside in 1958. It tells us that there were no peasants in the fields because they were working on the blast furnaces day and night. Klochko comments that this is because they are carrying out the orders of the party. He also says that they did not obtain any more iron than before and suggests the campaign was a waste of time. The source is valuable because it comes from a soviet observer who would be an outsider and therefore able to give an objective view of what was happening in the Chinese countryside. However, it is limited because it does not explain why the output of iron failed to increase, especially when it talks of peasants working night and day at the furnaces. This source is an official report so it will be valuable for historians as evidence of what Klochko submitted to his superior – probably in the USSR – after his visit, but it is limited because it does not tell us exactly where Klochko was visiting or who his companion was. Also, as a soviet scientist he was probably biased against the Chinese.

Examiner's comments

The candidate begins quite descriptively and the first three sentences fail to answer the question. The next sentence provides some comment on the value of the origin of the source, but the answer fails to point out the likely attitude of a Soviet observer in 1958, assuming he would view matters entirely objectively (although this comment is slightly contradicted in the final line). This means that the limitations of the source's origin are left unexplained as the following comment is about the limitation of the content, not of the origin or purpose. In reference to purpose the answer mentions that this is an 'official report' and tries to make some rather generalist comment about this, but the alleged limitations are more to do with omission than direct appraisal of purpose. The final sentence adds a further, unexplained comment on origin, which could have been developed further. Consequently, this answer cannot rise above Band 2, receiving 2 marks.

Activity

Can you improve on the student answer above? Start afresh with a plan that addresses each aspect of the question. You may incorporate some of the points made in this answer, but you will need to add others of your own and omit the irrelevant.

Summary activity

Make a table to explain why the Great Leap Forward failed:

Economic	Political	Social	International	Bad luck

Use your table to assess who or what was primarily responsible for the failure of the Great Leap Forward.

Paper 2 practice questions

1 Examine the reason for Mao's rise to power by 1949.
2 Evaluate the success of Mao's attempts to consolidate and maintain his power in the years 1949–53?
3 'In the years 1953 to 1967, Mao's economic planning was a total disaster.' To what extent do you agree with this statement?
4 Evaluate the impact of Mao's domestic policies on women and youth in China?
5 Examine the role of ideology in shaping Mao's domestic policies?
6 Evaluate the reasons why was Mao able to remain as ruler of China from 1949 until his death in 1976?

Further reading

Try reading the relevant chapters/sections of the following books:

Chang, J. 1991. *Wild Swans.* London, UK. Simon and Schuster.

Chang, J. and Halliday, J. 2005. *Mao: The Unknown Story.* London, UK. Jonathan Cape.

Cheng, N. 1986. *Life and Death in Shanghai.* London, UK. Grafton.

Feigon, L. 2002. *Mao: A Reinterpretation.* Chicago, USA. Ivan R. Dee.

Fenby, J. 2008. *The Penguin History of Modern China 1850–2008.* London, UK. Allen Lane/Penguin Books.

Short, P. 1999. *Mao: A Life.* London, UK. John Murray.

Spence, J. 1999 (2nd edn). *The Search for Modern China.* New York, USA. W. W. Norton and Company.

Spence, J. 1999. *Mao.* London, UK. Weidenfeld & Nicholson.

Xinran. 2008. *China Witness: Voices from a Silent Generation.* London, UK. Chatto & Windus.

Castro and Cuba

Emergence of an Authoritarian Regime in Cuba

Overview

- Before 1902, Cuba was a Spanish colony. Nationalist Cubans fought two Wars of Independence against Spain – from 1868 to 1878 and from 1895 to 1898. Following four years of US control, Cuba became independent in 1902.

- However, the US Platt Amendment of 1901, which the 1902 Cuban constitution had to include, gave the USA powers of supervision and intervention.

- Cuban politics was corrupt, and in the 1920s students and others launched radical protest movements.

- From 1927, Cuba was ruled by the dictator Gerardo Machado, but protests and a general strike in 1933 forced him to flee.

- The hopes of the 1933 radicals were dashed in 1934, when power increasingly passed to Fulgencio Batista. From 1934 to 1959, Batista ruled directly or through a series of puppet presidents.

- In 1953, Fidel Castro launched an unsuccessful attack on the army barracks at Moncada. In Mexico, his 26 July Movement planned Batista's overthrow.

- Before 1959, Castro's ideology was a radical mix, influenced by Cuban radical nationalists such as Martí and the leaders of resistance in the 1920s and 1930s. The main aims of his ideology were for fairness, social welfare, modernisation and independence from US interference.

- Also important was the idea of *cubiana* (see section 5.3, Nationalism and cubiana) – but there was little traditional socialism in the various manifestos published by his 26 July Movement between 1953 and 1959. This, along with his recourse to armed struggle, meant that the Cuban communists did not support him until after the Caracas Pact of July 1958.

- In 1956, Castro landed in Cuba with a small group of revolutionaries. The group included Che Guevara. By 1959, their guerrilla war had forced Batista to flee Cuba.

TIMELINE

1895 Feb: Jose Martí begins a Second War of Independence

1898 Jul: USA defeats Spain in Spanish–American War; Cuba is ceded to the USA

1901 Mar: the US Platt Amendment

1902 May: Cuba becomes independent, under US 'protection'

1927 May: Machado's dictatorship begins

1933 Aug: Machado flees – de Céspedes becomes president

Sep: Sergeants' coup takes place, led by Batista; Grau becomes president

1934 Jan: Batista increases his power; Grau steps down; opposition is repressed

1940 Aug: new constitution is passed

Oct: Batista is elected president

1944 Jun: Batista is succeeded by Grau

1952 Mar: Batista heads another coup

1953 Jul: Castro launches an attack on the Moncada army barracks; *Manifesto of the Revolutionaries of Moncada to the Nation* is published

Oct: Castro makes his 'History will absolve me' speech

1955 Jul: Castro goes to Mexico; 26 July Movement is formed

1956 Mar: Castro writes a letter publicly announcing the 26 July Movement

Dec: Castro's band of revolutionaries lands in Cuba; guerrilla war begins in the Sierra Maestra mountains

1958 May: Batista's unsuccessful offensive

Jul: Caracas Pact; communist PSP begins cooperation with the 26 July Movement

Dec: Batista resigns

1959 Jan: Castro enters Havana

Castro and Cuba

Figure 5.1 Fidel Castro (centre) entering Havana on 8 January 1959, following the 26 July Movement's victory over Batista's forces

5.1 How did conditions in Cuba before 1953 contribute to Castro's rise to power?

Castro's rise to power was unexpected – the start of his political revolt in 1956 was marked by lack of resources, early mistakes and mishaps. Nevertheless, within the space of three years, his movement succeeded in overcoming the armed forces of a brutal US-backed military dictatorship. The origins of a single-party state in Cuba lie in the political and economic problems of Cuba before 1956 – especially in the period after 1933 – and in Castro's guerrilla war of 1956–59.

The situation before 1933

During the 19th century, a strong independence movement had grown in Cuba. An unsuccessful revolt against Spanish rule, the First War of Independence (or Ten Years' War), took place between 1868 and 1878. This was followed by a Second War of Independence from 1895 to 1898. At first, this was led by **José Martí**, a revolutionary poet, political thinker and lawyer known as the 'Apostle'. By then, Cuba was Spain's last colony in the region. In 1898, when it looked as if the rebels were winning, the USA declared war on Spain. This short Spanish–American War ended in defeat for Spain, which was forced to give up Cuba in December 1898.

In many respects, Cubans had merely replaced one colonial power with another: in 1901, by the terms of the Platt Amendment, the USA claimed the right to intervene in Cuba's affairs. The USA did not grant the new republic of Cuba formal independence until 1902, and it insisted that the new Cuban constitution include the Platt Amendment. From 1902 to 1921, the USA intervened militarily four times to ensure that Cuban governments followed policies that were good for US investments, which increased greatly after 1902.

From the beginning, Cuba's politicians were corrupt, and elections were often rigged. Opposition to this and a desire to end Cuba's economic subservience to the USA inspired two radical student movements (1923 and 1927–1933), based on Martí's radical anti-imperialism and egalitarianism. Despite repression, opposition continued.

The revolution of 1933–34

On 12 August 1933, increasing unrest forced Machado (who, elected in 1925, had ruled as a dictator since 1927) to resign and flee to the USA. The USA then helped to put together a conservative-dominated and pro-US provisional government, headed by Carlos Manuel de Céspedes.

However, protests and strikes continued, and on 4 September army NCOs (non-commissioned officers, known as 'sub-officers' in some countries) staged a coup. With students and other civilian leaders, they proclaimed a new Provisional Revolutionary Government, led by Ramón Grau San Martín, a university professor. Grau's government,

Figure 5.2 José Martí (1853–95)

After the First War of Independence, Martí spent fifteen years in exile in New York, raising money to relaunch the struggle for Cuban independence and racial equality. He felt that the US party system was corrupt; he saw US imperialism as a threat to Cuban independence, was anti-capitalist and pro-labour movement, but was critical of Marx. In 1892, he set up the Cuban Revolutionary Party (PRC).

QUESTION

Why was the Platt Amendment of 1901 a disappointment for those Cubans wanting complete independence for their country?

Fact: By 1926, US investments in Cuba were valued at $1,360 million – mainly in sugar, railways, mining, banking, electricity, telephones, commerce and land. They reached their peak in 1958. Organised crime, controlled by the US mafia, also had considerable influence on Cuban political and economic life, especially as regards corruption.

Figure 5.3 A map of Cuba showing the regions of Cuba and the sites of Castro's 1956 Granma landing and the failed US-backed Bay of Pigs invasion of 1961

Figure 5.4 Fulgencio Batista (1901–73)

Batista was born on a sugar plantation. He joined the army at the age of 19, became a stenographer and rose to the rank of sergeant, participating in military tribunals. He dominated Cuban politics from 1934 to 1959 and, though remembered as a corrupt and brutal dictator, he enjoyed genuine popularity when he was the elected president from 1940 to 1944.

sworn in on 10 September, issued a manifesto promising national sovereignty, a new constitution, democracy and reforms for a 'new Cuba'. The Platt Amendment was abolished, women were given the vote, prices were cut and wages increased. These developments worried business people, and the US ambassador began to suggest US military intervention.

Batista's counter-revolution, 1934

The leader of the NCO army group in this 'sergeants' revolt' of September 1933 was **Fulgencio Batista**. The USA refused to recognise Grau's government because of its proposed reforms, and a split developed between moderates and a more radical left, led by Antonio Guiteras, who was minister of the interior, war and the navy. Another leader of the radical left was Eduardo 'Eddy' Chibás. However, unrest continued. Batista – concerned with military matters – then had meetings with the US ambassador, who persuaded Batista to take power by using his control of the army to impose a president and government that would 'protect' US economic and political interests in Cuba. On 16 January 1934, Batista transferred his support to Colonel Carlos Mendieta, a conservative politician who was immediately recognised by the USA. This ended the reforms of the short-lived 1933–34 revolution.

Puppet presidents, 1934–40

For the rest of the 1930s, Batista and the army were the real power behind seven civilian puppet presidents, who could only enact measures approved by Batista and the USA. During the years 1934–35, students resumed protests and over 100 strikes took place. Batista soon turned on the left, and used the army to crush and kill opponents. Guiteras formed the *Joven Cuba* (Young Cuba), which became an urban guerrilla movement, and called general strikes in 1934 and 1935. The general strike of March 1935 collapsed after a few days, and the severity of the military repression soon ended political protest. Mendieta and Batista imposed martial law: strike leaders were arrested and unions banned. Guiteras was later shot dead by soldiers as he tried to flee to Mexico in order to carry on the struggle, while many demonstrators were executed by firing squad.

Grau formed a new middle-class movement, based on Martí's old party: the *Partido Revolucionaria Cubano Auténtico* – known as the Auténticos. The communists – founded in 1925 – were renamed the *Partido Socialista Popular* (PSP). They agreed to cooperate with Batista and replaced revolutionary with reformist politics.

New constitution, new coup, 1940–52

In November 1939, Batista organised elections for a constituent assembly to draw up a new constitution – Grau's Auténticos won forty-one of the seventy-six seats. The assembly met in February 1940, and the new constitution was passed in August 1940. Batista was elected as president in October 1940. However, as a result of economic problems, Grau and his Auténticos party won a sweeping victory over Batista's preferred candidate for the role of president in the 1944 elections, and Batista – in charge of the army and with US support – went back to ruling from behind the scenes until 1952.

Grau's government of 1944–48, aware of Batista's power, soon abandoned the reforms expected by their supporters, and corruption continued. This disappointed those Auténticos wanting social reforms, so in 1947 Chibás formed the more radical PRC *Ortodoxo*, known as the Ortodoxos.

The 1948 elections were won by the Auténticos. According to Julia Sweig (a US scholar), this government of 1948–52 became one of the most corrupt and undemocratic in Cuba's history to date. Prior to the 1952 elections, Batista led another coup on 10 March 1952, cancelled the elections and ruled directly until 1959.

5.2 What were the most significant stages in Castro's struggle against Batista's dictatorship in the period 1953–59?

Batista's coup in 1952 met with little resistance from either the Ortodoxo or Auténtico parties, or the general public – especially as Batista promised an election in 1954. However, one person who was determined to oppose the coup was **Fidel Castro**.

QUESTION

Why did Batista use 'puppet presidents' in the period 1934 to 1940?

Figure 5.5   Fidel Castro (b. 1926)

Castro was the son of a successful Spanish immigrant. He followed the classic path of the son of a *peninsular* (the most recent immigrants from Spain and the Canary Islands, and from mainland Latin America). He was educated by Jesuits, and in 1945 he went to university to study law. He became involved in radical student politics, but stayed clear of the communists. After graduation, he travelled around Latin America, meeting other radical nationalists; he was caught up in the short-lived popular rising in Bogota in 1948.

Castro and the Moncada attack

On 26 July 1953, Fidel Castro and his brother, Raúl, led 165 youths in an attack on the Moncada army barracks in Santiago de Cuba in order to obtain weapons – but it was a failure. Half of the attackers were killed, wounded or arrested. Batista's police then began to slaughter any suspects, so the Castro brothers gave themselves up. They, along with about 100 others, were put on trial. Fidel Castro took on their defence.

SOURCE A

It looked as if his [Martí's] memory would be extinguished forever. But he lives. He has not died. His people are rebellious, his people are worthy, his people are faithful to his memory. Cubans have fallen defending his doctrines. Young men, in a magnificent gesture of reparation, have come to give their blood and to die in the hearts of his countrymen. Oh Cuba! What would have become of you if you had let the memory of your apostle die! … Condemn me, it does not matter – history will absolve me.

The concluding part of the speech Castro made at the trial following the attack on the Moncada barracks. No record was made of the two-hour speech at the time – he recreated it from memory later. Quoted in Gott, R. 2004. *Cuba: A New History*. New Haven, USA. Yale University Press. p. 151.

The five revolutionary laws:

- Return power to the people by reinstating the constitution of 1940.
- Land rights for all those holding (or squatting on) less than 67 hectares (165 acres).
- Workers in large industries and mines to have 30 per cent share of profits.
- Sugar planters to have 55 per cent share of the profits from their production.
- Action to stop corruption – property confiscated from those found guilty of fraud would be spent on workers' pensions, hospitals, asylums and charities.

Castro also promised reorganisation of public education, nationalisation of public utilities and telephones, and rent controls.

Castro's 'History will absolve me' speech (see **Source A**) later became the manifesto of his movement, and contained the '**five revolutionary laws**' that would have been published if his attack had been successful. Only twenty-six of the group were found guilty, and most were treated leniently. Fidel Castro was sentenced to fifteen years in prison and Raúl to thirteen years.

Batista won the 1954 election unopposed – in effect, Batista's control meant moderate political opposition had no way to present an alternative. His return to repression opened the way for armed opposition. During 1955 and 1956, armed groups such as *Directorio Revolucionario Estudiantil* (DRE) and the *Organización Auténtica* (OA) were set up to resist Batista's brutal repression. However, it was Castro who, in the end, organised the movement that ended Batista's dictatorship.

The 26 July Movement

On 15 May 1955, Fidel and Raúl Castro were among many prisoners released by Batista in an attempt to improve his public image. Immediately, they began to form what became known as the 26 July Movement. At first, Fidel Castro claimed that his new movement was just a different version of the *Chibasismo* (the Chibás wing of the Ortodoxos) but, in July, he and his supporters decided to go to Mexico, to plan Batista's overthrow.

Figure 5.6 Batista's troops looking at the corpses of some of the rebels killed during Castro's failed attack on the Moncada barracks in Santiago de Cuba on 26 July 1953

Preparing the revolution, Mexico 1955–56

Castro and his 26 July group stayed in Mexico for almost a year, plotting against Batista and raising money to print two manifestos. On 19 March 1956, he published a letter publicly separating his 26 July Movement from the *Chibasismo* and the Ortodoxos.

While in Mexico, one of Castro's early recruits was **Ernesto 'Che' Guevara,** who soon became a loyal collaborator and later became an important international symbol of rebellion.

By February 1956, Castro had begun to train his 'army'. However, the Mexican authorities discovered their plans and Castro, Che Guevara and some others were arrested. Once released, planning was renewed in greater secrecy. Following more

QUESTION

Why was Castro's movement known as the 26 July Movement?

189

raids by the Mexican police, Castro decided it was time to take his band of revolutionaries to Cuba – on the *Granma*, an old motor yacht. They left Mexico on 25 November 1956.

From Mexico to the Sierra Maestra

Castro had arranged for an armed rebellion to take place on 30 November in Santiago, under Frank País, the movement's leader in Cuba. This was intended to coincide with Castro's expected arrival in Cuba, but the revolt had been crushed before his group landed. On 2 December 1956, Castro and his small group of eighty-one revolutionaries landed on Cuban soil – in the wrong place and two days late. Batista's forces – alerted by the failed 30 November revolt – were there to meet him. In two days of fighting, several of the *Granma* party were killed, and twenty-two were captured and later put on trial. Only sixteen of Castro's group remained free and alive, and many of their weapons, ammunition and supplies had been lost.

The surviving **Fidelistas** retreated to the south-eastern mountain range known as the Sierra Maestra. It was from here that Castro began to organise a campaign of **guerrilla warfare**.

Batista responded to the guerilla campaign by forcibly clearing peasants from the lower slopes of the mountains – those remaining in the area were to be killed as they were considered revolutionaries. Batista also used bombers and paramilitary death squads, known as *Los Tigres*.

Attacks by the 26 July Movement were increasingly successful, and soon the movement began to attract recruits from the local population, allowing Castro to organise bigger offensives. However, until February 1957, most people thought Castro had been killed, as this was what Batista and the Cuban press reported.

What changed things were the reports of **Herbert Matthews**, foreign correspondent of the *New York Times*, who was taken to meet Castro by Frank País. Matthews reported Castro's successes, which encouraged Batista's opponents and brought extra recruits. Throughout 1957 and early 1958, the size of Castro's rebel army increased and the area of military operations expanded. The sympathy and respect they showed for the poor peasants gave them valuable support amongst the local population.

The urban resistance

Castro also organised a 'civic resistance movement' on a national scale, to get support from workers and liberal middle-class professionals. This movement was established first in Havana, and saw 26 July Movement supporters collaborating with middle-class Ortodoxos. In overall control was **Frank País**.

In July 1957, just before he was gunned down by Batista's police, País had persuaded leading Ortodoxo politicians and business people to issue a joint 'Pact of the Sierra', which called for a 'civic revolutionary front' to force Batista from power and hold new elections.

Fidelistas: Originally, this referred to the close group of early supporters of Fidel Castro and the 26 July Movement – in Mexico, the Sierra and in the first governments. They were a cross-section of Cuban society – workers, peasants, black people and middle-class liberals – who responded to Castro's charismatic appeal.

guerrilla warfare: This is the name given to war fought by small forces of irregular soldiers against regular armies, involving unorthodox methods; guerrillas tend to be most effective when they have the support of local people.

Herbert Matthews (1900–77)

Matthews, a reporter during the Spanish Civil War (1936–39), was a strong supporter of the republican cause against Franco in Spain. Castro's supporters contacted him and smuggled him up to Castro's armed group. His articles praised the bravery and commitment of the rebels, and exploded Batista's claims that Castro was dead. They also made Castro into an international figure.

QUESTION

What can you learn about the nature of Castro's movement from Figure 5.8? What is the significance of the armband Castro is wearing?

Figure 5.8 This photograph, taken in the Sierra Maestra, shows Fidel Castro (wearing glasses), with leading guerrillas in the 26 July Movement, Celia Sánchez (behind him) and Camilo Cienfuegos (right). Celia Sánchez was Castro's closest friend and his lover, and had been a political adviser to him since 1953

In early 1958, the communist PSP finally gave its support to Castro. Castro's movement then began to discuss plans for a revolutionary general strike in the cities. Faustino Pérez, the new leader of the movement and the 'civic resistance' in Havana, thought the time was ripe – Castro was less sure.

However, Castro let the planned strike go ahead. He and Pérez signed a manifesto, 'Total War Against Tyranny', calling for a strike and declaring that the struggle against Batista had entered 'its final stage'. The manifesto also outlined political plans for the post-Batista period. The date of the general strike was set for 9 April 1958.

Castro and Cuba

But the police and the army were ready, and the uprising was soon defeated. However, although this failure led Castro to decide to concentrate on the guerrilla war, the working class remained an important part of the movement's campaign against Batista, and was to be significant for developments after Castro's victory.

The final stage

By this point, Cuba was on the verge of revolution. In February 1958, Castro's 26 July Movement had announced a war on property and production in order to further isolate Batista by hitting the economic élites – both national and foreign – that had supported him up to then.

SOURCE B

[Commerce, industry and capital], which have whole-heartedly supported President Batista since he took over the government in 1952, are growing impatient with the continued violence in the island.

Comments in a telegram sent by the resident *New York Times* correspondent in Havana, 15 September 1957. Quoted in Bethell, L. (ed.). 1993. *Cuba: A Short History*. Cambridge, UK. Cambridge University Press. p. 90.

By mid-1958, four other guerrilla fronts had been opened up, while mergers with other rebel bands succeeded in gaining more local recruits for the 26 July Movement. In May 1958, Batista launched a massive 'liquidation campaign' to crush Castro's forces, involving over 12,000 troops. By then, Castro's forces were about 5,000 strong.

In July 1958, while the offensive was still taking place, representatives of the leading opposition groups met in Caracas, Venezuela, to organise a united front against Batista. The resulting 'Pact of Caracas' saw Castro recognised as the principal leader of the anti-Batista movement, with his rebel army as the main arm of the revolution.

Castro's counter-offensive

By August 1958, the government offensive had collapsed. This proved to be an important turning point, and in the late summer Castro's forces launched a counter-offensive. Within weeks, the government's forces in the east were overrun and cut off from reinforcements. More and more provincial towns went over to the rebels. After these successes, several leaders of the communist PSP, which had allied itself with Castro's forces in early 1958, took up positions within Castro's movement.

Castro now turned his attention to the west and Havana. Batista's increased use of terror (including torture and executions) at last provoked spontaneous uprisings across the island, and more and more people joined the urban resistance or the guerrilla groups.

QUESTION

What was the significance of the Pact of Caracas of July 1958?

Fact: The communist PSP had considerable support amongst workers and black people, but it was not trusted by groups on the left – especially as it had given limited support to Batista after 1937. In 1942, two communists even entered Batista's cabinet. However, after the start of the Cold War and his 1952 coup, Batista banned the PSP. By 1957, they were openly in opposition to Batista.

communist ideology: Before 1958, the communist PSP was opposed to Castro's insurrection, and had publicly condemned the 1953 Moncada attack for being 'guided by mistaken bourgeois conceptions' and inspired by 'putschist methods, peculiar to bourgeois political factions'. It was not until the mid-1960s that, for several reasons, Castro decided to carry his revolution into the communist camp.

By the end of 1958, Castro's guerrilla army numbered about 50,000 and was clearly in control of the countryside. This provoked several military plots against Batista, so, on New Year's Eve 1958, he resigned and fled with his family. Batista's army units then ceased to offer any resistance to Castro's forces. On 1 January 1959, after an unsuccessful US-backed coup, command of the army passed to Colonel Ramon Barguin, who on 2 January 1959 ordered an immediate ceasefire. On the same day, in Santiago de Cuba, Castro made a speech in which he said that 'The Revolution begins now', making it clear that this time, unlike in 1898, the USA would not be allowed to dominate Cuba's history.

A week later, on 8 January 1959, after slow progress through cheering crowds, Fidel Castro entered Havana to a hero's welcome.

5.3 How significant was the role of ideology in Castro's rise to power in 1959?

Although Castro adopted aspects of **communist ideology** after 1960, Richard Gott states that nationalism was more important in his ideology than socialism, and Martí was more influential than Marxist ideology with its emphasis on class conflict.

While the main factor in Castro's rise to power was his movement's guerrilla war against Batista, the stated aims of the movement were also important in gaining public support. These aims were publicised in various manifestos issued before 1959.

Manifestos

Castro saw manifestos as essential – 'Propaganda must not be abandoned for a minute, for it is the soul of every struggle.' According to Herbert Matthews, Castro's attack on the Moncada barracks in 1953 was inspired by patriotism, with aims similar to those of Martí and **Antonio Guiteras**. In the 1920s and 1930s, Guiteras had advocated a programme of radical reforms with vague socialist undertones. Castro was part of this radical Cuban nationalist tradition, as is shown by his first manifesto, 'Manifesto of the Revolutionaries of Moncada to the Nation', dated 23 July 1953. Prepared before the attack, it indicates the kind of revolution he had in mind: independence from foreign control, social justice based on economic and industrial modernisation, and restoration of the 1940 Constitution.

Castro's second 'manifesto', his 'History will absolve me' speech of 16 October 1953, developed these ideas. It included promises of agrarian reform, rent reductions, industrial development and modernisation, expansion of education and health care, and taking control of public utilities, which were mostly in the hands of US companies.

Fact: The 1940 Constitution – even though it was contradictory and impractical – was a symbol of democracy and freedom for most Cuban oppositionists and revolutionaries. It had a strong social democratic content (eight-hour day, paid holidays, pensions, social insurance). It gave the vote to all those over the age of 20, including women, and political rights such as multi-party elections. Following his 1953 *Manifesto*, Castro repeated his promise to restore the 1940 Constitution several times over the next six years.

QUESTION

How far does Castro's determination to remove poverty and inequality prove that he was a communist? Why did the US often see such social and economic programmes as being 'communist'?

Antonio Guiteras (1906–35)

Inspired by Martí, Guiteras had views that were a mixture of nationalism and anti-capitalism. In 1933, after the overthrow of Machado, Guiteras served in Grau's government. When Batista overthrew Grau, Guiteras formed *Joven Cuba* and began urban guerrilla warfare to spark off an insurrection. In May 1935, Guiteras was shot dead by soldiers (see section 5.1, Puppet presidents, 1934–40).

cubiana: This term was first used by the 19th century rebels struggling for Cuban independence and refers to the collective national interests of Cuba. *Cubiana* meant modernisation – the socio-economic and cultural development of Cuba – on Cuban terms, not on the terms set by liberal capitalism and foreign imperialism. Its aims were economic growth, a high level of social welfare, and socio-economic fairness.

Figure 5.9 Poor peasant housing in Oriente Province, Cuba, before 1959

Two formal 'manifestos of the 26 July Movement', issued by Castro while he was in Mexico, showed no signs of communism or Marxism–Leninism and lacked any systematic ideas or ideology. In fact, while Castro wanted a radical social revolution for all Cubans, he angrily rejected claims that he was inspired by communism.

During 1957–58, when Castro was in the Sierra, there was a continuous stream of manifestos – and, after the spring of 1958, talks on Radio Rebelde (the illegal radio station of Castro and the rebels). These only offered broad outlines of policies and reforms rather than a coherent programme. A manifesto issued on 12 March 1958, to help prepare for the unsuccessful 9 April general strike, mainly repeated elements of his 'History will absolve me' speech. In July 1958, the Caracas Pact, which was signed by all of the groups opposed to Batista – except the communist PSP – resulted in the issue of another manifesto. This manifesto mentioned agrarian reform but otherwise contained no radical socialist policies.

In fact, it was not until 1958 that serious contacts between Castro and the Cuban communists began. By July, Carlos Rodriguez, one of the leaders of the PSP, had joined the rebels in the Sierra and there was growing cooperation between the movement and the PSP. However, while Castro was prepared to accept support from all quarters, he made it clear that he was in charge.

Nationalism and *cubiana*

The main source of inspiration for Castro's ideology was the more radical version of Cuban nationalism, stretching back to 1868 and the First War of Independence, the student rebellions of the 1920s and 1930s, and the idea of *cubiana*. Castro believed that the 26 July Movement, as the custodian of *cubiana* and as the vanguard (the leading group that maintained and promoted revolutionary aims), needed to achieve Cuban independence and modernisation. Castro's political ideas before 1959 appear to have been more nationalistic and less radical than those of his two closest allies: his brother **Raúl Castro** and Che Guevara. According to Sebastian Balfour, even they (though more familiar with Marxism than Fidel) were 'unorthodox communists'. While it is possible that a Cuban version of 'socialism in one country' may have begun to emerge from the political discussions Fidel had with Raúl and Che in the Sierra, this was not reflected in the movement's manifestos.

Figure 5.10   Raúl Castro (b. 1931)

Raúl was the youngest of the five Castro siblings. Unlike Fidel, he was always known as a radical. At university, he became involved in the youth movement of the Communist Party. In 1953, he attended the World Youth Congress in Sofia and visited Bucharest and Prague. He fought alongside Fidel from 1953, and he was the first to welcome Carlos Rodrigues, the political leader of the PSP, to the Sierra in July 1958. His strong pro-communist views worried anti-communists in the 26 July Movement. At the time of writing, he was president of the Cuban Council of State and the president (as premier) of the Council of Ministers of Cuba.

SOURCE C

Because of my ideological background, I belong to those who believe that the solution of the world's problems lies behind the so-called iron curtain, and I see this movement [26 July] as one of the many inspired by the bourgeoisie's desire to free themselves from the economic chains of imperialism. I always thought of Fidel as an authentic leader of the leftist bourgeoisie, although his image is enhanced by personal qualities of extraordinary brilliance that set him above his class.

An extract from a letter written by Che Guevara to René Ramos Latour, national coordinator of the 26 July Movement in December 1957. Quoted in Franqui, C. 1980. *Diary of the Cuban Revolution*. New York, USA. Viking Press. p. 269.

As well as the 19th century nationalist struggles, Castro was inspired by the various Latin and Central American anti–imperialist movements of the 1930s and 1940s. Castro's movement was similar to these national liberation movements, which mobilised the masses against powerful traditional élites and attempted to escape from the controlling influence of US economic interests.

5.4 Why was Castro successful in his bid to overthrow Batista?

Military and political factors

One reason for the success of Castro's guerrilla movement was the quality of his commanders, including Che Guevara, Raúl Castro and Camilo Cienfuegos. Another

KEY CONCEPTS QUESTION

Continuity and **Significance**: To what extent does *cubiana* show continuity between Martí's ideas and those of Castro? How significant was it in relation to Castro's overall ideology?

reason was that, despite the disastrous start, the area in which his small group of survivors began operations was an unimportant part of the island, with only a few Rural Guard (a paramilitary police force) outposts. Moreover, the local population had been terrorised by commanders from the Rural Guard for decades and resented the central government in Havana. The growing success of the guerrilla group's military offensives meant that Batista was forced to divert troops to the rural areas from the cities, allowing opposition there to mobilise.

SOURCE D

The Cuban revolutionary struggle was a national one, encompassing all sectors of Cuban society. However, critical to its success was the working class, which 'provided a backdrop to the revolutionary struggle'. The labour movement was a dominant force in the political development and direction of the revolution. Workers were prominent actors throughout the urban wing of the revolutionary struggle, which complemented the rural armed struggle.

Saney, I. 2004. *Cuba: A Revolution in Motion.* London, UK. Zed Books. p. 11.

Batista's brutality and repression increased opposition to him and brought additional support for Castro's guerrillas. Furthermore, there were other problems facing Batista – as the rebel movement grew, so did dissent within the army ranks. This resulted in a series of army conspiracies that undermined Batista's confidence. By the late 1950s, Batista was thus facing mounting popular opposition and armed resistance, but with an increasingly unreliable army.

Economic developments

Another reason for Castro's success lies with the economic situation of Cuba in the 1950s. Between 1952 and 1954, the price of sugar declined, triggering the first of a series of recessions in the Cuban economy. In addition, the effects of the 1934 trade treaty with the USA, which removed tariffs, greatly contributed to the inability of Cuban industry to develop. Consequently, there was growing unemployment: by 1957, 17 per cent of the labour force were unemployed, while a further 13 per cent were underemployed.

Role of the USA

Another reason for Castro's eventual success was the attitude of the US government. In late 1957, the US government decided that, in order to protect US investments in Cuba and prevent Castro coming to power, it was necessary for Batista to give way to a caretaker government acceptable to US interests.

On 9 December 1957, a financier sent by the US State Department tried but failed to persuade Batista to retire. In March 1958, the US government began to reduce its support for Batista's dictatorship. Its first step was to place an arms embargo on both sides – this both weakened Batista's hold over his military and civilian supporters, and it made resistance to Castro's forces more difficult.

Historical debate:
Historians are divided over the importance of the urban resistance to Batista in the final victory of Castro's 26 July Movement. Read **Source D** again. Do you think this is a fair statement concerning the significance of the urban resistance?

Fact: Both Castro and Guevara had at first been inspired by Juan Perón's movement in Argentina. Castro was much inspired by the popular Colombian politician Jorge Gaitán, had attended the anti-imperialist student congress in Colombia in 1947, and had joined in the riots sparked off by Gaitán's assassination in that year. Guevara had been in Guatemala in 1954, where he witnessed the fall (as a result of a US-sponsored military invasion) of the reforming government of democratically elected Jacobo Arbenz. Both of these events showed how US interests and power made reform difficult if not impossible.

SOURCE E

According to US ambassador Earl E. T. Smith, intimations that Washington no longer backed Batista had 'a devastating psychological effect' on the army and was 'the most effective step taken by the Department of State in bringing about the downfall of Batista'.

Bethell, L. (ed.). 1993. *Cuba: A Short History*. Cambridge, UK. Cambridge University Press. p. 91.

Popular support

Apart from the growing successes of the rebel army, the deteriorating economic conditions in Cuba, and Batista's brutal repression, another significant reason for Castro's success was undoubtedly the increasing support obtained by the 26 July Movement. At the start of Castro's campaign, this had mainly been restricted to Cuba's rural areas. The rebels' policy of treating the peasants with respect, paying for food and helping with harvests – as well as their execution of the peasants' most brutal persecutors – gained them considerable support. It was this that enabled them to avoid detection by Batista's forces in the early stages of the guerrilla war. However, support soon spread to urban areas, where both the working class and student movements increasingly became involved in the urban resistance. In addition, Castro's movement also gained support amongst large sections of the middle classes and the intelligentsia.

Much of this growing support was achieved by Castro's increasingly skilful and coordinated use of the radio and the press. Ever since his student days, Castro had seen the value of using the media; once his rebellion had begun, he often staged publicity stunts – such as giving Herbert Matthews, a US journalist of the *New York Times*, an exclusive interview in the Sierra Mountains. The report, when it appeared, gave the impression – which Castro had cleverly stage-managed – that Castro's forces were larger and controlled more territory than in fact was the case. The regular broadcasts, from 1958, by their own Radio Rebelde were increasingly popular and so helped to build support – their deliberately accurate reports of military clashes, their affirmations of patriotism, and the repeated announcement of their planned reforms brought them new supporters and recruits. Towards the end, Castro's call for 'national regeneration' and economic reform even began to win him supporters amongst Cuba's business community. By 1959, his successful use of modern mass media had won the rebels considerable support – thus his slow journey from Santiago de Cuba in the east to Havana in the west was accompanied along the route by large cheering crowds who saw his movement as the one that would regenerate Cuba and introduce long-overdue reforms.

End of unit activities

1   Carry out some further research on the attitudes of the PRC Auténtico, the PRC Ortodoxo and the communist PSP in the 1940s and 1950s towards Castro and others who advocated armed struggle as the way to end Batista's dictatorship.

2   Reread section 5.2 and, using any extra information you can obtain from other sources, produce a table summarising the main steps in Castro's rise to power from 1953 to 1959.

Theory of knowledge

History, ethics and core values:
Many people believe it is a universal core value or moral principle never to resort to violence. So is armed struggle or resistance against a government ever justifed? What if there are elections, but they are manipulated or rigged? Is such a question related to moral relativism and the particular political and social contexts of different societies, or is it an example that falls under the heading of universal values?

KEY CONCEPTS QUESTION

Significance: What were the most significant factors involved in Castro's successful revolution in 1959?

3 Find out more about Raúl Castro and Che Guevara. Then write a couple of paragraphs to explain the significance of the roles they each played in the victory of the 26 July Movement.

4 Carry out some further research on the ideas of 'Eddy' Chibás and Chibasismo, and those of Antonio Guiteras. Then create a table, with the headings: 'Chibás', 'Guiteras' and 'Castro'. Underneath these headings, write down the main aims and/or policies of each in the period before 1959, trying to place similar ideas next to each other.

5 Try to find a transcript of Castro's 'History will absolve me' speech. Do you think history has, in fact, absolved Castro in relation to the legitimacy of his decision to resort to armed rebellion?

Overview

- After 1959, Castro began to create a politically centralised one-party state – with political, social and economic decision-making concentrated in his hands and those of his *Fidelista* élite.

- From as early as April 1959, when Castro announced the suspension of elections, relations with the USA became more and more strained. By January 1960, the USA had drawn up a plan to overthrow Castro.

- During 1959, Castro began to establish a situation of dual power by creating alternative organisations that increasingly bypassed the government.

- Castro also began to move against liberals opposed to his more radical policies. By July, Urrutia had been forced to resign and other liberals and anti-communists either resigned or were gradually removed over the following months.

- In 1960, Cuba made several trade agreements with the Soviet Union, East European states and China. As a result of increasing US economic restrictions, Castro nationalised US companies operating in Cuba.

- In April 1961, Castro made the first announcement of Cuba's move to socialism. This was reinforced by the Bay of Pigs incident. Over the next few years, Cuba moved closer to the Soviet Union – and to a Soviet-style economy and state.

- Between 1961 and 1965 the 26 July Movement, the DR (*Directorio Revolucionario*, the successor to the DRE) and the PSP were merged to form the Communist Party of Cuba (PCC) – taking action in 1962 against Escalante for attempting to promote his own supporters.

- In 1965, the numbers of Cubans leaving Castro's Cuba increased in what became the first large 'exodus' – this Camarioca Exodus and two others (the Mariel Boatlift in 1980 and the Malecón Exodus in 1994) effectively 'exported' potential oppositionists.

- From 1968, internal opposition also emerged within the PCC and from groups of intellectuals (such as the Varela Project): first it was against the growing ties with the Soviet Union; then in the late 1980s opposition developed in response to Gorbachev's liberal reforms in the Soviet Union; and later, in the 1990s, it emerged during the Special Period.

- On 18 February 2008, illness forced Fidel Castro to resign his leadership posts and his brother Raúl took over.

TIMELINE

1959 Feb: Castro becomes prime minister

Apr: Castro announces suspension of elections

Jun: Agrarian Reform Act

1960 Feb: trade deal is signed with Soviet Union

May: US oil companies in Cuba refuse to refine Soviet crude oil

Jun: Castro nationalises US refineries

Jul: US reduces quota for Cuban sugar; Soviet Union agrees to buy the surplus

Aug: main US businesses in Cuba are nationalised

Sep: Castro makes his 'First declaration of Havana' speech.

Nov: first US trade embargo on exports to Cuba

1961 Apr: Castro proclaims Cuba's socialist revolution; Bay of Pigs incident

Jul: 26 July Movement, communist PSP and Directorio Revolucionario (DR) merge to form the Integrated Revolutionary Organisations (ORI)

1962 Mar: The Escalante faction of the communist PSP is removed from positions

Oct: Cuban Missile Crisis

1963 Jul: ORI becomes the United Party of the Socialist Revolution (PURS)

1965 Oct: PURS becomes the Communist Party of Cuba (PCC)

1976 Feb: new constitution to establish *Poder Popular* is approved

Dec: first meeting of the new National Assembly; Fidel Castro becomes president

1992 Sep: Aldana is sacked; purge of reformists from PCC

1993 Feb: first direct elections to the National Assembly

2002 Jun: National Assembly amends constitution to make socialist system of government permanent

2008 Feb: Fidel Castro announces his resignation; Raúl takes over

---

KEY QUESTIONS

- How did Castro consolidate his power in the period 1959–75?
- To what extent did the reforms of 1959–75 mean that Castro had become a communist?
- What were the most significant measures taken to maintain Castro's power after 1975?
- How far did foreign policy help Castro to maintain power?
- What other methods did Castro use to maintain his power?

5.5 How did Castro consolidate his power in the period 1959–75?

In January 1959, a new government was installed. The president, as promised by Castro before 1959, was the moderate judge Manuel Urrutia. José Miró Cardona was prime minister. They presided over a cabinet in which there were only three members of Castro's rebel army (and only one of these was from the 26 July Movement). However, it soon became clear that the real power lay with Castro, who was appointed military commander-in-chief of the new Rebel Armed Forces.

As Castro had promised, there were trials (broadcast on TV) of several hundred of Batista's political supporters, especially senior police and torturers. Most were found guilty and many were executed by firing squad.

Dual power, January–November 1959

dual power: This term refers to a situation where political power, in reality, is shared between the formal government and an unofficial body. Such situations rarely last for long, as each authority tries to impose its power.

In January 1959, Castro formed the Office of the Revolutionary Plans and Coordination (ORPC), an unofficial committee composed of his closest advisers, including his brother Raúl and Guevara. This soon created a situation of **dual power** between the ORPC and the cabinet, as the ORPC began to push forward the revolution that Castro wanted.

In February, Castro became prime minister, taking on extra powers, and presiding over a government comprising both radicals and moderates. In April, he announced the suspension of elections, and in May 1959 the National Institute of Agrarian Reform (INRA) was set up, absorbing the ORPC. Castro was its president, and Núñez Jiménez – a Marxist economist – was its director. Its formal role was to deal with the issues of agrarian reform and industrial development, but INRA quickly became, in practice, the effective government.

In June 1959, several moderate members of the cabinet resigned over what they saw as 'communistic' policies. As communists were increasingly appointed to administrative

QUESTION

Why was Castro's formation of INRA important in establishing his power?

posts, Urrutia and others began to make public criticisms of the growing influence of communists.

Castro then decided to end the dual power situation. In July, Urrutia was forced to resign. He was replaced by a supporter of Castro, Osvaldo Dorticós. More sympathetic to the communists, Dorticós remained in post until 1976.

By the end of November 1959, most of the remaining moderates or liberals had either resigned or been forced out of office; four more went in 1960. The removal of anti-communists and non-communists resulted in a new coalition containing several communists.

Revolutionary consolidation

From 1960, Castro and this new leadership consolidated a centralised form of rule by Fidel and a handful of friends, via a cabinet that held all legislative and executive powers. By December 1960, the press had been brought into line – often through seizure by communist-led trade unions. Castro also assumed the power to appoint new judges.

However, from 1968 Cuba became increasingly dependent on the Soviet Union. New state structures and institutions were developed along Soviet lines. In 1972, the cabinet was enlarged, with an executive committee of eight that took over many of Castro's functions. The shift from individual to collective responsibility was designed to create a more formally democratic system and give greater political stability. At the same time, the Communist Party was also enlarged and reorganised along more 'orthodox' lines to make it more representative.

Castro thus no longer had the unlimited authority that he had in the 1960s. Despite differences at the top over later economic policies, Castro's regime remained fairly stable and united.

Opposition

There were many opponents of the regime in the early years. Many in the movement disliked the growing influence of the communists in Castro's regime. On 19 October 1959, Huber Matos, the governor of Camagüey province and one of the leading figures of the revolutionary war, resigned in protest. Matos, along with others sharing his views, was put on trial for 'rebellion'. Castro then used this crisis to further establish his own position by creating armed militias as part of the new revolutionary structure of power.

Some opponents, whose social and economic interests were threatened by the revolution, resorted to counter-revolutionary guerrilla warfare. This was often supported by the USA. Thousands of Cubans died in this civil war between 1960 and 1966. By 1966, however, these opponents had been convincingly defeated.

The US-sponsored Bay of Pigs incident (see section 5.6, The impact of US actions) in April 1961 had led to the immediate arrest of all suspected 'counter-revolutionaries'.

Fact: The Communist Party of Cuba (PCC), established in 1965, had never functioned as a mass party. It did not even hold its first congress until 1975. In 1972, it was given a new party structure, with a 100-strong central committee, as well as a smaller politburo and secretariat. It also produced new party statutes and a new programme. Membership rose steadily from 50,000 in 1965 to over 500,000 by 1980. By then, more than 9 per cent of all Cuban citizens aged over twenty-five belonged to the party. These changes turned it into more of a typical ruling party. At the same time, the proportion of military personnel in the leading bodies dropped significantly, making it a more normal civilian party.

Fact: The USA's offensive against Cuba, to undermine its government and society, was massive. Castro used these real US threats to increase his control, to bring about a one-party system and to mobilise the people to transform Cuba.

Figure 5.11 Fidel Castro in 1964, relaxing while planning consolidation of his revolution

About 3,500 counter-revolutionaries were detained in Havana alone. The resulting wave of nationalism and pride following Cuba's victory meant that those opposed to Castro's regime could be seen as traitors. However, the political centralisation and state control that followed was partly a response to genuine feelings of insecurity.

SOURCE A

According to US Senate reports, the CIA's second largest station in the world was based in Florida. At the height of the undercover American offensive [against Cuba] in the 1960s and 1970s … the CIA controlled an airline and a flotilla of spy ships operating off the coast of Cuba, and ran up to 120,000 Cuban agents, who dealt in economic sabotage, assassination and terrorism, and economic and biological warfare … Over 600 plans to assassinate Castro were devised. Nearly 3,500 Cubans have died from terrorist acts, and more than 2,000 are permanently disabled. As an ex-CIA agent has said, 'no country has suffered terrorism as long and consistently as Cuba'.

Balfour, S. 2009. *Castro*. London, UK. Longman. p. 190.

With the most serious oppositions defeated by the mid-1960s, Castro felt able to consider a more 'liberal' approach.

The Communist Party

As the 26 July Movement was mainly a guerrilla army, Castro needed the political experience provided by the communist PSP. The PSP had long experience of party politics and of organising mass movements such as the Confederation of Cuban Workers (CTC) and, unlike members of the 26 July Movement, it had prior governmental experience. Castro began negotiations with leading members of the PSP for the creation of a new Communist Party. He hoped to fuse this with the more radical wing of his movement, and so strengthen his control. In July 1961, the 26 July Movement, the DR and the PSP merged into the Integrated Revolutionary Organisations (ORI).

Initially, the old PSP came to dominate the ORI. Anibal Escalante, the ORI's Organisation Secretary, was particularly powerful – he gave preference to his old PSP comrades who were likely to be loyal to him. So, in March 1962, Castro denounced Escalante for 'sectarianism' and removed him from his post. A massive restructuring of the ORI then took place – almost half of its membership was expelled, most from the PSP faction. Huge efforts were made to recruit new members. In 1963, the ORI became the United Party of the Socialist Revolution (PURS); on 3 October 1965, the PURS became the Communist Party of Cuba (PCC). Thus, by the end of 1965, revolutionary power had been consolidated and Castro had established his pre-eminence over all potential rivals.

However, this did not mean that Castro was in full control of the new party. From 1965 to 1968, his criticisms of the Soviet Union over peaceful coexistence and revolution in developing countries (see section 5.6, The Soviet connection) were opposed by some traditionalist communists in the PCC. In February 1968, their leaders were put on trial for factionalism. The result of this 'micro-faction'

Fact: The organisation of party cells, selection of party members, and all promotions and dismissals had to be cleared through Escalante's office. Increasingly, party cells asserted their authority over administrators, and a preliminary system of political commissars was introduced in the armed forces. Much of this was similar to the methods used by Stalin as general secretary of the CPSU in the Soviet Union to establish a powerful position for himself during the 1920s. Stalin used his powers as general secretary to dismiss real or potential opponents, and to appoint his own supporters. This allowed him to draw up agendas and pack meetings with supporters, and this eventually gave him control of the party and, in a one-party state, of the country itself.

QUESTION

What were the main stages in Castro's formation of the PCC between 1961 and 1965?

affair was even greater control for Castro. After 1968, the party posed no serious challenge to Castro.

Mass organisations

As well as the communists, there were several mass organisations through which opposition could be expressed. In particular, Castro made early interventions to influence the trade union movement and university students in favour of unity between communist delegates and anti-communists within his movement.

Federation of University Students

On 18 October 1959, the election for president of the students' union, the Federation of University Students (FEU), was between Rolando Cubelas (the 'Unity' candidate, backed by the PSP) and Pedro Boitel, the 26 July Movement's candidate. After Castro intervened, the election was won by Cubelas, who later aligned the FEU closer to Marxism-Leninism (see Chapter 1, Terminology and definitions).

The trade unions

In November 1959, the Confederation of Cuban Workers (CTC) held its tenth Congress to elect a new leadership. The 26 July Movement's slate (list) of candidates seemed certain to win a clear majority, but Castro pushed for 'unity' with the communists.

However, in 1970, opposition emerged from the trade unions and the workers – shown by absenteeism and poor productivity. On 26 July 1970, in a long speech to a massive crowd, Castro admitted his mistakes and argued for more democratic methods of consultation at grassroots level, and greater delegation of powers from the centre. Up until this point, Castro accepted, the government had tended to treat workers as a production army.

5.6 To what extent did the reforms of 1959–75 mean that Castro had become a communist?

According to Balfour, before 1959 Castro had a radical programme of reforms but no clear view of the future direction of his revolution – suggesting he was not a communist before 1959. It was only after 1959 that Castro saw socialism as providing a structure within which to achieve the radical nationalist aims set out in his manifestos.

The impact of US actions

After Batista's fall, Manuel Urrutia, president of Cuba from January to July 1959, nominated a cabinet drawn from moderate members of the 26 July Movement, who

QUESTION

How far did the relationship between the mass organisations and the Cuban government, in the period before 1975, allow democracy?

ACTIVITY

Reread this section, and then write a couple of paragraphs to explain to what extent you think Castro had succeeded in establishing an authoritarian system in Cuba by 1975. Were there any limitations on his power? Keep this work to hand as a linked key concepts activity appears at the end of section 5.7.

Fact: Before January 1960, the CIA had proposed 'harassment' by CIA-funded Cuban exiles, using small planes to carry out sabotage attacks on Cuban sugar mills. Eisenhower asked for a more ambitious scheme to topple Castro. The result was the Bay of Pigs incident in April 1961 (see The Bay of Pigs incident, April 1961 below).

QUESTION

Is Figure 5.12 evidence to prove that Castro was a communist?

Figure 5.12 Fidel Castro (left) with Che Guevara (centre) and USSR deputy premier Anastas Mikoyan (right) during Mikoyan's visit to Havana in February 1960

Fact: In December 2014, US president Barack Obama and Raúl Castro, agreed to discuss the resumption of diplomatic relations between the two countries. Then, on 11 April 2015, during the Summit of the Americas in Panama, an historic meeting took place between the two leaders. Following this, in May 2015, the US agreed to remove Cuba from its list of `terror states'. However, in the following month, the US also announced it would give a further $30 million to organisations `sponsoring democracy' in Cuba. More importantly, there was no announcement concerning the ending of the US economic blockade of Cuba. By then, the blockade had been in force for 55 years, and had cost Cuba an estimated $116.8 billion.

were acceptable to most sections of public opinion in Cuba and even the USA. However, the US government's attitude altered after the May 1959 Agrarian Reform Act (see section 5.10, The early years, 1959–68). The USA issued a Note of Protest and began to plan Castro's overthrow. The threat from the USA, and frequent CIA-organised sabotage attacks by Batista's supporters and Cuban exiles, led Castro to establish trade links with other countries, including the Soviet Union, in order to reduce Cuba's dependence on the USA.

In June 1959, Guevara visited various developing countries to find new markets for Cuban sugar. In July, the Soviet Union placed an order for 500,000 tonnes, as they had done in 1955 while Batista was still in control. The Soviet Union was at first uncertain about Castro's intended direction, but in February 1960 Anastas

5

Fact: Since the early 20th century, US governments had attempted to ensure that Cuban governments followed policies that benefited US investments in Cuba. US companies owned large proportions of the main banks and public utility companies in Cuba (see section 5.1, The situation before 1933) as well as considerable amounts of the best agricultural land. In particular, the USA pushed for Cuba to concentrate on sugar production. Cuba also produced some tobacco, coffee and rice, but the production of sugar was the main source of income for Cuba. US governments agreed to purchase a large proportion – or quota – of Cuba's sugar crop at prices that were usually slightly higher than average world prices. However, in return, Cuba had to agree to give preferential access for US products (such as reducing or even abolishing import duties). This meant it was very difficult for the Cuban economy to develop and industrialise and it was heavily dependent on the US economy. Any reduction in US sugar quotas or in the price Washington was prepared to pay for sugar would seriously affect the economy. Consequently, many Cubans yearned for greater economic and political independence.

Mikoyan, the Soviet Union's deputy premier, arrived in Cuba to open a Soviet trade exhibition.

The Soviet Union then agreed to purchase a million tonnes of sugar each year for five years, and to provide $100 million credit for the purchase of plant and equipment. Cuba then signed similar agreements with several other Eastern bloc countries.

As early as January 1960, a draft plan to overthrow Castro had been presented to the US president, Dwight D. Eisenhower – he had pushed for more than the 'harassment' initially suggested by Allen Dulles, director of the CIA. These decisions were made well before May 1960, when the Soviet Union restored diplomatic relations with Cuba (these had been broken off following Batista's coup in 1952).

In early 1960, sabotage attacks were stepped up. On 4 March, a French ship carrying Belgian small arms was blown up in Havana harbour, killing 100 people and injuring over 300. At the mass rally that followed to condemn this outrage, Castro warned of the possibility of a US-backed invasion and, for the first time, used the now-famous slogan: '*Patria o muerte, venceremos*' ('Fatherland or death, we shall overcome').

The previous month, the first delivery of crude oil – cheaper than that sold by US companies – had arrived from the Soviet Union. The US government, wanting to break the Cuban economy, pressured US companies in Cuba into refusing to refine the oil – so Castro nationalised the oil companies in June 1960.

In July, the USA retaliated by reducing the import quota for Cuban sugar, leaving Cuba with 700,000 tonnes of unsold sugar. The Soviet Union agreed to purchase this and soon China signed a five-year agreement to purchase 500,000 tonnes a year. On 6 August 1960, Castro nationalised all of the main US-owned properties, including the sugar mills.

In September 1960, Castro made his 'First declaration of Havana' speech, in which he strongly condemned US imperialism. Following this, all US-owned businesses and public utilities, including US banks, were nationalised.

In November, the USA imposed an embargo on all exports to Cuba apart from food and medical supplies. The Soviet bloc then agreed to buy 4 million tonnes of Cuban sugar in 1961 – a million tonnes more than the USA usually purchased. The Soviet Union also agreed to make good Cuba's import gap (which had arisen due to the fact that Cuba was importing more goods than were being exported).

Castro first mentioned the 'socialist' nature of the revolution in a speech made on 16 April 1961, following air raids on 15 April (which preceded the Bay of Pigs incident on 17 April). His speech on 1 May, following the defeat of the US-planned invasion, spoke of 'our socialist revolution'.

The Bay of Pigs incident, April 1961

Two events – both related to US policy decisions against Castro's Cuba – contributed to the radicalisation of Castro's revolution. These were the Bay of Pigs incident in April 1961 and the Cuban Missile Crisis in October 1962. Both of these developments pushed Castro closer to the Cuban communists and the Soviet Union.

In March 1960, President Eisenhower had approved plans for US-backed Cuban exiles to invade Cuba. These invasion plans (Operation Zapata) were put into operation by John F. Kennedy, the newly elected (and strongly anti-communist) US president. On 15 April, CIA pilots helped exiles to bomb Cuban air bases. On 17 April, about 1,500 exiles – trained and armed by the CIA – left Nicaragua with a US naval escort and a CIA command ship. The exiles landed on two beaches – the majority on Playa Girón in the Bay of Pigs. However, the expected anti-Castro uprising never took place.

Castro immediately rushed from Havana to take charge of the defences, and the exiles were defeated after two days despite heavy air strikes, authorised by Kennedy, against the Cuban militia. Over 100 were killed and 1,179 were captured. Most of the Cuban exile commanders had been officers under Batista – five were executed and nine were sent to prison for thirty years. The rest were eventually returned to the USA in December 1962, in exchange for $53 million worth of baby food, medicines and medical equipment.

Despite this humiliation – and the obvious popularity of Castro as a nationalist resisting a 'Yankee' (US) invasion – Kennedy ordered the CIA to continue with sabotage and its attempts to overthrow or assassinate Castro.

The Cuban Missile Crisis, 1962

After the Bay of Pigs incident, Castro feared that the USA would attempt another invasion and, in November 1961, Kennedy did in fact authorise one. For protection, Castro asked the Soviet Union for more weapons; from May 1962, the Soviet Union delivered tanks and military aircraft and increased its troops on Cuba to 42,000.

Given the USA's big lead in nuclear weapons, Nikita Khrushchev, the Soviet premier, thought that placing nuclear missiles in Cuba would balance the threat from the US missiles in Turkey – this move did not originate from Castro. In September 1962, Soviet technicians began to assemble nuclear missile sites in Cuba. The USA was aware of this, and on 14 October a US U-2 spy plane took photographs showing sites almost ready for intermediate and short-range nuclear missiles, with warheads already on site.

For the next thirteen days, the world seemed close to a nuclear war. On 22 October, against international law, Kennedy imposed a naval blockade of Cuba. Although the Soviet Union said it would not comply, on 24 October Khrushchev ordered Soviet ships heading for Cuba to turn back. The USA then said it would invade Cuba if the missiles were not removed. Khrushchev – without consulting Castro – sent letters to Kennedy on 26 and 27 October, promising to remove the missiles if the USA promised not to invade Cuba and remove US missiles from Turkey. Kennedy agreed, but insisted that the US side of the deal should be kept secret. The threat of a nuclear Third World War ended.

Castro's revolution and communism

During the period December 1961 to March 1962, Castro proclaimed his Marxism-Leninism several times, claiming he had always been a Marxist 'in embryo', or a 'potential' or 'utopian Marxist'.

QUESTION

What were the Bay of Pigs incident of April 1961 and the Cuban Missile Crisis of 1962?

KEY CONCEPTS QUESTION

Cause and **Consequence**: Carry out some additional research, and then list the main causes and immediate consequences of the Cuban Missile Crisis. Then decide which cause was most important and write a short paragraph to explain your choice.

5

What is the value and limitation of Source B for historians trying to discover Castro's political views immediately before and after the Cuban Revolution of 1959?

Fact: In two important books Lenin had made comments that seemed to apply to developing countries such as Cuba. His *What Is to Be Done?* had argued for a revolutionary vanguard of intellectuals to lead the workers, while his *Imperialism: The Highest Stage of Capitalism* – developing Marx's points – had argued that imperialism created the conditions in which revolution in backward states was possible. Although the Soviet Union often only paid lip service to Marxist ideals, these ideals matched well with Castro's nationalist aim for Cuba to become independent.

Fact: While acknowledging Stalin's achievements in successfully modernising a backward economy, Castro criticised Stalin's repression. In many ways, Castro was too independent to fit into the 'orthodoxy' of Soviet Marxism-Leninism.

SOURCE B

At the time of Moncada I was a pure revolutionary but not a Marxist revolutionary. In my defence at the trial ['History will absolve me'] I outlined a very radical revolution, but I thought then that it could be done under the constitution of 1940 and within a democratic system. That was the time I was a utopian Marxist … It was a gradual process, a dynamic process in which the pressure of events forced me to accept Marxism as the answer to what I was seeking.

Extract from a conversation between Castro and the US journalist Herbert Matthews, 29 October 1963. Quoted in Matthews, H. L. 1970. *Castro: A Political Biography*. London, UK. Penguin Books. pp. 182–83.

However, the Cuban Revolution had not been led by the Communist Party, and was not directly the result of class struggle. Instead, Castro's revolution had more to do with economic growth and social reform in the conditions resulting from Cuban history, and the USA's military threats and economic embargo.

For Castro, socialism was mainly a strategy for a nationalist project of modernisation, based on state control of the economy, prioritising production over consumption – and hostility to US imperialism. Castro came to believe his revolutionary programme of reforms required central political and economic control – not private enterprise or even a mixed economy. The latter options could lead to political pluralism which, given the power and influence of the USA and its economic blockade, would be difficult to control. Socialism also provided the moral and ethical codes expected of Cuban citizens, and a vision of a world free from poverty, exploitation and injustice.

Soon after the 1959 revolution, Castro had talks with communist leaders, and several who were sympathetic to Castro's policies were given positions in the new government. Yet some of the PSP remained doubtful about Castro and tried to get more 'orthodox' communists into positions of power.

However, in March 1962, Castro asserted his authority and launched an attack on the PSP's leading member, Anibal Escalante, who was accused of packing the party with his own family and supporters, and of trying to undermine the government's authority.

Over the following decades, Castro's politics fluctuated between orthodoxy and heterodoxy as far as Marxism-Leninist ideology was concerned.

The Soviet connection

For some time after Castro's declaration of socialism in April 1961, the Soviet Union continued to support those in the PSP who were critical of 'Castroism'. However, it was not only US hostility that pushed Castro towards the Soviet Union and Soviet-style socialism. The Soviet command economy model of modernisation (see section 5.10, The early years, 1959–68) suited the Cuban leaders. They saw Joseph Stalin's industrialisation of the Soviet Union without any outside assistance as a way of constructing a fairer society in Cuba in the face of hostility from their powerful neighbour.

The Cuban Missile Crisis of 1962 temporarily disrupted good relations with the Soviet Union as Castro felt Cuba had been used. However, in April 1963, Castro and some other *Fidelista* leaders went to Moscow following an invitation from Khrushchev. Castro stayed until June, and had several important trade discussions. In January 1964, Castro paid a second visit to Moscow, promising to follow peaceful coexistence and to finalise economic deals. Relations cooled again when, in 1967, Castro attacked communist governments – including that of the Soviet Union – for trading with countries that applied a trade embargo against Cuba. Consequently, the Soviet Union delayed the signing of trade agreements and cut back on oil supplies to Cuba.

Cuba's economy then began to experience difficulties – as well as Soviet restrictions on oil supplies, there was a massive debt to the Soviet bloc. Less able to defy Moscow, Castro gave qualified support to the Warsaw Pact invasion of Czechoslovakia in 1968. This opened the way for Moscow to repair relations with Havana in the following decades.

Thus the decision to adopt Marxism for their new Cuban state was not just to do with the need for a strong power's protection from the USA. It was also based on the belief of Castro and his vanguard that communism offered the only possible model of economic growth and the only international movement with which they could identify – especially because of its anti-Americanism.

5.7 What were the most significant measures taken to maintain Castro's power after 1975?

By the end of 1975, Cuba had a well-established and well-organised communist system. The mid-1970s saw Castro attempt to consolidate his rule by changes to the system of popular representation. This was done in 1976, via a new constitution, which introduced a system of *Poder Popular* (see section 5.15 Constitutions and elections).

Rectification campaign, 1986–87

The changes to government and party structure in the early 1970s meant that Castro no longer had unlimited authority. However, he remained as head of the Communist Party and of the armed forces; and, on 2 December 1976, he replaced Osvaldo Dorticós as president. In the mid-1980s, Castro was able to use these positions and his personal authority to impose his will on domestic economic policy.

At the third Congress of the PCC, Castro had launched a new campaign – the 'Rectification of errors and negative trends'. While this was mainly connected to economic issues, it also became a drive against corruption and those who Castro felt were opposed to what he saw as Cuba's economic needs.

Fact: Castro was prepared to accept the Soviet Union's idea of a peaceful road to socialism, but he insisted that some roads might be non-peaceful. In the years 1965–68, Castro's relations with the Soviet Union suffered due to his attempts to establish revolutionary guerrilla groups in other Latin American and developing countries. These attempts conflicted with the Soviet Union's aim to establish good relations with the USA and the West (peaceful coexistence). In 1967, Castro seemed to be attacking the USSR for having 'capitulated' to capitalism by preferring good relations rather than supporting revolutionary groups.

QUESTION

Why did the question of 'peaceful coexistence' cause problems between Cuba and the USSR in the 1960s?

Fact: Trade agreements between Cuba and the USSR were based on Cuba providing a certain amount of sugar to the USSR in return for oil and industrial goods. However, a gap had opened between exports of sugar and imports of oil and industrial goods, leaving Cuba 7.5 million tonnes in arrears by 1969. Hence Castro declared 1969 to be the 'Year of Decisive Endeavour' – in an attempt to increase sugar production to 10 million tonnes.

Castro and Cuba

Fact: Gorbachev visited Cuba in April 1989. He was associated with three reforms – perestroika (economic modernisation), glasnost (greater openness about government mistakes) and *demokratizatsiya* (democratising the Soviet political system). He introduced these in the Soviet Union after 1985 and encouraged their adoption by the Eastern European regimes. Castro associated these policies with the fall of these regimes in the period 1989–91.

In the mid-1970s, the System of Direction and Planning of the Economy (SDPE) had been set up to introduce decentralisation of planning and management and to replace moral with material incentives to encourage greater productivity. In 1985, a plan was drawn up, in line with these principles, by the Central Planning Board (*Juceplan*). The board's director was Humberto Pérez, a Moscow-trained economist. However, Castro decided that this system and the new plan failed to take account of the new economic crisis in Cuba. So Pérez was removed from his post and from the politburo (the most important committee in the Communist Party). Castro then bypassed *Juceplan* by setting up a new committee to draw up a revised plan, which attempted to introduce some increased centralisation.

During 1986 and 1987, Castro widened his campaign, making a series of speeches in which he admitted 'errors', criticised the economic liberalisation of the 1970s and attacked signs of corruption. In particular, he singled out bureaucrats and technocrats, and those who had enriched themselves under the 1970s' market mechanisms that were introduced into the Cuban economy on the advice of the USSR. In large part, this campaign was a response to growing dissatisfaction amongst workers who were angry about increasing shortages and income differentials. Castro put himself at the head of this popular discontent as their self-appointed spokesperson, thus increasing his personal prestige.

Figure 5.13   Fidel Castro and Mikhail Gorbachev embrace during an official visit by the Soviet premier to Cuba in 1989

The Ochoa Affair, 1989

In June 1989, Cuba experienced its most serious internal opposition crisis since 1959. Four senior military and intelligence figures – including General **Arnaldo Ochoa** – and several others were arrested on charges of corruption and drug smuggling. They were tried by military tribunals. Four, including Ochoa, were condemned to death and executed on 13 July; others received prison sentences ranging from twenty to thirty years. There is speculation that Ochoa and the others, who favoured Gorbachev-style reforms, were planning a coup. The crisis caused serious divisions in Cuba. However, the economic crisis of the Special Period that soon followed (see section 5.10, The Special Period and beyond, 1990–present) brought about a new sense of unity.

Aldana and the 1992 purge

However, during the 'Special Period in Time of Peace' (see section 5.10, The Special Period and beyond, 1990–present), announced by Castro at the end of 1990, another reformist tendency emerged in the PCC and the Young Communist Party, where several members admired Gorbachev's policies. This opposition was led by Carlos Aldana, and called for some limited political pluralism.

The collapse of the regimes of Eastern Europe and then the Soviet Union in the period 1989–91 made Castro decide to move against this opposition as well as other groups of reformists. In 1991, with the Soviet Union no longer a reliable ally against the USA, Castro created Rapid Response Brigades of volunteers to act against potential 'fifth columnists'. These brigades often harassed oppositionist groups demanding political reform and the various organisations calling for human rights. In September 1992, Aldana was sacked from his party; and Castro, using his personal authority, began a purge of other reformists from the party.

To help diffuse this opposition, amendments to the constitution were made in 1992 to make *Poder Popular* more of a reality. Despite the post-1991 economic suffering, these reforms were relatively successful, and Castro's regime did not collapse like the Soviet bloc states in Europe, as some had speculated would happen. In part, this was because most Cubans saw the revolution as *their* revolution – whatever its failings, it had also had real successes.

US actions, 1992–96

The idea of a revolutionary Cuba under siege is part of the mythology of the revolution, and had led to mass mobilisations, revolutionary political offensives and popular militarisation. In the 1990s, moves against potential opponents were also a response – once again – to increased threats from the USA. The Torricelli Act of 1992 and the Helm-Burton Act of 1996, respectively, tightened US economic sanctions against Cuba and sought actively to 'assist' in the creation of the USA's form of democracy in Cuba. In March 1996, Castro acted against academics in the Centre for the Study of America (CEA). They did not lose their jobs, but they were moved to different posts.

'Re-moralisation' and the Varela Project

By 1996, most of the economic measures of the Special Period had been stopped; then, in 2003, Castro decided on a partial return to anti-market centralisation. This

Figure 5.14   Arnaldo Ochoa (1930–89)

Ochoa was in charge of the Cuban troops sent to Angola to fight against South African forces in 1988. The Cuban troops won an impressive victory at Cuito Cuanavale on 14 February 1988. This helped to force South Africa out of Angola and Namibia, contributing to the collapse of apartheid in South Africa. Two years later, Nelson Mandela was released from prison, and in July 1991 he visited Cuba to thank the country for its role in the struggle against apartheid. Ochoa had, as a result, become something of a hero.

QUESTION

What were the main reasons for the Ochoa Affair in 1989?

Castro and Cuba

also involved the 're-moralisation' of economic life (see section 5.10, The early years, 1959–68). Associated with this were further moves against potential opponents, dissidents and human rights activists. The minister for economics and planning and the minister of finance, both of whom were closely connected to the liberalisation policies under the Special Period during 1993–96, were replaced by ministers favouring centralised political control of the economy and society.

After the 2000 US presidential election, the USA stepped up its attempts to interfere in Cuba's internal politics and President George W. Bush included Cuba in his new 'axis of evil'. This led to renewed fears of an imminent US invasion. Castro then became concerned about the activities of members of the Varela Project, who were campaigning for a law of democratic reform and more private enterprise. Castro's government organised a counter-petition to amend the constitution to make the socialist nature of the Cuban constitution 'irrevocable'. This counter-petition included 8 million signatures – about 99 per cent of the electorate. At the same time, the Cuban authorities began to harass members of the Varela Project. On 15 March 2003, seventy-five members were arrested and many received long prison sentences.

Mass organisations

As well as with repression, Castro has tried to consolidate his regime by increasing the participation of citizens in a range of mass organisations. Since 1976, such organisations and methods have been used and adapted to make *Poder Popular* more of a reality, and so integrate the population of Cuba with the regime.

Unions

The main mass organisation is the Confederation of Cuban Workers (CTC), which unites all nineteen unions and organises national congresses for workers to discuss issues. These are preceded by months of meetings of workers' assemblies at local level. Castro and other leaders participate at times, to answer questions and to explain important issues. According to Saney, the workers' assemblies have considerable input and say in their workplaces and in major national political decisions. By law, workers meet twice a year in their workplaces to discuss their company's economic plans. They can reject management proposals, decide production norms and rates, and any new proposals are subject to ratification. Though they work closely with the PCC, they are independent of the government, which must consult the unions on all labour matters.

PCC

The PCC attempts to integrate citizens by 'promoting the development of a socialist consciousness and society' by trying to persuade people to put society's needs above those of the individual. While Hobart Spalding and others see the influence of the PCC as suffocating, according to Peter Roman the party does not meddle in the operation of people's power. Though it does 'screen' those selected as candidates, Carollee Bengelsdorf argues that Cuban citizens exercise significant political sovereignty.

About 1.5 million Cubans (15 per cent of the population) belong to the PCC and its youth body, the Union of Young Communists (UJC). Massive nationwide discussions – open to both party and non-party people – take place before the party congresses.

Fact: Set up in 1988, the CEA was mainly composed of academics, most of whom belonged to the PCC. By 1990, it had begun to suggest reform of Cuba's internal political system. After Castro made moves against the CEA in 1996, some members of the group went into exile to continue their opposition.

Fact: The Varela Project was named after Felix Varela, a 19th century advocate for Cuban independence, and was associated with the Catholic Church. Its leader was Osvaldo Payá, who had been involved in the Christian Liberation Group. Its members tried to use the clause in the Cuban constitution that said a new law could be proposed if a petition with 10,000 signatures was presented to the National Assembly. They managed to get 11,000 signatures, and presented it during a visit by ex-US president Jimmy Carter, who supported them.

QUESTION

What was the Varela Project?

Fact: In 1994, the CTC rejected plans to tax workers' wages; in 1995, it rejected proposed alterations to social security, which were sent back for amendment.

5.8 How far did foreign policy help Castro to maintain power?

Castro's early commitment to end US control over Cuba had been one of the reasons behind the support his movement achieved before and immediately after 1959. Castro saw the world as divided between developed and underdeveloped countries, and believed Cuba – because of its mixed Latin American and African history and culture, and its economic problems – had a special role in helping other 'Third World' countries overcome poverty and imperialism. His attitude to foreign affairs seems to have been widely shared by the Cuban people, and his foreign policies after 1959 often created feelings of pride amongst ordinary Cubans, as they saw their tiny island stand up to their powerful neighbour – not just in Latin America and the Caribbean, but also on other continents.

Latin America and the Caribbean

In 1962, US president Kennedy had been informed by the Director of the CIA that, because of the unequal social and economic conditions existing in so many Latin American countries, if Castro was able to maintain an independent and reforming Cuba, 'most of Latin America' would eventually 'fall'. Consequently, Cuba's early foreign policy was designed to promote similar revolutions in the region. Castro himself, in a speech in 1963, made it clear that Cuba's example and revolutionary ideas – if successfully spread – would increase Cuba's security. Cuba gave financial and logistical aid, and especially military training, to several revolutionary groups.

Bolivia, 1966–67

However, by the end of 1964, most of the guerrilla groups in Latin America that had received help from Cuba had suffered serious setbacks. It was in this context that probably Cuba's best-known attempt to 'export' its revolutionary ideas took place. In November 1966, Che Guevara (who had been supporting radical guerrilla groups in the Congo – see Africa below) went to Bolivia, with several other Cuban fighters, to help the **ELN guerrillas** in their struggle against the military dictatorship there, which had been established in 1964 following a US-backed coup. Guevara was keen to do this for several reasons: not just to end Cuba's isolation in the region and so improve its security, but also to help spread revolution as a way of ending US and Western imperialism.

In the end, the Bolivian insurgency that Che led lasted only a few months, from March to October 1967. On 8 October, a wounded Che was captured by a mixed group of CIA commandos and Bolivian special forces, trained by the US. He was briefly interrogated but refused to answer questions. On 9 October he was murdered by one of the Bolivian Rangers with the approval of the CIA. Despite this failure, this foreign policy exploit made many Cubans proud of their country's role – and of the fact that, after his death, Guevara became a worldwide symbol of resistance for many young people in the following decade. All this enhanced the popularity of Castro's regime.

KEY CONCEPTS ACTIVITY

Change and Continuity: Refer back to your earlier paragraphs on the extent to which Castro had established authoritarian control in Cuba by 1975. After reviewing the sections you have just studied, write two paragraphs – one to assess the degree of authoritarian control in the period 1975–2003 and one to show the extent to which Castro's power had changed or remained the same from 1959 to 2003.

Fact: Castro and the Cubans saw the events in Guatemala in 1954 – where the CIA had helped overthrow a reformist government – as a worrying example of what could happen to such governments in the Caribbean and Latin America: a region the US openly stated was its 'own backyard'.

ELN guerrillas: These were the *Ejercito de Liberacion Nacional de Bolivia* (National Liberation Army of Bolivia). Guevara went there to help them develop the *foco* system of revolution. This was based on the idea that, as in Cuba before 1959, small groups of guerrillas could act as a focus (*foco*) for popular discontent against repressive and/or elitist regimes and, eventually, come to power in a successful revolution.

Chile, 1970–73

Fact: At the Tricontinental Conference (which brought together anti-imperialist activists from Asia, Africa and Latin America) in Havana in 1966, Guevara made a speech in which he said: '*Wherever death may surprise us, let it be welcome, provided that this our battle cry may have reached some receptive ear and another hand may be extended to wield our weapons*'.

Despite the failure in Bolivia – and Che's death – in 1967, Castro's government at first continued to give aid to various revolutionary groups. This was despite increasing pressure from Moscow which felt such actions 'complicated' their relations with the US. However, by 1970, guerrilla groups that had been fighting in Venezuela, Colombia and Guatemala had also suffered serious setbacks. These defeats, and growing economic problems, led Castro to greatly reduce such aid and instead to seek Soviet economic aid.

Nonetheless, Castro continued to give political support, and sometimes limited aid, to various liberation groups and to the few reformist governments that came to power in Latin America during the 1970s. This included Allende's Popular Unity coalition government, which won the 1970 elections in Chile. Castro saw Allende's victory in Chile as a way of ending Cuba's isolation and reducing US domination of the region. This was shown by a banner headline in *Granma*, a Cuban government paper: 'Anti-Imperialist Victory in Chile'.

SOURCE C

The Cubans, [unlike the Soviet Union], welcomed Allende as a true friend. When Allende visited Cuba the year after Castro's tour of Chile [in 1971], the Cubans pledged solidarity, bread and forty tons of the Cuban population's sugar rations to help the Chilean Way. 'We must launch a gigantic wave of solidarity around our brothers the Chilean people,' said Castro, warning that what the Americans had 'tried to accomplish with bombs in Vietnam they are trying to accomplish in Chile by economic asphyxia'.

Guardiola-Rivera, O. 2014. *Story of a Death Foretold*. London, UK. Bloomsbury. p. 316.

AK-47 Kalashnikov rifle: When the coup against him was launched on 11 September 1973, in what was the world's first '9/11', Allende used this rifle against Pinochet's military rebels until his death in the afternoon of that day.

However, despite giving Allende an **AK-47 Kalashnikov rifle** with the words 'To Salvador, from a comrade in arms, Fidel' inscribed on the gunstock, no military help was given beyond providing personnel and training for a special bodyguard for Allende. When the expected US-inspired coup against Allende finally took place on 11 September 1973, Cuba did not send troops to help the Chilean resistance.

Grenada and Nicaragua

Although no serious aid had been given to Allende's Chile (in part, so as not to allow the US to claim that Allende was Castro's 'puppet') Castro continued to offer Cuban aid to other countries in the region after 1973. Once again, as portrayed in the Cuban media, this was popular with many Cubans, who continued to take pride in Cuba's continuing commitment to international solidarity in the struggle against US and Western imperialism.

In March 1979, the left-wing New Jewel Movement led a successful revolution in Grenada, a Caribbean island that was part of the British Commonwealth. When US President Reagan refused to give aid, Cuba sent construction workers to help build a new international airport for tourists, and military instructors to help establish a new police force. However, in October 1983, the US sent in troops from its recently created Rapid Deployment Force to overthrow the NJM government; twenty-five Cubans were amongst those killed in the fighting. This action – which led Castro to fear that a US attack on Cuba was imminent – was condemned by Britain and the UN, but the US used its veto in the Security Council to block the passing of an official resolution.

Also in 1979, following the overthrow of the US-backed dictator in Nicaragua by the **Sandinistas**, Cuba gave the new government considerable aid for its literacy, educational and medical reform programmes. This included sending 2,500 doctors, nurses, teachers and engineers. In addition, Cuba gave industrial aid and technical advice, and as the US-sponsored Contras began to attack and murder education and medical workers, it also provided military training. This Cuban aid was especially useful as, before 1979, most of Nicaragua's aid had come from the US. This had been cut off after the Sandinistas' victory in 1979 – Cuba almost immediately stepped in with grants and unconditional loans. Although the Sandinistas won elections (which international observers confirmed were free and fair), in 1984 US opposition continued; and in 1990, the Sandinistas narrowly lost the elections.

Venezuela and Bolivarian Revolution

More recently, Castro gave his support to Hugo Chavez, who was first elected president of Venezuela in 1998. Chavez was an admirer of Castro and Cuba and he immediately began a massive programme of reforms to reduce the great inequalities that existed in Venezuela. This won massive support amongst ordinary Venezuelans, enabling Chavez to win four presidential elections in succession, before dying in 2013. His rejection of neo-liberal capitalist economic policies, and his strong opposition to US imperialism, made him an obvious ally in Castro's eyes. Thus bilateral agreements were quickly reached: in return for sending large numbers of doctors to help Chavez implement his medical reforms, Cuba received significant supplies of badly needed oil. Cuba also received large amounts of grants, loans and investments. All of this greatly helped the struggling Cuban economy after 2003 and once again resulted in a foreign policy with popular outcomes for many Cubans.

Sandinistas: These were members of the Sandinista National Liberation Front (FSLN), which was a coalition that included Marxists, liberals, democratic socialists and Catholic priests who were united against the brutal dictatorship that was backed by the US. From 1909 to 1933, Nicaragua had been a US protectorate – after 1936, when Somoza seized power, the US had backed him. Almost immediately after the revolution in July 1979, the US (headed by President Reagan) gave aid to the Contras, a terrorist group opposed to the Sandinistas. When this aid was banned by the US Congress because of mounting examples of Contra atrocities, Reagan simply used the money from illegal arms sales to Iran in order to continuing Contra funding. This eventually led to the Contragate/Irangate political scandal.

SOURCE D

Within the [presidential] palace the assembled ministers and loyal officers began to discuss their options. Would it be possible to fight [against the army coup]? … At about midnight, Fidel Castro called from Havana to ask what was happening. Recalling the fate of Salvador Allende in 1973, he told Chavez that he was on no account to sacrifice himself in a useless battle of resistance – 'no te vayas a inmolar'.

'Save your people and save yourself. Do what you have to do. Negotiate with dignity. Do not sacrifice yourself, Chavez, because this is not going to end here. You must not sacrifice yourself.'

Chavez was too important a figure for the future of Latin America, Castro argued, for him to allow himself to be killed off in a coup.

Gott, R. 2011. *Hugo Chavez and the Bolivarian Revolution*. London, UK. Verso. p. 227.

QUESTION

How far do **Sources D** and **E** agree about Castro's attitude to Chavez's problems in Venezuela?

SOURCE E

The failure of the [management] strike to dent the support for our Revolution was the most important thing, but then we had to go on the offensive. How? I spoke with Fidel [Castro] who is a friend and a comrade. His advice during the coup was also very astute. 'Don't do anything rash', he told me, 'this continent does not need another Allende. Be very careful.' Now the Cuban comrades opened their doors wide. Within a fortnight ten thousand Cuban doctors, with field hospitals and Cuban medicines arrived in Venezuela. They set up clinics and began to treat people within twenty-four hours. Health facilities in this country have been the preserve of the well-off and often people in the barrios had to travel long distances for a doctor to even see them. Now they were being treated close their homes. Our medical profession was angered by this as were the Opposition leaders. They said openly that these Cuban doctors were 'terrorists' who had been sent to carry out violence.

Comments by Hugo Chavez in a conversation in 2004, about the 2002 coup and management strike against his government. Ali, T. 2008. *Pirates of the Caribbean: Axis of Hope.* London, UK. Verso. p. 81.

Castro also backed Chavez's 'Bolivarian Revolution', which was an attempt to overcome the great inequalities in Latin America and to resist US domination. In 2006, reformist politicians came to power in Bolivia and Ecuador. They then joined the ALBA bloc: the Bolivarian Alternative for the Americas (*Alternativa Bolivaraiana para Las Americas*). This had been set up by Chavez in 2004, with Cuban participation, as an alternative to the USA's Free Trade Area of the Americas (FTAA). Whereas the FTAA is committed to capitalist neo-liberalism and deregulation of economies to allow maximum profits, ALBA is a socially-oriented trade bloc for the countries of Latin America and the Caribbean, intended to eradicate poverty.

Africa

Much further afield, Castro also pursued an active foreign policy in Africa. As early as 1961, Cuba was helping Algerians in their independence fight against France. Once independence had been achieved in 1963, Cuba (despite its own problems) sent a medical mission to help establish a nationwide free health service for Algerians. From then on Cuban foreign policy focused on sub-Saharan Africa, especially on developments in southern Africa. Later, Nelson Mandela publicly acknowledged the important part Cuba played in helping to bring down the apartheid regime in South Africa. Most Cubans took great pride in this achievement and in the global recognition of its role there.

The Congo

By the mid-1960s, guerrilla groups in Portugal's African colonies were fighting independence wars. In addition, a civil war had broken out in the Congo, with the US sending a force of 1,000 mercenaries to defend its 'client' ruler. So, in December 1964, Guevara went on a three-month trip to Africa – much to the concern of the US, which feared Cuba might attempt to weaken its influence in the region – to see if any of these guerrilla groups needed Cuban help. On his return to Cuba, he called for black volunteers to go with him to help rebels in the Congo. In April 1965, Che and 120 volunteers entered the Congo. However, the odds against the rebels were too high, and in November 1965 Che and surviving volunteers were forced to return clandestinely to Cuba. His next venture was to be the ill-fated one to Bolivia.

Angola and southern Africa

Cuba's most successful foreign policy interventions in this region first began in 1966 when, in response to a request from rebels in the Portuguese colony of Guinea-Bissau, Castro sent doctors and military instructors. These stayed until Guinea-Bissau finally won independence in 1974.

However, Cuba's biggest commitment was to Angola where, in 1975, a civil war had broken out between three rival independence movements following the collapse of the Portuguese dictatorship the year before. Both South Africa and the US were determined to stop one of these groups – the Soviet-backed People's Movement for the Liberation of Angola (MPLA) – from coming to power. South Africa wanted to do this to ensure its illegal control of South-West Africa (known as Namibia after independence), which was between Angola and South Africa. As it looked as though the MPLA were winning, the US persuaded South Africa to send in troops to help the other two groups. Castro then decided to support the MPLA.

Fact: US documents, declassified in October 2014, have revealed that, in March-April 1976, US secretary of state Kissinger ordered the Washington Special Actions Group to draw up secret plans to 'crush Cuba', after Castro's decision to send troops to Angola. These US plans included air strikes and the mining of Cuban harbours. Kissinger discussed these plans with US president Ford who agreed with Kissinger that such action couldn't be taken until after the 1976 presidential election.

Figure 5.15   Some of the Cuban troops in Angola, which helped the MPLA government to resist the attempt by the guerrilla forces of Unita and the South African army to overthrow it

217

Although Soviet aid was very limited, Cuba quickly sent in troops when it looked like the South African forces were about to capture the capital. Despite heavy losses, the Cuban forces halted the South African advance. In 1976, as even more Cuban troops arrived, taking its total commitment to over 25,000 soldiers, the South Africans withdrew. Eventually, US politicians (including Kissinger) admitted that Castro had acted on his own initiative and not at the request of the Soviet Union. In fact, Castro's decision jeopardised Cuba's improving relations with both the Organization of American States (which had just lifted the sanctions it had imposed on Cuba in 1964) and west European governments (which were offering low-interest loans and development aid). However, Castro saw Cuba's intervention as helping to weaken South Africa's apartheid system. The victory of the Cuban forces over those of South Africa was the first time that the South Africans had been forced to retreat, and this greatly encouraged all those struggling against the apartheid regime. This included those trying to end South Africa's control of South-West Africa. With most of Angola now ruled by the MPLA, the forces of this independence movement at last had a sympathetic government across the border.

Cuban troops remained in Angola during the late 1970s, as South African forces continued to attack Angola from South-West Africa. US president Carter offered to normalise relations with Cuba and to end the sanctions if Castro would agree to withdraw Cuban troops. Castro, however, said that it was up to the Angolan government, and he made it clear that Cuba would not be bullied, bribed or blackmailed into withdrawing support from a government that had requested help. Once Reagan replaced Carter as US president in 1981, these US offers were quickly withdrawn. Thus Cuba paid a high price for its foreign policy.

SOURCE F

The intervention in Angola marked a dramatic shift in Cuban foreign policy – not of motivation or geographical focus but of scale. Before Angola, about forty Cubans had fought in Latin America and fewer than 1,400 in Africa. From the late 1970s through the late 1980s, more than 1,000 Cuban military advisers were stationed in Nicaragua but, once again, it was to Africa that the bulk of the Cuban soldiers went: tens of thousands remained in Angola and 12,000 went to Ethiopia between December 1977 and March 1978. It was a policy without equal in modern times. During the Cold War, extra-continental military interventions were the preserve of the two superpowers, a few West European countries, and Cuba. And West European military interventions in the thirty years between the rise of Castro and the end of the Cold War pale in size and daring compared to those of Cuba; even the Soviet Union sent far fewer soldiers beyond its immediate neighbourhood. In this regard, Cuba was second only to the US.

Gleijeses, P. 2009. *The Cuban Drumbeat*. London, UK. Seagull. p. 33.

Under Reagan in the 1980s, the US once more began to encourage South Africa to step up its actions against Angola. In September 1987, South Africa launched a major attack in south-east Angola. Although this was condemned by the UN, the US ensured no sanctions were imposed on South Africa and that no international aid was given to

Angola to deal with this invasion. The South African advance was finally halted at the battle of Cuito Cuanavale on 23 March 1988. South African forces had been trying to capture this town since the beginning of the year. This had been prevented by Cuban troops already in Angola. Castro then decided to send his best troops and most modern weapons to stem the South African advance. After their victory at Cuito Cuanavale, Cuban and Angolan troops pushed the South African troops back across the border with South-West Africa. In December, this threat of Cuban troops crossing the border eventually forced the US to push South Africa into agreeing to end its support of Angolan rebels, and to UN-supervised elections in South-West Africa. In return, Cuba gradually withdrew its troops from Angola.

Nelson Mandela later said that Cuban involvement in Angola had played a big part in the eventual fall of the apartheid regime in South Africa. By the end of Cuba's involvement in Angola, 2,400 Cubans had been killed. Their names are inscribed on the Wall of Names in Pretoria's National Park.

SOURCE G

Cubans came to our region as doctors, teachers, soldiers, agricultural experts, but never as colonizers. They have shared the same trenches with us in the struggle against colonialism, underdevelopment, and Apartheid. Hundreds of Cubans have given their lives, literally, in a struggle that was, first and foremost, not theirs but ours. As Southern Africans we salute them. We vow never to forget this unparalleled example of selfless internationalism.

Comments made by Nelson Mandela in his Address to the Cuba Solidarity Conference in Johannesburg, in October 1995. Source: *http://www.freedompark.co.za.*

Horn of Africa

In 1977, Cuba also sent about 12,000 troops to help the new government in Ethiopia resist an invasion by Somalia. Although Castro quite quickly agreed to send doctors and military advisers, he had at first refused the request for combat troops as he felt Cuba could not do this as well as help Angola. Cuba's intervention, which ended with the defeat of the Somali forces in 1978, was supported by most of the members of the Organization of African Unity.

Humanitarian aid

As well as military assistance to various countries, Cuba's foreign policy also included significant humanitarian aid, especially after 1975. Primary and secondary school teachers, doctors and nurses, construction workers and technicians went to places such as Nicaragua, Algeria and Guinea-Bissau. As with its military commitment, though, the biggest Cuban aid programme was in Angola. By late 1977, there were 3,350 volunteer Cuban aid workers in Angola. All of their salaries were paid by Cuba, despite the fact that it, too, was a poor country. Most volunteered because they shared Castro's commitment to internationalism and the duty to help others. More recently, in 2010, Cuba (followed quickly by Venezuela) was the first country to send help to Haiti after its terrible earthquake.

Many Cubans have also received help as a result of their country's foreign policy. For instance, in the wake of various destructive hurricanes in 2008 and 2012, Chavez's Venezeula provided massive amounts of humanitarian aid to Cuba. This included food and prefabricated houses.

In addition to sending aid workers, over 40,000 Africans, Latin Americans and Asians were given full scholarships to go and study in Cuba. These included medical professionals, educationalists, agriculturalists and scientists. As stated by many observers, there has been no other instance in which an underdeveloped country has carried out such massive and generous aid programmes. Despite its own economic problems (including during the Special Period), the Cuban government has retained the support of large sections of Cuban society. In part, this appears due to widespread support for, and pride in, Cuba's foreign policy.

5.9 What other methods did Castro use to maintain his power?

Fact: In later years, CDRs became involved in recycling drives, cultural and educational activities, and health campaigns (e.g. vaccination and blood donation). Though they are grassroots organisations, they do not necessarily function effectively as a way for people to express their views.

QUESTION

How did the large numbers of Cuban emigrants help Castro to consolidate his regime?

Historical debate:
There is considerable debate amongst historians about the support for/opposition to Castro's policies and the regime he created. Some, like Bethell, are negative, while others, such as Saney, present a much more optimistic picture. Which 'side' do you think presents the most realistic assessment?

Castro has also tried to maintain his revolution in other ways.

Committees for the Defence of the Revolution

With control over the FEU and the CTC established by 1960, the leadership created a militia with tens of thousands of members to build support, intimidate internal opponents and defend Cuba against external enemies. Particularly important were the Committees for the Defence of the Revolution (CDRs), established in September 1960 primarily for civil defence. CDRs were set up in every city district, in each large building, factory or workplace.

In the early days of Castro's regime, they involved the people in identifying enemies of the revolution and repressing counter-revolutionary opinions and activities (e.g. sabotage and terrorism). They are the largest of all the mass organisations, with a membership of over 7 million – helping many people identify with the revolution.

Emigration and exile

From the mid-1960s, waves of Cuban emigrants went into exile in the USA. The first wave were supporters of Batista, and especially those who had tortured or killed his opponents. Between 1959 and 1961, at least 40,000 emigrants left Cuba. The next wave of emigrants were disillusioned middle-class liberals, as well as members of the business and professional élites who opposed Castro's increasing moves towards communism after 1961. In the period 1961–62 alone, at least 150,000 left.

Since then, there have been several major emigrations – the Camarioca Exodus in 1965, the Mariel Boatlift in 1980 and the Malecón Exodus in 1994. According to Leslie Bethell, while the loss of professional and technical skills had a negative impact on Cuba's development, the 'exporting' of potential leaders of opposition or counter-revolution helped Castro to establish political centralisation and control.

Figure 5.16 Posters on a wall in a street in Havana. Che Guevara is depicted in the top-left poster

Castroism

Castroism, or *Fidelismo* – the idea that the Cuban Revolution is largely based on the teachings and principles of Fidel Castro – has not resulted in an obvious cult of personality, as happened for instance in the Soviet Union under Stalin or in China under Mao. In Cuba itself there are not many posters depicting Castro, although Che's image is found almost everywhere.

Castro certainly had great charisma (even liberals who went into exile acknowledged this) as well as the ability to speak well to crowds, sometimes for twelve hours at a time! This was apparent when, before 1959, he broadcast on Radio Rebelde. Since 1959, Castro has made good use of television to explain his aims and policies.

Despite difficulties, many still had faith in him. As long as he was in charge, they did not seem to mind what he did, even when he moved towards Marxism. Castro's legitimacy was also based on his identification with the heroic myths of Cuban patriotism and on his personal ethics: he has not used his position to amass a private fortune. His prestige was strengthened by the development of *Poder Popular* from the mid-1970s.

QUESTION

Who do you think is depicted in the top-right poster?

ACTIVITY

Using the information in this unit and any other materials you have access to, write a couple of paragraphs to explain how the USA's actions against Cuba made it easier for Castro to consolidate his power.

5

Figure 5.17 Raúl Castro, acting president of Cuba, looks at the empty chair of Fidel Castro during a session of Cuba's National Assembly in December 2006. Fidel finally resigned in February 2008, and Raúl took over as president

Yet Castro appears not to have wanted any adulation. His general style was much milder and warmer than other rulers of one-party states; and his good relationship with the public meant ordinary people felt able to approach him and speak of their problems and dissatisfactions.

On 18 February 2008, after almost two years of illness, Fidel Castro announced his decision to stand down as president and commander-in-chief of the armed forces. His brother Raúl, the acting head of state, took over.

Although he is no longer directly in charge, Fidel still exerts influence. Despite five decades of US economic and military actions against himself and his Cuban Revolution, he managed to turn Cuba into one of the best-educated and healthiest societies in the world.

End of unit activities

1 In pairs, carry out further research on the different opposition groups that emerged in Cuba after 1959 – both within the 26 July Movement and the Communist Party, and amongst intellectuals and artists. Then try to establish the reasons for their lack of success. You can present your findings in the form of two tables – one to show how the different groups were formed and what they did, and the other to show how and why they were defeated.

ACTIVITY

As you work through the next unit, try to analyse the relative importance of Fidel Castro's various economic and social policies in helping to maintain his power from 1959 to 2008. Were these more or less important than repressive measures?

2 Reread sections 5.5 and 5.6 and produce a table summarising the main steps taken by Castro between 1959 and 1976 in moving Cuba towards socialism/communism. Which one do you think was the most significant step? Write a short paragraph to justify your decision.

3 Carry out some additional research on the Bay of Pigs incident. How important was this event in helping Castro maintain support in Cuba for his regime in the 1960s and 1970s?

4 Find out more about the different reasons why so many Cubans emigrated to the USA. Were they mainly political or economic reasons? Why do you think Castro usually tolerated this emigration?

5 Carry out an investigation to explain why Castro's popularity remained so high among so many Cubans, right up to – and beyond – his resignation in 2008, despite Cuba's many political and economic problems.

Theory of knowledge

History and art:
Most people would agree that artists should be free to express their views and thoughts. Yet many governments – especially those in one-party states – have tried to confine art to those works that support their political and economic system. Is it possible to make a case for Castro's assertion in 1961 that creative freedom could be allowed 'within the revolution' but not 'against the revolution'; or his appeal in 1971 that art should be a 'weapon of the revolution'?

TIMELINE

1959 Mar: nationalisation of public utilities; Castro makes his 'Proclamation against discrimination'

May: Agrarian Reform Act

1960 Apr: Soviet crude oil is delivered

Jun: nationalisation of foreign oil refineries

Aug: Federation of Cuban Women (FMC) is set up

1961 Feb: Guevara becomes minister of industries

Apr: 'Year of Education' mass literacy campaign begins

1962 Feb: Kennedy announces full US embargo on exports to Cuba

1969 Nov: 'Year of Decisive Endeavour' is launched

1970 Jul: 10 million tonne campaign for sugar

1972 Jul: Cuba becomes a full member of Comecon

1975 Mar: Family Code

1976 Feb: new constitution to establish *Poder Popular* is approved

Dec: first meeting of the new National Assembly

1977 Centro Nacional de Educación Sexual (CNES) is founded

1979 Same-sex relations are decriminalised

1986 Apr: 'Rectification Campaign'

1989 Apr: Gorbachev visits Cuba

1990 Jan: Special Period begins

1991 Dec: Soviet Union collapses

1992 Jul: constitution is amended

1993 Jan: US embargo on Cuba is tightened; Castro introduces some market reforms

Feb: first direct elections to the National Assembly

1996 Feb: US trade embargo is made permanent

1998 Jan: Pope John Paul II visits Cuba

2010 State provides free gender reassignment surgery

Overview

- After 1959, Castro moved quickly to carry out earlier promises to help the poorer sections of society by redistributing wealth and resources. In May 1959, the Agrarian Reform Act gave confiscated land to landless and poor peasants.

- Castro nationalised public utilities in March 1959, and after foreign oil companies refused to process Soviet crude oil the refineries were nationalised in June 1960.

- Castro and his team wanted rapid industrialisation and diversification in agriculture. In February 1961, Guevara became minister of industries, and a central plan was quickly drawn up.

- During the years 1963–4, a more Soviet style of economic planning was adopted. This increased after 1968 and, in July 1972, Cuba joined the Soviet bloc's Comecon (the Council for Mutual Economic Assistance). From 1972 to 1982, Cuba experienced real growth during what became known as the 'Brezhnev Years'.

- From the late 1970s, increasing problems led to a rising trade debt. By 1986, Castro launched a 'rectification' campaign.

- The collapse of the regimes of Eastern Europe and then the Soviet Union in the years 1989–91 led to great economic problems. In January 1990, Castro announced the start of the Special Period.

- In the early years, Castro moved quickly to push through many social policy reforms. Priority was given to expanding health care. In 1961, a successful mass literacy campaign was launched.

- At the same time, moves were started to equalise educational access, pay and employment opportunities for women. Policies to end discrimination against, and improve resources and opportunities for, black people also began from the start of Castro's regime.

- The government was slower to tackle the discrimination and inequalities affecting gay men and lesbians. Until the 1970s, the government itself treated such people unfairly.

- In 1976, a new constitution was brought in to achieve *Poder Popular*, or People's Power. This constitution was amended in 1992, establishing direct elections to all three legislative tiers.

- As regards religion, the state at first moved to reduce the wealth and influence of the Catholic Church and, in 1976, formally declared Cuba to be atheist. However, in 1992, the constitution was amended, with 'secular' replacing the term 'atheist'.

5.10 What were the most significant features of Castro's economic policies?

A large proportion of Cuba's citizens seemed to share Castro's conviction that his government had a mission to help Cuba improve and serve its people. His redistribution policies in income – as well as education and healthcare – benefited people on lower incomes and so helped to solidify support for his regime. Even when Castro admitted failures, people were mindful of the successes of his redistribution policies. Thus Castro's social policy delivery and his redistribution of wealth – as well as his nationalism in the face of US power – all helped to maintain the legitimacy of his rule.

The early years, 1959–68

The new revolutionary government moved quickly in the first six months to benefit its supporters in the poorest sections of Cuban society.

Agriculture

In March 1959, a minimum wage was introduced for sugar-cane cutters and, in May 1959, Castro announced details of his plans for land reform in the Agrarian Reform Act. All *latifundia* (large estates) would be broken up into smaller units. Owners could keep 402 hectares (1,000 acres) – the rest were liable to expropriation. In all, about 40 per cent of Cuban farmland was expropriated and divided up into individual plots of 27 hectares (67 acres) for landless plantation workers and small farmers or peasants. Larger ranches and plantations were to be run as state farms (later to become co-operatives).

This was, in fact, quite a moderate land reform, but the landowning classes opposed the May 1959 Agrarian Reform Act. Many US companies and individuals owned large estates in Cuba, and the US government complained that compensation was inadequate.

In July 1960, the USA decided to destroy the Cuban sugar industry by cutting the sugar quota normally purchased by the USA. Castro's reaction was swift: 'They will take away

Fact: In Japan, after 1945, the USA had imposed a land reform that limited individual ownership to only 1 hectare (2.47 acres), and had given a lower rate of interest on the compensatory bonds. In 1963, Castro's government passed a second Agrarian Reform Act to nationalise the middle-size farms. By the end of 1970, the state owned 70 per cent of all land, with only small farms remaining in private ownership.

Fact: Compensation was based on the value that the landowners had placed on their land for tax purposes. These values were always deliberately lower than the land's real worth in order to reduce their tax bills.

Castro and Cuba

Why would some Cubans have supported the tearing up of the San José Declaration?

Figure 5.18 Fidel Castro, delivering his 'First declaration of Havana' speech in September 1960 to a large crowd in the Plaza de la Revolución. During his speech, Castro cancelled the 1952 Mutual Aid Treaty, signed between Batista and the USA, and went on to tear up the August 1960 San José Declaration, which was an agreement made between Latin American countries that supported the interventionist policies of the United States

What were the main steps that led to the USA imposing an embargo on all exports to Cuba in November 1960?

our sugar quota pound by pound, and we will take away their sugar mills one by one.' In August, Castro nationalised all major US properties on the island; in November, the USA announced a ban on all exports to Cuba.

The Soviet Union agreed to purchase Cuban sugar at the favourable rate of 6 cents per pound, at least until 1970. This would enable long-term planning, but it meant that Cuba would have to concentrate on sugar.

Before the revolution of 1959, unemployment had been high, especially in rural areas – but the new government's policies quickly reduced this. By the mid-1960s, there was in fact a labour shortage. However, production began to fall as the material incentives for better or more work were removed and were replaced with 'moral incentives' and calls for voluntary labour. Castro's response was to call for mass mobilisation for work in the sugar fields as well as in other sectors of the economy.

Industry

Immediately after 1959, the real wages of non-agricultural workers rose sharply and rents for the cheaper urban dwellings were reduced by up to 50 per cent. In March 1959, several utility companies were taken over and prices reduced. In April 1960, following Mikoyan's visit to Cuba in February (see section 5.6, The impact of US actions) and the signing of trade agreements, 300,000 tonnes of Soviet crude oil were delivered to Cuba. When the foreign-owned oil refineries refused to process it, Castro nationalised them in June 1960. Then, on 13 October 1960, 382 Cuban firms, including all of the sugar mills, banks and large industries, were **socialised**.

Castro saw his policies as necessary both for national security, given the growing confrontation with the USA, and as a pragmatic approach to ensure proper economic planning. A more centralised approach via a **command economy** was seen as the quickest way to ensure economic growth.

SOURCE A

We were carrying out our programme little by little. All these [US] aggressions accelerated the revolutionary process. Were they the cause? No, this would be an error … In Cuba, we were going to construct socialism in the most orderly possible manner, within a reasonable period of time, with the least amount of trauma and problems, but the aggression of imperialism accelerated the revolutionary process.

Comments made by Castro on the events of 1960–61. Quoted in Balfour, S. 2009. *Castro.* London, UK. Longman. p. 64.

The main aim of Castro's early economic policy was development via a programme of rapid industrialisation. This was seen as necessary as, since 1959, the Cuban economy had declined and was thus threatening the fulfilment of social policies for health, housing and education. By the end of 1960, the economic structure of Cuba had changed dramatically: 80 per cent of industry was under state control and state enterprises were producing 90 per cent of Cuba's exports. In November 1959, Guevara, who was determined to end Cuba's overwhelming dependency on the sugar industry, was made director of the National Bank. In February 1961, he became minister of industries.

However, there was considerable debate amongst the revolution's leaders about how best to bring about diversification and industrialisation. According to Balfour, there were two main models – the 'endogenous and exogenous models'. Guevara favoured the endogenous model, arguing that Cuba's links to the Soviet bloc meant it could jump 'stages' in the transition to socialism.

Fact: Although employment rose, productivity declined sharply. Inefficiency and underemployment became institutionalised in the new economic structures.

socialise: This term refers to the bringing of private companies into the public ownership and control of local co-operatives or collectives, local authority ventures or state/government enterprises. ('Nationalisation' refers specifically to the bringing of companies into government or state ownership and control.)

command economy: A command economy is directly opposed to a capitalist economy, which is based on the private ownership and control of major resources and businesses. When the state is in control, once businesses and banks have been socialised (i.e. taken into public ownership and control), the government can then make plans about investments, productivity and growth.

Fact: The endogenous model, favoured by Guevara, involved rapid industrialisation (similar to that adopted by Stalin in the USSR after 1928), central state planning, the elimination of the market laws of supply and demand, prioritising social need, and moral incentives. Supporters of the exogenous model argued for the need for an economic policy similar to Lenin's New Economic Policy (NEP) with its elements of capitalism (including market mechanisms, decentralisation and material incentives).

Figure 5.19 Guevara, minister of industries, taking part in voluntary labour at a public housing construction project in Havana in 1961; he gave most of his spare time to such activities

Fact: Mass mobilisation 'volunteers' (according to Bethell, many lacked the right to refuse) were used throughout the country, but were often not very effective. They were supplemented by a large number of the Cuban armed forces. Having defeated the prospect of internal counter-revolution by 1966, the armed forces were frequently used for direct productive economic activities.

Fact: Guevara went on a tour of African and Asian countries and on his return he resigned his government positions and Cuban citizenship. However, he and Castro remained close. Guevara returned to Cuba in secret in 1966 to gather and train a group of veterans for a new guerilla campaign in Bolivia, and to undergo plastic surgery to change his appearance. He was later captured and shot in Bolivia in 1967.

To bring this about, central state ministries were established, along with a Central Planning Board (*Juceplan*). In 1961, *Juceplan* was instructed to draw up a plan for 1962, and a draft four-year plan for 1962–65. According to Bethell, these plans were unrealistic and unrealisable. Despite this, during the first years there was an increase in consumption for the poorer sections of society who gained access to better food and housing.

During April–June 1963, Castro visited the Soviet Union and, in view of mounting problems, changes in economic policy were later announced – in particular, Guevara's plans for diversification were abandoned and his ministry was broken up. Instead, Soviet assistance would be given to get Cuba to concentrate on sugar production once again. Guevara left his post in 1965, just eighteen months after these changes, to undertake revolutionary work in Africa and Latin America. His ministry was divided into its former subdivisions.

However, by early 1968, there were signs of an emerging economic crisis – in part, because the Soviet Union was drastically reducing its supplies of fuel and gas.

The Soviet camp, 1968–90

Agriculture

From 1960 to 1990, production of sugar grew by 40 per cent, and the industry was employing over 375,000 people by the late 1980s. However, when unpaid overtime ('voluntary labour') became compulsory and material incentives were replaced by moral ones, mounting dissatisfaction led to falling yields. In 1966, a new deal with the Soviet Union saw Cuba agree to provide 5 million tonnes in 1968 and 1969, with a guaranteed price. But, despite Soviet investment funds to modernise the sugar industry, the harvests of 1968 and 1969 each only yielded 3.7 million tonnes. Hence Castro launched a spectacular plan to increase the sugar harvest for 1970 to 10 million tonnes – this 'battle for sugar' lasted from November 1969 to July 1970.

SOURCE B

The 10 million tonne harvest represents far more than tonnes of sugar, far more than an economic victory; it is a test, a moral commitment for this country. And precisely because it is a test and a moral commitment we cannot fall short by even a single gram of these 10 million tonnes … 10 million tonnes less a single pound – we declare it before all the world – will be a defeat, not a victory.

Extract from a speech by Castro, 18 October 1969. Quoted in Balfour, S. 2009. *Castro*. London, UK. Longman. p. 92.

Though it failed to reach the unrealistic target set by Castro, a fantastic figure – the highest in Cuba's history – of 8.5 million tonnes of sugar was reached: almost double the usual yield. The following year, production was 5.9 million tonnes. This improved production was maintained during the 1970s.

After 1970, Cuba was helped by the soaring price of sugar in the world market. As sugar accounted for about 80 per cent of all of Cuba's exports, this enabled Castro's government to successfully undertake new policies and directions. From 1980, once they had met state quotas, farmers were allowed to sell any surplus in markets where prices were no longer regulated.

Then, in 1986, new economic problems led to the 'rectification' campaign. The consequent policy changes mostly affected industry, but as regards agriculture, the newly legalised private farmers' markets were closed.

Industry

By 1968, Cuba had become increasingly dependent on the Soviet Union, and by 1970 the Cuban economy was in massive debt to the Soviet bloc. Castro then moved closer to the Soviet Union and his government increasingly turned to Soviet economic advisers along with some of the old Cuban communists. By November 1971, when Alexei Kosygin, premier of the USSR, visited, Cuba was already well integrated into the Soviet camp. Especially important was the supply of Soviet oil.

ACTIVITY

Working in pairs, develop arguments for a class presentation on:

1 Why Guevara resigned his government positions
2 What Guevara did abroad in the period 1965–67.

QUESTION

Why was voluntary labour seen as being important in the construction of a revolutionary Cuba?

QUESTION

What is meant by the term 'Soviet bloc'?

In July 1972, Cuba joined Comecon (the Council for Mutual Economic Assistance), the economic and trading union of communist states. In December, Castro went to Moscow, where he signed a 15-year economic agreement with Leonid Brezhnev that substantially increased the Soviet subsidy to the Cuban economy. This included increasing the price paid for sugar, deferring all debt payments for fifteen years (then to be repaid over twenty-five years, with no interest), and new investment credits (totalling $350 million over the next three years).

This marked the beginning of what some historians (such as Gott) and many Cubans have described as the 'Brezhnev years' – when, from 1972 to 1982, the Cuban economy was increasingly reorganised along Soviet lines. Soviet advisers helped the Cuban government to establish a new planning system: the System of Direction and Planning of the Economy (SDPE). The adoption of its first Five-Year Plan in 1975 was designed to industrialise the island by helping state enterprises to become self-financing, developing decentralisation and efficiency, and introducing profit and incentives.

Fact: Rectification involved moving Cuba away from market mechanisms in order to improve productivity and efficiency. It was not a return to the 'war economy' of 1966–70, nor a rejection of the new SDPE system of economic planning and management, but an attempt to restore a balance between the two.

However, at the third Party Congress in 1986, Castro argued that Cuba still lacked 'comprehensive national planning for economic development.' So, in April 1986, Castro launched his programme of 'rectification'. From May 1986, various anti-market measures were introduced and Castro repeated earlier calls for moral incentives as a way of motivating people to improve productivity and build a better society. Overall, there was a return to a more centralised command economy.

In 1985, Mikhail Gorbachev became the new ruler of the Soviet Union. He was determined to cut down on Soviet support for the Cuban economy. In April 1989, he made his first visit to Havana, where he spelled out the changes to come – especially the phasing out of the price subsidies to the Cuban economy, the aim to restore a greater balance of trade between the two countries, and the requirement for Cuba to pay for Soviet goods with US dollars.

QUESTION

Why did Castro launch the 'rectification' campaign in 1986?

By 1989, Cuba began to feel the impact of these changes and the effects of the collapse of the East European communist regimes. From 1989 to 1991, Cuban imports of petroleum products from the Soviet Union dropped by over 60 per cent. All former East European states cancelled their economic assistance programmes and reduced their trade with Cuba. From 1989 to 1991, the Soviet Union reduced its economic subsidies. With the collapse of the Soviet Union at the end of 1991, all subsidies were cancelled.

The Special Period and beyond, 1990–present

Agriculture

After 1959, while Cuba's economy was dependent on the Soviet Union, it was less affected by world prices. However, after the collapse of the East European communist states in 1989–90 and the Soviet Union in 1991, economic problems were inevitable. The ending of subsidies for sugar meant that Cuba was again dependent on the world market and its price fluctuations. In 1990, the average price of sugar to the Soviet Union, Eastern Europe and the West was $602 per tonne; by 1992, the world price had dropped to $200 per tonne. At the same time, external financing from the Soviet Union dropped from $3 billion in 1989 to nothing in 1992. This led to the 'Special Period in Time of Peace'.

SOURCE C

There may be other forms of aggression for which we must prepare. We have called the total blockade period a 'Special Period in Time of War'. Yet, in the face of all these problems we must prepare ... plans for a 'Special Period in Time of Peace'.

An extract from Castro's speech in January 1990 to the Cuban Workers' Federation, first announcing the Special Period. Quoted in Gott, R. 2004. *Cuba: A New History.* New Haven, USA. Yale University Press. p. 289.

Fact: Initiatives during the Special Period included:

- in October 1990, a 'Food Programme' was launched to encourage local production
- scarce funds were allocated for research and development in biotechnology
- a recycling campaign
- a far-reaching austerity drive
- a mass mobilisation of volunteers – with many (such as students) from outside the agricultural sector
- development of tourism in place of sugar.

In March 1990, farmers were urged to use draught animals such as oxen and horses, and food was rationed. Thousands of workers from industries that had to be closed because of their dependence on foreign imports were sent to the countryside to grow food. Before 1990, Cuba obtained 63 per cent of its food from the Soviet Union, and much food had been imported from Eastern Europe, so alternative sources of food supplies were needed. With no dollars available to buy from the West, food production at home had to be increased and various initiatives were undertaken.

However, by 1993 it was clear that further measures were needed. One of the three main measures was the establishment, in September 1993, of agricultural co-operatives (known as *Unidades Básicas de Producción Cooperativa* (UBPC)) to replace the state farms, which were reduced in size, as was the number of workers. The state agricultural sector – which had controlled 75 per cent of the agricultural economy – reduced to 30 per cent by 1996. The land remained nominally in the hands of the state, and the UBPCs still had to produce quotas at prices fixed by the government. Also, private farmers' markets, abolished during the 'rectification' campaign of 1986, were allowed once more.

The Special Period ended in 1996 but the constant fallback for the Cuban economy for centuries – sugar – was gone. In 2002, the government announced that 71 of the 156 sugar mills would be closed and half of the land devoted to sugar would be given over to other crops.

Industry

After 1975, few of the planned targets for increased productivity had been fully met and real economic growth had been modest. In addition, the Cuban economy had become increasingly reliant on the Soviet Union. Cuba imported 80 per cent of its machinery from the Soviet Union, while the Soviet Union purchased 63 per cent of Cuba's sugar, 95 per cent of its citrus and 73 per cent of its nickel. Since the 1960s, the regular deliveries of cheap Soviet oil had been Cuba's economic lifeline: in 1989, almost 13 million tonnes had been delivered – at very favourable rates. The Special Period really began in 1990, when oil supplies from the Soviet Union reduced dramatically: by 1993, supplies dropped to 5.3 million tonnes and replacement supplies had to be bought on the world market, at higher prices and with US dollars.

Castro and Cuba

QUESTION

How did *Poder Popular* help to protect Cuban workers from the worst impacts of Cuba's economic crisis? To what extent does this Cuban experience differ from the experiences of ordinary people in other countries suffering economic difficulties and implementing austerity policies?

The collapse of the Soviet Union in December 1991 removed the crucial role played by the Soviet bloc in keeping the Cuban economy afloat. Between 1989 and 1993, Cuban GDP fell by 35 per cent while exports fell by 79 per cent. By 2000, exports were still only 43 per cent of the figure for the pre-1989 years. In March 1990, gas, water and electricity supplies were cut off for short periods throughout the country. In August, oil and gas deliveries were cut by 50 per cent across the island, and electricity consumption was cut by 10 per cent.

However, because of *Poder Popular*, the economic crisis of the Special Period does not seem to have been resolved at the expense of the workers. Thus conflict between government and unions appears to have been limited. In 1992, the constitution was amended to allow for state property to become part of joint ventures with foreign companies. But, by 1993, it was clear that Cuba's internal economy was still experiencing huge problems. So Castro brought in a team of young economists led by Carlos Lage (the youthful vice-president) and José Luis Rodriguez (as minister of finance).

The first reforms were announced in Castro's Moncada speech on 26 July 1993. Particularly significant – and painful – was the Decree-Law 140 of August 1993, which made the US dollar legal tender in Cuba. Then, in September, the Decree-Law 141 reintroduced self-employment in some occupations and by 1995 more than 200,000 Cubans (about 5 per cent of the workforce) were registered as self-employed. Yet, throughout the Special Period, Castro maintained his opposition to capitalism.

SOURCE D

Authorising private commerce would be a political and ideological turnaround; it would be like starting along the path towards capitalism ... I find capitalism repugnant. It is filthy, it is gross, it is alienating ... because it causes war, hypocrisy and competition.

Castro speaking in January 1994. Quoted in Balfour, S. 2009. *Castro*. London, UK. Longman. p. 155.

Fact: The Torricelli Act banned foreign-based subsidiaries of US companies from trading with Cuba, and placed severe limits on travel to Cuba by US citizens. The Helms-Burton Act imposed penalties on foreign companies doing business with Cuba. In June 2012, the US Treasury's Office of Foreign Asset Control fined the Dutch bank ING $619 million for 'violating' sanctions against Cuba; in December 2012, the British bank HSBC was fined $665 million for the same reason. Such US actions led to many international banks and financial institutions withdrawing from Cuba.

To help the Cuban economy survive, tourism was strongly promoted and soon became Cuba's largest earner of foreign currency. The government invested heavily in it and worked with partner companies from Spain, France and Canada in particular. Yet just as things were improving, and Cuba might have been expected to benefit from the end of the Cold War, the USA turned up the pressure, passing the Torricelli Act in 1992 and the Helms-Burton Act in 1996 to tighten trade sanctions on Cuba. However, the European Union – by then the main investors in Cuba – objected strongly to US attempts to stop them trading with Cuba. Eventually, the USA was forced to exempt EU countries. The 1996 Act failed to stop Cuba expanding its world trade – though it remained as a potential threat.

In 2003, a new programme of anti-market re-centralisation was introduced: the dollar was no longer legal tender and the ministry for foreign trade was recreated to re-establish control over exports and imports.

5.11 How successful were Castro's economic policies?

The early years, 1959–68

Agriculture

Sugar production, already in trouble under Batista before 1959, was disrupted by managers fleeing to the USA during the period 1959–61. Early attempts at agricultural diversification away from sugar created further problems. As a result, the 1963 sugar harvest (down by over 30 per cent compared to 1961) was the worst since the Second World War, while agriculture in general suffered similar problems.

However, in 1964, the Soviet Union signed the first of a series of long-term agreements that guaranteed better and stable prices for sugar; sugar production then increased from the 1963 level of 3.8 million tonnes.

Industry

There were also problems in industry and, in 1962, the Cuban economy collapsed. Castro's government froze prices and had to bring in rationing for most consumer products. However, this meant that resources were distributed fairly. The fair distribution of food was a first for Cuba and contrasted strongly with other states in the region, which were marked by inequalities and mass poverty.

In 1963, the Cuban economy declined even further as imports of machinery for rapid industrialisation, on top of the decline in income from sugar, resulted in a balance-of-payments crisis. At the same time, the replacement of money incentives for workers with moral incentives proved ineffective as workers were paid the same regardless of effort or quality. Part of the failure of Guevara's plans was down to the US embargo – the US had previously supplied the raw materials and machine parts needed for factories producing consumer goods, and at first there was no alternative source. In 1963, industrial production fell by 1.5 per cent having grown by 0.4 per cent the previous year.

The Soviet camp, 1968–90

Agriculture

Problems in agriculture continued after the policy changes of the mid-1960s. Production in cattle-raising and forestry declined. Even fishing – the best performer – experienced some declines as well as successes. By 1970, Cuba's economy in general was in crisis; and by 1982, Cuba's terms of trade with the Soviet Union were over 30 per cent lower than in 1975 – largely as a result of lower sugar prices.

Industry

During the late 1970s and early 1980s, a new management system was introduced to give more autonomy to managers. Once again, higher wages and bonuses were paid for higher-quality work, increased productivity and overtime.

Fact: Material incentives included higher pay for certain types of workers, bonuses for increased productivity and payment for overtime. Those who saw money as a capitalist corruption wanted to stress moral incentives, such as taking pride in working to achieve a better society and resisting the efforts of the USA to undermine the gains of the 1959 Revolution, for example by volunteering to work overtime for no extra pay. Such people would be keen to be part of the movement to bring about a worldwide revolution and so create a better world for the majority of the people.

Consequently, the economy prospered spectacularly during the first half of the 1970s. From 1975 to 1985, there was good economic and industrial growth, with an annual growth rate of 4.1 per cent, and with a significant improvement in the early 1980s (the comparable figure for Latin America as a whole was 1.2 per cent). By 1982, its hard-currency debt reached about $3 billion; by 1986, Cuba had a record deficit of over $199 million and a foreign debt of $3.87 billion, 6.9 per cent higher than in 1985. An economic recession thus began in 1986 and continued for the rest of the decade.

The Special Period and beyond, 1990–present

Agriculture

Figure 5.20 Plaza Organopónico is one of many small organic farm co-operatives in Havana creating work and fresh food for the city's inhabitants

In 1990, with the start of the Special Period, Cuba experienced an economic disaster. Despite government measures to improve things, there remained mismanagement and shortages. After 1993, 'free' farmers' markets, in which farmers were free to sell directly to the public, were restored, with good results. By 2000, markets (known as 'kiosks') were established on almost every block in Havana, providing a wide variety of foods; they still exist in most towns and cities.

Despite such efforts, many areas of agricultural production in Cuba remained weak – apart from eggs and citrus fruits. However, the *organopónicos* – about 7,000 small organic plots, mainly located in urban areas – have been a success. These now produce 90 per cent of Cuba's fruit and vegetables, and obviously require no expensive (and harmful) pesticides or fertilisers. In addition, experts from Australia have taught the methods of permaculture – a sustainable agricultural system.

Industry

Cuba's import capacity dropped 70 per cent between 1989 and 1992 (from $8.1 billion to $2.3 billion). This was mainly because of the drop in earnings from sugar and the loss of external financing, mostly from the Soviet Union. As well as oil, there were also shortages of spare parts, chemical fertilisers and animal feedstuffs. However, the government maintained the revolution's gains of free education and a free health service – no hospitals or schools were closed during the Special Period.

After 1993, the economy slowly began to improve. GDP, at 0.7 per cent in 1994, stopped falling, and after 1996 it averaged out at 3.5 per cent a year. One important element in helping Cuba to overcome its biggest problems was Hugo Chávez, a great admirer of Castro, who became president of Venezuela in 1998. Chávez signed trade deals that were beneficial to Cuba.

In 2000, the first Cuba–Venezuela agreement was reached, to provide Cuba with considerable amounts of oil. By 2006, Cuba was importing 100,000 barrels of oil a day from Venezuela at a preferential price well below average world market prices. Meanwhile, in 2008, Russia agreed to help fund oil production off the coast of Cuba.

Theory of knowledge

History and ethics:
Utilitarianism is a theory of ethics that says that the supreme moral principle is the 'greatest good for the greatest number of people'. Do the social policies of Castro's government after 1959 justify the expropriation and nationalisation of land and businesses owned by wealthy Cubans and foreigners? Are the political theories of socialism and Marxism therefore more moral than those of neo-liberal 'free market' capitalism?

5.12 What were the main social policies in Castro's Cuba?

When Castro took power in 1959, Cuba ranked amongst the top five Latin American countries for literacy, infant mortality and life expectancy. In health care and medical services, it was third. However, these statistics are misleading as most services were based in Havana and the large regional towns. Conditions and services in the rural areas were very different – many rural areas had few doctors and few schools.

Living standards

Castro's policies to redistribute wealth have been very successful. By providing jobs for all those who are able to work, the goal of ending unemployment was met. Prices of basic goods were kept low, while rationing ensured fair distribution. In particular, the improvement in living standards for the rural poor was outstanding.

Health care

Health care is one of the most successful social policy areas for Castro's government. Health-care services were quickly established as the right of every Cuban citizen, and the system of free health care, which had existed before the revolution of 1959, was greatly expanded. This was especially true of the rural areas. However, the various political and military mobilisations – resulting from real or imagined threats from the USA – disrupted the expansion of medical services.

The improvement in the economy in the 1970s meant that great advances were made. By 1981, the infant mortality rate had fallen to 18.5 per 1,000 while pre-1959 diseases (especially those associated with poverty such as TB and diarrhoeal disease) had been greatly reduced.

Housing

Before 1959, only 15 per cent of rural inhabitants had running water (it was 80 per cent for urban dwellers), and only 9 per cent of households had electricity. However, the revolutionary government's performance in housing was less successful. There were inefficiencies in the construction and construction-materials industries, and insufficient production, as the government gave higher priority to the building of hospitals and schools.

From 1949 to 1959, when the Cuban population was half of the figure for the late 1970s/early 1980s, about 27,000 housing units were built each year. In the 1960s, figures dropped considerably, although they rose to 16,000 units per year during the first Five-Year Plan (1976–80). In 1973, a high of 21,000 units was reached, but by 1980 figures had declined again.

5.13 What has been the impact of Castro's policies towards women, ethnic and other minorities, and religion?

Women

The lives of women changed greatly under Castro's regime after 1959. As well as social policies affecting them – such as easier divorce, free abortions and subsidised family planning – the proportion of women in the labour force doubled from the late 1950s to the late 1980s.

SOURCE E

At present, more than 40 per cent of the workforce is made up of women, constituting an estimated 60 per cent of the upper levels of technicians and 67 per cent of professionals. Women constitute 61 per cent of prosecutors, 49 per cent of professional judges, 47 per cent of magistrates and 30 per cent of state administrators and ministry officials.

Saney, I. 2004. *Cuba: A Revolution in Motion.* London, UK. Zed Books. p. 94.

Fact: According to Bethell, the increase in the number of women in the labour force was not fundamentally the result of government policies (some of which did encourage women's participation in the job market), it was more a social trend of advancing modernisation.

Figure 5.21   Vilma Espin (1930–2007)

Espin was one of the leaders of the 26 July Movement in Santiago before 1959. She later married Raúl Castro and retained her power base in the FMC when they separated. In 1992, as president of the FMC, she challenged prejudices against gay men and lesbians, and formed a section to support the concerns of lesbians.

Cuban women are guaranteed equal pay, and the Women's Commission on Employment monitors hiring and workplace practices for discrimination. However, the highest paid jobs in mining, fishery and construction are restricted to men only on the grounds that they would damage women's health. Thus, on average, women's salaries are 15 per cent lower than those of men in the public sector.

There has been an impressive increase in the number of women throughout the education system. Cuba has one of the highest rates of school enrolment of young girls. Also, more than 60 per cent of university students are female, and 47 per cent of university instructors are women – in medicine, women actually outnumber men, forming 70 per cent of students. Although they remain under-represented in engineering and over-represented in primary and secondary school teaching and in the humanities, a fundamental shift has nonetheless occurred.

In August 1960, the Federation of Cuban Women (FMC) was set up. It has gone a long way towards changing sexist opinions and behaviour. For many years its president was **Vilma Espin**.

The FMC played a crucial role in getting an egalitarian Family Code adopted in 1975. This was designed to equalise the status of spouses in the family and obliged husbands to do half of all family chores. However, surveys suggest the persistence of Latin American *machismo* (male chauvinism) and gender stereotyping in the home. Women thus bear the brunt of the 'second shift' (i.e. household work), doing thirty-six hours of household work per week compared to ten hours for men.

Women's participation in politics has been significantly less equal than in the workplace. By the mid-1980s, only 19 per cent of the PCC members and candidate members and only 13 per cent of the PCC's Central Committees were women. There were no women in the party secretariat or the top government organ, the Council of State. However, by 2003, women formed over 30 per cent of the active membership of the PCC and 16.1 per cent of the Council of State, and five ministries were headed by women. Women also held 52.5 per cent of union leadership positions, and 31 per cent of all managers of state enterprises were women. According to historians such as Saney, Cuba compares favourably with other countries and ranks fifth in the Americas in terms of overall equality for women. In the 1988 elections, 27.6 per cent of delegates were women; in 2003, this rose to 35.9 per cent. Female representation in the National Assembly puts Cuba tenth in the world. Despite some problems, the Cuban Revolution maintains a strong commitment to achieving full equality between women and men.

Fact: Vilma Espin was the first woman to enter the party's politburo, in 1986. Women were also under-represented in the middle ranks of leadership.

QUESTION

How far have Castro's policies for gender equality overcome the pre-1959 traditions of *machismo* and patriarchy in Cuba?

Black people

Before 1959, Castro's programmes and manifestos had not alluded to the 'colour question'. However, after 1959, the improved treatment of black people soon became an important achievement of Castro's regime. In March 1959, he made his 'Proclamation against discrimination' speech, calling for a campaign against racial discrimination and making it clear that differences in skin colour were of no significance. The revolutionary government quickly repealed the pre-1959 laws that allowed or enforced racial discrimination. However, Castro did not support black separatism, and the societies and associations of black intellectuals and politicians that had existed before 1959 were closed.

As a result of government social and economic policies, Cuba's black and mulatto population – which was disproportionately poor – saw their living standards improve considerably after 1959. Consequently, surveys show that support for Castro's government is greater among black people than among whites.

The leaders of the 1959 revolution were overwhelmingly white, and white people have continued to fill the top political positions. Consequently, as with women, black people are still significantly under-represented in the top organs of both party and state. By 1979, only five of the thirty-four ministers were black; there were only four black members of the fourteen-strong politburo of the PCC; and only sixteen of the 146 members of its Central Committee were black. So, at the party congress in 1986, Castro declared it a priority to increase the black share of top political jobs.

Same-sex relations in Cuba

Today, same-sex relations are not illegal in Cuba. However, **homophobia**, though not violent as in many other states, persists in certain sections of society. The situation of gay men and lesbians has altered over the decades since the revolution of 1959. After 1959, same-sex relationships were at first seen as aspects of 'bourgeois decadence' resulting from capitalism. Such early attitudes were strengthened in the 1960s and 1970s as Cuba moved closer to the Soviet Union, whose laws reflected such prejudices.

As early as 1965, the Revolutionary Armed Forces forcibly recruited gay men into UMAP (Military Units to Help Production) work battalions. These military labour camps, however, were mainly intended for men who, as conscientious objectors, refused to do military service, or for young men who were considered unfit for military service. This led to significant criticism in Cuba – in 1967, Castro ordered the camps to be disbanded and the internees released.

However, this did not end discrimination in other areas of life. In 1971, the government described same-sex relationships as incompatible with the revolution – gay men and lesbians were expelled from the Communist Party and several artists, actors and teachers lost their jobs. However, this was overturned by the Supreme Court in 1975, and Armando Hart, head of the new ministry of culture, began to promote a more liberal approach.

As a result, during the second half of the 1970s, attitudes towards same-sex relationships were questioned in various ways. In 1977, the *Centro Nacional de Educación Sexual*

(CNES) was founded on the initiative of the Cuban Women's Federation (FMC) – this encouraged a more enlightened outlook on sexual orientation and started to undermine traditional sexual prejudices and taboos.

The work done by the CNES has contributed to changes in attitudes and laws. In 1979, the law was changed to remove same-sex acts between consenting adults as a criminal offence from the Penal Code. More recently, the age of consent for same-sex relations was equalised to that for heterosexual relations.

Figure 5.22 A meeting at *El Mejunje* (The Mixture), an arts and cultural centre in Santa Clara, established mainly, but not exclusively, for young LGBT people. It was founded by Ramón Silverio, and is partly funded by the authorities. One of its aims is to help parents of LGBT understand their childrens' sexual orientations

There have been further reforms, often emanating from Raúl Castro and his daughter Mariela Castro. These reforms include free hormone therapy in 2008 and free state-sponsored gender reassignment surgery in 2010. However, there is no recognition of same-sex marriage or civil partnerships or unions. Gay and lesbian organisations and publications are banned, as are gay pride marches. Yet since 1995, gay and lesbian groups

Historical debate:
Historians are divided over the degree of toleration of gay men and lesbians in Cuba today. Does the record of Castro's government on this issue since 1959 warrant the many criticisms that have been made of it – including those from some on the left, who have been otherwise supportive of the revolution?

239

have been allowed to participate in – and even lead – the May Day parades. Castro more recently criticised machismo and urged acceptance of same-sex relationships, describing these as a 'natural aspect and tendency of human beings, that must simply be respected'.

Religion

The Catholic Church had not grown deep roots in Cuba as in other Latin American states. By the late 1990s, out of a population of 11 million, only about 150,000 regularly attended Sunday mass. There were also various ecumenical Protestant sects, which experienced some growth in the 1990s. But the numbers of Catholics and Protestants combined was less than the 5 million who followed various forms of Afro-Cuban religion.

At first the Church leadership accepted the revolution; but the secularisation of education, and the reduction of the Church's role in government, changed the situation. By the end of 1959, the radical turn taken by Castro and his *Fidelistas* led to tensions with the Catholic Church.

However, during the 1980s, the Vatican and the Cuban and US Catholic Churches condemned the US embargo on Cuba. Pope John Paul II (who was strongly anti-communist) even mildly criticised the effects of neo-liberal capitalist economics.

In July 1992, amendments to the 1976 Constitution declared the state to be secular rather than atheist, while the PCC allowed religious believers to join. Then, in January 1998, Pope John Paul II visited Cuba, where he conducted four masses. The Pope negotiated the release of about 300 prisoners and gained greater room for activity by the Church, despite government concerns about faith-based oppositionist groups, which were still closely monitored.

5.14 What impact have the policies of the Cuban Revolution had on education, young people and the arts?

Education

Education has been the most impressive of Castro's achievements. Cuba in 1959 had a generally ill-educated population. As early as his attack on the Moncada barracks in July 1953, Castro had promised reform of education; in his speech to the UN in 1960, he promised that the revolution would end illiteracy within a year.

Fact: According to the 1970 census, illiteracy still stood at 12.9 per cent; by 1979, this had dropped to 5.6 per cent.

The drive to eliminate illiteracy began in 1961 – designated the 'Year of Education'. The revolutionary government took over all private and Church schools, and after some difficulties it achieved virtual universal attendance at primary schools. Over 100,000 volunteer student teachers, recruited into brigades, took part – most were teenagers.

Figure 5.23 A primary-school classroom in Havana in 2007 – note the poster of Che Guevara on the wall at the back

They were often the target of US-sponsored counter-revolutionaries, and more than forty were killed in these terrorist attacks. Yet these teachers taught over 1 million to read and write – thus allowing the fulfilment of Castro's promise. More than 3,000 schools were built in the first year, and over 300,000 children attended school for the first time.

The literacy campaign and school reforms continued throughout an extensive adult education system. Later, with some Soviet assistance, Cuba developed a greatly improved educational system, which was free to all and without parallel in Latin America.

As a result, average levels of education in the labour force jumped from bare literacy in the 1964 labour census to sixth-grade level in the 1974 census and to eighth-grade level by 1979. However, differences in access to quality education between urban and rural Cubans – though greatly reduced – did not completely end; but the improvements made in the late 1960s were built on in the 1970s. Many people deserve credit for these improvements: apart from Castro (who pushed for it as a priority), **José Ramón Fernández** played a key role.

Improvements in higher education were more limited. Departments were at first hit, both by the early emigrations and by the dismissal of 'politically unreliable' staff. There was a strong bias towards technical education, with engineering being prioritised over the humanities and the liberal arts; and academic study of the social sciences was neglected.

Figure 5.24 José Ramón Fernández (b. 1923)

During Batista's tyranny, Fernández was imprisoned from 1956 to 1959 for his involvement with the opposition group 'Los puros'. He took part in operations during the Bay of Pigs incident in 1961. He was first deputy minister of education until 1972 and minister of education from 1972 until 1990.

QUESTION

How far, and for what reasons, have Castro's educational policies since 1959 been successful?

241

Overall, Castro successfully carried through a real educational revolution after 1959. This has been not only a source of great pride for the Cuban government and people, it has also been an inspiration for other developing countries. Despite economic crises (including the Special Period) Castro has insisted that the 'historic socialist achievements of the revolution' – free education and free medical care – be preserved untouched.

The media and the arts

In 1960, all of the mass media came under government control; the only avenue of criticism was via the letters-to-the-editor pages – such letters had to relate to specific problems rather than criticising general policy.

There was greater – though still limited – freedom of expression and publication in the arts and the academic worlds for those who supported the revolution and who wrote on topics other than contemporary politics. However, in 1961 Castro said about culture: 'Within the revolution, everything; against the revolution, nothing'. Thus, material opposed to the revolution, or written by known opponents, was not published.

5.15 How far is Cuba's Castroist state authoritarian?

Since 1959, the Cuban state under Castro has been variously described as a 'communist dictatorship', an 'authoritarian democracy' and a 'guided democracy'. The siege conditions resulting from US hostility and threats have played an important role in the development of the Cuban state. In particular, Castro feared that a market/private enterprise economy and a multi-party political system would allow the USA to continue to influence the economy and politics of Cuba.

In 1959, Castro claimed that a people's government had come to power – but he also repeatedly stressed that the people were not yet ready to assume government. The movement's revolutionary vanguard, guided but not controlled from below, would carry out policy on behalf of the people. He summed it up thus: 'First the revolution, then elections'. Though the creation of an authoritarian government was not a stated aim of the revolution, the Cuban political system certainly shares some of the features of such a state. Present-day observers of the more recent political developments in Cuba differ over the extent to which Cuba has moved away from authoritarianism and towards greater political democracy. One reason for such differences is the fact that there are many perspectives on democracy: for instance, should democracy be representative or should it be direct? To what extent are 'free' elections really free, if political parties are dependent on funding by wealthy individuals and companies?

Theory of knowledge

History, the arts and truth: According to the novelist D. H. Lawrence (1885–1930), *'The essential function of art is moral.'* Study the poster, and then write a couple of paragraphs to show (a) what moral is being encouraged, and (b) how far it reflects the political realities of Castro's Cuba in the late 1970s.

Figure 5.25 A photograph taken in Havana in about 1977–78 of a poster depicting Karl Marx and Friedrich Engels, authors of *The Communist Manifesto*. The slogan at the top says: 'Workers of all countries, unite!'

Cuba and democracy

Prior to Castro's revolution in 1959, many Cubans had grown disenchanted with the corrupt multi-party political system that had operated throughout the first half of the 20th century, and with the external dependence that allowed the USA to dominate the Cuban economy and society.

Like Martí, Castro and the *Fidelistas* believed elections were less important than the things that governments do for the people. After 1959, at mass meetings, the people also apparently rejected elections and the old way of conducting politics. This was confirmed by Urrutia, president of Cuba from January to July 1959.

> ### SOURCE F
>
> The first time I heard the promise of elections repudiated was when Castro and I attended the opening of the library at Marta University at Las Villas. At the end of the meeting, Castro mentioned elections and a large number of his listeners shouted against them. After the speech, Castro asked, 'Did you notice how they spoke against elections?'
>
> Extract from a speech made by Manuel Urrutia. Quoted in Perez Jr. L. A. 1988. *Cuba: Between Reform and Revolution*. New York, USA. Oxford University Press. pp. 321–22.

Though Castro's Cuba was a one-party communist or socialist state until 1992, it was also populist – but with limits on individual and collective freedoms in the name of security and ideological correctness.

> ### SOURCE G
>
> What we have, obviously, is not the democracy of the exploiters … Now we are speaking of another democracy, the democracy of the people, of the workers, of the peasants, of the humble men and women, the democracy of the majority of the nation, of those who were exploited, of those who had no rights in the past. And this is the true democracy, the revolutionary democracy of the people, the democracy of the humble, by the humble and for the humble.
>
> Extract from a speech delivered by Castro in 1961. Quoted in Saney, I. 2004. *Cuba: A Revolution in Motion*. London, UK. Zed Books. p. 49.

Fact: Other political parties in Cuba include the Christian Democratic Party of Cuba, the Cuban Democratic Socialist Current, the Democratic Social-Revolutionary Party of Cuba, the Democratic Solidarity Party, the Liberal Party of Cuba and the Social Democratic Coordination of Cuba.

Since 1992, other political parties have been legalised. Nevertheless, the Communist Party of Cuba remains the official state party. However, all parties are prohibited from campaigning in elections.

Constitutions and elections

In April 1959, during a visit to the USA, Castro announced the suspension of elections in Cuba. From 1959 to 1976 there was thus no elected legislative body in Cuba.

The 1976 Constitution and *Poder Popular*

In 1976, a new constitution was introduced. This set up a three-tier system of *Poder Popular* (People's Power) – municipal, provincial and national assemblies to allow for democratic decision-making. However, only municipal elections were direct – those to the other two tiers were indirect.

Citizens and the various mass organisations (see section 5.5, Mass organisations) – *not* the Communist Party of Cuba – directly nominated the list of candidates for the different levels of representation. According to Isaac Saney, this formal socialist democracy had four elements: political participation, economic equality, the merging of civil and political society, and the **mandat imperatif**. However, Balfour argues that the 1976 reforms did not really shift power from the leadership to the people. The first meeting of the new National Assembly was in December 1976, at which the Council of Ministers, which had exercised legislative and executive powers for eighteen years, formally handed over these powers.

The 1992 constitution

In 1991, at the start of the Special Period (see section 5.10, The Special Period and beyond, 1990–present), it was decided to modify the 1976 constitution to allow a direct vote in elections for members of the National Assembly and the provincial assemblies. A draft was approved by the National Assembly in July 1992, with the first direct elections in February 1993. In the early 1990s, popular councils (*consejo populares*) were also established to increase the power of local government.

Poder Popular after 1992

The 1992 reforms have arguably resulted in more effective political participation for the Cuban people. The National Assembly chooses from its members the Council of State, which is accountable to the National Assembly. The Council of State also carries out the National Assembly's functions when it is not in session, but the next National Assembly must ratify any decisions.

The influence of the Communist Party of Cuba (PCC) was reduced by the 1992 reforms; it is prevented by law from playing any role in the nomination of candidates. According to Castro, this avoided the politicking and corruption often associated with multi-party political systems.

At the provincial and national levels there are candidacy commissions, made up of representatives from the various mass and grassroots organisations, presided over by workers' representatives chosen by the unions. The commissions sift through thousands of people and present their recommendations to the municipal assemblies for final approval.

Thus it is Cuban citizens who both nominate and elect representatives. Turnout in elections is usually high – about 90 per cent. There is no formal campaigning. Instead, a month before the elections take place, biographies of candidates are displayed in public places.

End of unit activities

1   Carry out some further research on the methods used by Castro to redistribute economic resources more equally amongst the citizens of Cuba. Then create a table, showing which groups have benefited most.

mandat imperatif:
This means elected representatives must listen to voters and respond to their complaints and suggestions.

Fact: Mass and grassroots organisations include the trade unions, the Cuban Confederation of Women, the Committees to Defend the Revolution, the National Association of Small Farmers, the Federation of University Students, and a range of professional organisations.

QUESTION

What do you understand by the term *Poder Popular*?

Historical debate: Historians are divided over whether Castro was or was not moving towards communism before 1959. Try to find and briefly summarise the views of at least four different historians on this question. Which arguments do you find the most persuasive?

Theory of knowledge

History, culture and bias: The post-1976 Cuban form of democracy known as *Poder Popular* is clearly different from the values and perceptions of democracy that hold sway in liberal democracies such as the USA and Britain. Is it possible for historians – and students of history – to evaluate in an unbiased way the values of a significantly different culture?

2 Re-read section 5.12 and produce a table summarising (a) the main social policies introduced by Castro's government since 1959, and (b) their results.

3 Find out more about the development of organic farming and recycling in Cuba during and after the Special Period. How significant do you think these have been in helping Cuba to survive the loss of support from the Soviet bloc?

4 Produce a newspaper article that examines the arguments for and against the view that Cuba is still essentially an authoritarian state.

End of chapter activities

Paper 1 exam practice

Question

Compare and contrast the views expressed in **Sources A** and **B** below on the impact of the Bay of Pigs incident as regards Castro's consolidation of power. **[6 marks]**

Skill

Cross-referencing.

SOURCE A

The victory at Playa Girón was celebrated amid national euphoria. It was as if the United States had finally received its comeuppance after a century of meddling in the affairs of Cuba. Castro's prestige among the population would never be higher … Later the same year, he declared on television that he was a Marxist and that the Cuban Revolution would have a 'Marxist–Leninist' programme. The words of a popular song of the post-Playa Girón days, 'Cuba Si, Yanquis No', suggest how collective faith in Castro seemed to override the residue of old ideologies; if Fidel was in charge, they implied, it did not matter which direction the revolution went.

Balfour, S. 2009. *Castro*. London, UK. Longman. p. 65.

SOURCE B

The invasion was one of the major strategic errors of the United States in the 20th century, reinforcing Castro's control over Cuba, ensuring the permanence of his revolution and helping to drive him into the Soviet camp … Before he left Havana [to supervise the military operation against the invaders], Castro had ordered the arrest of anyone suspected of counter-revolutionary activities, and 35,000 people were detained in the capital alone, including the auxiliary bishop of Havana. The CIA's hope that thousands would rise up against the revolution were thwarted on the first day.

Gott, R. 2004. *Cuba: A New History*. New Haven, USA. Yale University Press. pp. 190–94.

Examiner's tips

Cross-referencing questions require you to compare and contrast the information/content/nature of two sources, relating to a particular issue. Before you write your answer, draw a rough chart or diagram to show the similarities and the differences between the two sources. That way, you should ensure you address both aspects/elements of the question.

Common mistakes

When asked to compare and contrast two sources, make sure you do not just comment on one of the sources! Such oversights happen every year – and will lose you 4 of the 6 marks available.

Simplified mark scheme

Band		Marks
1	Both **sources linked**, with **detailed references** to **BOTH** sources, identifying both similarities **AND** differences.	6
2	Both **sources linked**, with **detailed references** to **BOTH** sources, identifying either similarities **OR** differences.	4–5
3	**Comments on both sources**, but treating each one **separately**.	3
4	Discusses/comments on **just one source**.	0–2

Student answer

Sources A and B give very different views of the impact of the Bay of Pigs incident on Castro's consolidation of power. Source A gives a much more positive view, pointing out how 'his prestige among the population would never be higher'.

However, Source B focuses on Castro relying on repression rather than the popularity mentioned in Source A, to consolidate his rule: it refers to how he used the invasion to reinforce his control by arresting any suspected counter-revolutionaries – '35,000 people were detained in the capital alone'.

Examiner's comments

There are some clear/precise references to both the sources, and one main difference/contrast is identified. Also, the sources are linked in the second paragraph rather than being dealt with separately. But only one clear difference is identified, so the candidate's answer is on the borderline between Band 3 and low Band 2 – this would score 3–4 marks. As no similarities/comparisons are shown, this answer fails to get into Band 1.

Activity

Look again at the two sources, the simplified mark scheme, and the student answer above. Now try to write a paragraph or two to push the answer up into Band 1, and so obtain the full 6 marks. Tip: try to identify any similarities.

Summary activity

Draw your own spider diagram, and using the information from this chapter and any other materials that you have available make notes under each of the headings. Where there are differences in the relative importance of the various reasons for Castro's success, or his ideology, try to mention the views of specific historians.

Summary activity

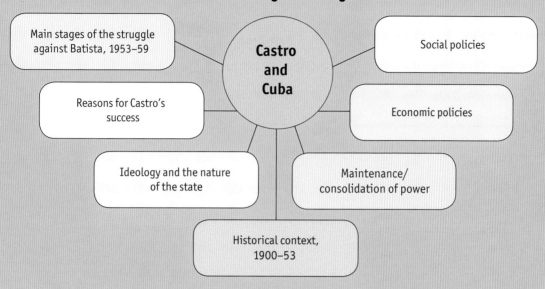

Paper 2 practice questions

1 Evaluate the conditions and actions that helped Castro in his bid for power.

2 'The main reason Castro came to power in 1959 was because of Batista's mistakes.' To what extent do you agree with this statement?

3 Compare and contrast the methods used by Hitler and Castro to obtain power.

4 To what extent, and in what ways, can Castro's ideology be described as Marxist in the years after 1953?

5 Examine the methods used by Castro to maintain power.

6 Compare and contrast either the economic or the social policies of Mussolini and Castro.

7 To what extent was Castro successful in achieving his aims?

8 With reference to one authoritarian state, examine the role of education or the arts in maintaining power.

Further reading

Try reading the relevant chapters/sections of the following books:

Balfour, S. 2009. *Castro*. London, UK. Longman.

Bethell, L. (ed.). 1993. *Cuba: A Short History*. Cambridge, UK. Cambridge University Press.

Coltman, L. 2003. *The Real Fidel Castro*. New Haven, USA. Yale University Press.

5

Gott, R. 2004. *Cuba: A New History*. New Haven, USA. Yale University Press.

Matthews, H. L. 1970. *Castro: A Political Biography*. London, UK. Penguin Books.

Reid-Henry, S. 2009. *Fidel and Che: A Revolutionary Friendship*. London, UK. Sceptre.

Sandison, D. 2001. *Che Guevara*. London, UK. Chancellor Press.

Saney, I. 2004. *Cuba: A Revolution in Motion*. London, UK. Zed Books.

Skidmore, T. E. and Smith, P. H. 1984. *Modern Latin America*. Oxford, UK. Oxford University Press.

Skierka, V. 2004. *Fidel Castro: A Biography*. Cambridge, UK. Polity Press.

Szulc, T. 1987. *Fidel: A Critical Portrait*. London, UK. Hutchinson.

Thomas, H. 1971. *Cuba: The Pursuit of Freedom*. London, UK. Harper & Row.

Exam practice

Introduction

You have now completed your study of the main aspects and events of 20th century Authoritarian States. In the previous chapters, you have had practice at answering some of the types of source-based question you will have to deal with in Paper 1. In this chapter, you will gain experience of dealing with:

- the longer Paper 1 question, which requires you to use both sources and your own knowledge to write a mini-essay
- the essay questions you will encounter in Paper 2.

Exam skills needed for IB History

This book is designed primarily to prepare both Standard and Higher Level students for the Paper 2 topic World History Topic 10: Authoritarian States (20th century). However, by providing the necessary historical knowledge and understanding, as well as an awareness of the relevant key historical debates, it will also help you prepare for Paper 1. The skills you need for answering both Paper 1 and Paper 2 exam questions are explained below.

In order to analyse and evaluate sources as historical evidence, you will need to ask the following 'W' questions of historical sources:

- **W**ho produced it? Were they in a position to know?
- **W**hat type of source is it? What is its nature – is it a primary or secondary source?
- **W**here and **w**hen was it produced? What was happening at the time?
- **W**hy was it produced? Was its purpose to inform or to persuade? Is it an accurate attempt to record facts, or is it an example of propaganda?
- **W**ho was the intended audience? Decision-makers, or the general public?

The example below shows you how to find the information related to the 'W' questions that you will need in order to evaluate sources for their value and limitations.

Paper 1 exam practice

Paper 1: skills and questions

This section of the book is designed to give you the skills and understanding to tackle Paper 1 questions, which are based on the comprehension, critical analysis and evaluation of different types of historical sources as evidence, along with the use of appropriate historical contextual knowledge.

For example, you will need to test sources for reliability and utility – a skill essential for historians. A range of sources has been provided, including extracts from official documents, personal diaries, memoirs and speeches, as well as visual sources such as photographs, cartoons and paintings.

Extracts from a speech
WHAT? (type of source)

need for fascist violence
WHY? (possible purpose)

Mussolini WHO?
(produced it)

fascists of Bologna WHO?
(intended audience)

April 1921 WHEN? (date/
time of production)

origin: 'Who, when, where and why?' questions.

purpose: This means 'reasons, what the writer/ creator was trying to achieve, who the intended audience was'.

content: This is the information or explanation(s) provided by the source.

Remember: a source does not have to be primary to be useful. Remember, too, that content is not the only aspect to have possible value – the context, the person who produced it, etc., can be important in offering an insight. Finally, when in the exam room, use the information provided by the Chief Examiner about the five sources, as it can give some useful information and clues to help you construct a good answer.

SOURCE A

And, however much violence may be deplored, it is evident that we, in order to make our ideas understood, must beat refractory skulls with resounding blows … We are violent because it is necessary to be so …

Our punitive expeditions, all those acts of violence which figure in the papers, must always have the character of the just retort and legitimate reprisal; because we are the first to recognise that it is sad, after having fought the external enemy, to have to fight the enemy within … and for this reason that which we are causing today is a revolution to break up the Bolshevist State, while waiting to settle our account with the Liberal State which remains.

Extracts from a speech about the **need for fascist violence**, delivered by **Mussolini** to the **fascists of Bologna** in **April 1921.** Quoted in Robson, M. 1992. *Italy: Liberalism and Fascism 1870–1945*. London, UK. Hodder & Stoughton. p. 51.

The 'W' questions will help you to become familiar with interpreting, understanding, analysing and evaluating a range of different types of historical sources. They will also aid you in synthesising critical analysis of sources with historical knowledge when constructing an explanation or analysis of some aspect or development of the past. Remember – for Paper 1, as for Paper 2, you need to acquire, select and deploy relevant historical knowledge to explain causes and consequences, continuity and change, and to develop and show an awareness of historical debates and different interpretations.

Paper 1 questions will thus involve examining sources in the light of:

- their **origin**, **purpose** and **content**
- their value and limitations.

The *value and limitations* of sources to historians will be based on the *origin*, *purpose* and *content* aspects. For example, a source might be useful because it is primary – the event depicted was witnessed by the person producing it. But was the person in a position to know? Is the view an untypical view of the event? What is its nature – is it a private diary entry (therefore possibly more likely to be true), or is it a speech or piece of propaganda intended to persuade? Even if the value of a source is limited by such aspects, it can still have value – for example, as evidence of the types of propaganda put out at the time. Similarly, a secondary – or even a tertiary – source can have more value than some primary sources – for instance, because the writer might be writing at a time when new evidence has become available.

Paper 1 contains four types of question. The first three of these are:

1 *Comprehension/understanding of a source.* Some will have 2 marks, others 3 marks. For such questions, write only a short answer, making 2 or 3 points – save your longer answers for the questions carrying the higher marks.

2 *Assessing the value and limitations of one source.* Here you need to assess the source over a range of aspects, AND comment on the source's relative value to historians studying a particular aspect of history. Remember to deal with all of the aspects required: origin, purpose, content, value and limitations.

3 *Cross-referencing/comparing or contrasting two sources.* Try to write an integrated comparison. For example, comment on how the two sources deal with one aspect; then compare/contrast the sources on another aspect. This will usually score more highly than answers that deal with the sources separately. Try to avoid simply describing each source in turn – there needs to be explicit comparison/contrast.

These three types of questions are covered in the chapters above. The other, longer, type of Paper 1 question is dealt with below.

Paper 1: judgement questions

The fourth type of Paper 1 question is a judgement question. Judgement questions require a *synthesis of source evaluation and own knowledge.*

Examiner's tips

- This fourth type of Paper 1 question requires you to produce a mini essay – with a clear/relevant argument – to address the question/statement given in the question. You should try to develop and present an argument and/or come to a balanced judgement by analysing and using the *four* sources *and* your own knowledge.

- Before you write your answer to such a question, you may find it useful to draw a rough chart to note what the sources show in relation to the question. This will also make sure you refer to all or at least most of the sources. Note, however, that some sources may hint at more than one factor/result. When using your own knowledge, make sure it is relevant to the question.

- Look carefully at the simplified mark scheme below. This will help you to focus on what you need to do to reach the top bands and so score the higher marks.

Common mistakes

When answering Paper 1 argument/judgement questions, make sure you do not just deal with sources OR own knowledge! Every year, some candidates (even good ones!) do this, and so limit themselves to – at best – only 5 out of the 9 marks available.

As with the other types of Paper 1 questions, a simplified mark scheme is provided to help you target the most important skills that examiners are looking for.

Exam practice

Band		Marks
1	**Consistently** focused on the question. **Developed and balanced** analysis, with precise use of **BOTH** sources **AND** relevant/accurate own knowledge. Sources and own knowledge are **used consistently and effectively together**, to support argument/ judgement.	8–9
2	**Mostly** focused on the question. **Developed analysis**, with relevant use of **BOTH** sources **AND** some detailed own knowledge. But sources and own knowledge not always **combined** to support analysis/ judgement.	6–7
3	**Some focus** on the question. **Some analysis**, using some of the sources **OR** some relevant/accurate own knowledge.	4–5
4	**No/limited focus** on the question. **Limited/generalised** comments on sources **AND/OR** some limited/inaccurate/irrelevant own knowledge.	0–3

Student answers

The student answers below have brief examiner comments in the margins as well as a longer overall comment at the end. Those parts of the answers that make use of the sources are highlighted in green; those parts that deploy relevant own knowledge are highlighted in purple. In this way, you should find it easier to follow why particular bands and marks were – or were not – awarded.

Question 1

Using **Sources A**, **B**, **C** and **D** *and* your own knowledge, analyse the reasons for Mussolini's rise to power by 1922. [9 marks]

SOURCE A

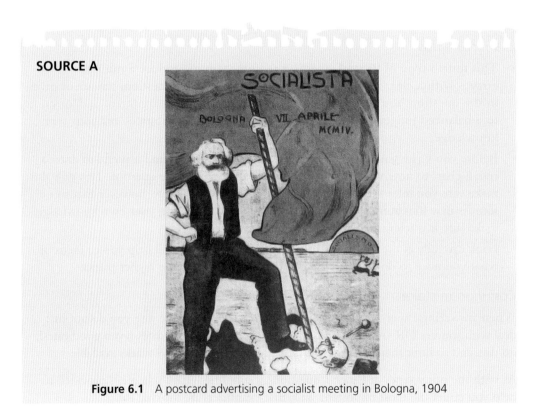

Figure 6.1 A postcard advertising a socialist meeting in Bologna, 1904

SOURCE B

Comments on the backgrounds of the fascist squadristi by Angelo Tasca, a member of the Italian Communist Party in the early 1920s.

In the Po valley, the towns were on the whole less red than the country, being full of landowners, garrison officers, university students, rentiers, professional men, and trades people. These were the classes from which Fascism drew its recruits and which offered the first armed squads.

Tasca, A. *The Rise of Italian Fascism 1918–22*. Quoted in Macdonald, H. 1999. *Mussolini and Italian Fascism*. Cheltenham, UK. Nelson Thornes. p. 17.

SOURCE C

Extracts from a speech about fascist violence by Mussolini towards the fascists of Bologna, April 1921.

And, however much violence may be deplored, it is evident that we, in order to make our ideas understood, must beat refractory skulls with resounding blows … We are violent because it is necessary to be so …

Our punitive expeditions, all those acts of violence which figure in the papers, must always have the character of the just retort and legitimate reprisal; because we are the first to recognise that it is sad, after having fought the external enemy, to have to fight the enemy within … and for this reason that which we are causing today is a revolution to break up the Bolshevist State, while waiting to settle our account with the Liberal State which remains.

Robson, M. 1992. *Italy: Liberalism and Fascism 1870–1945*. London, UK. Hodder & Stoughton. p. 51.

SOURCE D

There were sectors who assisted Fascism indirectly: although they could not bring themselves to support Fascism openly they were at least prepared to tolerate it in a way which would have been out of the question with, for example, socialism. One of these groups was the political establishment … Another was the aristocratic class, who were appeased by Mussolini's willingness to end his attacks on the monarchy. In fact, the Queen Mother, Margherita, and the king's cousin, the Duke of Aosta, were admirers of Fascism. A third sector was the Catholic Church, taking its cue from Pope Pius XI who, from the time of his election in 1922, remained on good terms with Mussolini. The Church undoubtedly considered a Communist revolution to be the main threat.

Lee, S. 1987. *The European Dictatorships, 1918–1945*. London, UK. Routledge. p. 95.

Student answer

The main reasons for Mussolini's rise to power were the old political system, the impact of the First World War, fear of socialism and the growing violence of Mussolini's Fascist Party.

EXAMINER'S COMMENT

This is a good introduction, showing a clear understanding of the topic and the question.

Source A is a postcard advertising a socialist meeting in Bologna in 1904. The Italian Socialist Party had grown rapidly since the late 19th century, and by the time the First World War broke out, it was gaining over 20 per cent of the vote. There were also many socialist-controlled unions – in 1904, the year of the postcard in Source A, there was a general strike. It was developments like that which worried the wealthy élites and the Catholic Church. This is why the social groups mentioned in Source B – the landowners, officers and professional people – began to look for a force to deal with this socialist 'threat'. This was because the liberal government did very little.

Source C is linked to this, as Mussolini refers to the 'enemy within' and the 'Bolshevist State'. The fear of socialism and communism increased amongst the wealthy élites in Italy after the Bolshevik Revolution in November 1917. These upper classes – and the Church – would have greatly appreciated the violence Mussolini talks about in Source C. These social groups liked the paramilitary nature and strength of Mussolini's Fascist Party which, before (and after) the 'March on Rome' in 1922, beat up, and killed, opponents on the left, often forcing them to drink castor oil (sometimes in such quantities that the victims died).

Source D ties in with the other sources – especially Source B – as it confirms that the political establishment and the Catholic Church gave support (whether passive or active) to Mussolini's party. These élites included the royal family, as Source D says. In fact, many historians argue that the main reason the March on Rome was successful was because the king refused to declare a state of emergency, as requested by Facta, the liberal prime minister. The reason they gave Mussolini support, despite the violence of the fascist squads (led by local ras such as Balbo and Grandi), and their takeover of many towns and cities, was because of their fears of socialism and their loss of faith in the Liberal Party.

However, the political system that existed in Italy before 1922 and the impact of the First World War were also important reasons for Mussolini's rise to power in 1922. Since unification in 1861–70, the Liberal Party had kept power through a rather corrupt system called trasformismo. Also important in Mussolini's rise to power was the rise in nationalism – especially after the peace treaties of 1919–20 had failed to give Italy what had been promised by the Treaty of London in 1915. Many called the outcome of the treaties the 'mutilated victory'. In 1919, d'Annunzio had led a force of blackshirted Arditi and captured Fiume, one of the areas claimed by Italian nationalists. Many of these Arditi later joined Mussolini's party.

Activity

Look again at all the sources, the simplified mark scheme and the student answer above. Now try to write your own answer to this question. See if you can use the sources to make some extra points, and integrate some additional own knowledge, to give a fuller explanation of the reasons behind Mussolini's rise to power.

Overall examiner's comments

There is good and clear use of sources throughout, but the use and/or integration of precise own knowledge to both explain and add to the sources is rather limited.
The overall result is an answer clearly focused on the question, but with own knowledge which, in the main, is not integrated with the sources. The candidate has done enough to reach Band 2 and be awarded 6 or 7 marks.

Question 2

Using **Sources A, B, C, D** *and* your own knowledge, explain why Mao came to power in China in 1949. [9 marks]

SOURCE A

Mao had an extraordinary mix of talents: he was visionary, statesman, political and military strategist of genius, philosopher and poet. To these gifts he brought a subtle, dogged mind, awe-inspiring charisma and fiendish cleverness … To Mao, the killing of opponents – or simply of those who disagreed with his political aims – was an unavoidable, indeed a necessary, ingredient of broader campaigns.

Short, P. 1990. *Mao: A Life*. London, UK. John Murray. pp. 630–31.

SOURCE B

Figure 6.2 The route of the Long March

EXAMINER'S COMMENT

The opening makes it clear that a number of factors will be considered and the grouping offers an effective structure for the answer. However, it fails to make any direct reference to the source material, even though some of the factors mentioned in it are directly linked to them.

EXAMINER'S COMMENT

The paragraph provides a lot of useful detail about military factors, but there is no source reference even though the point about switching from guerrilla to conventional warfare could have been exemplified from **Source D**.

Student answer

There are a variety of reasons as to why Mao came to power in China in 1949.
The main reason was the military victory that he achieved in the civil war, but underlying this are a number of different factors. These include Mao's own leadership, the military advantages of his forces during the civil war, and popular support, particularly among the peasants, which grew from his economic ideas on land reform. Mao's advantages must, however, be balanced against the weaknesses of the nationalists under Jiang Jieshi to understand why he was able to rise to power by 1949.

Mao's victory over the GMD followed a civil war that broke out after the surrender of Japan in 1945, which removed the nationalists' and communists' common enemy. Mao's forces were ably led by Lin Biao, who transformed the peasant recruits (increasingly swelled by nationalist deserters) into an effective fighting force. The communists' experience in guerrilla warfare was used to good effect in Manchuria, which they seized early in 1948, but they shifted to more conventional battles once troops were sufficiently trained. The communists understood the importance of seizing railway junctions and surrounding major cities, such as Beijing, which was captured in January 1949. The seizure of Nanjing and Shanghai in April and May 1949 were also crucial, allowing the PLA to march into the last nationalist strongholds in southern China and achieve victory, driving Jiang Jieshi from the mainland, so allowing Mao to declare the PRC in October 1949.

Mao's victory was also the result of his own leadership and 'extraordinary mix of talents' (Source A). Mao had established himself as an undisputed leader through the Long March (Source B) and during the days at Yan'an. He had removed his opponents and his own 'thought' had become the party's dogma. Communist troops were ideologically indoctrinated and were prepared to endure hardship for their cause. Mao maintained motivation and morale, ensuring unity and confidence, and was a pragmatic decision maker. It was Mao who had ordered cooperation with his former nationalist opponents in the fight against Japan, between 1937 and 1945, but then turned on them after 1945 (Source C). It was also Mao who ordered some restraint in communist persecution of landlords in 1948, when it threatened to get out of hand.

Another factor contributing to Mao's rise to power was the popular support that the communists received, particularly from the peasants. Mao's policy of land reform benefited the poorest peasants as large estates were confiscated in the programme of land redistribution. Furthermore, in communist-held urban areas, an effort was made to control corruption and crime, ensure supplies were fairly distributed and introduce fair taxation. By maintaining production and controlling inflation, the communists widened their support base considerably after 1948.

Much of the communist success, however, was due to the weaknesses of the nationalists. Although the nationalists had the military advantage at the beginning of the war with around 2.8 million troops and 6,000 artillery pieces as against the communists' 320,000 troops and 600 pieces of artillery, they squandered this and were ultimately overwhelmed. Jiang sent all of his best troops to Manchuria at the beginning of the war and never fully recovered from the losses there. The mainly conscript nationalist army suffered from low morale, made worse by meagre pay (and that was sometimes stolen by their officers), which led them to ill-treat local populations. The nationalists were also over-reliant on corrupt local warlords and foreign support, which added to their poor standing in the eyes of the Chinese people. They were associated with a dictatorial regime in the 1930s, which had done little to improve conditions in China and inefficiency, economic mismanagement, internal splits and Jiang's weak leadership all contributed to the ultimate Communist victory (Source D).

Mao therefore came to power in China for a variety of reasons, of which the military victory in the civil war was the most important. However, without the nationalists' weaknesses, it would have been far harder for him to have achieved political power, so this must also be seen as a very important factor.

Activity

Look again at all the sources, the simplified mark scheme and the student answer above. Now try to write your own answer to this question. In particular, see if you can make much more explicit use of the sources, and integrate this with own knowledge, in order to push the answer up to Band 1.

Overall examiner's comments

This answer shows a very good understanding of a variety of factors and provides plentiful and, in places, detailed own knowledge in response to the question. It is also a well-structured response that maintains its focus throughout and offers some judgement. However, its use of sources is minimal. Although each is mentioned, most receive only a reference in brackets and only once is a source directly cited. Despite the instructions in the question, much of the actual detail contained in the sources has been ignored and therefore the answer is not worthy of more than Band 3. Since there is a little more than just own knowledge, it would qualify for the top of the band – 5 marks – but an important aspect of this question that demands clear source reference has been missed.

EXAMINER'S COMMENT

This paragraph shows an understanding of Mao's leadership and makes reference to **Sources A**, **B** and **C**. However, it fails to look at the source detail in any depth and leaves the reader to work out the link between the source and essay text.

EXAMINER'S COMMENT

This paragraph makes some relevant comment on Mao's popular support. However, relevant material in **Source A** has not been included here.

EXAMINER'S COMMENT

This paragraph offers some balance and shows some detailed understanding of nationalist weaknesses. However, the reference to **Source D** at the end needed comment. Merely putting it in brackets has not made it clear which sections the student was referring to. Again an opportunity to incorporate source reference has been lost.

EXAMINER'S COMMENT

This is a weak finish to the essay. Although this conclusion repeats the view advanced in the introduction that military victory was the main reason why Mao came to power, it makes no reference to the sources and ends rather limply.

6

Paper 2 exam practice

Paper 2: skills and questions

For Paper 2, you have to answer *two* essay questions from two *different* topics from the 12 options offered. Very often, you will be asked to comment on two states from two different IB regions of the world. Although each question has a specific mark scheme, you can get a good general idea of what examiners are looking for in order to be able to put answers into the higher bands from the general 'generic' mark scheme. In particular, you will need to acquire reasonably precise historical knowledge in order to address issues such as cause and effect, or change and continuity, and to learn how to explain historical developments in a clear, coherent, well-supported and relevant way. You will also need to understand and be able to refer to aspects relating to historical debates, perspectives and interpretations.

Key Concepts

Remember – when answering essay questions, you will often need to consider aspects of one or more of the six Key Concepts. These are:

- Change
- Continuity
- Causation
- Consequence
- Significance
- Perspectives.

Make sure you read the questions carefully, and select your questions wisely. It is a good idea to then produce a rough plan for *each* of the essays that you intend to attempt *before* you start to write your answers. That way, you will soon know whether you have enough own knowledge to answer them adequately.

Remember, too, to keep your answers relevant and focused on the question. For example, do not go outside the dates mentioned in the question, or answer on individuals/states different from the ones identified in the question. Do not just describe the events or developments – sometimes students just focus on one key word or individual, and then write down all they know about it. Instead, select your own knowledge carefully, and pin the relevant information to the key features raised by the question. Also, if the question asks for 'causes/reasons' and 'consequences/results', or two different countries/leaders, make sure you deal with *all* of the parts of the question. Otherwise, you will limit yourself to half marks at best.

Examiner's tips

For Paper 2 answers, examiners are looking for clear/precise analysis, and a balanced argument, linked to the question with the use of good and precise relevant own knowledge. In order to obtain the highest marks, you should be able to refer, where appropriate, to historical debate and/or different historical perspectives/interpretations, or historians' knowledge, making sure it is both relevant to the question *and* integrated into your answer.

Common mistakes

- When answering Paper 2 questions, try to avoid simply describing what happened. A detailed narrative, with no explicit attempts to link the knowledge to the question, will only get you half marks at most.

- Also, if the question asks you to select examples from *two* different regions, make sure you do not choose two states from the same region. Every year some candidates do this and so limit themselves to – at best – only 8 out of the 15 marks available.

Simplified mark scheme

Band		Marks
1	**Consistently clear focus on the question**, with **all main aspects addressed**. Answer is **fully analytical** and **well-structured/organised**. There is **sound understanding of historical concepts**. The answer also integrates **evaluation of different historical debates/perspectives**, and reaches a **clear/consistent judgement/conclusion**.	13–15
2	**Clear understanding of the question**, and most of its **main aspects are addressed**. Answer is mostly **well structured and developed**, with supporting **own knowledge mostly relevant/accurate**. Answer is **mainly analytical**, with attempts at a **consistent conclusion**; and shows **some understanding of historical concepts and debates/perspectives**.	10–12
3	**Demands of the question are understood** – but some aspects **not fully developed/addressed**. Relevant/accurate supporting **own knowledge**, but **attempts at analysis/evaluation are limited/inconsistent**.	7–9
4	**Some understanding** of the question. **Some relevant own knowledge**, with some factors identified – but with **limited explanation**. **Some attempts at analysis**, but answer is **mainly description/narrative**.	4–6
5	**Limited understanding** of the question. **Short/general** answer, with very **little accurate/relevant own knowledge**. Some **unsupported assertions**, with **no real analysis**.	0–3

Student answers

The student answers that follow have brief examiner comments in the margins, as well as a longer overall comment at the end. Those parts of the answers that are particularly strong and well focused are highlighted in red; errors/confusions/loss of focus are highlighted in blue. In this way, you should find it easier to follow why marks were – or were not – awarded.

Question 1

Evaluate the methods used by one leader of a single-party state to ensure that opposition to his rule was ineffective. [15 marks]

Skill

Analysis/argument/evaluation.

Examiner's tip

Look carefully at the wording of this question, which asks for an *evaluation* of *methods* used in curbing opposition. This will involve consideration of the most/least important or most/least effective methods and does not require a detailed description of 'opposition' in itself.

6

Exam practice

EXAMINER'S COMMENT

This introduction is quite well thought through. It identifies the leader to be discussed and also itemises the range of methods that the essay will examine, but it fails to provide any further comment on those methods – for example, which of them might be considered the most important.

EXAMINER'S COMMENT

There is a full consideration here of the elimination of the opposition in 1933–34 and for the most part this succeeds in avoiding too much listing and descriptive writing. However, it is best to avoid 'then' in essays, and the second of these two paragraphs would have been more effective had it begun with a reference to the question and more comment provided on the significance of the events mentioned.

EXAMINER'S COMMENT

This is an effective paragraph that looks at how economic and foreign policies helped Hitler (although it does not mention any others – for example policies towards women, the Churches or youth). It has some depth of understanding in its reference to the traditional élites and the divisions among the opposition.

Student answer

Adolf Hitler was the ruler of an authoritarian state who was able to ensure that opposition to his rule was ineffective. He did this through a mixture of legal and illegal actions, policy decisions, propaganda and terror. As a result no individual or group opposed to his rule ever succeeded in removing him from power.

When Hitler came to power as chancellor of Germany in January 1933, he was faced with the task of destroying any opposition as swiftly as possible. At this stage he faced opposition from a number of groups, including the communists, the socialists and those within the army and on the right who regarded him as a rabble rouser and not to be trusted. His actions in 1933 were crucial to the later ineffectiveness of opposition. He took action against the communists following the Reichstag Fire and persuaded President Hindenburg to issue a decree whereby communists could be rounded up. He then proceeded to influence the elections of March 1933 and got the Enabling Act passed by intimidating the Reichstag. He pruned the civil service in April, and in May he destroyed the trade unions through which workers could have opposed his rule by joint strike action. Workers were brought into a new Nazi-controlled DAF, which made opposition impossible.

Hitler's consolidation of power was completed by overturning local governments and installing Nazi gauleiters, and the Night of the Long Knives of June 1934, which destroyed the power of the SA. Hindenburg's death in August 1934 enabled Hitler to assume the position of Führer and head of the armed forces, and the army took an oath of loyalty. A combination of legal methods and violence had made opposition virtually impossible.

Preventing opposition was also the result of the policy decisions adopted by Hitler. He brought about full employment – removing women from the workplace and setting up public works schemes and, although this was aided by circumstance, it brought him widespread support. Concern for jobs, sympathy with his aims – which included the destruction of the hated Treaty of Versailles – and a traditional respect for authority, which kept the civil service and army reasonably supportive, all played a part in weakening any opposition. The traditional élites were won over and, after the von Blomberg and von Fritsch affair of 1938, that included the army. Furthermore, what opposition there had been was weak and divided, whether between right and left, the SPD and KPD or the Protestant and Catholic branches of the Churches.

Opposition remained ineffective because of the heavy use made of propaganda in the Nazi state. Propaganda was used to win loyalty from all sections of society but particularly from the youth who were indoctrinated by the Hitler Youth movement. Germans were fed a diet of propaganda on their radios and only saw and heard of 'German splendour' in the art galleries and concert halls.

Finally and perhaps most importantly, opposition was ineffective because of the security apparatus of the state. The SS and Gestapo together with a network of informants ensured that everyone lived in fear of being found out for subversive activity and made the coordination of opposition virtually impossible. Arbitrary imprisonment, a Nazi-controlled judiciary and a concentration camp network enabled potential troublemakers to be readily identified and dealt with. This meant that opposition became largely individual and low-key, and when individuals tried to widen their net – as in the case of General Beck in 1938, von Stauffenberg in 1944 and Sophie Scholl, a leader of the student White Rose group – they were rapidly discovered and executed as a warning to others.

Hitler's methods to ensure that opposition was ineffective were similar to those of other authoritarians. By keeping the repressive activities of his regime reasonably unobtrusive or even secret, he was able to give the illusion of total support, which in itself acted as a curb to other potential opponents. There is little doubt that terror, intimidation and repression were the key elements in the prevention of effective opposition, but without Hitler's initial moves to consolidate his power, his propaganda and his successful policies, Hitler would probably not have been able to continue in power as easily as he did.

Overall examiner's comments

This answer provides some good focused material on the methods used by Hitler. It is also well organised. There are a few deficiencies in the style and content as outlined in the margin comments, but overall it is a strong survey worthy of a mark at the top of Band 2 –12 marks. To improve it further, more discussion of the individual methods employed and some *mention of relevant historians/historical interpretations* would be necessary and such would secure a Band 1 mark.

Activity

Look again at the simplified mark scheme and the student answer, and identify where it can be improved to ensure a Band 1 mark of 15. Try to provide a little more linkage and analysis as well as integrating some references to relevant historians/historical interpretations.

Question 2

Evaluate the methods used by Castro to maintain power between 1959 and 1996.   [15 marks]

Skill

Analysis/argument/evaluation.

Examiner's tip

Look carefully at the wording of this question, which asks for the methods used by Castro to maintain his power in the period 1959–96. If high marks are to be achieved, answers will need to consider a variety of methods, and their relative success. And remember – do not just *describe* what he did.

Student answer

Castro came to power in Cuba in 1959, at the head of a popular movement that ousted the dictator Batista, who had been supported by the USA. In order to remain in power, Castro used a variety of different methods – some of which were more successful than others – ranging from popular social and economic policies to repressive actions.

For many years, Cuba had been under the political and economic influence of the USA. This had begun after the Spanish–American War of 1898 and the Platt Amendment of 1901. In 1933, there had been a 'Sergeants' Revolt' in the Cuban army, led by Batista who, from 1934 to 1959, ruled Cuba.

Many Cubans came to resent the lack of democracy and the influence and power of the USA. One of those to do so was Fidel Castro who, along with his brother, Raúl, and some other supporters, launched an attack on the army barracks at Moncada on 26 July 1953. This failed, and they were imprisoned. On their release, Castro went to Mexico, where he formed his 26 July Movement and plotted the overthrow of Batista's dictatorship.

In 1956, Castro and a small band of guerrillas – which included Che Guevara – landed on the coast, and set up base in the Sierra Maestra mountains. Castro then began a guerrilla war that gradually became more and more successful. In January 1959, Batista fled and Castro's 26 July Movement took over.

EXAMINER'S COMMENT

These paragraphs look at propaganda and terror, as promised in the introduction. However, the material on propaganda is not fully linked to the ineffectiveness of opposition. The second paragraph is much better and shows some detail.

EXAMINER'S COMMENT

This is an effective conclusion. It stresses the importance of terror as the main reason behind the ineffectiveness of the opposition and explains why this is felt to be so important. It also shows how this relates to the other factors discussed in the essay, although it still assumes that all of Hitler's policies were successful.

EXAMINER'S COMMENT

This is a brief but clear and well-focused introduction, showing a good grasp of the key requirements of the question.

EXAMINER'S COMMENT

There is lot of accurate supporting own knowledge here – unfortunately, it is entirely focused on the period before Castro came to power and thus not relevant to the question.

Once in power, Castro used different methods to stay in power. One was the use of his charisma and speeches. He was a brilliant orator and was popular because he had put himself forward as a Cuban nationalist – this was especially true after the defeat of the US-sponsored Bay of Pigs invasion in 1961. Since the days of Martí in the 19th century, many Cubans had wanted Cuba to become truly independent. Castro claimed later that he had fused Martí with Marx – this proved a popular claim. On average, Castro made about two speeches a week – some of which lasted hours. This became a main way of staying in power. In fact, he had also used a radio station – Radio Rebelde – before 1959: this had spread messages against Batista and had been used by Castro to proclaim his policies if he came to power.

At first, Castro allowed moderates such as Urrutia to head the government, while he took charge of the Rebel Armed Forces. However, he soon set up an organisation of his closest friends, which began to take the most important decisions. Eventually, the moderates either resigned or were forced out, and members of the 26 July Movement or the communist PSP took over their posts.

Some of the things they then did helped Castro to stay in power – these were his social and economic policies. In particular, his health-care and educational policies were very popular and have been seen as his greatest achievements – such as the increase and redistribution of doctors, and the wiping out of diseases associated with poverty. These have played a key role in maintaining his power as dissatisfaction with other aspects of his rule were seen as less important than his social reforms. Castro also did much to improve the living standards of the poorer sections of Cuban society.

In addition, he has also tried to get ordinary people involved in mass organisations and movements as a way of staying in power – such as the Committees in Defence of the Revolution. Since 1976, when the constitution was changed, there have also been the many local discussions that take place on social and economic issues as part of Poder Popular, or People's Power.

At the same time, Castro has taken various steps to repress or contain any opposition that does arise. For example, in the first few months after January 1959, many of those who had acted as senior policemen and torturers under Batista were executed. This got rid of potential opponents, and led many more to emigrate to the USA. In subsequent years, Castro has encouraged others to leave – thus reducing potential opposition. However, there were some armed groups – often financed, trained and armed by the USA – who for the first few years carried out counter-revolutionary sabotage and terror against government facilities and personnel.

In conclusion, after 1959 and the winning of power, Castro did a variety of things to ensure he remained in power. Despite some opposition, and the failure of some of his economic policies, he was able to stay in power until his health problems forced him to hand over to his brother Raúl in 2008.

Overall examiner's comments

The candidate seems, in the main, to have understood the demands of the question, and there is some relevant own knowledge. However, this is often not very detailed; and there is a slight tendency to drift into narrative. One of its main weaknesses is the fact that, particularly at the beginning, there are sections that are not relevant, as they focus on the period *before* 1959 – these will not gain any marks.

The answer is good enough to be awarded Band 3, but probably only at the bottom end – 7 or 8 marks. To reach Band 1, some examination of economic policies and those relating to control of the media would have been useful; as would more specific details of those methods that have been identified. Also needed would be an examination of the creation of an authoritarian state, and the decision not to hold elections from 1959 to

1976. Finally, mention of the arguments/points of *relevant historians/historical perspectives/interpretations* would be useful.

Activity

Look again at the simplified mark scheme and the student answer above. Now try to write a few extra paragraphs to push the answer up into Band 1, and so obtain the full 15 marks. As well as making sure you address *all* aspects of the question, try to integrate some references to relevant historians/historical perspectives/interpretations.

Question 3

Compare and contrast the policies towards women and youth of two rulers of single-party states, each chosen from a different region.   [15 marks]

Skill

Analysis/argument/evalution.

Examiner's tip

Look carefully at the wording of this question, which asks for similarities *and* differences (comparing and contrasting) between the policies of *two different* rulers, each from a *different* region, towards women *and* youth. All aspects need to be addressed for high marks, so it is important to make a quick plan – ensuring two appropriate rulers are chosen and each part of the question considered. Describing the policies of each ruler in turn will score lowly. This question demands explicit analysis and comparison throughout.

Student answer

Mao Zedong and Adolf Hitler were rulers of apparently contrasting left- and right-wing single-party states in two very different regions. It might therefore be expected that their policies towards women and the youth would be very different. They do, however, have a surprising number of similarities, although there are also a number of differences. In this essay I will look first at Hitler and Mao's policies towards women and then at their policies towards the youth.

The main similarity between the policies of Hitler and Mao is that both regarded women as having a major role within the state. Propaganda was specifically directed towards them and in both regimes women were given a specific role alongside men that differed from the role they held in the previous regime. Both also emphasised the need for women to bear children for the state and to bring them up immersed in the ideology of their country. Their task was to ensure that children attended schools and youth groups, and were correctly instructed.

In Nazi Germany there was even talk of bearing a child for the Führer.

However, although both Mao and Hitler sought to change women's roles, for Hitler this followed a policy of reaction against the former liberal views of the Weimar Republic, whereby women played an active role in politics and public affairs towards a more traditional outlook, which placed women in the home, concerned only with domestic duties. In the peacetime Nazi years, women were discouraged from undertaking professional or factory work and even in wartime this was only permitted with reluctance. Women were expected to be child bearers with large families and there was even a system of medals to reward fecundity.

EXAMINER'S COMMENT

The first sentence provides a direct start that clearly identifies the rulers to be considered and shows an understanding of the question. However, the introduction does not go on to set out a view or argument to be maintained, and the last sentence is unnecessary.

EXAMINER'S COMMENT

These paragraphs are well structured and show good understanding in their consideration of similarity and difference. There are two incidences of extraneous detail creeping in and it is a shame that there are no specific examples to exemplify the Nazi policies or dates to accompany the mention of Maoist legislation.

Exam practice

On the other hand, Mao reacted against a system that had made women second-class citizens. In Maoist China, women were given full civil rights including the right of property owning, with legislation outlawing arranged marriages. They were expected to play a role in party committees (although few reached the higher eschelons of the party) and to work alongside men in the factories and mines. This made life very hard for women, who often had to combine their roles as mothers and workers. Few concessions were made for pregnancy and, from a few weeks old, children were placed in crèches and nurseries, the mother's task complete. Although births were encouraged in the early years to build communist support, these were increasingly discouraged once Mao was established in power.

With regard to policies towards youth, there were also important similarities. Both Mao and Hitler were aware that young people needed to be made 'ideologically aware' to ensure the continuation of their regimes. Both thus placed an emphasis on state-controlled education, with a restricted curriculum, censored materials and a heavily vetted teaching profession. They discouraged intellectualism and study for its own sake, seeing all education as developing idealism, patriotism and support for the values of the state. They also built up youth movements and saw these as an initial training ground for their powerful armies. Millions joined the Hitler Youth, but it was probably the adventurous activities and comradeship that were the main draw.

Whilst Hitler built on the traditional system of schooling in Germany, supplementing it with a few extra Nazi-inspired schools, Mao built a whole new educational system. He encouraged practical activities – even involving children in making things – as well as undertaking factory visits and sending young people for spells in the countryside. Although there were a few incidents of pupils reporting their non-ideologically pure teachers in Nazi Germany, this was far more widespread in communist China. Mao deliberately encouraged the Chinese youth to reject the older generation, ignore and shame 'bourgeois' teachers and, with the coming of the Cultural Revolution, to take the future into their own hands.

There was nothing in Nazi Germany to resemble the mayhem created when bands of Chinese youth, known as Red Guards, took to the streets, ransacked homes and caused near anarchy. Indeed, it was to prevent such activity that Hitler turned on the rabble-rousing youth of the SA in the Night of the Long Knives in 1934. Personal challenges and achievement were important in encouraging youth to meet Hitler's goals once he was in power, and discipline through military drill in the ranks of the Hitler Youth was crucial. Mao's youth, however, were expected to lead the way in rejecting the old or established and thus played a very different role.

There are clearly a number of similarities to be discerned in the policies of Hitler and Mao towards women and youth, but the differences are probably more striking, especially in the former's case.

Overall examiner's comments

This answer is very well focused and well planned to cover all of the issues that the question demands. It contains a good deal of analysis and avoids passages of description. However, it is rather thin on precise supporting detail and lacks the 'very specific and relevant own knowledge' that would be necessary for Band 1. Furthermore, it makes no reference to historical views. Some consideration of Hitler's policy of *Volksgemeinschaft* for example, or of the conflict between practical needs and Maoist ideology, could have

EXAMINER'S COMMENT

These paragraphs again address the similarities and differences with clarity and control showing some depth of understanding. There could sometimes be more specific references to policies, however, and the sections indicated in blue are either unnecessary or too general and unsupported.

EXAMINER'S COMMENT

This is a disappointing conclusion that makes a comment but fails to substantiate it. Its length might indicate a lack of time, but it is crucial to show an overall awareness at the end of an answer and provide some sensible judgement.

been included and shown some higher level understanding. The answer is therefore worthy of Band 2 – although not quite at the top because of the limitations of the factual evidence – 11 marks.

Activity

Look back over the material you have studied on both Hitler and Mao and select a number of relevant examples that could be used to provide supporting detail in this response. Reread the simplified mark scheme and consider where you might be able to refer to historiography and/or historical debate as required for Band 1. When you have gathered the necessary material rewrite the answer so that it would be worthy of the full 15 marks. Do not forget that the best essays state their argument in the introduction, sustain it throughout the answer and reach a clear and well-supported conclusion.

Further information

In addition to the attributions in the source panels, quotations in this book have been taken from the following publications.

Bracher, K. D. 1971. *The German Dictatorship*. London, UK. Weidenfeld & Nicolson.

Carr, W. 1987. 'Nazi Policy against the Jews', in Bessel, R. (ed.). *Life in the Third Reich*. Oxford, UK. Oxford University Press.

Chang, J. and Halliday, J. 2005. *Mao: The Unknown Story*. London, UK. Jonathan Cape.

de Beauvoir, S. 1958. *The Long March*. Cleveland, USA. World Publishing Co.

Feigon, L. 2002. *Mao: A Reinterpretation*. Chicago, USA. Ivan R. Dee.

Fest, J. C. 1970. *The Face of the Third Reich*. London, UK. Weidenfeld & Nicolson.

King Fairbank, J. 1998 (2nd rev. edn). *China, A New History*. Cambridge, USA. Belknap Press of Harvard University Press.

Lynch, M. 2008 (2nd edn). *The People's Republic of China 1949–76*. London, UK. Hodder Education.

Mao Zedong. 1963. *Selected Military Writings*. Beijing, China. Foreign Languages Press.

Meyers, S. and Biderman, A. (eds). 1968. *Mass Behaviour in Battle and Captivity: The Communist Soldier in the Korean War: Research Studies Directed by William C. Bradbury*. Chicago, USA. Chicago University Press.

Mitchison, L. 1970. *China in the 20th Century*. Oxford, UK. Oxford University Press.

Murray-Brown, J. 1979. *Portraits of Power*. London, UK. Octopus Books Ltd.

Payne, S. 1995. *A History of Fascism, 1914–45*. Madison, USA. University of Wisconsin Press.

Shirer, W. 1995. *Berlin Diary: The Journal of a Foreign Correspondent 1934–1941*. Edison, USA. BBS Publishing Corporation.

Short, P. 1999. *Mao: A Life*. London, UK. John Murray.

Spence, J. D. 1999. *Mao*. London, UK. Weidenfeld & Nicholson.

Stackelberg, R. and Winkel, S. (eds). 2002. *The Nazi Germany Sourcebook: An Anthology of Texts*. London, UK. Routledge.

Thurlow, R. 1999. *Fascism*. Cambridge, UK. Cambridge University Press.

Trevor-Roper, H. 1973. *The Last Days of Hitler*. London, UK. Pan Books.

Twitchett, D., King Fairbank, J. and MacFarquhar, R. (eds). 1987. *The Cambridge History of China: Vol. 14 Part I*. Cambridge, UK. Cambridge University Press.

Wegner, B. 1990. *The Waffen-SS: Ideology, Organisation and Function*. Oxford, UK. Blackwell.

Weston, A. 1975. *The Chinese Revolution*. London, UK. George Harrap.

Whitfield, R. 2008. *The Impact of Chairman Mao: China, 1946–1976*. Cheltenham, UK. Nelson Thornes.

Index

Index

Acknowledgements

The author and publishers acknowledge the following sources of copyright material and are grateful for the permissions granted. While every effort has been made, it has not always been possible to identify the sources of all the material used, or to trace all copyright holders. If any omissions are brought to our notice, we will be happy to include the appropriate acknowledgements on reprinting.

Text

Extracts on pages 36, 41, 55, 60, 71, 73: *Mussolini and Fascist Italy*, Blinkhorn, M, Copyright © 2006 Routledge, reproduced by permission of Taylor & Francis Books UK.

Images

1.1 Roger Viollet/Getty Images; 1.5 Library of Congress; 2.1 Topfoto; 2.2 PHOTOS. com>>/Getty Images Plus; 2.6 Amerigo Petitti/Mondadori Portfolio via Getty Images; 2.7 Library of Congress; 2.8 Library of Congress; 2.9 Wikimedia Commons; 2.1 © 2006 Alinari/Topfoto; 2.12 Wikimedia Commons; 2.13 Roger Viollet/Topfoto; 2.14 Wikimedia Commons; 2.15 Topfoto; 2.17 Wikimedia Commons; 2.18 Keystone/Hulton Archive/Getty Images; 2.19 Paul Popper/Popperfoto/Getty Images; 2.20 Alinari/ Topfoto; 2.21 Röhnert/ullstein bild via Getty Images; 2.22 Wikimedia Commons; 2.23 Hulton-Deutsch Collection/CORBIS; 3.2 Library of Congress; 3.3 Keystone/Getty Images; 3.4 © epa/Corbis; 3.5 Hulton Archive/Getty; 3.6 Hulton Archive/Getty Images; 3.7 Hulton Archive/Getty Images; 3.8 Hulton Archive/Getty; 3.11 Hulton Archive/ Getty Images; 3.12 Wikimedia 3.13 Getty Images;/Hulton Archive 3.14 Wikimedia 3.15 Topical Press Agency/Getty Images; 3.16 Galerie Bilderwelt/Getty Images; 3.19 Heinrich Hoffmann/Time & Life Pictures/Getty Images; 3.21 Imagno/Getty Images; 3.21 New York Times Co./Getty Images; 3.22 © Mary Evans Picture Library/Alamy; 4.2 Topical Press Agency/Getty Images; 4.4 CARL DE SOUZA/AFP/Getty Images; 4.5 AFP/Getty Images; 4.6 AFP/Getty Images; 4.7 AFP/Getty Images; 4.8 © Lordprice Collection/Alamy; 4.9 © Mary Evans Picture Library/Alamy; 4.10 Chen Xiaoxi, Guo Kekuan. Sichuan renmin chubanshe; 4.11 AFP/AFP/Getty Images; 4.12 AFP/ AFP/Getty Images; 4.13 AFP/AFP/Getty Images; 4.14 Keystone-France/Gamma-Rapho/Getty Images; 4.15 © Bettmann/CORBIS; 5.1 © Bettmann/CORBIS; 5.2 Library of Congress; 5.4 Library of Congress; 5.6 AFP/Getty Images; 5.7 Wikimedia 5.8 © ullsteinbild / Topfoto; 5.9 Elizabeth Frey/Three Lions/Getty Images; 5.11 akg-images/ullstein bild; 5.12 © Bettmann/CORBIS; 5.13 © Sygma/Corbis; 5.15 PASCAL GUYOT/AFP/Getty Images; 5.16 Getty Images; 5.17 © epa/Corbis; 5.18 Topfoto; 5.19 Alan Oxley/Getty Images; 5.20 © Adam Eastland/Alamy; 5.21 ADALBERTO ROQUE/AFP/Getty Images; 5.23 ADALBERTO ROQUE/AFP/ Getty Images; 5.25 Roger-Violett/Topfoto.